No Exit

No Exit

Arab Existentialism, Jean-Paul Sartre, and Decolonization

YOAV DI-CAPUA

The University of Chicago Press   Chicago and London

The University of Chicago Press, Chicago 60637
The University of Chicago Press, Ltd., London
© 2018 by The University of Chicago
Published 2018
Printed in the United States of America

27 26 25 24 23 22 21 20 19 18   1 2 3 4 5

ISBN-13: 978-0-226-49974-1 (cloth)
ISBN-13: 978-0-226-50350-9 (paper)
ISBN-13: 978-0-226-49988-8 (e-book)
DOI: 10.7208/chicago/9780226499888.001.0001

Library of Congress Cataloging-in-Publication Data

Names: Di-Capua, Yoav, 1970– author.
Title: No exit : Arab existentialism, Jean-Paul Sartre, and
    decolonization / Yoav Di-Capua.
Description: Chicago : The University of Chicago Press, 2018. |
    Includes bibliographical references and index.
Identifiers: LCCN 2017043645 | ISBN 9780226499741
    (cloth : alk. paper) | ISBN 9780226503509 (pbk. : alk. paper) |
    ISBN 9780226499888 (e-book)
Subjects: LCSH: Existentialism. | Philosophy—Arab countries—
    20th century. | Sartre, Jean-Paul, 1905–1980—Appreciation—Arab
    countries. | Sartre, Jean-Paul, 1905–1980—Influence. | Badawī,
    ʿAbd al-Raḥmān. | Decolonization—Arab countries.
Classification: LCC B5295 .D54 2018 | DDC 181—dc23
LC record available at https://lccn.loc.gov/2017043645
♾ This paper meets the requirements of ANSI/NISO Z39.48-1992
(Permanence of Paper).

To my family

Contents

Note on Transliteration

In the interest of simplifying the reading, I have used a modified version of the transliteration system of the *International Journal of Middle East Studies*, excluding diacritical marks except for the ʿayn (ʿ) and the hamza (ʾ). For names and terms that have a common transliteration in English (e.g., Gamal ʿAbd al-Nasser), I have used that spelling.

Acknowledgments

Like World War I, this book should have been finished by Christmas some four years ago. But now, now that it is all over and done with, there are a few institutions and a number of dear people whom I must thank. The first financial support was given by the College of Liberal Arts at the University of Texas at Austin, which generously covered all of my research expenses for the first three years. Based on this preliminary investment, I was awarded a National Endowment for the Humanities Fellowship for 2012–2013, which permitted precious and uninterrupted time for thinking. All along, I benefited immensely from continuous financial support from my home department, the Department of History. I am especially grateful to our own Institute of Historical Studies for granting me a fellowship for the 2015–2016 academic year, during which I completed the manuscript. Also at the university, I am grateful to the Office of the Vice President for Research for a generous subvention grant toward the publication of this book.

Books such as this one come to life in the context of a community, through multiple interactions with students and colleagues. In the History Department at the University of Texas, I wish to thank Tracie Matysik, Judy Coffin, and Ben Brower for being such excellent intellectual companions. Also at UT, I was tremendously lucky to be part of the Arabic Program collective, which, under the extraordinary leadership of Kristen Brustad and Mahmoud al-Batal, emerged as an extremely ambitious, creative, and intellectually dynamic group of scholars whose curiosity and energy knew no bounds. At the heart of this group is my dear friend Tarek El-Ariss, who surely deserves a few uninterrupted lines of acknowledgment all for himself. Before I get to that, however, I would like to thank Zeina Halabi and Angela Giordani, from whom I learned so much over the years. Undoubtedly, our community was strengthened by the unmitigated support of 'Arwa al-Shaibani and 'Aziz al-Shaibani, whose passion for high-quality intellectual work is surpassed only by their generosity.

As for Tarek, I am not sure where to start acknowledging my debt for his brilliance, lively spirit, big-heartedness, and friendship. I think of the many bottles of whiskey we drank together over the years; surely this book would have not been the same without them. I mean it, of course, in a sober way: as our single-malt-infused conversations influenced almost any major intellectual decision I have taken during these years. Perhaps it is better to say that regardless of what we ate and drank—and, admittedly, it was quite a lot—we held a decade-long dialogue, which is sure to continue for years to come and for which I will be forever grateful.

This book was already in production when our dear friend and colleague Barbara Harlow suddenly passed away. What a tremendous loss. Over the past decade, I borrowed freely from Barbara. I took books, ideas, political lines, cigarettes, and much more. She was never tired of giving and rarely asked for anything in return. Barbara was endowed with a rare peripheral moral outlook that brought the human concerns of decolonized people in Africa and the Middle East into sharp scholarly focus. She pioneered a hugely influential line of inquiry that centered on the relationship between the literary and the intellectual. I thank her for years of steady intellectual presence, for reading this manuscript, and for taking the time to comment, suggest, correct, and politely disagree with some of its contents.

Beyond Austin, I wish to thank Regina Longo for putting me in touch with Claude Lanzmann and persuading a grumpy old man to talk to me. He was the most difficult interviewee I ever had, and here, too, only a Rémy Martin bottle (this apparently is what he drinks) assisted in smoothing out a rough transaction. Thank you, Regina, for bringing this bottle. In Germany, I wish to thank Georges Khalil of EUME, Berlin, and Friederike Pannewick of Marburg University for their hospitality, support, and feedback. Many other colleagues read, commented, or provided valuable sources. I thank Sebastian Klor, Gary Wilder, Marilyn Young, Ronen Steinberg, Zur Shalev, Ussama Makdisi, Orit Bashkin, Yasmine Hanoosh, and Shereen Hamed Shaw for their help. Special thanks are also due to Omnia El Shakry, who helped me find a publisher. Robert Tignor, Eve-Trout Powell, Israel Gershoni, and Bob Vitalis wrote countless letters on my behalf to multiple institutions, institutions that often replied with a very thin envelope. Thanks are due to them for not giving up on this project. Another staunch supporter was Steven Sonneberg, who was instrumental in clarifying many of the issues at stake in this study and much more.

Cyrus Schayegh is one more friend who deserves his own lines of credit. Some people can see an issue from two different perspectives, but only a rare few of them can do so from four or five different cultural angles. Cyrus is a distinguished member of this elite club. Over the many years of our friendship, he has critically influenced the way I "think history." Lastly, I would like to thank my good fortune for providing me with the pleasurable opportunity of working with Priya Nelson at the University of Chicago Press. In the intricate and idiosyncratic world of academic publishing, Priya easily stands out as a beacon of clarity, good judgment, and efficiency. Also at the press, I wish to thank Dylan Montanari, Carol McGillivray for handling the copyediting of the manuscript, and the two anonymous readers who justifiably demanded a shorter manuscript.

Some parts of the book have been previously published. I thank Oxford University Press and Brill for allowing me to reuse this material: "Arab Existentialism: A Lost Chapter in the Intellectual History of Decolonization," *American Historical Review* 17, no. 4 (October 2012): 1061–91; "Homeward Bound: Husayn Muruwwah's Integrative Quest for Authenticity," *Journal of Arabic Literature* 44, no. 1 (2013): 21–52.

I encountered the story of Arab existentialism by sheer chance while preparing to write a very different kind of book, one that has absolutely nothing to do with Israelis and Palestinians or, at the very least, not both of them together, positioned in the same pages with Sartre stuck in the middle. Yet, against my expectations, the source material pointed toward the breakdown of the relationship between Arab intellectuals and Jean-Paul Sartre due to profound ethical disagreements. As it developed, Sartre's inability to establish a hierarchy of "otherness" between the Zionist victims of Europe and the Palestinian victims of Zionism had real-life consequences.

Today, five decades and counting into the Israeli occupation, the current moral dilemma is, of course, of a very different nature. In comparison with the surreal and violent world of the Occupied Territories, Sartre's philosophical dilemma seems benign, perhaps even irrelevant.

But from a historical standpoint and by the measures of the 1960s, a whole world seemed to hinge on the resolution of this dilemma. In that sense, this story provides the opportunity to explore the histories that exist in the impossible space between the Holocaust and the Nakba, the Nakba and the Holocaust.

This is a difficult space to navigate even from afar, and given my childhood in Jerusalem during the 1970s and 1980s and my specific family background, this was a rather personal book to write. I grew up in south Jerusalem with an Italian father who, along with his two brothers and sister, had survived the Holocaust. In the wake of disaster, Zionism, and especially Italian Zionism, helped them make a claim to life and, in that sense, saved them. On the other hand, my mother came from a Yemenite family whose Arab culture and religious-mindedness was the obvious enemy of Zionism and the subject of ridicule and much shame. It was a confusing terrain to navigate. As a child, synthesis between these two worlds eluded me, and I squarely went with the Zionist tribe. I stayed there for decades.

I was by no means the only one who was compelled to choose sides. Everyone else was too. Our working-class neighborhood comprised Jews who came from elsewhere due to severely unfavorable circumstances: Egyptians, Romanians, Germans, Algerians, Russians, Moroccans, Iraqis, Poles, and Iranians, to name a few. In hindsight, it was a rich, multilingual world with outstanding food, an awe-inspiring reservoir of curses and insults, and myriad other rich traditions. It was also an environment in which no one had anything in common and in which we rarely got along. Since difference was everywhere and conflicts were endemic, it was natural to let the kids build their own consensus around the world of tomorrow. We built it like kids do. A "Lord of the Flies" type of childhood like this, however, rarely manages to establish communal certainty and a sense of safety. Indeed, for us, nothing was ever clear-cut.

Half of the city was undeniably Palestinian, and the surrounding villages were all Arab. Some of these villages, or rather what was left of them, were literally under our feet. At least that was the case in my neighborhood, and whatever we made of these ruins as kids, the fate of Palestinians was never an abstraction but something quite physical and present: a broken wall, a fig tree, a spring, a stone house. While physically hanging out in their ruined world of yesterday, in our minds we nurtured exclusively our own sense of the past. We paid reluctant annual school visits to Yad Vashem, the Holocaust memorial that was situated on a hilltop adjacent to our neighborhood. We excessively commemorated dead soldiers. We tended solely to our own tragedies, and these were admittedly many.

We never heard the word *Nakba*. On the surface, our denial seemed to work; except, as it turned out, it meant that we were ignorant not only of the Palestinian past under our feet, but also of the past inside our own houses: that of our own parents. We were therefore heirs to a kingdom of silence covered up by hollow commemoration. We were surrounded by silence and knew absolutely nothing of that which really mattered. This was as true collectively as it was privately. Indeed, I learned of the sad history of my Italian family—the Di-Capuas and Ottolenghis—under fascism and Nazism in my early forties: only a few years ago. I know close to nothing of the Yemenite side of the family, though I do owe them my current profession.

Working through this contested terrain, of course, is not simply a professional matter of writing a book, but the business of my life. That is, a life that began in one country and continues in another. And, in life, I was fortunate to find my dear wife Stephennie Mulder. Sometimes it seems like a small human miracle that two people who grew up in such radically diverse environments can still find such a broad common ground (particularly considering the wife repeatedly refuses to drink whiskey). But thanks to her wisdom and patience we certainly have. I thank her for many years of friendship, for intellectual companionship, for putting up with a clueless immigrant, and, of course, for our three lovely daughters, Daniela, Naomi, and Alma. Thanks to all four, I now have a home away from home.

Introduction

As the colonial era in the Middle East drew to a close, a restless generation of young intellectuals vowed to rethink their culture and invent what they called "a new Arab man": self-confident, authentic, reflective, worldly, independent, self-sufficient, proud, and, above all, free. Since during this era existentialism was taken to be the comprehensive philosophy of the individual, this generation's project of radical self-fashioning led them to Jean-Paul Sartre. Taking seriously the existentialist battle cry "be yourself at all costs," they forged a homegrown tradition of Arab existentialism, or, as it is known in Arabic, *wujudiyya*. By offering a wide spectrum of intellectual possibilities, Arab existentialism germinated the culture of decolonization and functioned as the intellectual foundation of an entire generational endeavor. Indeed, by the late 1950s, the Arab world boasted of having the largest existentialist scene outside of Europe. A random walk into a bookstore, a quick glance at one of the dozens of literary journals, or an afternoon in a downtown café in Beirut, Cairo, Baghdad, or Damascus would suffice to establish the fact that Sartre had become, among Arab intellectuals, a household name. As the progressive Egyptian writer Ahmad 'Abbas Salih put it in a public letter to Sartre, "Your influence in this region is deeper and wider than that of any other writer. We have known you for a long time, and from the first contact with your ideas . . . their appeal grew deeper until our publishing houses were working daily to translate and print your work. . . . You are the only Western writer that all Arab newspapers follow closely."[1] Indeed, so avidly read was

Sartre in the region that at one point in 1963, upon the publication of his celebrated autobiography *Les Mots* (*The Words*), the Lebanese translator and publisher Suhayl Idris bragged of bringing the Arabic edition to the market ahead of the original French one.[2]

The daily French newspaper *Le Monde* took appreciative note of the fact that Sartre and Beauvoir topped the Arab best-seller lists. This fame, it noted, was not simply due to intellectual fashion, Sartre's support for Algeria, or his well-known declining of the Nobel Prize in Literature. Rather, it was because "twenty years later, the questions that Sartre posed in his 1947 essay *Qu'est-ce que la littérature?* [*What Is Literature?*] still resonate in the Middle East."[3] Echoing this enthusiasm and dedication to his work, intellectuals wrote passionately to Sartre (but curiously not to Beauvoir) about their deep love for him and recounted in great detail how the awkward-looking philosopher had changed their lives by teaching them how to become fighter-intellectuals (*munadil-mufakkir*). Mostly they were touched by his sincere effort to simply and meaningfully recognize who they were, and they felt validated by and through his writings.[4]

Indeed, with the possible exception of Karl Marx, for the last two hundred years—roughly during the entire course of Arab modernity—no other foreign intellectual was more translated, read, debated, engaged with, and admired than Jean-Paul Sartre: his philosophy, literature, theater, and his global politics. Furthermore, moving beyond the usual one-way relationship between metropolitan stars and peripheral thinkers, Sartre warmly reciprocated and humanely recognized his Arab interlocutors and established an ongoing rapport with a host of them. In the modern annals of the Middle East, especially its Eastern Arab lands, it would indeed be difficult to find another cross-cultural moment more intimate, intense, and hopeful than this one.

On both sides of the Mediterranean, Sartre, his intellectual circle, and their new Arab interlocutors were eager to demonstrate that, against the polarizing logic of the Cold War and the sociopolitical stagnation of Europe, decolonization could produce revolutionary societies that were as egalitarian, free, and patriotic as they were anti-imperialist and humanistic. For Europeans of the Left and colonized people of recently liberated domains, that, in a nutshell, was the promise of Third Worldism, and, far from being a provincial African, Asian, or Arab project, it was, in a variation on the old theme of colonial universality, a promising universal counter-project of its own.

Arab existentialists, those who actually thought with existentialism in order to decolonize their world and construct a new one, were endowed with impressive peripheral vision and a taste for worldly engagements. At the same time, they were not made of one political cloth. They embraced diverse ideological orientations and held opposing political commitments. Some were sworn enemies. Yet, in order to argue about the meaning of freedom at the close of empire, about individualism, alienation, cultural authenticity, solidarity, and the need to invent what was known at the time as a "new Arab man"—this new citizen of the world—they used the referential grammar of existentialism.

Reconfiguring the European tradition, Arab existentialism yielded an effusive stream of political tracts, manifestos, op-eds, novels, poems, short stories, plays, philosophy books, and works of literary and cultural criticism. Numbering in the thousands, these original formulations of existentialism were penned and read by countless pundits, artists, philosophers, students, revolutionaries, politicians, political prisoners, state officials, refugees, feminists, social reformers, peacemakers, would-be martyrs, and universal justice seekers. The intelligentsia of the Eastern Arab lands (and to some degree that of Iran) wholeheartedly embraced *wujudiyya* and, in the course of doing so, turned Sartre into its mentor. But a mentor for what, exactly? As it turned out, finding a way out of colonialism was no easy task. One of the first thinkers to grasp this complexity was the Algerian thinker Malek Bennabi, who imagined decolonization as "an exit from the colonial situation" with all of its related racial, psychological, social, political, and economic implications.[5] In search of such an exit, Arab thinkers began trusting Sartre to intellectually mark a way out, or an exit, from the colonial condition.[6] Yet, unfortunately, for all the optimism, enthusiasm, and hope that this movement engendered, the story of Arab existentialism, and of Sartre's Arab celebrity, did not have a happy ending, nor did it provide an easy exit from the colonial condition. It is, quite sadly, a postcolonial story of no exit.

In more than one way, the eventual collapse of the Arab world's personal relationship with Sartre was a foreshadowing of things to come. While at the beginning of 1967 Sartre was still an uncontested Arab hero, whose impact, reputation, and legacy seemed as enduring and long lasting as the Algerian independence he staunchly supported, by the end of that same year, in the wake of the devastating Six-Day War, he was branded a traitor and a Zionist in disguise. Accused of signing a pro-Zionist manifesto (which indeed he did sign), Sartre's Arabic books were banned, burned, or voluntarily boycotted, and an entire course of thought was quietly disowned. Suppressed and virtually forgotten, the legacy of Arab existentialism and its association with Sartre was replaced with a sense of colossal betrayal and an argument against the suitability of existentialism to Arab liberation.

Decades later, the memory of an iconic betrayal still lingers: "Nearly everything he [Sartre] wrote," reflected Edward Said in 2000, "is interesting for its sheer audacity, its freedom (even its freedom to be verbose) and its generosity of spirit." Once an admirer of Sartre indebted to his advocacy on behalf of any just cause around the globe, eventually even Said saw in him "a bitter disappointment to every (non-Algerian) Arab who admired him."[7] It is hard to argue with this emotional judgment, but what was the intellectual basis for this pervasive sense of betrayal? Was Sartre a Zionist in disguise all along? Did he and Beauvoir share the same opinions of Israelis and Arabs? What role did other intellectuals in Sartre's circle play in the drama of Zionism versus the Arab Cause? What positions did Arab and Israeli intellectuals take vis-à-vis Sartre's 1965 decision to engage the Arab-Israeli conflict? And, of course, how did the still-unprocessed trauma of the Holocaust and the legacy of anti-Semitism affect those who were part of this trans-Mediterranean intellectual and political network? As we shall see, on a remarkably narrow evidentiary base, some of these questions have, at least in theory, already been addressed. But here *No Exit: Arab Existentialism, Jean-Paul Sartre, and Decolonization* draws on a plethora of recently discovered and previously unconsulted Arabic and Hebrew sources to finally draw a fuller and more nuanced understanding of the accusation that Sartre, Beauvoir, and the entire French Left were traitors to the Arab Cause. Of equal importance, we can begin to recognize—as well as to make sense of—the Arabs' deep sense of betrayal.

Yet, important as these aspects are, aside from the drama of Sartre, the French Left, and Zionism, there is the story of Arab existentialism itself: its makers and its believers. Though largely forgotten even in the region, the rich legacy of Arab existentialism elucidates a moment when the emancipating promise of global citizenship for recently colonized people became a real possibility. Moving from the vast landscape of economic and political decolonization to consider the specific architecture of intellectual decolonization at its narrowest scope, *No Exit* uses Arab existentialism as a prism that reveals how this process looked from within. Though primarily an intellectual and political affair of the Eastern Arab lands rather than of North Africa, it nonetheless raises important questions about the intellectual specificity of Arab decolonization: What was Arab existentialism, and why did it achieve such a grip on the thought and practice of the postcolonial generation? To what degree was Arab existentialism, and decolonization more broadly, distinctively Arab rather than simply a standard transnational project with a global imaginary and a superstar philosopher—Sartre—as its ultimate symbol?

Obviously, there is much to consider in relation to these questions, but—except in passing—this is not a study of Arab intellectual history in the so-called postliberal era. Rather, by tracing Arab existentialism, *No Exit* provides a snapshot of the beginning and end of a hegemonic project for decolonization, one that was worlds away from the current dark domains of fundamentalism. In addition to the scholarly arguments this study seeks to make about freedom, authenticity, sovereignty, and Sartre's global ethics of engagement, at the most basic level, this is a story about people who tried to change their world for the better. That is, it is an account of the intellectual hopes, struggles, imperfections, setbacks, and small victories that shaped the Arab experience of decolonization.

Taken collectively, it is the tale of the postcolonial Arab generation or, as they proudly called themselves, *al-jil al-jadid* (the new generation). Born sometime during the 1920s, members of this generation grew up during the tumultuous and disorienting era of the 1930s and intellectually matured in the anxious moment of colonial closure. Even today, as these thinkers, writers, journalists, and essayists quietly leave our world, their lives remain virtually unknown, not only beyond the Mediterranean and on the other side of the ocean but also, in some cases, at home. In addition to a critical engagement with the global intellectual history of decolonization, this book is also a modest attempt to collect a record of their lives and situate scholarly arguments not within a body of theoretical work but within a constellation of human biographies.

Here are some of the protagonists that appear in these pages. At times working alone in the solitude of a study, at other times making public spectacles of themselves in bustling cafés, the Beirut-based writer and Sorbonne graduate Suhayl Idris and the translator ʿAida Matraji Idris worked as a couple. Casting themselves as a local take on Sartre and Beauvoir, they made books happen and careers flourish (or wither). Writing, translating, editing, and endlessly corresponding with the who's who of Arab letters, this power couple produced *Al-Adab*, the ingenious laboratory of Arab existentialism and easily the most important Arab magazine until the tragic 1975 Lebanese civil war. Even today, their publishing house remains hard at work in the trusted hands of their son. Arab intellectual decolonization and Beirut's rise to prominence as the capital of Arab thought would make no sense without them.

It is also the story of Egyptian philosopher ʿAbd al-Rahman Badawi. Crowned as the first modern Arab philosopher, Badawi had a breathtaking intellectual scope and a maniacal scholarly manner. A difficult man by all accounts, he brought Heidegger to the region and was the first—as well as the most consistent and prolific—local philosopher of European existentialism. Energetic and highly creative, his all-consuming project was to fuse Heideggerian existentialism and Sufism as means of engendering cultural authenticity and bringing Islamic philosophy up to date. When that theoretical project was eclipsed by what he saw as a shallow Sartrean-style commitment to politics, he left Egypt in frustration, wandered the region for a time, and eventually settled in Paris as a teacher at the Sorbonne. Condemning himself to voluntary exile, Badawi died with hundreds of books to his name, a corpus that became a source of continual reference and inspiration for generations to come.

As a former student of Badawi, communist literary critic Mahmud Amin al-ʿAlim went beyond the abstract theories of his professor to tie thought to concrete political action. Seeking to revolutionize the role of intellectuals, al-ʿAlim appropriated Sartre's notion of commitment and selectively applied it in order to purge culture of the influence of ivory-tower thinkers and steer it toward the people. His most famous victim was Taha Husayn, the doyen of Arab letters and the man who, much to his own regret, introduced Sartre to Arab readers in the first place. Always up for a good fight, al-ʿAlim nonetheless was a man of good nature, rare political stamina, a will to sacrifice, and a remarkable capacity for scandal making. It comes as no surprise, therefore, that he was also no stranger to the prison cell. Unlike many of his comrades, he survived the 1960s to enjoy an enduring and long-lasting presence in public life.

The Palestinian philosopher and activist Fayiz Sayigh also makes an important appearance in these pages, as does his compatriot, friend, and philosopher peer Hisham Shrabi. Sayigh was a native of Tiberius who, in the wake of the Nakba, the destruction of Palestinian society and the founding of Israel, was forced to take refuge in Beirut. Trained in existentialist philosophy at both the American University of Beirut and the University of Chicago, for much of the 1950s and 1960s he persistently deployed an existentialist perspective in order to elucidate the impact of the colonial condition on the Arab subject. Staunchly committed to individual freedom and a just solution in Palestine, he was one of the most courageous and clearheaded observers of decolonization. As one of the most well read thinkers of his generation, he applied Sartre's critique of neocolonialism and racism to Zionism and insisted that what applies to Algeria, Congo, and Vietnam should apply also to Israel.

Liliane and Lutfi al-Khuli were another remarkable couple whose engagement with Sartre's circle and its ideas was anchored in their generation's quest for a new society. Living in Paris during the high fever of Left Bank existentialism, they befriended Sartre and Beauvoir and established a personal relationship that hinged on the possibility and promise of global ethics and universal citizenship. Al-Khuli was a principled man of many talents and unlimited energy. A trial lawyer by education, a journalist by choice, and a political prisoner by virtue of his commitments and intellectual designs, al-Khuli, along with Liliane, hosted Sartre and Beauvoir in their much-anticipated 1967 visit to Egypt and Gaza. Working with Sartre toward elucidating the ideological divide of the Arab-Israeli conflict and charting the contours of the universal Left, this worldly Egyptian couple witnessed and chronicled the painful and extremely personal collapse of the Arab relationship with Sartre. For both Liliane and Lutfi al-Khuli, Sartre and Beauvoir's unexpected support of Israel was not simply an intellectual disappointment but a very personal one as well.

Alongside these idealistic figures were dozens of so-called existentialists, such as the Lebanese feminist writer Layla Ba'albaki, the Syrian novelist Hani al-Rahib, and the Iraqi *poète maudit* Husayn Mardan. All three used existentialism to form a counterculture that exposed the repressive nature of mainstream Pan-Arabism and authoritarian state politics. Thus, inasmuch as this is the story about the circulation of an idea, it is much more the story of a bold and proud generation that strove for intellectual dignity and freedom, believed that words could change the world, and dared to dream of big answers to big questions; a generation that sought to destroy an established order and replace it with another. The fact that, in the wake of the 1967 war, this effort disintegrated and was branded a failure should not deter us from finding out for ourselves what intellectual decolonization was like. If this is a story of "no exit," what exit did Arab intellectuals imagine during these years?

On Intellectual Decolonization

Regardless of geographical, historical, and cultural differences, all over the postcolonial world, decolonization faced similar tasks. First, and most urgently, it needed to secure the physical liberation of the population and define its space. Second, newly liberated societies faced the formidable challenge of overcoming decades of extreme poverty, low literacy rates, poor hygiene, low life expectancy, and the colonial destruction of the sociocultural fabric. The postcolonial quest for social justice was a response to this malaise, and, whether conceived as part of a Euro-American mold or a Soviet one, it called for radical projects of development. The third, and by far the most elusive, aspect of decolonization involved the question of *being* in the wake of empire or, for lack of better terminology, the question of identity. Viewed as a whole, it was widely believed that a successful engagement with all three aspects of decolonization would turn the moral value of human dignity (*karama insaniyya*) from an abstract ideal to a material condition. If Arab decolonization ever had a popular object, that was it.

Roaming the frontiers of human dignity (while occasionally slipping into the trap of self-glorification), the political elites of the 1950s understood that the project of decolonization hinged on the question of being. What does it mean *to be* a person after colonialism? After decades during which Arabs were struggling objects in the closed world of European consciousness, who and what dominated the definition of the self and the community to which it belonged? It is here, on this entirely subjective and ultimately elusive aspect of decolonization, that I'd like to focus our attention.

As a recent book about mid-twentieth-century American intellectual life nicely illustrates, obsession with what writers of the time called the "destiny of man" was a ubiquitous preoccupation.[8] Who were we, fundamentally, and how could we justify this "being" to ourselves as well as to others? Some of these concerns may seem odd today, but after World War II, anxiety about the self was a sign of the age almost everywhere in the West. Existentialism made its debut as a response to this crisis, and one can persuasively argue that this preoccupation also marked the beginning of the cultural revolution of the 1960s. Yet, though some parallels certainly exist, in the decolonized world the preoccupation with the problem of existence assumed an entirely different level of complexity as well as of urgency. Indeed, postcolonial ontology is a world unto itself.

The ontological problem of subjectivity had three subaspects: free-dom (*hurriyya*), authenticity (*asala*), and sovereignty (*siyada*). Being free, authentic, and sovereign meant owning the capacity for self-determination. The Arabic name for self-determination, *haqq taqrir al-masir*, clearly connotes the ontological meaning of the right to decide one's own fate, destiny, and path in life. Entrusted with the forward-looking mission of giving meaning to life after colonialism, self-determination was both the end result of successful decolonization and, at the same time, a rallying cry for the deepening and widening of this process.

It is against this background that we can begin to appreciate why ex-istentialism had so much to offer Arab societies in the East whose print culture, education system, intellectuals, and politicians were ready to embrace decolonization as a generational project. Clearly, not every-body was equally well positioned to participate in this endeavor. As opposed to the Algerians, who were yet to start and finish their strug-gle for liberation, the Eastern Arab lands of Egypt, Palestine, Lebanon, Syria, Iraq, and, to a lesser extent, Jordan, were certainly ripe for in-tellectual decolonization. But how could a philosophical fashion from Paris seriously address Middle Eastern needs? For existentialism to be meaningful, it had to be so for all people. That is, "it had to address questions that appear meaningful to those who are not white European men."[9] What were these questions?

Driving the spread of existentialism in the Arab world was the basic proposition that there was no such thing as *human nature* but only a *human condition*. In the long view, during colonialism, the effort to de-termine human nature, or essence, summoned fixed characterizations of Arabs as lazy, superstitious, and irrational, to name a few of the ac-colades that determined their prospects in the world. In contrast, exis-tentialists like Heidegger and Sartre shifted the discussion to the ques-tion, *What does it mean to be human?* Thus, rather than asking, what is an Arab, existentialism was neatly equipped to elucidate the daily Arab experience in the world. It was a fundamental difference.

From the perspective of the colonized, this fundamental alteration announced the possibility of being human in the universal sense of the word. In that new order, the colonized could now reject the Car-tesian dictum "I think, therefore I am" for its radical separation of the individual from the surrounding world of human beings. They were no longer required to be subjected to a universe of sharp ruptures between object and subject, true knowledge and daily experience, body and mind. Authored by Husserl and Heidegger, this philosophical proposition automatically discredited a host of existing colonial ideas about Oriental people, such as the notion that the essence of Islam, to cite one famous example, is fundamentally incompatible with reason, science, and democracy. Likewise, it liberated the colonized self from the shackles of this binding characterization, thus opening up the possibility of reshaping it along new lines.

The meaning of the shift from "essence" to "existence" in the lives of Middle Easterners becomes more concrete once we realize that, since the "primary ontological condition for humans is freedom," existentialism suggested itself as the foremost philosophy that explains, safeguards, and works to advance the spread of human freedom.[10] Sartre was very clear about this and "held fast to a conception of freedom in which human beings create future-oriented projects that transcend what is given in the present."[11] "We are free," clarifies philosopher Charles Taylor, "when we can remake the conditions of our own existence, when we can dominate the things that dominate us."[12] Nothing defines a postcolonial project better than this.

Right from the start, existentialism urged the individual to wholly embrace its own freedom and develop without hindrance. Sartre's call to refuse submission to any externally imposed condition of life was, basically, a call for authenticity. This strongly resonated with colonized people, as it did with Beauvoir's assessment of the female condition. Indeed, inner truthfulness to oneself, or authenticity, became a primary existential value.[13] And though "existential authenticity must not . . . be confused with the popular notion of authenticity as 'as being true to one's roots and heritage,'" in its call to live fully, openly, decidedly, and authentically, existentialism helped expose the immense void that the marginalization of Islamic heritage and the debilitating absence of cultural continuity (*istimrariyya*) opened for both individuals and society at large.[14] It therefore became clear that the colonial demand that Arabs should become European ended up creating individuals and societies that were fundamentally inauthentic, alienated from their true selves, and, ultimately, unfree. The idea behind the popular talk about a "new Arab man," was to heal the schism in the Arab self and render it once again an authentic and sovereign whole.

Politics was part of the existentialist menu. For that, Sartre devised the powerful principle of engagement "as a form of authenticity with relation to the political."[15] This principle instructed intellectuals to be *engagé* and influence their civic circumstances, through which identities could be shaped and sustained. The call for commitment and direct political action was probably the most embraced and debated Sartrean principle in the Arab world. It was also the easiest to understand and put to work. Authenticity, therefore, could also be addressed politically, not only philosophically.

Healing the problem of authenticity and engaging in the process of self-formation and taking responsibility for it were some of the stepping stones toward full sovereignty, freedom, and, eventually, self-determination. Existentialism was relevant to all of these subaspects of the ontological problem of subjectivity. Dealing with similar concerns, Africana philosophy long ago acknowledged the immense potential of existentialism to elucidate and argue for the humanity and freedom of black people.[16] While black and European existentialism share similar concerns about consciousness, trepidation, meaninglessness, hopelessness, fear, despair, servility, and abasement, they differ markedly from one another. As theorized by Lewis Gordon and summarized by Magnus Bassey, although European existentialism is "predicated on the uniqueness of the individual as well as on a universalist conception of humans and their obligation to self, Africana critical theory or Black existential philosophy is predicated on the liberation of all Black people in the world from oppression."[17]

Similarly, little in the career of Arab existentialism is identical to Europe. The acculturation process of Arab existentialism was never a straightforward business that was clear, coherent, and free of contradictions. To the contrary, it seems that existentialism's entry into the Arab world raised as many questions as it promised to answer, and that its development was messy and contentious. Some, as we shall see, even ridiculed it. Thus, European existentialism, and Sartre's work in particular, did not arrive in the region as a ready-made philosophy waiting to be "implemented." Rather, as one would expect, it arrived slowly, from multiple sources, and via several agents over an extended period of time. Consumed as a fragmented body of work, it was modified to the point of reinvention. This is why it is so redundant to speak of "passive reception" or "borrowing from the West," tropes dominated the East-West literature for decades.[18] Concomitantly, insisting on a neat definition of Arab existentialism is somewhat counterproductive. What really counts are its features and tasks and what it reveals to us about intellectual decolonization.

Indeed, disorderly as it was, the reception of Sartre's work raised many concerns, for instance, with regard to freedom. Granted, all political groups called for freedom, but of which kind? That of radical individualism, which instructs the individual to follow a personal path of self-realization? Or that of the nation? If it was the freedom of the nation, was it the freedom that speaks of individual political rights, or the one that calls for the collective rights of the political community to override individuals? Did political sovereignty, in the national sense of the word, equal freedom? Could freedom realize itself only within the confines of the nation-state? Recent scholarship suggests that questions concerning the meaning of freedom (and justice) as autonomous from the institution of the state animate much of the intellectual history of decolonization.[19] Arab existentialism took many of these concerns as its subject matter.

On the ideological level, addressing the standard challenges of decolonization through the prism of existentialism meant that Arab intellectuals had to reckon with two interrelated issues that underlined the reception of Sartre's work globally. First, they had to deal with the alleged incompatibility of existentialism and Marxism, which enjoyed a significant Arab tradition in its own right. Second, they had to make sense of the inability to translate the relationship between Marxism and existentialism into sound global ethics that would apply to the troubles of the region. Taking issue with this difficulty, Marxists relentlessly attacked existentialism for its radical individualism, which revolved around a conception of an isolated individual consciousness obsessed with authentic self-discovery and self-creation. Such self-referential projects came at the expense of articulating a constructive and scientific plan for progressive collective change on behalf of all of society. Targeted for embodying these severe shortcomings, Sartre promised to deliver a philosophical work that would reconcile existentialism and Marxism.

But if the idea was to articulate "a grounding for the view that the actions of individuals would lead to the creation of a single meaningful history" of the sort that Marxism envisioned, Sartre had famously failed to deliver it.[20] Against the nagging absence of a unifying theory, during the 1960s Sartre practiced actual politics, from which his followers were welcome to deduce or, rather, to guess at general principles of conduct. His relentless global engagements in the uncharted ethical domain of decolonization and the Cold War presented Sartre as the ultimate model for the ethical subject of the Left whose stage, as well as his judgment, was truly universal. These engagements, however, were so ahead of Sartre's philosophy and so out of sync with it that they left behind a rather confused audience. This confusion was particularly apparent in the Middle East.

With no philosophical consideration of global ethics and no reiteration of moral genealogies of any kind, progressive Arab circles called for consistency in telling "rights from wrongs." Thus, they argued that if a certain principle were upheld in one part of the globe it must also be embraced and defended elsewhere. Specifically, they declared that if racism and neocolonialism were condemned in the cases of Algeria, South Africa, and Rhodesia, then they must also be condemned in the case of Israel. Indeed, in the absence of theory, Sartre's promise of a global ethics hinged almost entirely on how his global actions (with which Arabs identified automatically) translated to the case of Palestine. This kind of selective ethics by example was built into the tradition of Arab existentialism and conditioned its politics. This is why it would be a mistake to regard this tradition as a simple matter of words.

Even though Sartre's ethics were left unfinished, his overall work was immensely influential. By writing about racism, neocolonialism, settler colonialism, otherness, subhuman existence, human dignity, hegemony, justice, and the emancipating possibilities of violent resistance, his philosophy helped Arab intellectuals to rearrange the essential domains of freedom, authenticity, and sovereignty. By doing so, Arab existentialism slowly emerged as a meaningful tradition armed with principles, concepts, behavioral modes, and political expectations that were readily available so that the culturally committed classes could begin to sort through the rubble of colonialism.

Reinvented as "their own," Arab existentialism no longer adhered to its European provenance and could not be comfortably positioned within a European intellectual genealogy. As Mahmud Amin al-'Alim succinctly put it, "When we discuss existentialism, we do not discuss French or German philosophy but an intellectual movement with roots in Arab culture."[21] In that, existentialism opened a horizon of significance to help overcome the troubles of the age. In a word, it suggested an exit.

The Problem of Invisibility

If, on the relatively thin account of Sartre's popular reception in Africa, V. Y. Mudimbe and Robert Young branded Sartre an "African philosopher," what then should Arab intellectuals, who read Sartre for breakfast, call him?[22] With such a ubiquitous presence, how exactly is it that one of the longest and most extensive engagements with Sartre and existentialism outside Europe has been overlooked? How did it happen that local adaptations of existentialism as well as the women and men who forged them became so invisible to us? What does this invisibility tell us about the kind of history we are used to writing, reading, and telling about the Middle East?

Thinking ahead, what kind of historiography can successfully account for the intricate global habitat of the postcolonial generation, which is characterized by linguistic multiplicity, increased access to texts in circulation, and a prevailing sense of political immediacy? The multivalent story of Arab existentialism has relevance for a range of fields, including decolonization studies, postcolonial studies, Middle Eastern studies, French studies, and Cold War studies, all of which would be enriched by decoding and situating this experience in the context of their traditional interests. Yet, regardless of the intense interest in this era and the vast and impressive literature that these fields continue to yield, the globetrotting circulation of existentialism's ideas, the synchronized role of intellectuals in this movement, and the new linkages they forged remain invisible.

The same applies to what could be described as the global Sartre, the first and most important postwar intellectual to cast his net so widely and build a web of relationships and texts with multiple thinkers, liberation movements, and Third World regimes. This omission, I would like to argue, is not an empirical coincidence, as in something that simply has not been discovered yet. No new archive can solve this problem. Neither is it an oversight due to a lack of scholars who can work in three, four, or five languages. Much more significantly, it is a lapse built into the historiographical makeup of those scholarly fields, and one that potentially could be overcome by practicing historiographical cross-pollination. In other words, each of these fields has unique access to some aspects of the story, but we can tell it in its entirety, and appreciate its distinctiveness, only when we combine and corroborate these perspectives vis-à-vis each other.

Let us review one field at a time. In spite of the booming interest in decolonization and the consensus within this field with regard to the central role of intellectuals in shaping postcolonial societies, historians have typically reduced intellectuals to their function as anticolonial thinkers and hence cast them as one-dimensional ciphers for decolonization. Indeed, for many decades scholars emphasized the centrality of anticolonial nationalism as the focal point of interaction between colonizer and colonized and, hence, as a salient feature of decolonization. Early scholarship in this field focused on the "transfer of power" as a unidirectional process that extended from the metropole to the periphery in the face of the so-called onslaught of nationalism. For obvious reasons, much of this work came from scholars of the British Empire.

A later variant of this literature illustrated how power was not simply transferred but in fact demanded, even taken by force. This process was further explained in terms of provincial anticolonial nationalisms (freedom movements) and higher-level political solidarity (Pan-Asian, Pan-Arab, Pan-African). But solidarity and resistance have functioned largely as tropes rather than empirical points of reference, with scholars generally assuming that anticolonial nationalism was similarly constituted wherever and whenever it occurred and that the history of anticolonial nationalism accounts for the role of ideas during this era. Related to this emphasis is the largely defunct assumption that decolonization happens only, or mainly, vis-à-vis the colonizer and not internally among members of the same nation.[23]

Taking issue with this flat characterization, over the last decade a growing number of scholars have taken internal decolonization seriously and explored its inner workings in diverse locales ranging from London, or rather "Black London," to sub-Saharan and West Africa and the Caribbean.[24] Understanding the complexity of the matter at hand, Frederick Cooper recently asked: "What lies between the 'colonial' and the 'post'? Not an event, not a moment, but a process," which, as he and others show, was as profoundly inward oriented as it was outward.[25]

This richer understanding of decolonization has not yet informed the otherwise highly impressive field of Cold War studies, whose treatment of ideas stops at big ideologies such as liberalism, socialism, and communism and their interface with the classic political spheres of the war. The daily role of ideas in organizing the local experience of people in Africa, Latin America, Asia, and the Middle East during the Cold War is almost completely absent from the larger consideration of this field.[26]

Postcolonial studies could be credited for being the only field that has made a point of studying the "decolonization of the mind." Yet, it, too, has done little to rehabilitate local thought in a systematic fashion. While it offers an important corrective to Eurocentric scholarship on empire as well as an effective critique of the practices of the nation-state, the realities of colonized peoples are almost always projected against the essentialized epistemology of colonial Europe, with the ultimate goal of investigating the persistence of "colonial discourse." With a rarefied and far-from-rigorous historical method that uses epistemology as the omnipresent referent for all forms of thought, we are left with the false notion that colonialism was uninterrupted by the process of decolonization. While postcolonial studies powerfully uncovers tacit modes of domination, it has done little to date by way of presenting a systematic and comprehensive account of how people on the ground put their thoughts together during the period of decolonization.[27]

Even as excellent scholarship on labor, Third World diplomacy, race (*négritude*), and gender is breaking new ground, the otherwise ongoing absence of empirically grounded intellectual history prevents us from fully appreciating the constructive nature of decolonization.[28] Indeed, in recent years, the intellectual history of decolonization took a hypertheoretical turn with heightened interest around iconic thinkers such as Frantz Fanon and hardly any attention to the hundreds of invisible intellectuals without which there would be no decolonization to begin with.

Within area studies, an emphasis on nationalism has also dominated the study of the Middle East and, possibly, other area studies fields as well. Though the period that preceded World War II witnessed an impressive array of studies on contingent forms of thought such as feminism, anarchism, Darwinism, and Islamic law, the immediate postwar era in the Middle East is suffering from an extremely narrow focus on nationalism.[29] Indeed, the history of decolonization in the region is still considered to be the exclusive domain of Pan-Arab nationalism.[30] However, notwithstanding this emphasis, the era of Pan-Arabism hasn't been studied for several decades now. Somewhat curiously, most studies conclude at the beginning of World War II while others resume the history after the 1967 war.[31] Not unrelated, even beyond the era of decolonization and the study of nationalism, two senior scholars have reached the grim conclusion that "it would be more fruitful (and perhaps more correct) to admit our own failure to give voice to the individual intellectuals, intellectual schools, discursive systems, or other thought processes that have emerged and developed in the Middle East."[32] Given this harsh judgment, revealing the contribution of Arab existentialism as an effort to "decolonize the mind" becomes quite urgent.

Properly speaking, an appreciation of Sartre's global role as a thinker of decolonization and a consideration of the spread of existentialism across the globe to places like China, Vietnam, and the Middle East is not really the business of French studies, and perhaps more properly belongs in the field of francophone studies.[33] However, given the fact that scholars of Sartre have established an entire subfield equipped with its own professional societies, journals, and conferences, a reconsideration of Sartre's oeuvre from an Arab perspective should be of serious benefit to these fields. However, for many years now, Sartre's intellectual legacy has been stuck on two narrow, albeit important, issues: his problematic rapport with Soviet communism and his ambivalent stand on violence.

These two concerns date back to the 1970s, when the focus of the post–May 1968 generation shifted away from the cause of Marxist-driven revolution and Third Worldism and began engaging with questions of ethics, human rights, and the law. In this entirely new context, a self-described group of "New Philosophers" took issue with Sartre's legacy and critiqued its easy association with Soviet communism and credulous Third World resistance.[34] Following a similar agenda, in the post–Cold War English-speaking academia, the late Tony Judt condemned an entire class of postwar French intellectuals, chief among them Sartre, for "intellectual irresponsibility" and moral blindness in the face of communist totalitarianism. Others joined him in this critique.[35] As for the criticism of Sartre's ambivalence toward violence, though the political criticism is legitimate, and the historiographical discussion is mature and substantial, it is characterized by a wholesale theoretical perspective, one that is for the most part nongenealogical and thus excludes the course of his intellectual development. It is also oblivious with regard to how Sartre's position on violence was received by those who actually practiced it, for example Palestinian resistance fighters.[36] In these two respects, Sartre's legacy is still open for reconsideration.

Critical of the Sartrean historiographical *terroir*, Alexander Zevin opined,

These approaches, dominant since at least the mid-1980s, are in need of revision. It is not just that they have aged poorly since the polemics attendant upon the end of the Cold War, but that they depend on the most pious and rudimentary of *mise-en-scènes*. Sartre is given the role of a villain in an anti-totalitarian passion play in which his anti-colonialism is all but ignored: essays, newspaper articles, speeches, interviews, correspondence and well-publicized speaking tours and voyages that extended from the immediate post-war period up through the 1970s. . . . Such a reassessment is necessary not only for making sense of Sartre's diverse theoretical insights into racism and anti-Semitism, the extent and shape of human freedom, or the meaning of literary engagement, but just as much for appraising the intellectual constellation within which Sartre was enmeshed.[37]

To this I would add that attention must be given to his interlocutors around the world, as during decolonization he pioneered a new form of politics: the politics of mutual recognition.

To be sure, there is the famous Sartre of Algeria, who has been the subject of multiple studies, commentaries, and celebrations, especially by the pens of his biographers.[38] Yet, the focus on the Algerian Sartre is one that tends to severely constrict Sartre's involvement in the Third World and in the Arab world to his role in Algeria. The invisibility of Arab existentialism, a cultural preoccupation that was exclusively the business of non-Algerian Arabs, is the obvious consequence of this approach, but so is the invisibility of the impact of existentialism and Sartre's thought on decolonization elsewhere in the world.[39]

Nonetheless, the current historiographical state of the field is by no means static or uniform. Paige Arthur's *Unfinished Projects: Decolonization and the Philosophy of Jean-Paul Sartre* excavates an entire corpus of Sartre's thought on freedom, race, human rights, global responsibility, ethics of violence, and international justice and situates it within the historical context of decolonization. This work correctly reassigns the forgotten intellectual origins of postcolonial studies to Sartre and opens new vistas for research outside Europe. A similar view could be taken with respect to Jonathan Judaken and Robert Bernasconi's *Situating Existentialism*, which, as its title suggests, very effectively situates multiple variants of existentialist philosophy within new religious, cultural, and social contexts.[40]

The presence of historiographical ghettos, however, is not the only reason the contours of global intellectual circulation remain difficult to parse with clarity. There is also the serious problem of archives. Systematic destruction of records and their removal from the public domain by the colonizers or the militarized postcolonial state that followed is fairly common and well documented.[41] Yet, the perennial elegies mourning ruined archives should not blind us to the presence of a more significant difficulty. In explaining why "some elements of decolonization have been difficult to see," historian Jordanna Bailkin notes that "The longstanding distinction between the high politics of decolonization overseas and its domestic aspects need to be called into question. This distinction has not been merely conceptual in the minds of historians, but rather has been embedded into the structures of archives upon which histories of decolonization have been based."[42] In other words, the archives register the assumption that decolonization took place "over there" as a limited, unidirectional, and final event that, once it occurred, no longer informed the history of the colonizer. Ignoring the characteristic interplay across the seas, over time, and within societies, and inscribing this unidirectional and temporally bounded notion into the very logic and structure of the archive, the invisibility of intellectuals and the circulation of ideas is almost guaranteed.

Cognizant of the fact that the historical record of decolonization is structurally compromised, Omnia El Shakry asks: "In what ways, then, have historians remembered, forgotten, or appropriated the various intellectual traditions that belonged to the era of decolonization in the Middle East? What compositional logics enable certain individual thinkers to be archived as part of the history of decolonization and others not?" Facing the intentional erasure that regularly took place in the Arab archival ecosystem, she concludes that "The uses and abuses of both paper and what we might term nondocumentary archives have led to 'subjugated knowledges,' 'excluded socialites,' and aporias, the implications of which we have yet to fully explore."[43] This difficult reality underscores the need for the intellectual historian of the Arab world to develop an alternative archive and, as I suggest below, a slightly different method of reading the source material.

To add insult to injury, conditioned by this list of factors that collectively render aspects of the intellectual experience of decolonization invisible, scholars inevitably end up portraying the persona of the Arab intellectual as a static signifier of an idea rather than as a contextualized and dynamic human being. Thus, whereas Euro-American intellectuals regularly benefit from a fine-grained consideration of their inner motivations, urges, and character, most Arab intellectuals, especially those associated with decolonization, remain fundamentally unknown. Their habits, their surroundings, their friendships and fallouts, their body language, their politics, their emotional and intimate lives, their letters from prison, their relationship with their parents, and their overall humanity—with all its beauty, promises, weaknesses, strengths, and vulnerabilities—are only rarely associated with their ideas in a meaningful way. Just like many black intellectuals during decolonization (and in general), their humanity is compromised from the point of departure, thus severing the link to "who they really are," that is, their inner self, and their ideas.[44] This powerful form of fragmentation between the person and the fruit of the mind dehumanizes Arab thinkers and, admittedly, is perhaps the most difficult-to-overcome aspect of the invisibility problem.

How can we do right by the life and times of people such as Suhayl Idris, Fayiz Sayigh, Lutfi al-Khuli, Mahmud Amin al-ʿAlim, ʿAbd al-Rahman Badawi, and ʿAida Idris? How can we take their ideas seriously? How can we overcome their empty, fragmented, and dehumanized status and portray instead a more integrated, balanced, and intimate portrait that takes into consideration their motives, realities, ambitions, and shortcomings? Of equal importance, how can we retrieve the meaning of their ideas and the scope of their circulation in the context of their lives? Below, I offer two possible solutions that address these concerns. The first is a simple proposition about historiographical cross-pollination, and the second is a return to old-fashioned storytelling as a way of capturing the humanity of the thinker.

Toward Visibility

As David Armitage recently argued, whereas "historians in all fields have more recently been moving toward studies they describe variously as international, transnational, comparative, and global," intellectual historians, who trace the circulation of ideas as others would otherwise track commodities, have always occupied such an international position.[45] Yet, the recent trend of global intellectual history and the journal that is associated with it aimed to deepen the commitment to an international line of inquiry.[46] Trying to make sense of the global space of intellectual exchange, scholars in this field invest considerable energy in identifying the specificity of non-European thought and situating it within a larger intellectual context. The basic assertion is that "an implicit holism according to which cultural, social, linguistic, civilizational or geographical boundaries are always occupied by mediators and go-betweens who establish connections and traces that defy any preordained closure."[47]

Decoding the grid of intellectual circulation and accounting for the various "exchange rates" that ideas are assigned in a time of cross-cultural translation are worthwhile tasks that intimately concern this book and its relation to similar accounts of intellectual entanglements. Recent scholarship in this field begins to do just that and whether we associate these studies with global intellectual history or with transnational intellectual history is beside the point.[48] What is of importance, however, is how not to fall into an uncritical celebration of every global exchange at the expense of the cultural specificity of the various participants. At the same time, we should draw on the strength of this trend in empirically connecting historical realities that had long been assumed to have no connection and in bringing into one conversation diverse historiographies that rarely intersect; for example, in this case, Arab and French intellectual histories.

This is not an easy task. Though global intellectual history certainly amplifies the voice of the Arab intellectual, considering the pervasive invisibility of their personas and the archival void that surrounds them, the acoustic reverberation of the Middle Eastern voice in the global space does not automatically lead to the humanization of the writer and the restoration of their ideas.[49] My admittedly somewhat old-fashioned response to this problem is to return to storytelling.

My adoption of this method is part of a broader trend. Marking the return of storytelling in fiction and history writing after a long period of absence, recently, a group of philosophers have restated the unique properties of narrative: namely, that it allows the writer to embed human subjectivity in the original social context in which the subject spoke, wrote, and acted. In that sense, storytelling is functioning "as a sense-making practice that is integral to how subjects who act in the world interpret and share their experiences with others."[50] Understanding that we become who we are by virtue of operating in such contexts—rather than viewing narrative as a violent and imprisoning agent of modern power—(as we have become accustomed to do following our repeated engagements with a certain bald French philosopher), we are newly invited to reconsider storytelling as a tool that validates the deeds, memory, perception, and cognition of the human subject.

In particular, this group of philosophers invites us to regain appreciation for the significance of narrative in capturing human experience in the following domains: "epistemological (concerned with questions such as how we know and understand), ontological (concerned with questions of being, existence and reality such as what is real and how we exist) and ethical (concerned with questions such as what is right and how we act in the world with others)."[51] In all of these important respects, narrative is emerging as "a crucial form of historical inquiry" that can sensibly assist us in reconstructing the fragmented persona of the Arab intellectual and thus render it both visible and human on the global stage on which he or she was originally a player.[52] There are grounds to believe that especially the non-European spheres of global intellectual history can benefit from the cognitive and humanizing qualities of narrative. In other words, contrary to some 1990s entrenched assumptions, narrative can represent.

But how can we write such full representative narratives in the absence of archives, the other cause of invisibility? The answer is that we should reconstruct an alternative archive. Though Arab state archives are virtually absent, and though official state publications are often misleading, an alternative archive untainted by the aforementioned problems could be established. Arab intellectuals wrote a lot. They wrote a lot about themselves and even more about each other. They left books, articles, essays, letters, and interviews in which they articulated their ideas, debated them, and quarreled with each other. This immense trove of information can be retrieved and needs to be read very carefully. It is never enough to read one edition of a book but several, as later editions will often tell us about the trials and tribulations of the first edition and reveal the misfortunes that befell its author. As we shall see, debates and scandals, such as the obscenity trial of Layla Baʿalbaki for extravagant sexuality and disrespect for patriarchy, often arrive to us in just such a roundabout manner. The history of the postcolonial Arab book and its author is indeed complex and multilayered, but ultimately it exists, and it is decipherable.

Another archive can potentially emerge from situating old subjects in a new global context. Sartre, for instance, says nothing about the young Egyptian student who, for a whole year, tutored him about the realities of the Arab world, but the memoir that this student wrote later in life and an Israeli intelligence report on this young man tell us quite a lot. Simone de Beauvoir and Claude Lanzmann did not leave detailed accounts of their involvement with Sartre's foray into the Arab-Israeli conflict, and even when interviewed Lanzmann was somewhat reluctant to "return" to this era. Beauvoir's biographer writes, "In 1967 they were official guests of the Egyptian and Israeli governments, but she spoke very little to her friends about these trips beyond what she wrote in her memoirs."[53] They might indeed have spoken very little, but the unpublished diary of a socialist Israeli emissary to Paris, a kibbutz member in the big city who was in on the secret dealings of the whole affair, does tell us in detail about this effort. Reconstructing these lost connections is the standard work of any historian, but, in the context of the Middle East, we have grown accustomed to believing that the absence of archives and the poverty of narrative are two inevitable sides of the same coin.

Understandably, given the centrality of critical theory in the humanities and its huge explanatory potential, many scholars would rather see the future of intellectual history as one that would depart from basic narrative and continue to move toward an engagement with critical theory. There is indeed no doubt that such an approach has paid handsome intellectual dividends for some of its advocates.[54] Such work often engages with intellectual decolonization through the prism of Frantz Fanon, Aimé Césaire, and Léopold Sédar Senghor, some of the most studied, celebrated, and humanized intellectuals of decolonization.

But who ever heard of Lutfi al-Khuli, one of Sartre's and Bertrand Russell's main Arab interlocutors? Al-Khuli wrote a whole book—still untranslated—about his debates with Sartre and Russell, and it might be a good idea to read it and learn something of the life, intellectual trajectory, and ideological position of the author before we rush to theorize it. Indeed, most Arab intellectuals benefit little from a theoretical approach that precedes their humanization. They need to be brought back to life first. A global historiographical positioning that relies heavily on multiple fields, including the assets of area studies—that historiographical bête noire of recent decades—coupled with the critically reconstructed vignettes of old-fashioned historical narration can begin to accomplish that.

Approaching Arab Existentialism

The rendezvous between Arab intellectuals, Jean-Paul Sartre, his French circle, and existentialism spans nine chapters. The first chapter picks up this story toward its conclusion, when Sartre finally decided to intellectually intervene in the Arab-Israeli conflict and—on the eve of the June 1967 war—to visit Egypt, the Gaza Strip, and Israel on a fact-finding mission. Focusing on the minute details of this engagement as they appear in newly discovered material in Hebrew and Arabic, we learn that, in reality, Sartre's visit was not strictly his own idea but also that of Simone de Beauvoir and Claude Lanzmann, the managing editor of *Les Temps Modernes* and the chief architect of this visit. In fact, nothing in Sartre's engagement with the conflict makes sense without considering this triangular relationship, its disagreements, its silences, and its effort to coproduce Sartre's position of neutrality or, as he called it, of absence. Opening this book at the peak of Sartre's celebrity in the region, it becomes clear how high the stakes were for those on the Arab side of the conflict. But how did existentialism achieve such a dominant status in the Arab world to begin with? The following six chapters examine this process from its early beginnings in the 1940s to the apex of existentialism's influence in the 1960s.

Chapter 2 begins with the self-described post–World War II crisis of the Arab self and the problem of authenticity as a disjuncture between being and meaning. Responding to this crisis, Egyptian and Lebanese intellectuals developed two strands of existentialism. By way of Alexander Koyré, the first was inspired by Heidegger while the second drew from Sartre's idea of *engagement*.

Continuing with the theme of engagement, chapter 3 offers a conceptual history (or *Begriffsgeschichte*) of Sartre's notion of engagement and analyzes its rise to a position of intellectual prominence. Known in Arabic as *iltizam*, the main purpose of engagement was to decolonize Arab culture by way of politicizing it and purging the old-guard generation of the *udaba'*, whose thought was seriously in debt to colonial humanism. This effort was conducted by a new generation that had recently "graduated" from Paris's Left Bank cafés and Moscow's communist seminars.

Chapter 4 shows how in the wake of the 1955 Bandung Conference, the 1956 Suez War, and the ongoing struggle in Algeria (1954–1962), a new revolutionary and hypernationalist Arab state (Nasserist and Ba'thist) appropriated the Sartrean notion of commitment for the sake of sacrificial politics. Identifying the masses as the touchstone of political authenticity, and seeking to redeem them from colonialism, the call for sacrifice as a liberationist act of freedom became the dominant notion of freedom during this era and the decisive generational choice of millions. With a skeptical view that rejected the suffocating collectivity of Pan-Arabism, minorities such as women and Palestinians drew on existentialist themes in order to expose the absence of freedom and signal their abandonment by fellow Arabs.

Chapter 5 takes us to Baghdad, the ostensible capital of Arab existentialism. Baghdad's existentialism was not a textual philosophical phenomenon but rather a carnivalesque, artistic scene that showed profound disinterest in the workings of the state and ridiculed all forms of iltizam. Seen by many as intellectually superficial, the much-maligned debauched existentialism of Baghdad was no less consequential or significant than Abbie Hoffman's East Village performances during the 1960s.

Chapters 6 and 7 are concerned with the intellectual movement from the specificities of Arab nationalism to the 1960s global culture of resistance and left-wing politics. Inspired by Che Guevara, who visited the region twice, and taking their cues from Sartre's position on Algeria, Vietnam, Cuba, and Congo, Arab intellectuals jointly translated Sartre's writing on sites of anti-imperial resistance and used them to join the global movement of Southern resistance to Northern oppression. They also used Sartre's vocabulary to theorize Zionism as a classic neocolonial phenomenon of settler colonialism and asked Sartre to acknowledge these ethical similarities. Against this background, and with war looming on the horizon, Sartre visited the Middle East.

Finally, chapters 8 and 9 pick up where the first chapter left off to examine Sartre, Beauvoir, and Lanzmann's actual visit to the Middle East and its dramatic aftermath, which brought about the total collapse of Sartre's relationship with the Arab world. Did Sartre intentionally betray his Arab followers? If so, why, in which sense, and under what circumstances? Closely dissecting the dynamics around the 1967 war, the chapters show how Sartre's ethical ambiguity toward the Arab-Israeli conflict slowly crumbled and brought him to politically side with Israel. Stunned, Arab intellectuals broke off all communication, and Sartre's work was publicly disowned. Gone was Sartre, Arab existentialism, and with them, too, the hope of a smooth exit from the dire straits of colonial ontology.

ONE

The Visit

In 1965, at the height of his popularity in the Middle East,
Sartre finally decided to weigh in on the Arab-Israeli conflict, visit the region, and see for himself. It was expected
that following the tour he would, characteristically, publish his opinion on the conflict and perhaps even take
sides and name names. But, before that, Sartre wanted
the quarreling parties to collaborate and contribute their
respective impressions of each other to a special issue of
his journal. Since both Arabs and Israelis were reluctant to
cooperate, more than two years would pass before Sartre,
Beauvoir, and Lanzmann would finally board an airplane
bound to Cairo. This chapter registers the many political
maneuvers it took to produce this visit. Outwardly, this
might look like a classic case study of Sartre's famed global
politics of engagement leading to a clear ethical statement
and a solid political commitment to a venerable cause. But
would it be the same this time around?

It would not. The irony of that noble effort lies in the
fact that in the case of the Middle East, and particularly
in the case of the Arab-Israeli conflict and the question
of Palestine—in other words, in this case where Sartre's philosophical convictions should have provided the
greatest clarity—his otherwise powerful ethics of engagement seemed inapplicable to the realities of the Middle East. All of Sartre's international engagements were
framed by a sharp postcolonial perspective, a committed
text, and an unambiguous set of principles. But here, in
his dealings with Arabs and Israelis, he uncharacteristi-

cally resisted taking sides, refused to pass moral judgment, and found himself unable to craft a convincing text. Even his body language betrayed confusion.

Consistently evasive and facing the dilemma of how to establish ethical hierarchy between survivors of the Holocaust and Palestinian victims of the Nakba, the philosopher repeatedly failed to produce clear language. Consequently, clear-cut dichotomies that had become a staple of decolonization, such as those between colonizer and colonized, perpetrators and victims, masters and "others," did not result in an organized ethical framework that would point toward a just solution. This uncharacteristic position left heads of state, politicians, activists, journalists, commentators, and, later, scholars second-guessing Sartre's politics. In the absence of a logical explanation for the politics of ambiguity, many Arabs subscribed to the idea that Sartre's ambiguity was no ambiguity at all and that the celebrated philosopher had been a staunch supporter of Israel all along.

Though many decades have elapsed since Sartre's visit, this conclusion has become only more firmly entrenched. In 2000, Edward Said wrote that "For reasons that we still cannot know for certain, Sartre did indeed remain constant in his fundamental pro-Zionism. Whether that was because he was afraid of seeming anti-Semitic, or because he felt guilt about the Holocaust, or because he allowed himself no deep appreciation of the Palestinians as victims of and fighters against Israel's injustice, or for some other reason, I shall never know."[1] Most commentators were far blunter. 'Aida al-Sharif, Al-Adab's special correspondent who covered Sartre's tour in Egypt, wrote that Sartre "came to visit Egypt, met who he met, visited the Gaza Strip, spoke to its inhabitants and to the refugees, but everything he heard and saw did not influence him even one iota. . . . That is because Zionism was smarter and more focused than us in navigating him toward its goals."[2] But was it really so?

Al-Sharif, Suhayl Idris, and others placed much of the blame on the person who had produced the Middle East tour, Sartre's close associate Claude Lanzmann. Lanzmann, the famed managing editor of *Les Temps Modernes*, was a bold journalist, a filmmaker, a former resistance fighter and, yes, a pro-Zionist French Jew. Did he have to be there? Did he really have to be part of this project? Absolutely yes, said Sartre plainly, "I cannot move without Lanzmann."[3] But his presence, as we shall see, was hard to swallow. According to al-Sharif, Lanzmann sabotaged the visit by conspiring and manipulating Simone de Beauvoir, who in turn influenced Sartre to distance himself from the Arabs.[4] "Haven't we been naive that we agreed to the presence of Lanzmann as a guarantee for the neutrality of the visit? Why didn't we stipulate that a pro-Arab individual accompany Sartre to Israel?" asked ʿAida.[5] She placed the blame squarely on the naïveté of the Egyptian hosts for not realizing the true interpersonal nature of the triangular relationship between Sartre, Beauvoir, and Lanzmann, which made such a betrayal inevitable.[6]

But why had this triangular relationship remained unknown to an Arab audience that "read everything"? After all, in her memoir *La force des choses*, Beauvoir was quite forthright about her long romantic relationship with Claude Lanzmann. Their life together during the 1950s was never a secret. Yet, in 1964, when *Quwwat al-ashyaʾ*, the Arabic translation of Beauvoir's memoir, appeared in print, there was no trace of her relationship with Lanzmann there. As it turned out, Suhayl Idris had intentionally removed these passages from his wife's translation of the memoir.[7] Could it be that such crippling practices of willful not-knowing prevented Sartre's Arab interlocutors from understanding the true nature of his thought and thus prevented them from politically maneuvering their case? Could it be that a simple romantic entanglement prevented Sartre's enrollment on behalf of the Palestinian cause?

The story of Sartre's visit is a dramatic one, a key development of the European intellectual response to the Arab-Israeli conflict and especially to the question of Palestine. Over the years, and as recently as 2016, numerous scholars, observers, and politically interested parties have felt compelled to comment, analyze, and reflect on Sartre's overall failure to "figure out" the conflict and its many complexities. Explanations for this failure vary considerably and range from an exploration of his genuine ethical difficulties to deterministic arguments about his inherent pro-Zionism. Drawing on Sartre's few public declarations, several French-Algerian and Moroccan scholars registered his ambiguity and concluded, rather inaccurately, that Sartre was and remained pro-Zionist. Much of this work falls under the category of engaged intellectual commentary and does not represent systematic historical study.[8] As we shall see in chapter 8, an exception to this type of history writing is the work of Jonathan Judaken and Paige Arthur, who engaged the topic through a very close reading of Sartre's texts.

However, though Judaken and Arthur's work certainly strikes a chord, Sartre's words fall short of exposing the real stakes behind this drama and, in fact, obscure far more than they reveal. As a result, they fail to account for the historical process by which Sartre arrived at his understanding, and they remain silent on the intellectual milieu with which he interacted so intensely. Obviously, for an inherently committed intellectual such as Sartre, adopting an uncommitted position did not come naturally. Furthermore, the long process of arriving at this position had a serious impact on his engagements elsewhere in the world, as well as—in this particular case—on the two sides of the conflict, who were eager to persuade Sartre that they were the ultimate model for true revolutionary socialism. The process by which Sartre came to an ambiguous and uncommitted position needs to be spelled out. Thus, although Sartre's role in the conflict has been considered, it has been so far only from the position of Sartre as the exclusive subject, meaning that everything around him has, until now, received little attention. The operating mode of *Les Temps Modernes* and the small circle of people in Paris and the Middle East who worked tirelessly for two long years in order to produce Sartre's visit have not yet been studied. His Arab interlocutors are largely unknown to scholarship and, overall, the visit that initiated the total collapse of Sartre's Arab legacy remains a moral, political, and historical enigma.

To understand what happened during and after Sartre's visit to the Middle East, a new perspective is needed: one that turns away from the exclusive focus on Sartre and instead situates this episode as a drama with multiple actors on both sides of the Mediterranean. Hopelessly entangled in everything that came to pass between Jews, Arabs, Zionists, and Europeans, Sartre's engagement with the Middle East suggests a level of historical complexity that has thus far escaped our attention. Who initiated Sartre's foray into the politics of the Middle East? What was the goal of this engagement, and what were the politics behind it? Why was the visit to the region necessary to begin with? Did Arabs and Israelis have an impact on the visit's agenda, and, if so, what were their expectations? Were the Israeli and Arab camps united in their respective oppositional positions toward each other? If not, what were the allegiances or divisions, and how did they play out politically? What was the role of the French government in facilitating this visit? This multitude of questions will here be the subject of a straightforward narrative, one that shifts the analytical strategy from Sartre's broken words to a careful reconstruction of the effort to engage the conflict. We will return to the two final acts of this story, Sartre's travel in the region and its aftermath, in the last two chapters of the book.

The Interlocutor

Sometime in 1958, a patriotic Egyptian student by the name of ʿAli al-Samman arrived in Paris. He held a law degree from the University of Alexandria and had just graduated with an advanced degree in law and political science from the University of Grenoble.[9] Revolutionary Egypt was thirsty for young talent, but al-Samman did not want to go home. He wanted to live in Paris. Hopelessly poor, he took a low-paying job as a porter in the busy wholesale marketplace of Les Halles. He also enrolled in a PhD program in political science. But his real business was neither that of Les Halles nor that of academia. It was people. Equipped with sharp social skills, an endearing personality, and a talent for self-promotion, he also happened to have rented a room in Boulevard Raspail. A few years later, after the bombing of Sartre's house in rue Bonaparte by supporters of French Algeria, he would move there as well. They became neighbors.[10] Like many other young students in those years, al-Samman too headed for the cafés, where he quickly found his true métier.

In the late 1950s, there were dozens of Arab students in the cafés of the Latin Quarter, and though these were the days of high nationalist fever and growing enthusiasm for Arab unity, Arab students were in an obvious state of disunity. Iraqi communists occupied one café, Syrian Baʿthists another, Egyptian Nasserists yet another, and others with an obvious dislike for politics found their own corner. Interaction between these ideological circles was minimal. Realizing the untapped social and political potential of this scene, al-Samman, along with his Lebanese friend Faruq al-Muqaddam, set out to break down these divisions and bring the community together. Moving from one café to the next, they gradually formed an informal circle of patriotic students who shared the same diaspora experience. Al-Samman showed his friends that what they shared in common was stronger than what divided them, and, as part of that project, he pushed for the establishment of the Association des Étudiants Arabes en France (Arab Students Association of France, Ittihad al-Tulab al-ʿArab fi Faransa). Being the first Arab organization of its kind, it was a political startup that would assist al-Samman in representing what he now called "the Arab cause in France" and, also, in making a name for himself.[11]

And a name for himself he made. At the height of the Algerian war of liberation, metropolitan France took increasing interest in the collective affairs of the Arabs. Surprisingly, there were very few articulate

Arab voices to represent these affairs and forcefully argue on their behalf. As a recognized leader of students in France, al-Samman would gradually emerge as the face, voice, and pen of the Arab Cause.

He started small. In late 1958, al-Samman was asked to publicly rebut an Israeli official in a discussion about the Arab-Israeli conflict. It was the first proposed public debate of its kind, and his fellow students were divided on how to approach it. Most members called for a boycott of the event, but al-Samman thought otherwise and, despite harsh opposition and a stream of telegrams of protest sent directly to Gamal 'Abd al-Nasser and the Egyptian security service, al-Samman attended the debate and delivered an eloquent speech about Zionism and racism. It made a serious impact, and from that point things happened quickly for al-Samman.

French diplomat Pierre Rosso introduced him to André Ulman, editor of the foreign affairs journal *Les Tribune de Nations*. Ulman was impressed and, according to al-Samman, "proceeded to teach me the art of political journalism."[12] Working with André Ulman, a Jew and a former resistance fighter who survived the Nazi extermination camp of Mauthausen, al-Samman developed a set of sensitivities that most of his fellow compatriots did not. And, thus, when it came to critiquing Israel, al-Samman understood very well the post-Holocaust French and European sensitivities. "We oppose Israel," he is reported to have said on one occasion, "because of politics, not because of anti-Semitism!"[13] The head of the Middle East desk at *Le Monde*, Egyptian Jew Eric Rouleau, also noted al-Samman's sophisticated take on Zionism. Impressed, he invited him to contribute periodically to *Le Monde*.[14] His moment had arrived.

Under al-Samman, the activities of Arab students gained so much traction and publicity that they soon drew the attention of the Egyptian security service, which was displeased with the students' independence and which made public its decision to monitor their activities. The French government was also spying on them.[15] While this attention was quite expected, little did al-Samman and his friends realize that the Israelis were watching, too. In a classified Israeli file, al-Samman is described as the highly competent head of Association des Étudiants Arabes en France and its network of at least ten other satellite Arab-student groups all over France.[16] Al-Samman was now an up-and-coming leader and writer who no longer needed to lift heavy things for a living. With the value of his work acknowledged, he regularly met Egyptian intellectuals who visited Paris, such as Luwis 'Awad, Husayn Fawzi, and Lutfi al-Khuli. Of equal importance, he had also made friends in French intellectual circles. Raymond Aron was one such friend. They meet frequently and found common ground in their deep skepticism toward communism or, as Aron famously called it, "the opium of the intellectuals." With more writing and connections under his belt, greater opportunities presented themselves, and al-Samman soon became a busy Parisian journalist with the Cairo-based Middle East News Agency.[17]

Recognizing his value, the Egyptian embassy stopped spying on al-Samman, included him in the official visit of Egypt's chief of staff, ʿAbd al-Hakim ʿAmr, and sought his advice on matters of public opinion and even policy.[18] And so, quite rapidly over the course of the early 1960s, al-Samman emerged as a dynamic journalist, a self-appointed spokesman, and a one-person public-relations firm, all in the cause of Egypt and the Arabs. Apparently, during the French negotiations with the Algerian National Liberation Front (FLN) at Évian, he was even asked to carry a personal message from Charles de Gaulle to Nasser, asking him to tone down the anti-French propaganda of Voice of the Arabs, Cairo's international radio station.[19]

It was hard to ignore al-Samman, and, one day, his neighbor's secretary called and said that Jean-Paul Sartre would like to meet him. It was early 1965. Sartre called on al-Samman because he was interested in his position on "fighting racism" in the context of the Arab-Israeli conflict. As we shall see, since the late 1940s, Sartre had spearheaded postcolonial thought about race (through *négritude*), otherness (through the Jewish experience), alienation from the self, and these theories' relationship to neocolonialism more broadly. Yet, Sartre had never written anything about Zionism as a racist system. Though 1965 was nine years before the United Nations passed a resolution that equated Zionism with racism, the idea was already circulating, albeit in a rather crude fashion. Over the course of their conversations, al-Samman explained to Sartre that the Arabs experienced Zionism as a system of racial differentiation. It was a viewpoint about which Sartre knew close to nothing at that point, as until then he had been mainly focused on Algeria. In fact, not since 1948 had Sartre paid any intellectual attention to Palestine. Indeed, one could say that, when it came to the issue of Palestine and the Eastern Arab lands, Sartre was quite ignorant.[20] But he was a fast learner.

By the mid-1960s the Arab-Israeli conflict, as it came to be known, was getting more international attention. Unable to refuse participation in any cause célèbre, Sartre began to systematically study the position of each side in the conflict and, in the process, to define his own position. He assured al-Samman that he was a member of neither camp, Arab nor Israeli, and that his one and only commitment was to freedom. Their first meeting went well. Sartre was eager to learn about the region and certainly would have found al-Samman to be a smart, knowledgeable, and engaging interlocutor. Al-Samman, for his part, wanted to bring Sartre to Egypt. In concluding their first meeting, Sartre suggested that from now on they would meet every Sunday at noon. They did so for about a year, in *Le Dôme Café*, a few steps from their apartments. During this time, al-Samman saw that Sartre's situation was complex. On one occasion, he arrived at *Le Dôme* and noted a young Tunisian woman packing to leave. It was Arlette Elkaim, the Jewish philosophy student whom Sartre had just adopted as his child.[21] During these meetings al-Samman registered that Sartre had strong opinions about Gamal 'Abd al-Nasser. They were quite negative. He called Egypt "a country which eliminates freedom" and cited this as a major reason for his refusal to visit the country.[22] While respectful of Sartre's principled position, al-Samman vowed to change his mind. He told Sartre about Egyptian socialism, the agrarian reforms, the effort to educate and lift millions out of poverty, the quest for dignity, and the profound revolutionary position of his country with regard to all Third World issues including those of Congo and Vietnam.[23] Besides my personal interview with al-Samman, no additional record exists of his and Sartre's Sunday meetings. And, although what Sartre asked and what al-Samman replied is known to us only in general terms, the Israeli intelligence file on 'Ali al-Samman reveals in full his position on Judaism and Zionism.

On December 14, 1966, al-Samman gave a keynote address in front of eight hundred Arab students. His words were transcribed by an Israeli agent in the crowd. Introduced by the organizers as a progressive intellectual, he directly addressed two painful issues: "It is sad to read in the European press how the Arabs are always to be blamed as the aggressor whereas Israel always has the right to defend itself." He related this profound imbalance to the fact that "the world still ignores the Palestinians." Like many Arabs he thought that the current "status-quo perpetuates injustice, an injustice the Israeli people need to fix. No one can force the Arab states," he maintained, "to sign a peace treaty before the injustice is reversed." He then moved to his second concern and spoke about the Arab disappointment with the French Left, which with few exceptions supported Israel, as would become painfully clear six months later. Al-Samman was acutely aware of the linkage between this unequivocal support of Israel, the French legacy of anti-Semitism, and the still-unprocessed trauma of the Holocaust, which in those days began to be addressed via the so-called Treblinka Affair.[24] He addressed this link carefully and, given his audience, very courageously: "The Arabs are at the forefront of the battle against Colonialism [and, as progressive international actors] Arab students fight anti-Semitic manifestations. I join every demonstration against anti-Semitism and fascism. We will take to the street with you in order to fight fascism. We will never let anybody hurt a Jew for who he is as long as we are here!" In return he asked "the French Left, which always protected the oppressed peoples . . . to protect the Palestinians as well."[25] We can assume he told Sartre the same thing.

One day, while al-Samman was telling Sartre about Egypt's economic development, the philosopher cut him short: "I am ready to visit Egypt," he said.[26] Sartre explained that the visit to Egypt was part of a larger project of *Les Temps Modernes* to investigate the causes and dynamics of the Arab-Israeli conflict. The idea was to visit Egypt and Israel on the same trip. In tandem with these visits, the journal wished to publish a special issue in which both Israeli and Arab intellectuals would lay out their cases side by side. The special issue was designed to be—and indeed was—the most comprehensive exposition of the conflict to date. Explaining his goals, Sartre asked al-Samman to produce the Arab side of the special issue. He also consulted with Palestinian writer Dawud Talhami.[27] It was a risky job that might have alienated al-Samman from his Arab environment, as the overall mood opposed any collaboration with Israelis. Yet, since appearing side by side in the same journal could hardly be considered collaboration, al-Samman accepted Sartre's offer.

Elated by the prospect of bringing Sartre to Egypt, al-Samman left for the Egyptian embassy and delivered the news to Nasser's secretary. Arrangements were made by the embassy in close consultation with al-Samman, who was asked to advise which government agency should host Sartre. He thought that the publishing house of *Al-Ahram*, run by Nasser's confidant Muhammad Hassanein Heikal, would be an excellent choice. Al-Samman also insisted that the pro-Israeli, Jewish manager of *Les Temps Modernes*, Claude Lanzmann, be invited. He made a strong case for Lanzmann by explaining that Jews and Zionist Israelis should not be confused as one and the same. Shortly afterward, *Al-Ahram* sent Lutfi al-Khuli to officially coordinate the visit, and December 1966 was set as the official date.[28] Sartre now set out to find an Israeli counterpart to al-Samman.

The Other Interlocutor

On November 17, 1965, a resourceful and highly idealistic Israeli man arrived in Paris as the representative of the Israeli Socialist Party (MAPAM, a Hebrew acronym for the United Workers Party) in Europe. His name was Simha Flapan, and he spoke no French. Born in Poland in 1911, he immigrated to Israel during the 1930s and became the director of MAPAM's department of Arab affairs as well as its secretary. Being a relentless peace activist but also a party man, he cofounded and edited the nonpartisan magazine *New Outlook*, which promoted a better understanding of Middle East affairs and called for a peaceful solution to the Arab-Israeli conflict. It had a modest circulation and struggled to survive. While his official job was to establish a strong relationship with the Jewish community in Europe, promote the goals of his party among the various power brokers of Paris (journalists, activists, and politicians), and invite and coordinate pilgrimages like the one undertaken by the young Paul Ricoeur to experience the miracle of the kibbutz—his unofficial business was searching for peace with the Arabs. He was the perfect man for Sartre's project and a much better choice than his skeptical predecessor in the directorship of MAPAM, nicknamed Buma, who was reluctant to cooperate with Sartre's circle.[29]

And so, exactly two days after Flapan's arrival, Claude Lanzmann invited the Israeli to a meeting in the offices of *Les Temps Modernes*, where Lanzmann briefed him about the special issue and the planned visits to Egypt and Israel. Flapan then participated in a preparatory meeting, which included Professors Robert Mizrahi (pro-Israeli) and Maxim Rodinson (pro-Arab) as well as Egyptian and Israeli diplomats, who attended unofficially. Unlike his predecessor, who would soon be out of the picture, Flapan was engaged. To begin with, as al-Samman's counterpart, his job was to organize the contributions of Israeli writers to the journal and help coordinate Sartre's visit to Israel. Yet, above all, his most pressing job was to persuade his comrades back home that Sartre's project had merit.[30]

It was a tall order. Upon hearing of the project, MAPAM's party boss Meir Ya'ari wrote to Flapan: "I am not enthusiastic about writing to Sartre's magazine" and suspect Sartre's "objective neutrality. . . . It's better if you write to the magazine yourself."[31] Flapan responded: "I do not agree with you about Sartre. He stands before considerable Arab pressure, and thus far, they failed to get from him any anti-Israeli statement. . . . His decision to tie the Egyptian and the Israeli visits together is courageous . . . as for the special issue, it is a serious enterprise and not cheap propaganda."[32] Like Ya'ari, the Israeli Ministry of Foreign Affairs was equally suspicious of Sartre.

During the course of several more meetings in December and January, the organizers insisted that, rather than Sartre being the official guest of "the Israeli government," MAPAM would host him. The Israeli embassy emphatically rejected the idea. The organizers then suggested that Flapan's *New Outlook* sponsor the visit, thus creating parity with the invitation from the Egyptian *Al-Ahram*. MAPAM liked the idea but the Israeli Ministry of Foreign Affairs objected, saying that, unlike the state-owned and widely circulated *Al-Ahram*, *New Outlook* was both marginal and partisan.[33] Instead, they proposed the Hebrew University as the hosting institution. This time Sartre refused and, citing the growing friction between MAPAM and the Israeli embassy, threatened to cancel the Israeli leg of the tour altogether. Just like the Egyptians, since the 1950s the Israelis had been eagerly expecting a visit from Sartre to acknowledge the socialist achievements of Zionist revolution. They therefore took the threat of cancellation seriously and moved to quickly settle their differences.[34]

By 1966, still unsure of MAPAM's ability to pull the visit off, on February 21 Lanzmann arrived in Israel to test the ground. His job was to assure the Israelis of the sincerity of Sartre's intentions and to defuse the establishment's suspicion. In return he wanted to hear from MAPAM a solid commitment and a unified voice. Upon Lanzmann's arrival, the popular press announced the visit of "Sartre's confidant."[35] He started with the socialist party MAPAM. In a short yet highly effective meeting, he persuaded party boss Meir Ya'ari to contribute to the special issue and lift his opposition to the visit.[36] Other key members of MAPAM fell into line, and while they were still skeptical of the prospect of Sartre's visit, as he had already "disappointed us so many times," they were willing to give it a chance.[37] Lanzmann also assisted in brokering a compromise between the Ministry of Foreign Affairs and MAPAM, who agreed that a bipartisan public committee would welcome Sartre.[38] For the time being, the Israeli side was in order.

An Exclusive Egyptian Agenda

While over the course of 1965 al-Samman and the Egyptian embassy were able to bridge their differences, the rest of the Arab community, especially Syrians and Palestinians, refused to attend the various meetings preparatory to Sartre's visit and indicated their reluctance to participate. Cognizant of the political meaning of this rejection, Sartre instructed his representatives to do whatever it took to bring them on board.[39] With the Arab side completely fragmented, Egypt pushed forward and articulated an Egypt-centered agenda that served only to further alienate the rest of the Arabs. As we shall see in chapter 7, beginning in 1962, Egypt's political elite was eager to show the world that Egypt was not simply a Middle Eastern nation in search of sovereignty but a powerful force in the global revolution of socialism against imperialism. Engaging Sartre from that universal standpoint and seeking his acknowledgment for this vanguard revolutionary position was a major need of Egypt's political elites.

With Egypt unilaterally setting the program for the entire Arab side, in December 1965, in anticipation of the ensuing multiparty dialogue and visit, Sartre sat with al-Samman for a long interview in *Al-Ahram*. The interview's main theme was highly partisan: to inquire why Sartre and the French Left continued to refrain from a dialogue with the Arab Left and to ignore Egypt's objective revolutionary achievements. Though cordial, al-Samman put Sartre on the defensive. He maintained that Egypt's positive role in the high-profile Congo conflict and in fighting neocolonialism in Yemen was worth acknowledgment as a global revolutionary achievement. He noted that Egyptians were committing their meager resources to such struggles, while, at the same time, toiling to transform their society from within by fighting feudalism at home. As we shall see ahead, all of this was true, and Egypt had indeed taken a leading role in the global fight against imperialism in Africa and elsewhere.

Though obviously aware of this, Sartre responded in general terms and spoke of the difficulty for outsiders to engage a foreign place. He acknowledged collective blame on behalf of the French Left, which he characterized as "unorganized, confused and diverse," but which was nonetheless still very interested in, and quite knowledgeable about, the challenges of the Third World.[40] Shifting to the personal, Sartre said that he had been meeting Egyptians for years, and that they had even invited him to visit on several occasions. Yet, he added, "unfortunately, several of those who came to meet me were put in jail right afterward, and the visit could not take place. This put us in an impossible situation especially when my information about Egypt was quite disjointed. If I commit to a cause, I better know it thoroughly." "In any case," he assured *Al-Ahram*'s readers, "we have great interest in Egyptian affairs."[41]

Al-Samman then opined "that (all over the world) revolutionary movements are losing ground to the forces of reaction." He wanted to know "what the reason for that might be and what role could Cairo play" to offset this development. Sartre answered that Fanon's *The Wretched of the Earth* described this very situation and explicated how the bourgeois middle class accommodated colonialism and capitalism and, by doing so, frustrated the progress of the revolutionary cause. Sartre then explained the inner workings of neocolonialism and, dramatically, concluded that Egypt's revolutionary international role was so obvious that "for my part I have sided with it since 1956."[42] These words, "I have sided with Egypt since 1956," were powerfully meaningful for the Egyptians—but they would also come to haunt Sartre once his affiliation with Israel was fully exposed, and his inability to side only with the Arabs became painfully obvious.

As in most of the meetings that Sartre would eventually have in Egypt, al-Samman wanted to talk about existentialism. Given the fact that so many Arabs "identify themselves as existentialists," he asked Sartre if he could "clarify what (exactly) is existentialism?" Sartre gave the usual speech about his philosophy of freedom but elaborated on how his recent philosophical work (*Critique of Dialectical Reason*) elucidated the ways existentialism complemented Marxism, thus substantiating and updating the famous notions of commitment and collective responsibility.[43] As we shall see in chapter 6, this clarification would eventually help settle the decade-and-a-half-long debate between Arab existentialists like Suhayl Idris and committed communists like Mahmud Amin al-ʿAlim, both of whom subscribed to competing notions of political responsibility

Shifting pace, al-Samman asked Sartre to comment on Egypt's role in the context of global revolutionary movements. Sartre said that "in his mind, Egypt did for the Yemenite revolution more than (Leon Blum's) Socialist government did for the Loyalists during the Spanish Civil War."[44] It was a stunning answer that revealed the depths of Sartre's ignorance with regard to the brutal realities of Yemen. Far from being a true revolutionary cause against British neocolonialism in Aden, if anything, the conflict in Yemen resembled the folly dynamics of the Vietnam War, with Egypt playing America's role.[45] In addition to the frequent violations of human rights, including the Egyptian use of poison gas against civilians, it was a war about which Egypt's leadership repeatedly lied to itself as well as to its citizens. Quite simply, it was a colossal military, political, and human disaster about which Sartre and his circle knew absolutely nothing. Indeed, when he was asked during his visit to Israel about resemblances between the wars in Vietnam and Yemen, Sartre answered sternly that "only clowns will see similarities."[46]

Concluding the interview, al-Samman turned to discuss the purpose of *Les Temps Modernes'* project on the conflict. Sartre was very careful not to take any position and explained that the sole purpose of this work was to elucidate the problem: that is, to untangle the various positions of those involved in the conflict. "I am fully committed to this objective position," said Sartre, "and for that reason I will visit Egypt as well as the Palestinian refugee camps. I will then visit Israel."[47] He then wished the Egyptian people success in the global revolutionary cause and the building of a just and equal socialist society. The translated interview appeared in full in MAPAM's daily newspaper *Al Ha-Mishmar.*[48]

The next day, the journalist and intellectual Lutfi al-Khuli published a programmatic piece in the same pages, titled "Beginning a Dialogue with Sartre." Al-Khuli was the intellectual who in 1958 had invited Sartre to visit Egypt and had been imprisoned shortly afterward. Traveling to Paris frequently, al-Khuli and his wife, Liliane, a friend of Beauvoir, were familiar faces in Sartre's circle.[49] In Egypt, al-Khuli was a revered playwright, journalist, lawyer, and political activist. A man of principles who already had already seen, and would continue to see, a prison cell from within,[50] he was an independent Marxist and a freethinking humanist who struggled on behalf of poor peasants, workers, Palestinians, and all globally disenfranchised Third Worlders.[51] As a member of the intellectual revolutionary vanguard, an unofficial circle of Egyptian leftist thinkers, al-Khuli wrote a daily political column in *Al-Ahram* and edited the revolutionary magazine *Al-Tali'a* (the vanguard). A close friend of Muhammad Hasanayn Haykal, he had an indirect access to Nasser, who closely followed his work even as he was instrumental in imprisoning al-Khuli and his comrades. His part-commentary, part-sponsorship of Sartre's forthcoming tour was therefore very influential.

When it came to politics, al-Khuli was no amateur, and when he called for a dialogue with Sartre he had a model in mind. Over the previous six months al-Khuli had successfully conducted a critical dialogue with the man who would collaborate with Sartre on the Vietnam tribunal, Bertrand Russell. In March 1965, the ninety-three-year-old British philosopher had surprised *Al-Tali'a's* editors with an open letter, in which he criticized Arab societies for nondemocratic political practices and, especially, for curtailing freedom of speech. Al-Khuli drafted a short response, explaining the complex dynamics of the revolutionary process and assuring Russell that they hold the same democratic principles dear.[52] Shortly after, in September, Russell invited al-Khuli to spend the weekend at his house in Wales. Thus, on the agenda for dialogue was the very past, present, and future of Middle East affairs.

Al-Khuli shared Russell's key positions on the state of the world, but when it came to the Middle East they held very different views. Like Sartre, Russell believed that Egypt was in the hands of a military dictatorship that systematically infringed on basic freedoms. He also thought of the problem of Palestine in terms of the so-called Jewish problem. He did not distinguish between Jews and Zionists, was quite sympathetic to Zionism, and believed that Arabs aspired to exterminate the Jews. "Frankly," he asked al-Khuli, "aren't Arabs anti-Semites?"[53] With such a starting line, al-Khuli had a lot of heavy lifting to do, but by the end of a long weekend, during which al-Khuli reconceptualized regional affairs as a neocolonial struggle and explained why Zionism and Judaism are two separate issues, the philosopher had changed his mind. Indeed, shortly before his death in 1970, in his last public statement, Russell openly expressed an obvious change of heart with regard to the Zionist project and the state of the Palestinian refugees.[54] Satisfied with his gains, al-Khuli hoped for a similar success with Sartre.

And, thus, for his interview with Sartre, al-Khuli crafted an agenda based on his recent exchange with Russell. He began the interview by addressing the specificity of Egypt's double revolution, namely, the revolution it conducted at home against reactionary forces, and the revolution it waged externally, in the Third World. He wanted to ensure that Sartre fully understood that though, they were partners in the fight against racism, fascism, neocolonialism, and exploitation, Arab revolutionary thought was very different from European revolutionary thought.[55] Similar to his conversation with Russell, after establishing the parameters of the deeper common denominators of the global 1960s, al-Khuli conveyed to Sartre his dismay with the French Left. He recalled a meeting with Lanzmann in which al-Khuli had complained about the superficial French understanding of the Middle East and, concomitantly, of bad policies. Lanzmann had acknowledged the problem and promised that the community of *Les Temps Modernes* had already begun to "pay attention to the manifestations of the new revolutionary experiments" such as that of Egypt.[56] Again, seeking recognition for Egypt's universal ambitions was both a paramount political concern of the Egyptian state as well as a deep psychological need of the intelligentsia.

At the center of his piece, al-Khuli offered a key distinction between Judaism and Zionism. This message was directed to Arab ears, as he wanted to make sure that all those who were going to be involved with Sartre's visit and the ensuing dialogue would not use the terms Israel, Zionism, and Jews interchangeably. "Our issue with Israel and Zionism," he told his readers, "has absolutely no relation to the Jewish Question."[57] He condemned the discrimination and persecution of Jews anywhere in the world just as he condemned "the suppression of Africans in South Africa and Rhodesia."[58] And, thus, al-Khuli characterized Zionism as a movement that had "colonized Palestine and established in it a militarized and racist system" that systematically inflicted violence on the Arabs, independently of the fate of the Jews.[59] Clearly, and as we shall see in chapters 6 and 7, al-Khuli applied to Zionism Sartre's very own understanding of neocolonialism. The fact that al-Khuli liberally employed Sartrean categories of thought with relation to Zionism placed the two men on a collision course as Sartre had thus far showed no inclination to judge Zionism by the measure of neocolonialism or the terms he reserved for the struggle in Algeria. Yet, at the time, neither of them could yet foresee their inventible and tragic collision.

Importantly, in insisting on separating the Jewish question from Zionism, al-Khuli, like ʿAli al-Samman, was pushing for a new understanding of the conflict in Arab circles. He did so because he truly believed that Zionism and the Jewish question are two separate issues. But also because, as an intimate interlocutor of the French Left, al-Khuli knew that any confusion between Zionism and Judaism would result in an immediate alienation of Sartre's circle and the collapse of the dialogue. In hindsight, this was quite a challenge since even the powerful Egyptian official radio, the Voice of the Arabs (Sawt al-ʿArab), by then the largest broadcasting radio station in the world, frequently referred to Israel as al-Yahud (the Jews) and had expressed openly anti-Semitic views.[60] After all, for most Arabs, Zionists were simply Jews. As we shall see shortly, eighteen months later, an unfortunate violation of al-Khuli's principle of the neat separation of Zionism and Judaism occurred in the most politically sensitive of circumstances.

Push and Shove

Sartre's persistent efforts to bring all Arabs on board with his agenda gradually paid off when in February 1966 Fayiz Sayigh, a member of the executive committee of the PLO (Palestinian Liberation Organization), director and cofounder of the Palestinian Research Center in Beirut, and above all an avid existentialist and admirer of Sartre, announced that he supported the project and would travel to Paris to meet Sartre. The young Syrian philosopher Sadiq Jalal al-ʿAzm recalled being in the offices of the Palestinian Research Center when the invitation from Sartre to participate in the project arrived: "When Sartre requested our participation, our position was that we reject any dialogue. However, we were concerned that Sartre would blame us for the failure of the initiative. We felt that we couldn't ignore his request because the implication would be that either we do not have a position or that we are unable to defend it. The world might think that maybe the Palestinians have no case. So, we decided that our papers could appear next to those of the Israelis but not in conversation with them."[61]

It was an important decision and, more so, a critical endorsement by Sayigh, a well-connected individual. Sayigh had his reasons for endorsing the project, as over the past two years he had customized Sartrean neocolonialism to the situation in Palestine: as we shall see in chapter 7, a few months earlier he had published the influential *Zionist Colonialism in Palestine*.[62] We have no record of his meeting with Sartre, but we do know that Sayigh's brother Anis, who directed the Palestinian Research Center in Beirut, supported Palestinian participation. Needing approval from Ahmad al-Shuqayri, head of the PLO, Anis Sayigh flew to Cairo, met al-Shuqayri in the airport, and boarded the same airplane back to Beirut with his approval in hand.[63] Attention now shifted once again to the Israeli side.

Answering the doorbell on March 16, 1966, the Israeli socialist activist and sponsor of Sartre's visit Simha Flapan was surprised to find Simone de Beauvoir on the doorstep of his apartment. She came unannounced. It was their first meeting. "My wife and I were astonished and confused," he later recalled.[64] What did Beauvoir want? What was so urgent? It took them some time to get their bearings, and when they finally did Beauvoir said that she had come to explain "Sartre's delicate position." What was this delicate position? It was the night before Sartre was scheduled to give Flapan an interview to be published in *Al Ha-Mishmar*. Keeping symmetry between the Israelis and the Arabs, this interview was the equivalent of the one Sartre gave to *Al-Ahram*. Beauvoir told Flapan that Sartre had preconditions—the exact stipulations that al-Samman had agreed to grant him—namely, that "Sartre would not be asked any question about the Arab-Israeli conflict or any other question that would force him to say something against Israel. This time Sartre wants to avoid a similar situation with the Arabs."[65] Put differently, Beauvoir requested that Sartre be given ample space for ambiguity. Flapan accepted, and then set out to explain this delicate position to his superiors in Israel: Sartre's neutrality absolutely prohibited him from making any supportive statement on behalf of Israel or Zionism, Flapan explained. He could not take sides or even appear to be taking sides. If he did, the Arab partners would withdraw from the project. "By the way," Flapan concluded his report to Ya'ari, "Simone was charming."[66]

The following day, as they sat down to do the interview, "Sartre appeared pleasant and supportive. He apologized once again for the various constraints and explained that it was for the benefit of both sides. His answers were fluent, spontaneous, and free of any effort to control the message. They were full of meaning and substance." "He is," wrote Flapan, "an outstanding individual, and I finally understood the myth that surrounds him."[67] As for Sartre's message to Israelis, his famous declaration was that "As long as one Jew is threatened around the world no Christian would enjoy security."[68] Acknowledging directly the presence and weight of anti-Semitism and its connection to the "Jewish Condition," he did not think that Israel was the only place Jews could reclaim their authenticity. Yet, nonetheless, the experience of the war had brought Sartre to support the Zionist struggle against the British. For the exact same reasons, he also sided with the Algerian struggle against colonialism and made sure that the Israelis understood his deep connection to the Arab side. As a result of this dual engagement, Sartre stated, he and his friends were "torn between contradictory friendships and loyalties . . . and live this opposition as if it was our personal tragedy."[69]

With this dilemma fully explained, Sartre then told Flapan that Arabs and Israelis were not ready for a dialogue, and that all he was asking from them was to elaborate their respective positions. Flapan then guided the discussion toward exploring the idea that socialist intellectuals on both sides could make a difference in regional politics: "There are two sides, both socialists, that would like to see the Middle East outside the competition of the two superpowers and of the Cold War, free of foreign interests and bases and free of the arms race and the nuclear threat."[70] Was this joint struggle being held hostage to the dynamics of the Arab-Israeli conflict? Sartre said that when it came to the Middle East he was not sure that nuclear nonproliferation was a pressing mission and that he hoped that one day socialism would transgress its internal paradox of being both nationalist and internationalist so that it could fulfill its universal mission. The rest of the interview was dedicated to the expected themes of Marxist philosophy and praxis, Third Worldism, Vietnam, and the prospects of socialist Europe.

The interview was well received. The popular daily *Yediot Ahronot* was pleased with the fact that "the spiritual leader of the Arab intelligentsia," as Sartre was known to Israelis, had taken a strong position against anti-Semitism and was genuinely preoccupied with the Jewish question.[71] For the time being the December tour and the special issue could proceed as planned, and, as the project progressed, al-Samman and Flapan took a liking to each other. Both were also close to Lanzmann and would eventually become lifelong acquaintances of his. Flapan was very impressed by al-Samman's courageous position against anti-Semitism and heard from him in detail about his troubles with fellow Arab activists. He saw in him a natural leader who "believes that war is avoidable and hence calls for an open debate for finding a solution to the conflict."[72] Beyond the various technical aspects of the tour Flapan and al-Samman also dared to dream big about high-level political maneuvers they had absolutely no power to initiate or control.

As a member of MAPAM, a marginal political partner in a coalition government, Flapan's belief that Sartre's project would mobilize socialist intellectuals on both sides to jumpstart a peace process seemed particularly surreal. The more he met with al-Samman and other Arab personalities, the more Flapan surrounded himself with an air of secrecy and self-importance. His letters to party headquarters were now marked "Top Secret." Later that year, when Flapan met Lutfi al-Khuli to discuss the situation in Egypt, Arab unity, American imperialism, anti-nuclear-proliferation, Israel and Palestinian guerrillas, he wrote to his superiors "I would rather not name him at this stage," thus concealing al-Khuli's identity. Turning from an open participant to a secretive convert, he alienated some important Israeli allies in his environment. Many simply disliked him.[73]

As the summer of 1966 came and went, rumors spread that the special issue was in jeopardy due to an Arab "writing strike," upon whose cause we can only speculate. Indeed, by this time there were thirty Israeli articles on Sartre's desk and only two from the Arab side. Most notably, Fayiz Sayigh and his circle did not deliver their material. In a meeting between Sartre and Lutfi al-Khuli, the philosopher warned that "if the Arabs fail the publication he will cancel his tour to Egypt."[74] Once again, threats were used to mobilize the participants, and al-Samman was immediately sent to the Middle East to collect the Arab contributions. He knew fairly well that while Egyptian intellectuals badly wanted Sartre to acknowledge their revolution, they had no motivation to engage Israel and the Palestinian issue. So, instead of going to Cairo, he traveled to Beirut, which he rightly considered a more open environment; at the time it was the capital of Arab freethinking. In Beirut he brought Palestinian and Lebanese intellectuals and activists such as Sami Hadawi, Munthir 'Antabawi, 'Abd al-Wahhab Kayyali, and Jibran Majdalani on board. Burhan Dajani, the cofounder of the Institute for Palestine Studies, also joined. By October he had at his disposal a total of seventeen articles including one by himself and two by Egyptian leftists Khaled Muhyi al-Din and, of course, Lutfi al-Khuli.[75] The threat of cancellation was averted.

With publication still scheduled for late December 1966, Sartre insisted that al-Samman would accompany him to Egypt. It was a great honor but, unfortunately, al-Samman's final PhD examination, his "defense," had already been scheduled for the date. Should he go with Sartre or stay behind to defend his dissertation? He told Sartre about his dilemma and, quite astonishingly, the philosopher postponed the trip. They kept the real reason secret and cited instead a busy schedule with Bertrand Russell and the Vietnam tribunal. Back in Cairo the news was a major cause for concern, and Lutfi al-Khuli rushed to Paris to find out if Zionist pressures caused the cancellation. He was assured that technicalities alone were at play. All sides agreed on a new date: February 1967.[76]

Conclusion

That *Les Temps Modernes* was an intellectual powerhouse of the Left with clear universal ambitions is well known. Less understood perhaps is its function as a lubricated political machine that occasionally mimicked a government executive branch. Seemingly informal and at times even casual, in reality the journal was coldly calculated, business oriented, and tenacious.[77] As the locomotive of Sartre's political train, it carried the philosopher through the difficult terrain of Egyptian hegemony, Palestinian suspicion, Israeli skepticism, multiple political schisms, independent agendas of various individual actors, state politics, and metropolitan needs and expectations. Clearly, both Arabs and Israelis realized that behind the machine stood not simply a man but the entire noncommunist French Left and, possibly, that of Europe as a whole. The stakes, though exceptionally high, were not distributed equally.

Whereas the Israeli government, and much of the public for that matter, were highly suspicious of Sartre's intentions and believed that, almost by definition, he could not support Zionism, the Egyptian side was elated and considered the visit a golden opportunity to win recognition and capture the moral high ground. This asymmetrical enthusiasm emerged from the fact that whereas Sartre's intellectual influence in Israel was quite marginal, in the Arab world it was so significant that one can only wonder how Sartre had never visited it before. Indeed, even Israelis realized that Sartrean thought was constitutive of the postcolonial Arab project and hence regarded him as the philosopher of the Arabs. In other words, the asymmetry between the two sides had to do with the quality of the validation they sought to receive for who they were. Both sides sought this validation, but only the Arab side depended upon it. That is to say, only Arabs took Sartre personally. Why so? To gain a full appreciation of why and in which ways the Arab world became intellectually dependent on Sartre we need to take a long view that begins somewhere in the early 1940s and moves slowly through the decades to consider how the abstract issues of freedom, authenticity, sovereignty, and agency conjoined to assemble a Sartrean tradition of Arab existentialism, a tradition that sought to work through the painful legacy of colonialism toward a happier human condition.

Why Existentialism?

In May 1944, when the Egyptian philosopher 'Abd al-Rahman Badawi defended his dissertation on existential time, Taha Husayn, the doyen of modern Arab letters and its most celebrated intellectual, declared it the birth of modern Arab philosophy. The six-hour-long defense was a national event, and hundreds of onlookers, students, teachers, and journalists came to celebrate. The widely distributed Egyptian daily *Al-Ahram* immediately shared the news with its readers.[1] But why did a standard PhD examination on an arcane philosophical topic attract so much attention to begin with? What factors made it an event? Was this some sort of a beginning and, if so, of what and to what end?

Taking this event as its symbolic point of departure, this chapter explores the kind of existentialisms with which young intellectuals experimented. To explore these early engagements is not to say that they were necessarily successful or would become hegemonic. As we shall see, Badawi's project, for instance, was nothing but a brilliant theoretical proposition that was completely lost on realpolitik. But there were also other propositions that drew on existentialism, embraced the political, and sought to engender change from that exclusively engaged angle. This chapter tells the story of two existentialist strains that were acculturated and reinvented in the Arab East during the late 1940s. The first, of course, was Badawi's creative attempt to fuse together Heidegger's phenomenological existentialism with Islamic mysticism, or Sufism, as a platform for addressing the problem of cultural authenticity.

The second strain was Suhayl Idris's adaptation of Sartrean existentialism, specifically the theme of commitment, to the concrete cultural and political needs of Arab decolonization. Though both options developed independently of each other they illustrate how existentialism could potentially address the pressing issues of the day. We begin this exploration by acknowledging the fact that these early experiments were entertained against the backdrop of collective anxiety and a prevailing sense of alienation among the youth.

Down and Out in Cairo and Beirut

There are many reasons why Badawi's dissertation defense became such an ecstatic event. None has to do with the confident student who became a doctor of philosophy that day. Smart and accomplished as Badawi was, and though by that point he was already quite famous for his 1939 biography of Nietzsche, the first philosophical best seller in the Arab world, the cause for the attraction is to be found elsewhere.[2] As World War II slowly came to a close and British control over Egypt began its long and expected retreat, Egyptian youth braced for a sweeping change, which would touch upon every aspect of life from high politics to the intimacy of love. Faced with the totality of decolonization but lacking any assuring leadership with a credible plan for the future and an orienting cultural agenda to go with it, the age yielded anxiety, and plenty of it. Not only in Egypt but elsewhere in the region as well, Arab youth were in need of a clear direction. Such was the case, for instance, of Fayiz Sayigh, a Palestinian refugee in Beirut who embraced existentialism in order to register the profound implications of the Nakba and decolonization: "The key to the character of Arab youth is . . . dissatisfaction: our dissatisfaction with the way our leaders, or our rulers, look upon things in general, manage our affairs, and run our lives. . . . Our dissatisfaction has transformed itself into rejection. We have lost respect for our traditional values, virtues, and way of life. We have become a generation at odds with its world. We no longer belong to our immediate world: We are no longer at home."[3] This basic insight of inner alienation was shared by young people all over the region and served as a catalyst of the search for a new form of citizenship.[4] It was not lost on Badawi either.

Sensitive and worried as he was, a year after graduation, Badawi expressed this collective sense of alienation in a fictional text that exposed the depths of Arab anxiety in the wake of its colonial experience.

As a precursor to the rise of existentialism, it is worth quoting at length. Titled *Humum al-Shabab* (The youth's anxiety), in this work Badawi harnessed his sharp analytical skills to compose what is arguably one of the best local texts about colonial trauma. His motto? "We are a generation of youth who were cast down [*alqa bina*] into the unknown of a foreign world."[5] Focusing on the lack of sovereignty and the loss of physical freedom experienced by colonial subjects ("We became desperate pawns in the hands of European powers."[6]), Badawi understood that the Arab human condition is not restricted to that domain alone and extends quite deeply into the spiritual realm as well: "We, the Egyptian and Arab youth . . . are unable to bear our situation and surrender to our wretched fate. . . . We find ourselves in the same state of destruction of Eastern youth from India, Japan and China. . . . In our minds we live the tribulations of European youth and we became spiritually preoccupied by them . . . [but when attached] to our own actual painful experiences, enormous charges of revolt, anxiety, spiritual confusion, and psychological disorder generated in us an exceptional sensitivity."[7]

This heightened sensitivity was a result of a deep cultural schism that forced Arabs to think of themselves in cultural terms that were completely foreign to their actual historical and daily experiences. Sadly, it was a major side effect of the Arab project of Enlightenment, or the Nahda.[8] Compounded by the physical loss of freedom, Arab youth all over the region suffered from what Badawi defined as "psychological disorder," namely, an overwhelming sense of loss, humiliation, helplessness, shame, desperation, powerlessness vis-à-vis oneself and others, spiritual and material deprivation, a broken—if not castrated—father figure, and a general sense of emptiness and anxiety. This mental state was not simply an individual matter but a reality that greatly affected the political, social, cultural, and economic fabric of collective life. "These," Badawi wrote, "are the main characteristics of the generation that was born between 1910 and 1920."[9] He wrote these words a decade or so before Albert Memmi, Aimé Césaire, and Frantz Fanon ventured into the topic of mental slavery, thus opening the field of mental decolonization.

Badawi's own life was a fine example of the turmoil and tribulations of postcolonial Arab youth. During the 1940s he was heavily involved in radical, and sometimes violent, nationalist organizations. By his own admission, he was a member of the semifascist Young Egypt organization and, early on, a self-proclaimed Nazi sympathizer.[10] Indeed, many intellectuals, politicians, and pundits were well aware of the lure that radical solutions posed to Arab youth. The link to violence was obvious, too. Seeking an escape from the trap of colonialism, Arab youth began to experience decolonization as an ideologically guided, violent process.[11]

This phenomenon had its origins in the 1930s when the fear and fascination with the energies of youth and their attraction to political violence yielded a certain discourse of "youth crisis," in which youth "were recast as a problem in need of regulation and control."[12] The fear of youth as unbridled political and sexual subjects brought observers like social scientist Ibrahim Batrawi to characterize youth as being in "a psychological stage of social adjustment, sexual repression, and existential anomie."[13] Fellow social scientists were in the same opinion and so were lay observers of youth action in the region. Indeed, from Cairo's student demonstrations to Baghdad's urban riots against the British, the political violence of the late 1940s spoke volumes of the mental toll that colonialism took on Arab youth and laid bare a visible state of crisis.

The emerging realization of colonial trauma also bore within it the seeds of decolonization as a powerful and, at times, violent rebirth: "What should we do with the overflowing vitality that fills us like a bomb about to explode?"[14] All too aware of the dangers of political violence, Badawi charted a larger project: "This time our role is to be creators and not representatives, transmitters and guardians of (someone else's) light."[15] The question was how to do that. How exactly to reclaim a sense of cultural authenticity and agency so that contemporary Arabs could work through the psychic wound of colonialism and reinvent themselves anew? Answers to these questions varied all over the region.

For the countless followers of the Muslim Brotherhood, the largest grassroots movement in the Middle East, the answer to colonialism was a "return" along classic fundamentalist lines to an allegedly pure and unadulterated premodern Islamic past. For Iraqi communists, the largest political party in the Middle East, the straightforward answer was Marxism-Leninism and deep socioeconomic and political reform. However, for the majority of young people, there was no obvious straightforward path to inner peace and communal success.[16] Though eventually Pan-Arab nationalism would emerge as a popular albeit limited way forward, Badawi and numerous other intellectuals began searching for more substantial and decidedly unideological answers in the philosophy and political example of existentialism. And so, as colonial rule in Iraq, Lebanon, Syria, Palestine, and Egypt gradually came to a close, existentialism suggested itself as a way out of the generational impasse of colonialism. But how could existentialism offer a healing antidote to colonialism? An initial response to this question arrived somewhat unexpectedly.

Healing the Fragmented Self

In June 1940, as German forces headed toward Paris, Russian émigré philosopher Alexander Koyré left his teaching position at the École pratique des hautes études (EPHE) and crossed the Mediterranean hoping to enlist with the British army in Egypt or, alternatively, with the newly organized forces of Free France.[17] Instead, he settled for a life of less action as a professor of philosophy in Cairo's Fu'ad University, where his work with 'Abd al-Rahman Badawi, then an advanced graduate student, would critically influence the reception and reformulation of existentialism in the Middle East.[18] Joining André Lalande (1867–1963), a Sorbonne retiree, Koyré arrived at a young and highly ambitious university in which students took classes with some of the most accomplished European scholars, and often traveled to the continent in search of knowledge.[19] Koyré was a student of Edmund Husserl's phenomenological circle and a follower of Martin Heidegger's existentialism. Whereas until the 1930s epistemology (represented in France by Bergsonian philosophy) had been the central philosophical subject, dealing with what we can know and with what degree of certainty, existentialism prioritized the problem of *being* above that of *knowing*.[20] Moving to France, Koyré was "serving as a bridge between Germany and France and between Husserl and Bergson."[21] Koyré strongly believed that "[Heidegger's] philosophy of existence would not only determine a new age of the development of Western philosophy but would form the departure point for an entirely new cycle."[22] As part of his efforts to expose French intellectuals to contemporary German philosophy, Koyré started a journal (*Recherches philosophiques*) and a seminar.[23]

Among the participants in this vibrant and experimental forum were Alexandre Kojève and Henri Corbin. Kojève was a Russian émigré who studied with Karl Jaspers and after 1932 was responsible for a systematic introduction of Hegel and Heidegger to French thought.[24] Corbin was an Orientalist and the first French translator of Heidegger's *Being and Time* and other seminal texts whose translations Koyré prefaced. Raymond Aron, the person who introduced Sartre to phenomenology and Heidegger, was also a member of this circle. For obscure reasons, in 1933 Koyré departed for his first academic year in Cairo and left the seminar in the skilled hands of Alexandre Kojève.[25] Thus, as an intimate insider of the Franco-German philosophical scene, Koyré brought an incredible heritage to Cairo; whatever impact he had there was, ultimately, a function of a simple one-on-one philosophical transaction between him and Badawi.

But Badawi, who came from a rural Suni background and had an excellent Islamic education under his belt, was also interested in Islamic philosophy. He therefore studied with the eminent scholar Mustafa 'Abd al-Raziq (1886–1947), a towering figure of Islamic thought in the first half of the twentieth century. 'Abd al-Raziq taught Badawi logic in the tradition of Ibn Sina (980–1037) and offered close, and sometime excessive, readings of original texts. He was also interested in mysticism, or Sufism, a topic that Badawi would later explore in terms of Koyré's existential philosophy. Even though he spent five years as a student of Islamic philosophy in France, when 'Abd al-Raziq was asked about the many ways in which modern philosophy or the study of Orientalism, challenged medieval Islamic philosophy he simply smiled.[26] Indeed, the painful disjuncture between Islamic and modern philosophy was never a matter of personal or disciplinary dispute among faculty members and students. They were simply treated as two parallel universes and, in 1937, when Lalande moved to Cairo, as a token of recognition for his unflinching commitment to Egyptian education, 'Abd al-Raziq conceded the position of chair to him. This cordial arrangement, in which faculty members did not articulate Islamic and modern philosophy as mutually exclusive systems, opened for Badawi critical space for intellectual experimentation.

Following an inspirational 1937 tour in Germany, Badawi was ready to write about "Death in Existential Philosophy," a topic about which Alexander Koyré had much to say.[27] Indeed, Badawi received from Koyré a new philosophical frame of reference: Max Scheler, Karl Jaspers, Martin Heidegger, Gabriel Marcel, Jean Wahl, and Emmanuel Levinas. These thinkers nourished the rise of Arab phenomenology[28] and taught Badawi that death is not simply an event that happens by the end of one's life, but an experience that shapes one's entire way of being and, especially, illuminates the condition of authenticity upon the eventual encounter with death itself.[29]

He also began to think in Heideggerian terms, specifically, to view existence in terms of time and to understand it from a circumstantial perspective in which existence is not historical, linear, or continuous but fragmented, ruptured, and synchronic. In other words, Badawi subscribed to two main themes of existentialism: first, *existence precedes essence* (i.e., who a human being is [his essence] is the result of his or her choices [existence]), and, second, *time is of essence* (i.e., human beings are time bound and experience lived time in a way dissimilar to measured clock time).[30] Yet, by the time Badawi came to think in this entirely new way, Charles de Gaulle visited Cairo and enlisted Koyré in the efforts to represent the cause of a free France in the United States. In late 1941 Koyré left for New York City, where he reinvented himself as a historian of science.[31]

So what did Koyré leave behind? Badawi credited him with shaping his methodology, introducing him to modern philosophical notions and the contemporary philosophical scene, teaching him phenomenology (which was new to the Arab world and was given the name *ilm al-zahriyat*), and, most importantly, encouraging him to draw a link between existentialism and Sufism.[32] Four months after Koyré's departure, Badawi graduated.[33] He was now ready for his PhD. His ability to practice philosophy at the highest level was not in question.

Titled *Al-Zaman al-wujudi* (Existential time), Badawi's dissertation investigated how time shapes individual existence. It argued that "true existence is that of the individual. The individual is the subject that necessitates freedom. The meaning of this freedom is the very existence of possibility."[34] From here he followed a classic Heideggerian interpretation of subjectivity[35] and embraced Heidegger's key concept *Dasein*, which was not a conscious subject, politically or otherwise, but the way human beings (both as real people and in the abstract form of "being human") are in the world among things.[36] In doing so he embraced two more axioms of existential philosophy (four overall): *radical individualism* (i.e., humanistic focus on the individual's quest for meaning and identity) and *freedom* (i.e., the only guarantee for individualistic self-reflection and responsibility). As mentioned above, upon graduation Badawi was celebrated as Egypt's first modern philosopher.

The year was 1944, and Badawi was now a busy man traveling, lecturing, and publishing at an incredible pace. His new major project aimed at achieving an intellectual synthesis between Sufism and existential philosophy. In some metaphorical sense, Badawi tried to synthesize his two beloved professors, 'Abd al-Raziq and Koyré. The reason for this particular synthesis was that Badawi identified existentialism as the future of post–World War II European philosophy, and he thought that by fusing it with Sufism he would instantly update Arab philosophy to a level of parity with that of Heidegger.[37] If achieved, the project would heal the schism that made Islamic cultural heritage, or *turath*, intellectually redundant and would thus allow the postcolonial Arab generation to join the modern world on equal philosophical terms.[38] This is how he thought of doing it.

According to Badawi both existentialism and Sufism are predicated on individual subjectivity, which maintained that we are in the world by a relationship of being in which the subject is our body, our world, and our situation. To make this fusion happen, he sought to update the medieval Sufi doctrine of the Perfect Man (*al-Insan al-Kamil*) as an "isthmus [*barzakh*] between necessity [*wujub*] and possibility [*imkan*], . . . which combines the attributes of eternity and its laws with the attributes of the generation of being."[39] In what followed, he mined this mystic doctrine for the key principles and concepts of Heideggerian existentialism, arguing that he was drawing on medieval Sufism in the exact same manner in which Heidegger built on Kierkegaard. In no uncertain terms he promised his readers that this exercise would result in no less than the birth of a new Arab subject and "a comprehensive philosophy for our generation."[40]

In hindsight, however, Badawi was in the same boat with Vietnamese, Chinese, and especially Japanese philosophers who had "discovered" Heidegger already in the late 1920s and found his work very suggestive in terms of its relation to mysticism. In the East Asian context, Heidegger's widely noticed compatibility with Daoism boiled down to nothing more than "Correspondences, congruencies and resonances" but by no means synthesis.[41] This is also the case with relation to Sufism. For all his work, Badawi's search for philosophical synthesis consisted only of the discovery of Heideggerian and phenomenologist categories of thought in Sufism. An actual merging of these spheres in a fashion that, to borrow from Nietzsche, would have allowed Arab philosophy as a whole "a past *a posteriori* from which [it] might spring, as against that from which [it did] spring" never really occurred.[42] Indeed, years later, Mahmud Amin al-ʿAlim, a former student of Badawi, mused that his teacher "lived" two distinct forms of existentialism (Western and Sufi) rather than one.[43]

Though Lebanese philosopher Charles Malik taught Heidegger's work in the American University of Beirut and even studied at the University of Freiburg shortly after Heidegger stepped down as rector in 1934, it was Badawi who dominated the philosophical discussion of his day with this promise of a new philosophy.[44] Because this promise was about transforming colonial subjectivity into a healthy postcolonial Arab interiority, it was quickly acknowledged by other intellectuals, such as psychoanalyst Yusuf Murad, and the burgeoning community of Egyptian psychologists.

Murad was to Arab psychology what Badawi was to modern Arab philosophy, and the two shared ideas, influences, hopes, and students, such as Mahmud Amin al-ʿAlim. Indeed, Murad had trained "a generation of thinkers who then went on to become literary critics, translators, university professors, and mental health professionals in Egypt, Syria, and Iraq; he left a wide imprint on psychology, philosophy, and the wider academic field of the humanities and the social sciences."[45] Murad himself "had been trained in philosophy and psychology at the Sorbonne in the 1930s and was extremely active in the translation and dissemination of psychological theories in Egypt after World War II, founding the Jamaʿat ʿIlm al-Nafs al-Takamuli (Society for Integrative Psychology) and the Egyptian *Majallat ʿIlm al-Nafs* (Journal of psychology) in 1945."[46] Like many other intellectuals during the 1940s, Murad was fascinated by the new analytical category of "adolescence" and the subjective experience of Arab youth, their selfhood, and their soul. "Murad and others writing in *Majallat ʿIlm al-Nafs* shared a set of assumptions about adolescent psychology as characterized by introspection and acute self-perception, the manifestation of unconscious sexual impulses, and philosophical turmoil. Adolescence, in other words, marked the developmental beginnings of a cavernous interiority and represented a new category of analysis that hailed new modes of being."[47]

How to integrate a new mode of being organically and in an integrative and unitary way was a major preoccupation of Badawi, Murad, and others in the academic community. Given what these psychologists identified as turmoil, aberrant behaviors, and other "unconscious conflicts that manifested themselves in [the] ontological and existential anxieties" of Arab youth, Murad searched for the authenticity of Arab subjectivity, and the unique circumstances of its own specificity dovetailed neatly with Badawi's work.[48] Thus, from the very beginning, the two conversations about existential philosophy and youth psychology were not as distinct from one another as one would expect. In fact, since the 1930s, psychology had been taught in the philosophy department where Badawi got his degree.[49] Reviewing Badawi's work on existential time, Murad was quick to acknowledge this nexus: "This is a book that presents the contours of a new philosophy whose roots extend deep into the study of psychology."[50]

Academic understandings aside, by 1950, young Arabs who wanted to read about existentialism in Arabic found Badawi's work about individualism, authenticity, angst, responsibility, and freedom readily available.[51] The terminology he had worked so hard to establish began appearing in Lebanon and Iraq as other aspiring philosophers pitched in with their own explanations of subjectivity and commitment and why existentialism was so relevant.[52] On the popular level Badawi also wrote of Sartre's fiction and of how existentialism nourished a new literary sensitivity that allowed the individual to actualize its possibilities through radical liberty.[53] Badawi was also not free of existentialist sentimentality and romanticism. In a series of fictional dispatches from Paris he wrote of love, longing, loss, and the self.[54] Popular content on existentialism was now circulating so regularly that accusations of recycling and plagiarism began to appear.[55]

Yet, despite this circulation and the philosophical promise of existentialism to liberate Arab subjectivity from the constraints of European cosmology and reestablish it on authentic grounds, it was not clear what could young people could *do with it*. How exactly did one go about actualizing her possibilities through radical liberty or reconfigure her subjectivity? Was this an individual effort, a group effort, or both? Even though Badawi was the most serious existentialist philosopher during the 1950s and 1960s, being primarily an academic pursuit undertaken for its own sake, Badawi's existentialism was not, so to speak, "operational" enough; it lacked a real-life goal and a political and ethical community to support it. It was, as the philosophy itself held, a one-man project of radical individualism, one which would eventually function mainly as an important philosophical reference shelf for writers in the Arab world as well as in Africa.[56] There was also another problem: Badawi had nothing to say yet about "commitment" and about Jean-Paul Sartre, "the other" existentialist.[57]

A Tighter Grip on Culture

While Badawi's existentialism made its very slow debut as a general frame of reference for a new postcolonial culture, the storm of Sartrean existentialism was gathering in the East. It arrived to the Arab world on the eve of an intellectual change of guard and thus was initially met with the skepticism of established writers. The text that represented Sartre in the Middle East was not his major philosophical oeuvre *Being and Nothingness* (1943), which was translated only in 1966, but his 1947 essays in *Les Temps Modernes*, which were later delivered publicly and published as *Qu'est-ce que la littérature?*[58] As far as the udaba' were concerned, Sartre's politicization of culture was a threat that required their immediate attention. The first person to react to Sartre's challenge was Taha Husayn.

Gifted as he was, Husayn was not a disinterested intellectual communicator. Though a model for Badawi's generation, he was also at odds with them as his work and public persona, like the rest of the udaba', were seriously conditioned by the problematic nature of colonial Enlightenment. No text captures this discrepancy better than Husayn's 1938 *Mustaqbal al-Thaqafa fi Misr*, a seminal call for cultural renewal. The book was published in a moment of great cultural optimism following the 1936 Anglo-Egyptian Agreement and the 1937 Montreux Convention, when Egypt expected to finally win its unconditional independence. Thinking of the postcolonial era with youth in mind, Husayn asked them to embrace Europe and, in fact, to become culturally European. Concomitantly, his notion of cultural self-criticism was inevitably reduced to a calculation about what should be done in order to become European. Critical chapters in *Mustaqbal al-Thaqafa fi Misr* follow this logic.[59] Clearly, the classic tale of the Nahda, the nineteenth-century Arab project of Enlightenment, as an unproblematic and progressive liberal march toward human betterment finds its apex with Taha Husayn's cultural vision.

There were other problems as well. Taha Husayn was well aware of the dire sociopolitical circumstances, and, even though the postcolonial concerns of Egypt, the Arabs, and the rest of the colonial world were not yet fully theorized, they were, nonetheless, very visible. Most visible, and most urgent, were the profound levels of social inequality manifest in poverty, illiteracy, and disease. This was not merely an economic problem of wealth distribution but a political and cultural issue that Egyptians did their best to comprehend.[60] Then there was the lingering impact of colonial culture, which had resulted in cultural disorientation, yielding the quest for one's authentic cultural stance. This element was perhaps the most elusive, subjective and difficult issue to entertain. Finally, Taha Husayn's vision was narrowly Egyptian. Husayn had little to say about the Arab world and, indeed, like most of the udaba', he seems to have subscribed to the classic post–World War I order in which the Egyptian udaba' write, and the rest of the Arab world reads and follows.[61]

With the end of World War II, many other individuals and groups understood that youth would be the makers of the postwar era. For instance, in May 1945, as soon as the war was over, a group of Egyptian Marxists established *Al-Fajr al-Jadid* (The new dawn) a journal that focused on the problem of social justice and the critique of capitalism and imperialism. Drawing firm connections between these seemingly separate issues (e.g., by writing about poverty, distribution of wealth, class differences, literacy, and economic policy), the journal presented a comprehensive analysis of Egypt's ailments and suggested that radical change was overdue. It is perhaps not a coincidence that the Free Officers who came to power in Egypt in 1952 borrowed much of the journal's platform.[62] But the Free Officers are only an example of what Taha Husayn and his fellow udaba' were up against in Cairo. Political and cultural fermentation was under way in Baghdad, Damascus, and Beirut as well.

Drawing on his successful experience as a hegemonic cultural leader during the 1930s, Husayn sought to compete in this emerging space of youth radicalization by providing cultural leadership. His plan was to revitalize *Mustaqbal al-Thaqafa fi Misr*. Since *Mustaqbal al-Thaqafa fi Misr* offered only an abstract vision, Husayn collaborated with the Harari Brothers publishing company to establish a new platform for his ideas. They called it *Al-Katib al-Misri* (The Egyptian scribe) and "it owed its name to the famed ancient sculpture of the amanuensis or seated scribe." The pharaonic figure of the amanuensis "idealizes Egypt's mythohistorical role in world culture as the inventors of writing and . . . as a bridge between ancient and modern Egypt."[63] Thus, more than being simply another mainstream journal, *Al-Katib al-Misri* was designed as a robust cultural front that consisted of an Arabic journal of the same name, two French journals on literature, culture, and history (*Valors* and *La revue de Caire*, cowritten by Arab and French writers), and a series of two dozen translated classics by foreign writers such as André Gide, Oscar Wilde, and Antoine de Saint-Exupéry. In presiding over this enterprise as editor in chief, Taha Husayn propagated a novel view of world literature, which he seemed to have developed while corresponding with André Gide.[64] This impressive literary front was also in serious debt to the British literary journal *Horizon*, which published the best of European and American writing and closely followed new cultural trends. This was Taha Husayn's arsenal in combating the emergence of postwar radical subjectivity.

In his opening statement for the first issue of *Al-Katib al-Misri* Husayn made it clear that this was an elitist enterprise designed for a vanguard of a select few. He told readers that the journal had an exclusive agreement with the best European and American intellectuals to publish material in *Al-Katib al-Misri* before it appeared in print anywhere else. He connected this opportunity to the old theme of Egypt as a

Mediterranean bridge between civilizations, thus underlining the pivotal role of the journal. Notwithstanding the strong emphasis on Egyptian exceptionalism, somewhat paradoxically, the journal saw itself as relevant to all Arab countries. In that sense, it was another cultural enterprise that, as in the 1930s, positioned Egypt as the main producer of "Arab culture" and the rest of the Arab world as its passive consumer.[65] In a burgeoning Pan-Arab era, this was a gross miscalculation that would take Taha Husayn a decade to acknowledge.

Another thing that had changed since the 1930s was the local understanding of colonialism. Though Husayn was not oblivious to the harmful effect of colonialism, his editorial line treated it as a geopolitical problem external to the constitution of the Arab self.[66] In that sense he differed markedly with the young generation, who would follow existentialism precisely because they felt that the colonial process had damaged their selfhood. Social justice was another pressing issue, but here Husayn was much more involved. First, he translated Voltaire's *Zadig ou la destinée* (1747) to Arabic. This work of fiction was a veiled attack on the sociopolitical order in Voltaire's time, prior to the French Revolution. Second, drawing on Voltaire's fictional formula, Husayn wrote *Al-Mu'adhabun fi-l-Ard* (The wretched of the earth), a socially conscious work that blamed the government and the king for the troubles of the struggling masses. *Al-Mu'adhabun fi-l-Ard* was first circulated in *Al-Katib al-Misri* but later had to be published in Beirut because of government censorship. Husayn's efforts to connect to the "concerns of the youth," as his student Badawi put it, were conducted with a clear intention to actualize, repackage, and make relevant again his vision of inclusive cosmopolitan Enlightenment. Cognizant of the rise of "ideologies" (Marxist, socialist, and communist) as wholesale packaged solutions, Husayn made a herculean effort to offset, derail, or, at the very least, postpone the drive of young people to ideologize and thus politicize culture. Refuting Sartre became part and parcel of this effort.

Finely attuned to France's intellectual milieu, Taha Husayn's interest in Sartre began as soon as the existentialist scene became "an event." Early coverage was inquisitive and even admiring. There were essays that explained the philosophical genealogy of existentialism, its deep meaning, and the reasons behind Sartre's fame and the craze of existentialism.[67] Exactly a month after it was first published in Sartre's revolutionary magazine *Les Temps Modernes*, a fine translation of Sartre's "La nationalisation de la littérature" ("The Nationalization of Literature"), appeared in *Al-Katib al-Misri*. Shortly afterward and still with Paris in mind, Taha Husayn introduced the black American existentialist writer

FIGURE 1   *Al-Katib al-Misri*: "All over the Arab world"

Richard Wright to Arab readers. Wright had left America for France, where he befriended Sartre and collaborated with him on various projects concerning race and otherness.[68]

Still unsure what existentialism really was, some readers asked the editor for a more comprehensive essay on the topic. In response, *Al-Katib al-Misri* contracted Didier Anzieu, a French philosophy student and "real existentialist" to explain what French youth found in Sartre and existentialism. Anzieu, who later became a student of Jacques Lacan and an influential psychoanalyst in his own right, started with an enticing account of the mystique of the postwar existentialist atmosphere, thus communicating the power of a certain historical moment. Only then did he move to hardcore philosophy and an explanation of the "I."[69] Although this and other essays joined the existentialist bookshelf that Badawi had established, it was still unclear how exactly Arab youth could use existentialism. That changed when Sartre published the articles that would become known as *Qu'est-ce que la littérature?*

Taha Husayn was the first local thinker to grasp the intellectual appeal and political meaning of Sartre's articles in *Les Temps Modernes*, and, beginning in August 1946, he reacted to them with a clear sense of urgency. In his reckoning, *Qu'est-ce que la littérature?* critically examined the relationship between the writer and society, and argued that, since writing is a consequential form of acting/being, intellectuals should assume political responsibility for their work and the circumstances that condition it. This call for responsibility qua professional action was conjoined in Sartre's concept of commitment (*engagement*). Though the philosophical concern of commitment was human freedom and authentic existence, its practical application was "something for which (one) is prepared to die." This "something" was widely understood as a political cause, and almost overnight the notion of commitment as total submersion in the political became a mainstay of Sartrean existentialism. Even though often understood in this way, Sartre's notion of commitment was far from a straightforward call for politics. In fact, it was just one essential element in Sartre's quest for authenticity or, in his words, the "complete consciousness of being embarked."[70] Nonetheless, since Sartre himself led a politically engaged life, his example of action overrode the complexity of his philosophy.

This point was not lost on Taha Husayn, who argued that, historically speaking, writers had always had more options to choose from than the alleged two Sartrean choices of engaged/progressive versus detached/reactionary. He also argued that engagement was a specific response to the unique European realties of the 1930s and to the much-regretted passivity of Sartre's generation prior to and during the war. Since these European circumstances had no parallel in the Middle East, Sartre's notion of commitment was culturally void.[71] In his lengthy meditation on Sartre's concerns (what do we write, why do we write, and to whom do we write), Husayn invoked his generation's apolitical sense of literature as "art for art's sake."[72] He was truly concerned that any other formulation would "kill literature."[73] As we shall see, this specific apolitical notion of intellectual labor became the focus of a fierce generational debate. Lastly, not losing focus on his mission to discredit committed literature, Husayn criticized Sartre's unfortunate exclusion of poetry and the visual arts from the rank and file of committed literary engagement.[74]

The reception of Sartre's articles took place against the background of an overwhelming demand for action, in fact, for revolution. Its manifestation in the political violence of the mid-1940s—specifically the murder of Egyptian Prime Minster Mahmud Fahmi al-Nuqrashi in 1949, three consecutive military coups in Syria, anticolonial riots in Iraq during 1948 (the *wathba*), and violent student politics everywhere else—indicated that young people did not believe in the separation of the intellectual and the political. They wanted ideas to instigate real and immediate change and rejected the ineffectiveness of democratic institutions and their tendency for endless and fruitless deliberations. As a senior member of the udaba', who, as already mentioned, perceived politics as an indirect extension of culture, Husayn feared the potential of commitment to embed the cultural in the political. This total erasure of "borders" rendered commitment a dangerous cultural menace.[75]

So, was Taha Husayn afraid of an abstraction, of a simple notion of action? Not quite. What made Husayn so fearful was the sad precedent of his friend André Gide. Until the end of the war, Gide still represented the Dreyfusard legacy of the universal intellectual who makes courageous moral interventions, such as exposing the vicious side of colonial Congo and an early rejection of the USSR (at a time, one must add, when Sartre and much of the French left-wing intelligentsia failed to acknowledge the ways in which the horror of the gulag constituted the very essence of Soviet communism). Though he spent the war away from occupied Paris, in Tunis, and embraced the highly problematic position of a "nonparticipant," the magazine with whom Gide was closely associated, *La nouvelle revue Française* (The new French review), continued to operate under the Nazis. When the Nazis were driven out of Paris, the journal was charged with collaborationism and banned. Gide's reputation took a serious hit, and his intellectual model, and that of his entire generation, was now under constant attack by Sartre's *engagement* and its mass of young followers. The fact that only a few years earlier Gide had guided Sartre and his generation was all but forgotten. Amnesia is indeed constitutive of youth rebellion.

Indeed, *Qu'est-ce que la littérature?* included numerous references to Gide, and they were all negative. For instance, writes Sartre, "When one considers the work of Gide . . . one cannot help seeing in it an ethics strictly reserved for the writer-consumer. What is his gratuitous act if not the culmination of a century of bourgeois comedy and the imperative of the author-gentleman."[76] Behind Sartre's literary agenda there was a well-orchestrated attack on the older generation of French littérateurs and a blunt call to replace them. Though the irritated Gide did receive the 1947 Nobel Prize for Literature, there was very little he could do about the departure of the youth from his legacy.[77]

Husayn followed these debates closely and took Gide's side (or, as he put it, that of the "French *Shuyukh*").[78] He never hid the fact that he saw in Gide a role model and that to some degree he saw himself as an Egyptian Gide. Gide was the leading literary figure in France and a conscious universal intellectual of the first rate. Husayn held a similar position in the Arab world as a courageous defender of liberal humanistic values against constant attack by the religious and political establishments. Thus, seeing in Gide an unjust victim of existentialism, Husayn translated his work, as well as their correspondence, and made it available in *Al-Katib al-Misri* and its Franco-Arabic twin *Valors*.[79] He had done so in order to avoid Gide's fate and he held to this line until 1948. But then, due to the 1948 war in Palestine, Husayn's Jewish publishers, the Harari Brothers, abruptly closed down their operation and left the country. It was rumored that the king's hand was behind this closure and Husayn was not even given the opportunity of writing a concluding editorial. With the encouragement of Gide, he was nominated twice for the Nobel Prize in Literature (1949 and 1950) but did not receive it.[80] In January 1950, Husayn became Egypt's minister of education; it would be his last hurrah before he and his generation were swept away by revolution.

Though Husayn's fear of commitment proved to be prophetic, not all members of his generation saw Sartre's existentialism in the same light. Salama Musa, an Egyptian Fabian ideologue and a perennial prisoner, published *Al-Adab li-l-Shaʿb* (Literature to the masses), a text that embraced Sartre and challenged Taha Husayn to answer Musa's question: "What is his message and how does it serves humanity?"[81] ʿAbbas Mahmud al-ʿAqqad, a prolific humanist, rejected existentialism's individualism but commended it for protecting freedom. He also reminded his readers that, beyond Sartre, existentialism was a substantial and complex philosophical tradition.[82] Somewhat ironically, in warning the young away from the dangers of commitment, Taha Husayn gave this burgeoning intellectual movement its Arabic name: iltizam.[83]

Doing Sartre in Arabic

It was only a matter of time until someone in the Arab world connected in a meaningful way to the theme of commitment and successfully tied it to the "concerns of the youth." That someone was the young journalist, literary critic, and novelist Suhayl Idris. In a matter of years, under his leadership, the new culture of iltizam overshadowed Badawi's philosophical enterprise, thus indicating the triumph of literature over philosophy as a vehicle for postcolonial thought. Born in Beirut in 1923 to a middle-class Sunni family, Idris grew up in a colonial atmosphere in which the urban middle class tried to appropriate the culture of the French occupier while, paradoxically, also resisting it. This explains how Idris matured as both a francophone and an avid nationalist who systematically nourished two paths: the universal and the particular.

Idris's gift for letters became evident in an early age, and, against all odds, especially financial ones, he pursued his passion all the way to the Sorbonne. There, between 1949 and 1952, Idris wrote one of the first studies of the Arabic short story. Upon his return to Beirut as Dr. Idris, he published the literary magazine *Al-Adab*, which immediately became a reference point for culture and the key literary venue for decades to come. Since *Al-Adab*'s agenda was modeled on Sartrean existentialism, Idris's Parisian sojourn merits close attention.

Whoever visited Paris following World War II could not escape its cafés, the focal point of intellectual, social happenings and exhibitionist behavior.[84] Existentialism, then in full flower, was a philosophical activity conducted in cafés. The sharp contrast between the lived freedom of Paris and the strict code of social (and in particular sexual) behavior at home had surfaced periodically in Idris's correspondence. In the eyes of a foreigner like Idris, who made a point of writing one of his first letters from a café, existentialism was an active scene of people who participated in things like sex, jazz, and crazy dancing. As Sartre's biographer Annie Cohen-Solal put it, "to people in their twenties the area [of the cafés] became synonymous with disenchanted nonchalance, frenzied freedom, and the discovery of excess. The public space of a café and the intimate corners of a village were the privileged places in which one could speak freely and abandon oneself to dreams and chance encounters."[85] Much of this "spiritual surrender to dreams," as Badawi called it, was organized around the literature and theater of the existentialists and the Sartrean idea that words are action.[86] Idris instantly subscribed to this idea, and he was not the only young Arab intellectual to do so.

As the Arab world entered the phase of decolonization, an entire cohort of young Arab intellectuals chose the freedom of Paris as a place where they could redesign Arab culture. There were so many of them living in the Latin Quarter that they renamed it the Arab Quarter, thus making their foreign environment a bit more familiar.[87] High on sugar and caffeine, the cafés of the Arab Quarter were where the phenomenon of Third Worldism gained momentum. For example, Egyptian economist, political prisoner, and future Third World activist Isma'il Sabri 'Abdallah explained that "the important thing in the late 1940s was not only to free our country, but to acquire the knowledge to do so."[88] In fact, around 1950, a short visit to Dupont Café would suffice in order to meet the next generation of Arab intellectuals, such as existentialist playwright and future minster of education in Tunisia Mahmud al-Mas'adi.[89] It was also a historical juncture where young Arab intellectuals encountered likeminded people from Congo, Senegal, Cameroon, Togo, Upper Volta, Cambodia (including Pol Pot and his future murderous junta) and elsewhere. As developmental economist Samir Amin noted, he and his peers shared in common the association of freedom with personal and collective dignity as a new Third World condition.[90]

In this atmosphere of existentialism-as-performance, Idris took the daily and unexpected personal freedom that he experienced as a representation of the philosophy of existentialism and a model for collective cultural renaissance at home. "Life here," Idris wrote to his friend and mentor, the Egyptian literary critic Anwar al-Ma'dawi,

is characterized by a kind of freedom that has no parallel in the East. We are in desperate need of such freedom. Freedom in our lands is suffocated. . . . In Paris people can say and do whatever they want . . . and live humanism to its fullest extent. . . . However, our freedom of speech is repressed, the freedom of thought is massacred, and the freedom for life outside the boundaries of inherited tradition is virtually nonexistent. We need to learn from the West the love of freedom as it is this love alone that would guarantee us our aspired freedom.[91]

On the receiving end of Idris's letters, al-Ma'dawi had the impression of an endless Parisian carnival. He half-jokingly inquired, "Are you spending your time in the nests of the existentialists, have you seen Simone de Beauvoir, have you walked behind the coffin of André Gide?"[92]

Idris answered with a semiautobiographical novel. "I believe that French literature now influences my work," he wrote al-Maʿdawi in October 1951.[93] Two years later his novel *Al-Hayy al-Latini* (The Latin Quarter) became an instant best seller. In this self-described existentialist narrative, Idris dealt with the individualistic anxiety and conflicts of an Arab intellectual torn between East and West, tradition and modernity.[94] It is hard to ignore the similarities to Sartre's *La nausée* (1938), which also dealt with the overwhelming dilemma of an individual. Yet, the fact that Idris's protagonist is a former colonized subject whose anxious encounter with the metropolitan significantly affects his sexuality set the two novels apart. Indeed, the character's "excessive sexual obsession with European women" ends up arresting "cultural contact at the level of sexuality," thus reducing the metropolitan, in all of its intellectual, social, and cultural complexity, to the single trope of sex.[95] Fiction aside, the frantic sexuality that Idris captured so vividly, corresponds with the way in which Arab psychologists characterized the postcolonial adolescent "as first and foremost a psychosexual subject, that is to say, as a subject forged at the vortex of unconscious sexual impulses."[96]

In December 1949, after having his first Parisian love affair, Idris wrote to al-Maʿdawi: "After I suffered in Beirut intense emotional deprivation, I feel emotionally flooded. Here it is possible to meet a girl who would lovingly and dedicatedly respond to your feelings and would grant you the pleasures of the world that you have been missing for so long. Here they cherish affection and love as part of their life whereas we in the East renounce this quality."[97] Thus, in his fiction as well as in correspondence, Idris's emotional and sexual experiences were taken as freedom in the raw and, by extension, as an existentialist experience par excellence.

With so many young Arabs in search of a new tomorrow, Idris was not the only Arab writer who tried to reposition his own subjectivity vis-à-vis the dominating atmosphere of the Latin Quarter. A certain Hassan al-Shamaʿil became such an integral part of the existentialist spectacle that he was nicknamed Paris's Mayor (*ʿUmdat Baris*), thus giving the disenfranchised immigrants the fantasy of total control.[98] Using fiction and the allure of the literary, others tried to entirely reinvent themselves. Such was the case of ʿAbd al-Rahim al-Shalabi, a young Syrian who sought to "create (from scratch) an entirely new literature that emerged from his specific experience of life." He worked on this novel for close to a decade. It sold two copies.[99]

Badawi, who recorded these episodes, took them as an example, actually as a caricature, of compatriots who lived existentialism as style without content and as practice without philosophy. Back in the Middle East, some older opponents of this conduct believed that existentialism would bring nothing but egotistic indifference and social decay.[100] Some parents took this image seriously. The father of a young Egyptian girl by the name of Liliane (later Liliane al-Khuli) refused to let her leave for a city of sin, a "place where people kissed one another in the streets."[101] Yet, against all odds, Liliane and a score of other Arab students and would-be writers flocked to the Latin Quarter to take part in its carnivalesque atmosphere. Badawi lamented this entire scene and the fact that Arab journalists associated the newly found sense of freedom with existentialism and therefore viewed it not so much as a philosophy but as a corrupting platform for moral laxity and sexual misconduct.[102] That was what the older generation thought of existentialism.

As for Idris, he did not come to Paris merely to enjoy life and submerge himself in existentialist action. Quite the contrary, he had an ambitious plan: "I would like to return quickly to Lebanon so I can take part . . . in raising the cultural, social and political level in the country."[103] Far from wasting his time in the cafés and writing of sexual freedom á la Sartre, Idris intended to bring Paris home by publishing a groundbreaking literary journal that "Lebanon, Syria and Iraq desperately need."[104] Al-Ma'dawi concurred: "We are indeed in need of an excellent journal as it is for a long time now that the Arab lands have lacked such a journal. And believe me when I say that I am ready to collaborate with you, even if it means I have to quit my editorial position in *Al-Risala*."[105] Like al-Ma'dawi, Idris also believed that *Al-Risala* and several other classic journals of the interwar period were in decline. One Lebanese writer challenged the suitability of the classic journals to postcolonial times because their contents had remained virtually unchanged since 1937![106]

The fact that Idris was writing for *Al-Risala* and that al-Ma'dawi was a staff member mattered very little. It was time to invent a journal—in fact an entire scene—that, like Paris's cafés, would connect Arab intellectuals to fellow postcolonial intellectuals and to the Third World condition as such. Given the growing irrelevance of the classic literary magazines (including the Lebanese veteran *Al-Adib*, for which both Idris and al-Ma'dawi were writing), Idris's business plan made sense. In August 1952 he wrote to his Egyptian friend, "we are aiming for literature which is called '*iltizam*' or '*indiwa*' [i.e., committed literature]."[107] Al-Ma'dawi immediately knew what Idris was talking about. Influenced by their correspondence, already in 1948 he argued that the connection between literature, art, and life in the Arab world was in need of repair. He dedicated the article to Idris.[108] Readers from Iraq wrote to the editor of *Al-Adib* with observations about intellectuals and iltizam.[109] A modest momentum gathered, and Idris and al-Maʿdawi saw a chance to start something new. The magazine, which Idris eventually called *Al-Adab*, prioritized Sartrean engagement as literary and political action that conceived life and literature as one.

At times it seems that putting the magazine together and doing research for his dissertation were, for Idris, the same work. For both projects he drew heavily on al-Maʿdawi, who, at the young age of thirty, was already a rising, yet frustrated, star in the field of literary criticism. Idris repeatedly asked al-Maʿdawi to invite Sayyid Qutb to join the board because, Idris said, "I consider him to be in the first rank of modern Arab literary critics."[110] Qutb's departure to America and his famous transformation into a postcolonial born-again believer did not deter Idris from seeking his contribution.[111] Idris also asked al-Maʿdawi to persuade Taha Husayn and Tawfiq al-Hakim to serve on the board. Given the fact that al-Maʿdawi had already started to revolt against the cultural hegemony of the udabaʾ and that Taha Husayn deplored existentialist commitment, this was an odd choice that revealed a certain lack of cultural confidence.[112] Idris also needed to know more about the Iraqi literary scene: "My knowledge is fragmented, lacking, and is in need of both [better] focusing and comprehensiveness."[113]

Al-Maʿdawi generously contributed his knowledge, and a year later the first issue of *Al-Adab* was out. Its bold mission statement reads like the creed of an entire generation: "The present situation of Arab countries makes it imperative for every citizen, each in his own field, to mobilize all his efforts for the express object of liberating the homeland, raising its political, social and intellectual level. In order that literature may be truthful it is essential that it should not be isolated from the society in which it exists. . . . The kind of literature which this Review calls for and encourages is the literature of commitment (*iltizam*), which issues from Arab society and pours back into it."[114] A near-copy of Sartre's agenda for *Les Temps Modernes*, *Al-Adab*'s message spread through the capitals of Arab thought with incredible speed, with the first issue selling out in Baghdad in a mere two days.[115] The organizing framework was built around the three questions that Sartre had asked in 1945: *What is writing? Why do we write? For whom does one write?* These questions allowed the new generation to use literature as a tool for broad cultural, social, and political criticism. They could now write about everything from a standpoint that acknowledged that Arab culture was in a state of deep crisis and that intellectuals could change that situation through writing.[116] For an opponent of Sartrean iltizam like Taha Husayn, Al-Adab's creed meant that young writers might start to blame members of the old-guard udaba' for living in uncommitted and segregated ivory towers.

A Palestinian Testimony

Though inhabitants of the Syrian Hawaran area are often ridiculed for their brainlessness and lack of cultivation, the Hawrani priest 'Abdallah Sayigh fathered six outstanding children. Moving from Syria to Tiberius, Palestine, four of them were destined to dominate Palestinian public life in the second half of the twentieth century: Yusuf, the economist (b. 1916); Tawfiq, the poet (b. 1923); Anis, the historian (b. 1931); and Fayiz, a curious teenager infatuated with Kierkegaard and existentialism. Born in 1922, Fayiz pursued his interest and became a philosopher and later an internationally renowned Palestinian diplomat and intellectual.[117] Fayiz, however, was not the only Palestinian teenager who was taken by existentialism. His friend Hisham Sharabi (b. 1927) was another conscript. Born to an established Sunni family in Jaffa, Sharabi lived a cozy life removed from poverty and the poor: "It did not occur to us to imagine a relation between our wealth and their misery."[118] Yet material comfort could not compensate for other deficiencies, and for this Sharabi had to study philosophy: "My choice of philosophy as a subject of study was a result of my persistent desire to get rid of the state of psychological anxiety and intellectual disarray I was in."[119]

Indeed, unlike the intellectual pioneers Suhayl Idris and 'Abd al-Rahman Badawi, Fayiz and Sharabi were not occupied with the cultural translation of existentialism to Arab culture. Instead, they used it to understand, but also to alleviate, the state of uncertainty in which they lived during the transwar era and the British Mandate. Then, after the 1948 war, when their land was no more, their society was defeated, and their families destroyed, these young Palestinians became intimate-outsiders of the Arab world; at once of it and perpetually outside of it. Pivoting on the axis of being / not being, they acquired a dual perspective on virtually everything that involved Arab affairs. Thinking on all of this in existentialist terms, the penetrating views of Sayigh and Sharabi captured the vicissitudes of Arab subjectivity during the early stages of decolonization.

The quest for higher education brought Sayigh and Sharabi to en-
roll in the Philosophy Department at the American University of Beirut (AUB). Both worked under the supervision of Charles Malik. Fayiz's
examination notebooks from his undergraduate years contain essays
on "the nature of Being," "the problem of existence," "the existential
philosopher," and "the problem of subjectivity."[120] These interests cul-
minated in his MA thesis, titled *Personal Existence: An Essay*. Holding
approximately four hundred pages, it was a long and impressive exercise about individualism that was in serious debt to Christian existentialism and much less so to phenomenology.[121]

Similarly, Sharabi wrote papers that followed Charles Malik's religious Kierkegaardian Christian existentialism. The phenomenological
existentialism that Malik studied at Freiburg was left out of the cur-
riculum "for faith was the prevailing mode at the philosophy department since the days of Dr. Malik."[122] The differences between the two
were fundamental explains Judaken: "Man in search of God plays the
central role in religious existentialism, whereas human alienation plays
a key role in phenomenological existentialism."[123] And since Sharabi's
main preoccupation was with alienation and orientation, he had a
very negative assessment of Malik: "Doubtlessly, the kind of thought to
which I was exposed at AUB strengthened my alienation from myself
and increased the distance between me and the reality of life, which, I
yearned to understand and grasp. . . . In the religious idealist frame of
mind adopted by Malik and our other professors, there was no room for
another manner of thinking."[124] And so, though "when we graduated,
we considered ourselves to be existentialist followers of the idealist religious Kierkegaardian school. . . . The purpose of the process of our
education at the university, as in the family and at school, was basically
to render us obedient and subjugate us psychologically to a patriarchal
ethos."[125] Put differently, Sharabi, Fayiz, and many others were exposed
to everything that phenomenological existentialism, especially in its
Sartrean version, sought to replace.

The expected result of the inability of their society to tend to their
deepest psychological needs brought these two young men to seek radical alternatives. And in Beirut of the 1940s, radicalism meant joining
the Syrian Social Nationalist Party (SSNP) of Antun Sa'ada, a charis-
matic yet authoritarian and whimsical leader who insisted he be addressed as "The Leader" (*al-za'im*). Sharabi writes, "I yearned to become
part of a greater whole, an entity in which my individual identity would
merge with my general communal identity. . . . All this— . . . my lone-
liness, my idealistic yearnings—led me in the end to join the Syrian

Nationalist Party."[126] Fayez did the same and joined his older brother Yusuf, who was already a party member. But even the party was not a perfect solution: "Our leaders and teachers hated the West and loved it at the same time. The West for them was the source of their humiliation and misery. They ingrained in us an inferiority complex toward the West, as well as a complex to sanctify it. Our national idea, thus, took on a fanatical quality. Sound social and historical conceptualization was totally alien to us."[127] This is one reason why the paradoxes of colonial humanism were experienced as an existential crisis.

Since its establishment in 1932, the SSNP was an "anti-establishment conspiratorial party" that sought to overturn the political designs of the Lebanese elite and fuse the country into a Pan-Syrian political entity. The party developed an extreme top-down hierarchical structure and a cult of leadership in which Sa'ada's job was to establish sovereignty by way of delivering the Syrian masses from bondage and submission into a brighter future. Thirsty for action, its members aestheticized and valorized violence not simply as means for liberation from French rule but as a regenerative force in the service of a mystical and redemptive nationalism. It therefore had a militia, uniforms, and a militarized body language. All over the region, these were the standard manifestations of youth in revolt.[128]

Since the SSNP was the only political group with a clear Palestinian agenda, both Sharabi and Sayigh saw in it a home and a family that answered their call for ideologically guided youth action better than any other organization. As a senior party member, Fayiz Sayigh held various editorial and intellectual responsibilities. In contrast, though close to the leader and highly committed to the cause, Sharabi's role was rather passive. Sharabi reminisced: "When the disturbances came to an end and the French forces withdrew from Beirut. . . . That was the beginning of independence and the inception of a new era of our lives. That was my first experience with political action."[129] Yet orienting and comforting as membership in the SSNP was, in all other respects, the experience was at odds with their liberal upbringing.

Thus, in 1946, when the leader single-handedly changed the ideology of the party with no prior consultation, Fayiz had enough. Rather than simply quit the party, he registered his differences with the leader in the acerbic treatise *Ila Ayna?* (1947, *Where To?*).[130] In it, Fayiz accused the leader of running a totalitarian institution that completely dominates the life of its members with no legal or procedural grounds. Sayigh exposed in great detail the leader's authoritarian style and its unfortunate personal as well as ideological consequences.[131] Though this attack did much to discredit the party and foretold its eventual collapse as serious player in Lebanese and Syrian national life, Sharabi remained a member: "Saʿada's personality had overpowered me so completely that it was impossible for me to conceive of questions such as those that Fayiz Sayigh, Ghassan Tuwayni, Karim ʿAzqul and others had begun to raise concerning matters of principle, doctrine, and organization."[132] He then added, "I did not feel any aversion, as I do today, to pyramidical systems based on hierarchical authority."[133]

Though authoritarian, the leader did not object to Sharabi's departure for the United States to pursue a PhD in philosophy.[134] Fayiz, too, was a free man. And so, writes Sharabi, on a cold day in December 1947, Yusuf Sayigh drove his car to Lydda Airport in Palestine. "He was taking his brother Fayiz and me to the airport as we were on our way to America for higher studies. Fayiz was going for Georgetown University and I to the University of Chicago."[135] It would be their last time in Palestine, and they had no sense that by leaving they might be giving up the struggle: "We had come to see things from an odd angle—the viewpoint of abstract thought. Thus, the world appeared to us as the subject of our speech and thought, not as a space for the realization of action. . . . The strange thing was that both Fayiz and I were politically committed."[136] Thereafter, the Nakba happened, and they became two refugees whose preoccupation with existentialism took two different paths.

The loss of Palestine and the execution of Antun Saʿada in 1949 devastated Sharabi, who gradually turned inward and became an uncommitted academic, a philosopher of existentialism rather than an existentialist philosopher (however, after 1967 Sharabi would renew his intellectual and political connection to the Arab world once again). Sharabi enrolled in multiple classes, which bit by bit discredited much of what came to pass as existentialism in the Arab world prior to the proliferation of Suhayl Idris's commitment. His most revealing relationship, in this respect, was with the influential French philosopher Jean Wahl, who was on leave from the Sorbonne. Sharabi writes:

Jean Wahl was a short man and had small body shaped like Sartre's. Like Sartre, he wore round eyeglasses, but he did not squint like him. . . . From Wahl's lectures, it became clear to me that what I had studied in Beirut of Kierkegaard's thought and existentialist philosophy was very little and hardly worth mentioning. . . . I mentioned to Wahl one day that the Egyptian philosopher ʿAbd al-Rahman Badawi had authored a book on existentialist philosophy. . . . He expressed interest in it and suggested that I take Badawi's book as the subject of my research paper for that semester. A few weeks later, I presented my paper to him, in which I reviewed the principal points of the book and translated a few passages from it. Wahl called me to his office after reading my paper and said, "This book is ordinary. The translated passages and Badawi's ideas seem to be derived mostly from Heidegger's book *Sein und Zeit*. There is nothing new in them."[137]

Unlike Sharabi, Sayigh became a committed intellectual whose existentialism was both a sharp diagnostic tool and a possible framework for the organization of postcolonial Arab identity. He arrived at this formulation through his academic work. Thus, his dissertation at Georgetown, "Existential Philosophy: A Formal Examination" was "devoted to the establishment of distinctions between, and the characterization of the varieties of, the 'existential.'" This typology of existential philosophy taught Sayigh how to extract meaning from human experience, which in his case included displacement: "As an experience of cognition, it [existential philosophy] is realistically directed toward its object, seeking to find there the source and measure of knowledge and truth. As a human experience, it represents the exister's striving not merely for truth but also for adequate knowledge . . . thus constituting an 'existential experience' and pointing to the meta-philosophical domains of human Existenz."[138] Put differently, upon graduation in 1950, Sayigh saw the recent human situation in the Middle East in all its complexity, and he believed he could use this newly gained clarity to intervene politically.

At that point, Philip Hitti of Princeton University, the don of Arab students in America, advised him to abandon academia and take a position in the UN. He joined hands with his former adviser Charles Malik, a major contributor to the Universal Declaration of Human Rights and a sworn anticommunist.[139] Having the powerful Malik as a patron helped Sayigh launch a career in public and diplomatic life and later join the Arab delegation to the UN.[140] All along, his academic work continued to nourish his understanding of Arab affairs. In 1953, just as Suhayl Idris pushed forward Sartrean existentialism in Arabic, Fayiz reworked his academic insights into a popular statement about the state of the Arab world. Though existentialism famously prescribed that existence precedes essence, and Sayigh even dedicated a dissertation chapter to this understanding, he nonetheless selected an essentialist title: *Understanding the Arab Mind*. In this smart small book, Sayigh powerfully cast the work of decolonization as a movement that sought to establish freedom, authenticity, and sovereignty: "The Arab's search for basic existential orientation—for light and love and loyalty, for poise and purpose, for destiny—is a search for being, for effective participation in history. . . . No matter what the outcome of this search may be it is bound to assume historic significance. . . . The search for basic existential orientation is going on. Hence the anxiety and the dread; hence the hopelessness; hence the mobilization and the struggle; hence the suspense and expectation and thrill."[141] He framed this existential quest in philosophical and political terms that few members of his generation could understand or even cared to follow. Written in English, the text was by no means influential. But it did do one important thing, which was to tie the postcolonial condition of the Arab individual with terms that would later be recognized globally as Sartrean internationalism. Thus, without any of Sartre's foundational text yet translated to Arabic, Sayigh illustrated why existentialism made so much sense in an era of decolonization.

But Sayigh was also very concerned about the rebelliousness and politicization of youth.[142] Perhaps because in his student years in Beirut he was a member of a radical party, he understood the dangers of reducing the momentous challenge of decolonization to a mere politics of sacrifice as Pan-Arabism and Baʻthism would increasingly demand. This aspect put him in the same unlikely camp as Taha Husayn who, once again, feared that a distorted form of Sartrean existentialism might become the vehicle for the total politicization of Arab life.

Conclusion

Undoubtedly, until the 1950s, the presence of existentialism in the Arab world was limited to small academic circles and high-level cultural journalism. Even within this embryonic scene, existentialism did not appear as a coherent idea or an organized system of thought. The few individuals and academic units engaged with the existentialist tradition differed significantly in their opinions of foundational issues such as religious faith, politics, cultural orientation, and, in Charles Malik's case, even ethics. Though one can think of these differences in terms of the European genealogy of existentialism (i.e., as a question of which thinker to follow: Kierkegaard, Heidegger, or Sartre), they also reflect a real divergence in the Arab world itself; namely, Christian religious existentialism in Beirut versus phenomenology and Islamic mysticism in Cairo. This divergence helps explain why, in the late 1940s, Arab existentialism was not yet "ready" for a public conversation that transcended the localities of Beirut, Cairo, and to a lesser extent Baghdad.

As the 1950s began, Arab youth could draw on two strains of existentialism in different stages of articulation: that of Badawi and that of Idris. Sayigh's contribution, though very critical and self-reflective, was essentially his own analysis of Arab youth, culture, and politics, rather than a cultural platform positioned to influence these realities. As the most systematic thinker of the three, Badawi sought to repair the colonial cultural schism with a philosophical synthesis intended to heal the Arab self. Beyond the collective civilizational focus of this proposal, Badawi's work introduced an intellectually coherent terminology that presented an entirely new way of thinking and formulating existential concerns. Whether he wrote of angst, being-in-time and toward death, authenticity and inauthenticity (as states of turath), and radical individualism, his lexicon was extremely useful for thinking about the state of the Arab subject during the impending era of decolonization. The fact that this conceptual cluster could intimately relate to the emerging field of psychology and the practice of psychoanalysis made Badawi's work relevant in other quarters of the academic world as well.

In contrast with this academic perspective, Suhayl Idris took from Sartrean existentialism the political doctrine of commitment as a liberating act of individual as well as collective self-assertion. He was also taken by the existentialist mood of Paris as an informed lifestyle choice. This too was about self-assertion. Prioritizing this sense of freedom at the expense of systematic thought, Idris was intellectually selective. Though he was well aware that Sartre was also, and perhaps primarily, a philosopher, he ignored his philosophical writing and read only plays and novels.[143] For instance, Idris never ventured into Sartre's *Being and Nothingness* or to the work of Gabriel Marcel, the author who coined the term existentialism. As we shall see later, there were also some more serious omissions, such as *Anti-Semite and Jew* and "Black Orpheus." Though this form of selective reading might come at a price, in and of itself selectivity is a hallmark of any form of intellectual translation and does not constitute a problem as such.

Though very different from each other, both Badawi and Idris thought in existentialist terms not simply as an act of cultural recovery but as a generative force toward the invention of a new Arab subject, one who was confident, politically involved, independent, self-sufficient, and, most importantly, liberated. For this new Arab self to emerge, youth had to transcend the traumatic legacy of colonialism, which manifested itself in a prevailing sense of humiliation, helplessness, loss, shame, desperation, powerlessness, spiritual deprivation, emptiness, and anxiety, of which Badawi, Sayigh, Sharabi, and others wrote eloquently. Though there is no straight line of progression between colonial trauma and postcolonial recovery, it is highly suggestive to think of Arab existentialism as an open-ended intellectual system that enclosed important antitraumatic properties and aimed at healing the colonized self.[144]

Whether intellectuals had been using existentialism to promote individual and collective self-awareness, call for the acceptance of responsibility for one's circumstances, or organize political action, there is no doubt that existentialism was beginning to make its cultural mark. As we shall see in the next chapter, as part of the quest for a new Arab self, Suhayl Idris and his peers embarked on a generational revolt against old-guard intellectuals in a battle to redefine the borders of legitimate culture and create a revitalizing space so that a new self could indeed emerge.

THREE

Commitment

Out of the existential crisis of the 1940s came the expectation that in the 1950s "everything" would change. Not simply politics but culture itself, and not in some superficial way but in a profound, sweeping, and long-lasting fashion. Transitioning to this new era, the Palestinian thinker Ishaq Husayni wrote of how nationalism could help resolve a deep "crisis of Arab thought" whose unfortunate manifestations were confusion, an incapacity for self-criticism, a loss of intellectual freedom, irrationality, overdependency on tradition, and an overall lack of intellectual seriousness.[1] Aware of the prevalence of such self-critical sentiment, Fayiz Sayigh opined that, due to profound changes in the international and domestic arenas, the Arab world was in dire need of a new intellectual leadership that would be able to affectively deal with the multiple challenges of decolonization and the unique threat of Zionism.[2] Concerned by the disorienting impact that colonialism had inflicted on Arabs, the up-and-coming critic Raja' al-Naqqash registered a "crisis of critical thought which is not confined only to the literary field but encompass all other areas of art" and extended beyond to the Arab human condition as such.[3] It was against this backdrop that the idea of replacing the established intelligentsia began to gain momentum.

For that to happen, the new generation needed literature, poetry, history, social and political thought, and many intellectuals who could inhabit new cultural spaces, debate new ideas, and proliferate a new critical spirit. The problem was, since the end of World War I, the cultural arena had been occupied by the well-entrenched generation of the udaba' and their commitment to high culture. It was they who wrote the books, edited the journals, organized the literary field, and held the key positions in academia, the press, and government. Would they voluntarily vacate their powerful positions as public-opinion makers? Most certainly not. As could be expected, the change of the intellectual guard proved to be a complex, rancorous, and painful. In the battle over the future of Arab culture, 1954 proved a pivotal year; a year of intellectual rebellion, in which a group of former students and disciples challenged their mentors. Their weapon of choice was the new doctrine of iltizam, and their target was to redefine the purpose of artistic work as a gateway for more comprehensive intellectual change.

Following its early articulation by Suhayl Idris, iltizam emerged as a doctrine of cultural action: a framework of thought that could organize, systematize, and rationalize the quest for postcolonial culture. By 1954 the new doctrine of commitment was making its mark on the capital cities of the Arab East. As one committed commentator boasted, "The idea of committed literature dominates the Arab world now."[4] Such a rapid proliferation raises questions: How could a concept, a mere abstraction, be utilized to marginalize established writers and thinkers? How did it undermine their ideas and corner them into a defensive position? What intellectual properties were at play during this process, and what was their relation to existentialism? Related to this question, if the origins of iltizam could be traced back to Sartre, how much influence did Sartre's writing have over the formation of Arab commitment during the 1950s, and what exactly about that process was Sartrean? And last, given the fact that the Arab public was ideologically divided, was there any broad consensus or unity of thought as to what constituted proper commitment?

These questions interrogate the heart of the intellectual process of decolonization, revealing the scale and depth of the effort to fully decolonize Arab societies and articulate a new collective agenda. A discussion of this process should put to rest the claim that Arab nationalism, or for that matter any other form of nationalism, be it Pan-African, Indian, or Indonesian, was the central intellectual mechanism at play during decolonization.

The culture of iltizam was obviously not the sole answer to all the problems of decolonization, but its stunning popularity does call attention to its power as a doctrine of intellectual engagement. This chapter tells the story of the intellectuals who made iltizam, those who employed it, believed in it, and those whom it victimized. Notwithstanding its success, the debates, exchanges, and confrontations of the time—especially those of and around 1954—reveal the divided intellectual origins of iltizam. What started as a classic Sartrean project that even today still carries Sartre's familiar trademark of *engagement*, faced a hostile theoretical takeover by Soviet-inspired proponents of socialist realism. With both groups calming ownership of iltizam and struggling to establish some measure of control over its reception and usage, the culture of commitment became forever divided between two opposing camps. While the first camp looked for intellectual inspiration from Paris, the second swore allegiance to Moscow. Between these two poles, iltizam was articulated as a moral imperative that polarized the Arab intellectual field as good versus bad, just versus unjust, true versus false, and progressive versus reactionary. Though the proponents of iltizam did not target individuals as such but only their modes of thought, a real person, an *adib*, always had to answer back and defend the assumptions underpinning his or her thought. With no choice expect that of choosing sides or being forever silenced, udaba' such as Taha Husayn and Tawfiq al-Hakim launched a last-ditch effort to stay relevant. They lost.

The Symbolic Battle for Egyptian Culture

During the years 1953 and 1954 a polite and reserved debate about the connection between the "aesthetic," the "literary," and the "political" took place in the cultural pages of the daily *Al-Jumhuriyya*. The young poet and literary critic Luwis 'Awad served as the section's editor and had already made a name for himself as a bold literary thinker. 'Awad hosted a debate in which Taha Husayn and Isma'il Mazhar took opposing views on the question of "art for art's sake" (Husayn) or "art for the sake of society" (Mazhar). At times passionate, the debate was conducted however between two members of the same generation who, by and large, shared the same cultural working assumptions.[5] The troubles began when Taha Husayn decided to "pick a fight" not with his esteemed peers but with a younger generation for whom he had little if any respect.

And so, on February 5, 1954, Taha Husayn returned to the pages of *Al-Jumhuriyya* and published what seemed to be another routine piece of literary criticism. His topic of choice was "The Form of Literature," a subject that usually elicited little public interest and was ostensibly guaranteed to arouse little debate. In this concise piece, Husayn called

79

for the creation of works of art with high aesthetic value, suggesting that beauty (*jamal*) alone should be the primary purpose of art and the main standard for its evaluation.[6] While there would seem at first glance to be nothing controversial in this modest proposition, Husayn's arcane literary request was, in fact, designed to upset the younger class of writers and critics. And indeed, almost immediately, it unleashed a storm in literary circles, one that pitted a young generation of writers against the established intellectual class of the udaba'.

What was the debate about? In a nutshell, most young writers correctly understood Taha Husayn's piece as an offensive move in the ensuing battle over the shape and role of culture, and especially of literature, in the postcolonial era. In more specific terms, the debate revolved around the desired relationship between writers, writing, and society; that is, at issue was *commitment*. Taha Husayn's provocation did not go unchallenged. In a matter of weeks, the desired relationship between art, its creators, its critics, and Arab society at large became the single most contested cultural issue. It remained so for the next two years. Though started in Egypt where its exclusive subject was Egyptian literature, the debate quickly became a symbolic regional affair articulated in terms of commitment. Here is how the scandal of Taha Husayn triggered the rise of iltizam as a new cultural imperative.[7]

Though Husayn's "The Form of Literature" elicited various reactions from critics like Luwis 'Awad, Muhammad Mandur, and other established figures, it was the reaction of two marginal figures that mattered most: philosopher Mahmud Amin al-'Alim and mathematician 'Abd al-'Azim Anis. Both were young and inexperienced professors pursuing standard university careers. Both were communists. Though they were not trained as literary critics, they fancied themselves as such and hence responded to Taha Husayn with the confidence and verve of established authorities. Al-'Alim was especially gifted in this field and would eventually emerge as one of the most influential Arab critics in the second half of the century. Another figure who was about to play a major role in this saga was Husayn Muruwwa, the young Shi'i seminary student from Najaf whose infatuation with Taha Husayn and his peers during the late 1920s had created sufficient internal conflict in Muruwwa to drive him to a nervous breakdown. Afterward, Muruwwa had moved to Baghdad, where he worked as a teacher and a journalist. Witnessing firsthand the dire socioeconomic and political conditions of Iraq, he felt compelled to understand a socioeconomic and political reality that made no sense to him at all.[8] As in many other postwar cases around the world, the holistic nature of

Marxism-Leninism—articulated in the fundamental insight that imperialism is the highest stage of capitalism—made everything connect. In Muruwwa's own words, "Given the nature of WW II, there was no other option but Lenin."[9] Thus, two decades after his mental collapse, this fragile teenager emerged not only as a *mujtahid* but also as a powerful communist literary theoretician and as the man who gave al-'Alim and 'Abd al-'Azim both a coherent voice and a communist-inspired theory of commitment.

As avid readers of Arab literature, especially that written by members of their own generation, al-'Alim and 'Abd al-'Azim fully appreciated the quest for literary experimentation. Indeed, as new styles of writing emerged all over the region, the traditional balance between literary form (*shakl*) and content (*madmun*) began to shift. At first, this shift was slow and measured, but with time, as was the case with the Free Verse Movement in Iraq (see chapter 4), young writers openly challenged the literary style of their predecessors' work and, especially, its sociopolitical implications. Thus, in response to Taha Husayn's dismissal of the literary structure that underlay these new trends, the couple began writing a series of aggressive articles in the daily *Al-Misri*, which deepened the growing generational rift with the udaba'. Husayn replied, saying that al-'Alim and 'Abd al-'Azim were ignorant, superficial, and hopelessly incomprehensible.[10] In Beirut, the Sartrean *Al-Adab* and the communist *Al-Thaqafa al-Wataniyya*, the two most dynamic venues of the time, joined the fray. At times reporting on the Egyptian scene and at others contributing their own thoughts, the debate spread to other intellectual communities in Syria and Iraq.

"The literary struggle between young and old writers," wrote the editors of *Al-Thaqafa al-Wataniyya*, "is raging on."[11] The journal explained in detail Taha Husayn's argument that the aesthetic beauty of literature emerges organically from its form and not from its carefully chosen meaning or content. "There is no doubt," the editors quoted Husayn, "that, regardless of the content, words turn into literature only due to their beauty."[12] Next to this argument, the journal brought the response of al-'Alim and 'Abd al-'Azim, who maintained that, essentially, literary content should reflect social realities, that the role of the literary form is to create this social content, and that this social focus does not undermine the aesthetic value of literature but instead strengthens it. Calling to defeat the "old school of literary critics," they presented a committed literary vision in which the discovery of the social reality is the unified goal of new writers and critics alike.[13]

Their young Iraqi colleagues agreed. They attacked Husayn, lamenting the fall of a progressive and revolutionary father figure who now, under the pressures of Egyptian military tyranny, wrote for the government newspaper while "writers who opposed dictatorship are abducted one after the other." Depicting him as a detached aristocrat, the Iraqis wrote that as long as Husayn's villa in the luxurious neighborhood of Zamalek and his summer vacation (in Europe) were not interrupted, he could not care less about the condemning reality that surrounded him.[14] The Lebanese intellectual Muhammad Sharara, a close friend of Muruwwa, who also replaced the clerical culture of Najaf with the revolutionary intimacy of the Iraqi Communist Party, was another disappointed follower. Sharara listed Husayn's heroic battles against political and cultural oppression during the last two decades and reminded readers of Husayn's progressive compositions such as *Al-Muʿadhabun fi-l-Ard* (The wretched of the earth). He was especially grateful for Husayn's early articles in *Al-Katib al-Misri* about Sartre's commitment (published before Husayn turned against Sartre). Given this legacy, Sharara expected Husayn to be at the forefront of "[our] glorious, yet hard, battle against colonialism and reaction," as this was a battle for life—the battle of a new generation that was, Sharara wrote, "still fond of you."[15]

But Husayn was not vulnerable to persuasion, as his heart was elsewhere. Even during Liberation Holiday, the public celebration that commemorated the six-month anniversary of the July Revolution, Husayn still believed that a heavy dose of mass Enlightenment, a self-imposed *mission civilisatrice*, was the only solution to a postcolonial society.[16] This attempt to infuse the meaning of "liberation" with Enlightenment values was made at a time when Marxist-Leninist and even existentialist thought spread as an obvious alternative to this vision. As Pierre Cachia put it, Taha Husayn was "dedicated to the spread of enlightenment to the masses and convinced that when this was done the masses would inevitably be one with it."[17] Indeed, regardless of the political mood, Husayn was committed to the idea that, against the backdrop of a democratic political marketplace, the three key issues of the postcolonial era, social justice, physical liberation, and the problem of the self, would resolve themselves without recourse to a revolutionary phase. This belief was a political mainstay of pre–World War II, and emerging literary disagreements with former followers and disciples were about something much bigger than art per se.

Suhayl Idris intuitively understood that. Less polemical than the communists', Idris's journal placed the literary debate with Husayn in the overall political context of the 1952 revolution and the postcolonial desire to create cultural space for new intellectual forces. Far from being an arcane academic debate about literary taste, *Al-Adab* was aware of the fact that young intellectuals used the theme of commitment in order to accelerate the pace of generational change and create "free intellectuals like those of the French Revolution."[18] Seeking to aid this process, it reiterated the Sartrean idea that words can change reality and published a survey in which a Syrian, Lebanese, Iraqi, Egyptian, and even a Bahraini writer were asked to answer the Sartrean question "To whom and why do we write?"[19] In one way or another, they all echoed Sartre's notion of commitment as a vehicle for sociopolitical change through writing.

This trans-Arab commotion only strengthened the resolve of al-ʿAlim and ʿAbd al-ʿAzim to take the fight to the next level, and a year later they copublished *Fi-l-Thaqafa al-Misriyya* (On Egyptian culture). Inspired by Leon Trotsky's *Literature and Revolution* but also, especially, by Ralph Fox's *The Novel and the People*, two books that attacked bourgeois realism, *Fi-l-Thaqafa al-Misriyya* was a direct response—indeed a refutation—not only of Taha Husayn's present literary choices but of his entire 1938 cultural agenda, *Mustaqbal al-Thaqafa fi Misr* (The future of culture in Egypt).[20] In order to better understand what the book was about and how it functioned as a refutation of Taha Husayn, a few words about its making are in order.

It so happened that in late 1954, shortly before their book was ready for publication, the two young professors became victims of Nasser's great purge of the academic system. In search of income, ʿAbd al-ʿAzim took a teaching position in Beirut. As a foreigner in an unfamiliar city, he made new friends in communist circles. Not long afterward, he met the energetic Red Mujtahid Husayn Muruwwa, who resettled in Beirut after being deported from Baghdad for subversive politics. Muruwwa and ʿAbd al-ʿAzim had much in common. Muruwwa had just returned from the Second Congress of Soviet Writers in Moscow, where he witnessed how Soviet-style socialist realism and its notion of commitment could destroy the old intelligentsia. Inspired by his experience, he saw socialist realism as a new postcolonial aesthetic with the potential to revolutionize Arab life.[21] On his part, though he lacked any systematic intellectual platform, ʿAbd al-ʿAzim thought of literature as a tool for effective cultural and social criticism.

It was a meeting of the minds, one that provoked the Lebanese Communist Party, which sponsored Muruwwa's trip to Moscow, to suggest publishing *Fi-l-Thaqafa al-Misriyya* in Beirut rather than in Cairo.[22] Muhammad Dakrub of the communist magazine *Al-Tariq* took care of the logistics.[23] Undoubtedly, the intellectual openness of Beirut as well as its rising status in Arab letters made it a much better place to undertake such an enterprise than Cairo with its growing state-led dogmatism and stifling atmosphere. The two Egyptian thinkers asked Muruwwa to preface their book.[24]

By far, the best articulation of the book's intentions was Muruwwa's preface, which ultimately set the tone for much of what was to happen in Arab letters during these tumultuous years. Muruwwa wrote of a new postcolonial Arab situation prevalent not only in Egypt but throughout the Middle East. According to him, this situation necessitated a new culture and a new generation willing to destroy "old" culture. He saw much promise in a book that called for a new relationship between writers and reality and expected that writers would become actively involved in not only the "accurate" depiction of this reality but also its transformation. Muruwwa believed that *Fi-l-Thaqafa al-Misriyya* was the first step in launching an objective scientific process of cultural change.[25] This effort is an example of the unique nature of postcolonial Arab culture, which sought to change public culture by creating a new form of literary criticism that was essentially political. Al-ʿAlim and ʿAbd al-ʿAzim were very pleased with how his contribution furthered their agenda.[26]

What was the agenda? In brief, it was a more thoughtful and detailed articulation of their differences with Husayn, except that they now extended their argument to include not just Husayn but the entire intellectual class of the udabaʾ. The axiom was that, given that "the troops of colonialism" were still at work in Egypt, there was an urgent need to purge the culture.[27] Taha Husayn and Tawfiq al-Hakim, two of the leading representatives of established culture, were singled out as bearers and propagators of colonial cultural assumptions. As al-ʿAlim and ʿAbd al-ʿAzim put it, by submerging himself in the universal culture of Europe, Taha Husayn failed to account for the uniqueness of "our" culture and could only vaguely state that "Egypt has its own special expressive and intellectual schools."[28] The specific characteristics of Egypt, they contended, could not be found in Enlightenment's universalism but in Egypt's unique social realities. "If culture reflects the workings of social reality," they wrote, "and if our social reality is struggling toward liberation, then we need to define the meaning of Egyptian culture from within this social reality."[29]

In other words, in contrast with the alleged universal culture of colonial Enlightenment and its Eurocentric ethos, the authors believed that "culture is not founded on one firm basis but is the result of a multi-factored and interactive operation by society at large."[30] This agenda resonated with many young writers across the region. As Iraqi poet 'Abd al-Wahhab al-Bayyati succinctly put it, "The search for poetic form which did not exist in our old poetry . . . brought us to discover the wretched reality in which the masses live."[31] By way of addressing this regional problem, they hoped to create a new Arab subject.

Making its case specific, *Fi-l-Thaqafa al-Misriyya* also described Taha Husayn and his class as disconnected "ivory tower" intellectuals removed from the social struggles of ordinary people. In particular, it argued that, both structurally and stylistically, their literature was interested in "art for its own sake" and thus perpetuated the gap between the elite and the people.[32] In place of this literature, they called for realism as a tool for committed literature (*adab multazim*) in the service of the people.[33] Their exemplar of "right" literature was 'Abd al-Rahman al-Sharqawi's *Al-Ard*. In such literature, the social content reflects the commitment of the writer to social change. It was indeed an excellent example of socialist-realist literature that aimed to change society rather than function for its own aesthetic sake as a pleasure maker. The problem was that there were not many books like it.

To those who were well versed in the intellectual world of the mid-1950s, the conceptual proximity of communist iltizam to that of *Al-Adab*'s Sartrean existentialism was quite evident. With this conceptual closeness in mind, al-'Alim and 'Abd al-'Azim made a deliberate attempt to appropriate Sartrean iltizam and submerge it in the Marxist-Leninist schema. They did so by attacking Badawi's Heideggerian existentialism as the alleged godfather of radical individualism that supposedly underlay *Al-Adab*'s iltizam. They began by admitting that Badawi's existentialism was a significant school of thought with indigenous foundations in Islamic mysticism.[34] However, they found it ethically flawed because it promoted a self-centered and socially alienated human being, void of social responsibility.[35] They agreed that individualism was a valid value "yet not as a detached and entirely independent entity but as an element of a socio-economic reality." For them, therefore, "[Badawi's] existentialism was a deep-reaching individualistic philosophy which denied the objective truthfulness of human reality."[36]

Badawi's existentialism was indeed apolitical, as it was a pledge to one's authentic way of being, which, modeled on Heidegger, refused "to be tied down by . . . a self-imposed commitment to attitude and action."[37] Since Badawi was the most systematic Arab writer on existential philosophy, al-'Alim and 'Abd al-'Azim took him as the official representative of the existentialist line of thought as a whole. This was intellectually dishonest, and it was based on a misreading of the differences between Sartrean and Heideggerian existentialism.[38] Yet such technicalities in reading made little difference. In their highly influential book, al-ʿAlim and ʿAbd al-ʿAzim replaced the individual in existentialism with society and harnessed it to their cause. In a complementary step to this intellectual "takeover" of iltizam, al-ʿAlim, who had previously contributed to *Al-Adab*, left the journal and started writing for *Al-Thaqafa al-Wataniyya*.[39] An obvious rift had opened between the two postcolonial literary pioneers.

However manipulative this move was, by this communist application of commitment to Arab letters, all three men—Muruwwa, al-ʿAlim, and ʿAbd al-ʿAzim—had by 1955 emerged as literary/cultural critics. Their book could be credited with pioneering a postcolonial Marxist literary criticism that, in the next two decades, would become an influential field.[40] Yet, much work lay ahead. Though their book was very successful in singling out individuals and literary problems, intellectually speaking, its narrow Egyptian focus and its incoherent method of realism called for further development.[41] The task of elaborating a more systematic introduction to realism along credible socialist lines fell to Muruwwa. But, before that happened, the other champions of iltizam, the Sartrean community of *Al-Adab*, began to challenge the Marxist version of iltizam and resist the intellectual attempts of cooptation.

Sartre's Commitment in Arabic

Encapsulating the spirit of a new generation, *Al-Adab* hosted literary critics from across the region, supported the Free Verse Movement of Nazik al-Malaʾika, Badr Shakir al-Sayyab, and others in Iraq, published political analysis from Syria and Lebanon, and circulated a healthy dose of Sartrean existentialism from the growing community of Arab existentialists.[42] Most writers were new to the Arab literary scene. By the mid-1950s, in what seemed no time at all, *Al-Adab* had emerged as one of the most dynamic and influential cultural venues; a bastion of the postcolonial intelligentsia. What held this diverse community of people together and gave their work a lasting resonance as a comprehensive cultural phenomenon? Without doubt, it was the notion of Sartrean commitment.

Building on *Al-Adab*'s 1953 revolutionary opening statement on iltizam, Idris now called for a comparable revolution in literary criticism. He contended that since current criticism "falls short of fulfilling its mission" the Arab reader is left "wandering in the dark" in a perpetual state of confusion and anxiety.[43] Seeking to change this dismal state of affairs, he wrote that "the mission of the literary critic is much greater than the mere proliferation of culture" as it was practiced in the present. Instead, it was "to create a conscious reader" who could use the meaning that the critic extracts from the text for the greater goal of changing Arab reality.[44] Thus, just as in Marxist circles, the critic who "simultaneously lives the experience of the writer as well as that of the reader" emerged as the new intellectual hero of the postcolonial era. Granted there were developmental economists, political scientists, psychologists, historians, philosophers, journalists, and other intellectuals who toiled hard to create a new Arab world. But, the fact that Idris and, as we shall see, many others placed the literary critic at the forefront of intellectual decolonization was at least in part due to Idris's understanding of Sartre's *What Is Literature?* Though still not available in Arabic translation, Sartre's text on postwar France was the most influential example of how literary criticism could be used to advance cultural change.

Yet, even at times when the Marxist doctrine of socialist realism began to pose a theoretical challenge to Sartrean criticism, Idris left the precise designs and technicalities of how exactly to create committed critics, writers, and readers to people such as Anwar al-Maʿdawi. His skills were neatly tailored to the work. Al-Maʿdawi began his programmatic piece on developing the notion of committed literature (*al-adab al-multazim*) by declaring that "commitment should be the essence of each work of literature and the mission of each writer." To become an "existentially committed" writer one is required to be socially submerged in life, "connected to his surroundings, close to the people and their feeling," and never separated from the big "questions of his generation."[45] However, he added, "the existentialist writer" is different from the communist writer. Whereas the former writes *committed* literature the latter composes *socialist* literature. And the two, as Sartre himself insisted, are in opposition to each other as "committed literature demands the complete freedom of the writer as well as that of the reader." This "exemplary goal of the principle of commitment" could be achieved only if the writer distanced himself "from allegiance to any political party," including the Communist Party. "Sartre's goal," continued al-Maʿdawi, "was to establish a clear separating line between his committed literature and that of the communists."[46] This hostility toward the Communist Party and the emphasis on separating Sartre from it quickly became a key principle of *Al-Adab*.

During its first two years in print, *Al-Adab* dedicated much space to the methodological and theoretical mechanics of committed litera-ture. Critic ʿAbdallah ʿAbd al-Daʾim, for instance, took on the question of artistic creativity, asking what is creativity, which creativity do we need, and what is its relation to Western culture? In answering these questions he argued that the creative intellectual should be embedded in "the new atmosphere that engulfs his society."[47] Following Kierke-gaard, al-Daʾim tied creativity to freedom of the self and argued that "the creative intellectual is that which liberates himself" from the shackles of old traditions and habits of mind toward the achievement of real freedom.[48] Yet, according to al-Daʾim, the major obstacle facing the rise of Arab creativity was the problem of cultural borrowing and its relation to "liberation from servitude to the West."[49] Addressing this classic postcolonial problem, he warned against the solitary dangers of cultural fundamentalism (or exclusive self-reliance) and argued that re-lation to Western culture must not come at the expense of indigenous creativity. Dealing like many others before him with the problem of authenticity and continuity in Arab culture, he focused the debate on the method of borrowing and the quality of the borrowed object. "In the context of borrowing," he wrote, "the first criterion for creativity is that we fully and perfectly understand what are we borrowing," thus avoiding the consumption of culture "in the same way in which we import bottles of Whiskey." To avoid this, "our goal is to transmit the inspiration behind the ideas and not only the ideas themselves." Only then can foreign ideas be processed creatively, thus avoiding the preva-lent pitfall of superficial Western thinking that yields "poor literature, poor art, and poor thought." "The public," al-Daʾim concluded, "is thirsty for real creativity" and fully knows how to identify it.[50]

Other critics took on equally pressing concerns. In "Fi risalat al-adab" (The mission of literature), the Syrian critic ʿAli Baddur raised the ubiquitous question of the time regarding the purpose of art. Does art exist for its own sake of for that of society at large? Though supporting the standard requirement that writers should be connected to their so-cieties, adhering to Sartre, he argued that the writer should never com-promise his or her freedom for the sake of pursuing social change. It was another gentle reminder that Sartrean iltizam has a fine membrane that clearly separates it from communist and socialist commitment.[51] No other person was better prepared to deepen the meaning of Sar-trean commitment than the twenty-five-year-old Syrian philosopher and critic Mutaʿ Safadi.

Writing of the intuitive commitment of literature, Safadi took the first step in reacting to the meteoric rise of socialist realism in Syria as an alternative model of commitment.[52] His argument was that realism is more real, so to speak, when the external world is processed by a free committed individual rather than by a committee. Equipped with a good background in phenomenology, Safadi argued that the writer's function of "being-in-the-world" was a subjective existential act that accentuated the freedom of that writer. In turn, this freedom then contributed to a better articulation of realism as well as to a more democratic engagement with the world.[53] Building on this understanding, the Egyptian critic Ahmad Kamal Zaki reminded the reader that intellectual responsibility had been the ethical foundation of various types of commitments throughout history. This sense of responsibility resided and thrived exclusively within the writer and not outside it through an external structure such as a political party. Once again, the idea was to anchor commitment in the stormy water of contested individual freedom.[54]

Perhaps the greatest advocate of this approach was the Lebanese writer and critic Ra'if Khuri. Unlike young intellectuals who called for commitment, Khuri, who was born in 1912, had a mature perspective on the promise and dangers of being committed. In his youth during the 1930s, his main object of commitment was Palestine. Like European and American activists who went to fight for a free Spain, in 1936 he took an active role in the Palestinian revolt against Zionism and the British. As a result of his political choices, he lost his teaching position in Palestine and was forced by the British to return to Beirut, where he collaborated with 'Umar Fakhuri, a towering Marxist figure in letters and politics. During the 1940s Khuri went as far as embracing communism and accepted Soviet leadership in matters of politics and culture alike. Though he wrote regularly for Beirut's leftist venues such as *Al-Tariq*, when the Soviet Union instructed its followers to support the establishment of Israel, he at once broke off with communism. Clearly, the communist request to follow a strict party line was in sharp opposition to Khuri's freedom to choose commitment to Palestine.[55] Losing his communist comrades and their press, in 1953 he found a new home in Idris's *Al-Adab* and became one of its most important and prolific theorists of commitment. The vantage point of Khuri's commitment was individual humanism as the ultimate addressee of any political theory, system, or school. By specifying freedom as the central human feature, he placed it as the premier objective for any literary, intellectual, political, or social project. In that, Khuri critiqued Marxist iltizam, which submitted the individual to a collective order and called instead for a culture that conceives of the individual as the highest so-cial value.[56]

Another important principle that distinguished Khuri's commit-ment from that of Marxists was his insistence that literature should take an active role in criticizing the state. He was one of the first intel-lectuals to identify the Arab state of the 1950s as a menace to intellec-tual freedom rather than its guardian. Not confusing Arab nationalism, which he wholly supported, with statism, which he feared, Khuri's committed writer found its political inspiration in the street rather than in party headquarters.[57] Just like al-Safadi, Khuri was clear about how free literature written by free writers should mediate between the people and the big social, political, and economic circumstances that defined their existence.[58]

Yet, the individualistic human vantage point of *Al-Adab*'s commu-nity and its staunch noncommunist stance did not mean it took a prin-cipled adversarial position toward key Marxist notions such as class, workers' oppression, or the tight link between political control and economic submission. As one critic put it, the point was that, when literature descended from "the ivory tower to the marketplace, through the street and into the factory," it should remain an ideologically un-bounded human enterprise, true to the free and ever-changing nature of life itself.[59] Though Suhayl Idris and his writers never thought of iltizam in terms of strict methodological and stylistic guidelines that dictated what could be considered good committed literature and criti-cism, they did, nonetheless, have something of a doctrine. This doc-trine sought to abolish the gap between the writer and society in a way that accentuated the idea of intellectual responsibility to one's age, historical era, and generation. At the same time, like Sartre, they en-shrined the absolute freedom of the writer to choose his or her own subject and style of writing. Not so was the case with advocates of so-cialist realism.

Anticipating the struggle over the meaning of iltizam, in March 1954 a Marxist critic published a review of Suhayl Idris's celebrated novel *Al-Hayy al-Latini*. The review's personal and acerbic message was that the novel provided the ultimate example of noncommitment: instead of seriously exploring "the important issue of sex in our so-ciety . . . the novel does not address any social problem. All it does is dealing with one sick individual."[60] Whereas for Idris the sexual tribu-lations of one individual revealed something greater about society, for the Soviet-inspired critic, the novel was nothing but an obsessive sex-ual account devoid of social merit. This was a difference not simply of taste but one that spoke of the fundamental divergence in the 1950s between two groups who, though both rejected the udaba', disagreed sharply over the desired form of culture and its relation to the political.

Occasionally, as part of the struggle over iltizam, the entire tradition of existentialism was vilified as corrupting and immoral. Responding to these charges, *Al-Adab* wrote,

It is clear that most of those who attacked existentialism . . . manufactured an imaginary existentialism which has absolutely nothing in common with existentialism . . . as stream of thought in the contemporary world. Clearly, when it comes to existentialism, and many other issues, Egyptian journalists have a very superficial understanding. . . . As for the real existentialism, it continues to grow quietly among our loyal and responsible youth not as a trend which is detached from life, but as an intellectual movement . . . that responds to the current circumstances of life and succeeds . . . in defending the reality of life as well as life itself.[61]

Communist Commitment Ascending

Muruwwa was neither the only nor the first critic to understand the potential of socialist realism to change the power structure of the literary establishment. Emerging critics like al-ʿAlim and ʿAbd al-ʿAzim also sought to appropriate the notion of iltizam as a Marxist intellectual staple and frame popular political energy in new theoretical terms. This largely successful project, however, was preceded by the pioneering and now largely forgotten work of Shahada Khuri, a young literary critic from Damascus.

Published ahead of its time in 1950, *Al-Adab fi-l-Maydan* (Literature in the field) was true to its title and demanded that writers "enter the field" and change it from within. By "field," the author meant the social, economic, and political battlefield, which, in his assessment, had seen dramatic changes since the end of World War II. Changes in the field reflected even "deeper and fundamental" changes in "the thought and actions of Arabs."[62] But which kind of literature could credibly account for this change and further engender it? Was existing literature synchronized with this change? Shahada Khuri thought that it was not: "Our emerging literature is powerless and still lacks a framing theory. It looks to the past more than it does to the future; it takes interest in the individual more than in society, and it is affiliated with dreams more than it is with reality. It is pale literature which is completely empty of the pulse, energy, and ambition of life."[63] In place of this, "we want literature to be both influential and influenced. We want it to describe that which exists in order to create that which should be. We want to carry a message but not on the basis of dreams and delusions but on the basis of historical truth and human development."[64]

Interestingly, the writer argued that the main obstacle facing this new literature was not the hegemony of the udaba' but a new spirit of existentialism that prompted the youth to "turn their attention to amusement, dancing, and cafés and throw themselves into the bosom of failure and defeat which characterizes 'existentialist youth.' They fail to distinguish between good and bad, beauty and ugliness, right and wrong, and justify this failure by calling it the new urban 'atmosphere' of our times . . . [in which] they live the teachings of Heidegger the Nazi and Sartre, the (so-called) hero of resistance!"[65] Alarmingly, the young generation was surrounded by culture that "spreads pessimism and despair, thus fleeing to ideological solutions such as self-awareness, sentimental examination, and painstaking psychological attentiveness."[66] In light of this state of affairs, Shahada Khuri called to establish a new form of "fighting literature" (adab mukafih).[67]

Other intellectuals also felt a deep need for change. The Lebanese critic Jurj Hanna, for instance, wrote that the prevalent notion of humanity in Arab letters was narrowly focused on radical individualism to the complete exclusion of collective existence.[68] Since Arab Marxists predicated their notion of commitment on society at large and went as far as taking it as their ontological base, they rejected Sartrean individualism as the basis for commitment. Reflecting on this position, Hanna had a Soviet-inspired expectation that Arab writers would function as "engineers of the human soul."[69] That is, that their commitment should actively reshape human reality rather than simply reflect its social aspects.

Yet, regardless of Shahada Khuri and Jurj Hanna's contribution to Marxist commitment, their work was theoretically insufficient to ground the practice of committed Marxist-Leninist culture and compete with Al-Adab's existentialist momentum. Indeed, compared to Sartre, Al-Adab's direct source of inspiration, Al-Thaqafa al-Wataniyya's muse and source of intellectual legitimacy was the legacy of the Lebanese writer, critic, and committed activist 'Umar Fakhuri. Though an outstanding figure who led by example, Fakhuri, who passed away in 1946, left little by way of a systematic theory of literature and culture. Muruwwa set out to close this gap, and, just like Suhayl Idris in Paris, to do so at a high intellectual level, he needed international experience.

Thus, in his first foray into likeminded international circles, Muruwwa attended the 1954 meeting of the Soviet-sponsored World Peace Council in Berlin where he gave a public address. He spoke of the paralyzing effects of intellectual colonialism (isti'mar fikri), which yields a cosmopolitan culture that detaches intellectuals from the real-life concerns of the people. He exposed the absurdity of a Lebanese state that allocates only 8 percent of its budget to education and 20 percent to internal security. He also lamented the complacency of the udaba' with the regrettable phenomenon of intellectual colonialism. Finally, he condemned Arab intellectuals for copying decadent foreign traditions such as impressionism, surrealism, and existentialism.[70] Yet, much more important than what Muruwwa said to the Berlin delegates is what he heard from them.

For the first time, Muruwwa was exposed to the emerging global front against imperialism and to its intellectual stars. Though this was a year before the Bandung Conference, the powerful assertion, as well as demonstration, of Third Worldism was already circulating. His impressions from the conference speak for themselves: "I saw myself as part of a vast movement that takes on an enormous cause. I felt as if I grew to represent inside me all these delegations of peoples and nations."[71] Thus, the parochial cultural struggle at home was now informed by the larger context of similar realities everywhere else. Seated at the dinner table next to writers and poets from China, Brazil, India, Cuba, and Argentina, Muruwwa was exposed to the many historical commonalities that these nations share. This sense of camaraderie only strengthened his conviction. But beyond conversations with Jorje Amado of Brazil or Nâzım Hikmet of Turkey, Muruwwa also got a taste for the intellectual complexity of this international project.

What was so complex? One of those dining next to him was the prophet of radical individualism, Jean-Paul Sartre. What was he doing there? Could the radical individualism of existentialism coexist with Marxism? It turned out that the global front against imperialism was indeed a complex ideological affair, in which the commitment of existentialists like Sartre was by no means weaker or in contradiction with that of communists.[72] Did it mean that existentialism and Marxism were compatible? What were the implications of Sartre's stand for the growing Arab debate about the theory of iltizam? There was no denying that Sartre's commitment nourished the fast rise of Third World liberation theology and that he saw individual responsibility in global terms. As we shall see, with this rise also grew the global intellectual demand that Sartre reconcile existentialism and Marxism. For the time

FIGURE 2 Poet Pablo Neruda on the cover of *Al-Thaqafa al-Wataniyya*

being, Muruwwa got a first taste of the burgeoning international front against imperialism and its keen interest in the Third World.

Six months later, Muruwwa attended the Second Congress of Soviet Writers in Moscow. By all accounts, especially his own, this short visit in December 1954 was a transformative experience that exposed him to the tremendous potential of socialist realism to usher in and guide postcolonial Arab culture.[73] Traveling once again outside the familiar parameters of the Arab world, Moscow appeared to Muruwwa as a larger-than-life human experiment. His travelogue glows with admiration for Moscow's sheer size, beauty, and authority. Standing in front of the Kremlin (Russian for "fortress"), the huge gates opened to welcome the delegations of Soviet writers from the golden wheat fields of Ukraine to the barren ice fields of Siberia . . . as well as from the thirty-nine nations that comprise the Soviet Union. Here we are now, behind the walls of the Kremlin, inside the formidable fortress . . . entering the big hall where the Supreme Soviet Council holds its sessions. This space is now at the disposal of Soviet writers as they open the great Second Congress of Soviet Writers. In their capacity as the people's intellectuals they are its rightful representatives.[74]

As Muruwwa made his way in to the hall, he spotted Marshal Zhukov, the legendary Soviet general who, only nine years earlier, had conquered Nazi Berlin. He was in awe.

Muruwwa: What do military personnel have to do with this celebration of writers and writing?
Translator (laughing): Here writers and soldiers are part of the same people. There are no barriers and boundaries. Marshal Zhukov attends this meeting not as a military man, but in his capacity as a writer and a friend of writers.
Muruwwa: And who are the people with the decorations on their chests?
Translator: These are also Soviet writers, ten of which wear the Stalin Medal, and four of them are war heroes.[75]

Thus, in a few brief pages, Muruwwa is welcomed and, in turn, introduces the reader to the wonders of Soviet utopia: an egalitarian classless society where writers play a concrete social role and are admired and celebrated in return.

With his critical guard down, over the next ten days, Muruwwa got a crash course in socialist realism, the congress's topic of choice. His first impression was that because Soviet writers had a definitive social mission they fundamentally differed from their Arab counterparts. Musing on Maxim Gorky, the man who convened the First Congress of Soviet Writers (1934) and was responsible for the elaboration and proliferation of socialist realism, Muruwwa, as well as everybody else, saw in him the ultimate role model for what a writer should be: a literary Stakhanov of sorts.

Taking their cues directly from Stalin's industrial metaphors, which imagined writers as "engineers of human souls," the congress's discussion revolved around their role in forging a new society and a new Soviet Man/Woman.[76] With this mission in mind, Soviet cultural architects conveyed the sense of a mystical relationship between writers, literature, and reality. And, though he did not yet properly understand the tenets of socialist realism, Muruwwa was smitten: "the marvelous interaction between the life of the people and literature is unprecedented in human history . . . we have seen this wondrous phenomenon throughout the Congress."[77] If the main business of the writer is to apply socialist realism to writing, the function of self-criticism, of which the congress was proud, was to identify and purge "mistakes" in the application process.[78] As one delegate put it, "Gorky became Gorky . . . only because Lenin corrected his mistakes."[79] For Muruwwa as well as for most Arab writers of the time, the concept of "literary mistake" was a novelty, one that made sense only if one thought of art in pure Marxist terms as a carefully structured scientific process. In other words, the practice of socialist realism made perfect philosophical sense only within the framework of Marxism-Leninism.

As the official Marxist-Leninist standpoint on art, socialist realism did not stop with the internal quest for purifying art of its "mistakes." Since this form of realism was locked in a fateful battle with capitalism, the cosmology of the writer was a "black and white" adversarial worldview in which "good" writers fought against "bad" ones, and "progressive" literature was pitted against "reactionary" literature. As the cofounder and chairman of the Union of Soviet Writers, Alexander Alexandrovich Fadeyev, put it, if "the role of realist literature is to fight capitalism," then socialist realism could be easily distinguished from capitalist literature, which was nothing but cosmopolitan "Art for Art's sake."[80]

And, thus, during the congress Muruwwa was exposed to the elementary tenets of socialist realism, namely, that literature should resonate with Marxism-Leninism, convey class consciousness, and personify class heritage, adhere to party mindedness (*partynost*), and endorse the interests and viewpoint of the people (*narodnost*).[81] In addition, as his later writing revealed, Muruwwa understood this doctrine in light of the philosophical proximity of the Soviet writer to reality. This aspect was first articulated in the First Congress of Soviet Writers when Andrei Zhdanov (Stalin's cultural tsar) decreed that, as the official style of Soviet culture, the art of socialist realism should "depict reality in its revolutionary development."[82] To summarize, the congress taught Muruwwa how and why to contrast socialist realism with the corrupt capitalist form of art for art's sake. Evidently, this reactionary capitalist art was divorced from social reality and lacked the historical momentum of revolutionary development. As such it should be destroyed.

Thus started Muruwwa's quest to bring socialist realism to Arabic literature with greater consistency and theoretical coherence than his colleagues Ra'if Khuri and 'Umar Fakhuri had thus far provided.[83] Though

Muruwwa was a committed believer, he was not dogmatic. Returning from Moscow, Muruwwa surmised that "There is no intention to
simply 'import' the meaning of Socialist Realism to Arabic literature."
Instead of wholesale application, the idea was to identify the unique
circumstances of the Arab world and thus to follow the method of various Soviet peoples, which enabled "scientifically applied Socialist Realism" in accordance with their own cultural peculiarities. He now had a
transnational *madhhab* (denomination) and a local mission.[84]

Rising to the challenge, Muruwwa's 1956 book, *Qadaya Adabiyya*,
was a careful blueprint of why and how to apply socialist realism in the
Arab world. A decade later he published another, more complete, literary agenda: *Dirasat Naqdiyya fi Daw' al-Manhaj al-Waqi'i* (1965). Both
books established him as the most systematic Arab theorist of socialist
realism. He now talked about his approach to literature in terms of a
methodology (*manhaj*) of total critique, a form of philosophy for life
that illuminates "the most important issues of the era . . . whether they
were intellectual, social or political."[85]

Taking his statement of purpose in *Fi-l-Thaqafa al-Misriyya* to the
next theoretical level, Muruwwa began his new book along more explicitly polarizing lines. "It is the nature of the 'new,'" he writes, "to
wish, from deep inside, to eliminate 'old' ideas, values and meaning
which belong to an era whose social progressive moment is gone. And
it is in the nature of the 'old' not to leave the field to the 'new' without
firm resistance."[86] The necessity to define, locate, and then eliminate
the "old" is derived from Muruwwa's dissatisfaction with how cultural
and political power was divided. In search of a political and cultural
revolution, the elimination of the "old" would inevitably make space
for "new social groups," which would then usher in a better phase of
historical development.[87]

According to Muruwwa, literature was the linchpin of an ongoing
effort to claim culture as a revolutionary political space through "literary battles" (*ma'arik adabiyya*), a notion that during this era became
extremely popular in Arab letters.[88] Indeed, those who subscribed to
socialist realism soon celebrated the birth of "fighting literature" (*adab
kifahi*).[89] Aside from the fact that this literature was the precursor to the
1960s Palestinian literature of resistance (*adab al-muqawama*), there is
the issue of the Marxist militarization of culture. Clearly, as the language of the speakers in the Second Congress show, "The diffusion of
military expressions is associated with the strong sense of militancy
inherent in Socialist Realism, and necessary for its didactic purposes."[90]

With this militant mentality in mind, the dividing line that Muruwwa charted was clear: while the old-guard reactionary udaba' like Taha Husayn, Tawfiq al-Hakim, and, to a lesser degree, al-'Aqqad insisted that "politics corrupt literature" and hence called for a separation of writers, literature, "and arts as a whole from the general affairs of life," the progressive socialist-realist generation insisted on activist "art for society's sake."[91] This act of total politicization was another characteristic of the postcolonial era that sought to replace the allegedly neutral (yet in actuality Eurocentric and equally political) critique of the udaba'.

By insisting that writers "define the social position of literary works," Muruwwa sought to distinguish progressive from reactionary writers.[92] But he also took time to define these differences philosophically. According to Muruwwa, reactionary writers drew on an idealist philosophy in which individual reason and consciousness constitute the first line of existence from which everything else is derived. That which is external to the individual, including society and economy, is relegated to a marginal level with minimal historical agency.[93] On the other side of this philosophical divide were the materialists, for whom individual actions and thoughts were projected onto the world that, in turn, rendered them meaningful. The material world, therefore, enabled the thoughts of the self and should hence be the focus of all intellectual efforts.[94] With a clear line separating the two camps, Muruwwa maintained that the inevitable outcome of idealist-inspired art was self-referential art. Divorced from reality, this art emerged exclusively from within the self, reflected mere individual experiences and, ultimately, was directed back at the selfish concern of the individual.[95]

With this philosophical division in mind, Muruwwa offered to rethink the position of the literary critic vis-à-vis literature. Unlike the politically disengaged literary criticism of the time, Muruwwa called upon the critic to become a revolutionary fighter (*munadil*) enrolled in the ranks of the avant-garde. As his friend and colleague 'Amil Mahdi argued, "A critic without a [political] position [*mawqif*] is a critic without methodology" and hence without social utility.[96] Hence, practically, the task of the progressive literary critic was to comb through the text and determine the degree to which materiality and the social position were articulated in a satisfactory fashion. By this time there was already an acknowledged international pool of progressive writers who could serve as role models, such as Pablo Neruda, Federico Garcia Lorca, Louis Aragon, and Nâzım Hikmet.[97] Once the position of the writer and the critic was redefined, the udaba' clearly emerged as a group of detached ivory-tower writers, a category to which some of their young-est followers, such as Naguib Mahfouz, were also consigned.[98]

Lastly, as the brainchild of a communist milieu, in addition to il-tizam, Muruwwa identified a Marxist theoretical justification for the project of "locating progressive elements in *turath*."[99] Similar to the USSR, which encouraged the many Soviet nationalities to connect to their heritage, Muruwwa identified *turath* as the strategic depository of socialist realism and, by extension, of a new revolutionary culture.[100] Like ʿAbd al-Rahman Badawi, Muruwwa too was troubled by the schis-matic consequences, linguistic (colloquial versus literary Arabic) as well as cultural (Enlightenment versus Islamic heritage), that colonialism left behind. As the collective cultural reservoir of Arab Muslims, the tu-rath was a victim of this split, thus causing the people to live as if they had no past experience to draw upon and hence no present authentic existence. In a postcolonial era, maintained Muruwwa, "the (broken) relation between the present Arab generation and its old intellectual/ religious tradition" should be repaired so that cultural authenticity could be reclaimed.[101] Yet, whereas Badawi devised a philosophical ma-neuver to overcome this divide, Muruwwa turned to Marxism.

Muruwwa strongly believed that "Marxist methodology is capable of placing the problem of turath in its correct context and respond to the issues and complexities that turath raises in a methodologically cor-rect and practical manner."[102] That was because in the context of post-colonialism Marxism constituted a new form of objectivity, one that was historically grounded. Approaching the turath from this uncon-ventional angle and reading it in light of historical materialism raised the question of what is knowledge and what is a revolutionary standing vis-à-vis this knowledge. In other words, through the Marxist prism Muruwwa and his circle sought to redefine the meaning of knowledge in the age of revolution.[103]

Thus, in an intellectual project that today, when debates on turath proliferate, remains largely forgotten, Muruwwa began to systemati-cally reread, rediscover, and then reinvent Islamic tradition.[104] Fully en-gaged, in 1954 he declared this effort "Our Lifetime Project" (*mashruʿ al-ʿumr*).[105] His home journal, *Al-Thaqafa al-Wataniyya*, and the entire Marxist community were on board: "The mission of our journal is . . . to treat the connection between the present Arab generation and its ancient heritage [*turath*]."[106] By the time Muruwwa had finished elabo-rating his vision, militancy was in the air: "We call to fight the (reac-tionary) benighted *adab* which propagates desperation and pessimism.

This literature, which aspires to rule over people by promising a better tomorrow, instead turned its oppression and pessimism into a 'philosophy' and the future into a sealed wall."[107]

The Coup: Taha Husayn in Beirut

For a heavyweight intellectual like Taha Husayn, a person who had courageously endured the scandals and political pressures of the 1920s and 1930s, post–World War II cultural debates should have been easy to navigate. Yet, this time, all signs showed that Taha Husayn was growing tired, frustrated, and perhaps even desperate. That much became obvious in April 1955. Four months earlier Suhayl Idris had invited Taha Husayn to publicly debate the question, For whom does the intellectual write: the elite or the people? Husayn accepted and arrived in Beirut for a much-publicized debate with literary critic Ra'if Khuri.[108] It was yet another round in the ongoing conversation about iltizam and socialist realism as "literature for life." Two lectures were planned for the debate: Taha Husayn delivered "The Man of Letters Writes to the Elite" and Khuri lectured on "The Man of Letters Writes to the Masses." These opposing visions summarized the cultural tensions of the last decade.

Ra'if Khuri lectured first. He was polite yet polemical: "Dear Doctor, to whom do we write? To the people or to the elite? . . . According to you, you write for the elite."[109] In the spirit of the times, Khuri invoked a theory of literature that took the people as its subject, emerged from life-oriented popular dynamism and returned to inform and nourish it.[110] While Khuri did not call explicitly for the strict application of Soviet-style realism, he nonetheless embraced Stalin's mechanistic 1934 idea that "writers are the engineers of the human soul."[111] He was careful enough to qualify this statement, saying that as long as writers did not follow blindly what had been engineered for them by the state and the party, they would benefit society as a whole. "This is the free socialism that I believe in," he concluded, and this was his vision for Arab writers.[112]

When his turn came to deliver "The Man of Letters Writes to the Elite," Husayn immediately said that he was "neither committed to defend the elite nor the people." "I simply received an invitation from Suhayl Idris . . . who asked me to talk about writing to the elite."[113] Indeed, the provocative title of Husayn's lecture was given by Idris himself, who sought to dramatize the event and the ensuing publication in *Al-Adab*. "As much as I am concerned," Husayn declared, "the entire debate is artificial and baseless . . . as, in anything I had ever written, I never applied 'elite' or 'people' as literary parameters. [All] I understand is literature and readers who read this literature."[114] In fact, he added, "I do not believe at all in this debate."[115] Why not? Because, he said, "it is all politics."[116]

Yet, a debate is a debate, and, not to be undone, Husayn also took a polemical approach: "Did Sophocles write on behalf of a political party?"[117] Homer too wrote poetry to the elite few, but "who does not read Homer now?"[118] What bout medieval Islamic praise poetry (*madh*), is this political?[119] As far as Husayn was concerned, the literature of commitment was nothing but a "literature of propaganda."[120] Raising the painstaking issue of language accessibility, he said that those who truly want to write to the masses should do so in their colloquial language (*'amiyya*) and not in the standard literary Arabic (*fusha*), which the masses do not understand.[121] This was a strong point as, in reality, much of what the new generation was writing was entirely inaccessible to the vernacular-speaking masses.

Pleasantries aside (and the debate featured many formalities), the two writers and their respective generations shared very little. In hindsight, this debate marked the inevitable inability of the udaba' to continue their role as the prime shapers of public culture. Besides many anti-udaba' follow-ups to the debate, there were other indications of this state of affairs;[122] for instance, the 1953 closure of two leading *nahdawi* journals, *Al-Risala* and *Al-Thaqafa*. As *Al-Risala*'s editor, Hasan al-Zayyat, sadly admitted, this was the end of an era.[123] In fact, even before his arrival at the debate, Taha Husayn already had noted that Beirut was emerging as the capital of Arab thought, at the expense of Cairo, and Anwar al-Ma'dawi seemed to agree with some elements of this prognosis.[124] That same year, committed writers had established the Arab Writers Union, and its first two congresses (1954, 1956) marked a gradual shifting of the literary center from Cairo to Beirut, as well as the emergence of a hegemonic form of committed literature. As one of the organizers noted, Taha Husayn, who attended the Second Congress in Bludan, Syria, was obviously out of place.[125]

Perhaps so, but nonetheless Husayn did not budge. After decades of intellectual activity Husayn was confident in his own criteria for what defined good literature. Upon his return from Beirut, he published *Naqd wa Islah* (Criticism and reform). In it he republished a critique of the interplay between "pessimistic philosophy" and "pessimistic literature." He traced the genealogy of this relation all the way from Sartre,

Camus, and Marcel deep into the nineteenth century and took its current manifestations to indicate the unfortunate condition of the "European soul" in the wake of two devastating world wars.[126] On his part, Ra'if Khuri also continued the debate and extended his criticism to the canonical Lebanese writer Mikha'il Nu'ayma, an innocent bystander of a debate he did not care much about.[127] Insisting on the mandatory presence of politics in literature, in 1959 Khuri wrote, "While politicians should not exploit writers, literature that would not make a political statement would become escapist."[128]

Finding themselves displaced, the udaba' confronted their marginalization as individuals and not as a group. In fact, rather than uniting they fought among themselves. The old-fashioned socialist ideologue Salama Musa argued that the social problem in the Arab world had a linguistic side to it—namely, the division between literary and colloquial Arabic. With hardly any colloquial literature in existence, the majority of the population was left speechless, so to speak. Taking after Sartre, he argued for a connection between language and thought and said that he could trust nothing that could not be expressed.[129] A year later, in 1956, Musa published *Al-Adab li-l-Sha'b* (Literature to the masses), a text that further embraced Sartre, challenged 'Abbas Mahmud al-'Aqqad, and pressed Taha Husayn to answer the question, "What is his message, and how does it serve humanity?"[130] Musa argued that the literature of the udaba' was meant for kings and rulers (*muluk*) and not for the people. Husayn and al-'Aqqad responded in kind, and the generational unity of the udaba' quickly disintegrated.[131] Two years later Salama Musa passed away.

Tired of the debate, al-'Aqqad decided that he "does not debate communists."[132] Tawfiq al-Hakim, who was still the most active *adib* and received the bulk of the criticism, could not afford to do the same. Taking the debate to heart, he responded by publishing *Al-Ta'duliyya: Madhhabi fi-l-Haya wa-l-Fann* (The equilibrium: My creed in life and art), in which he called for a dialectical and hence inclusive process of cultural change: "[My usage of] the word equilibrium should not be taken here literarily to mean balance, symmetry, or even moderation and intermediateness," he wrote. "[Instead], in this book, equilibrium means the movement of both acceptance and opposition to another (human) undertaking."[133] Though heavily in debt to existentialism, his call went unanswered.[134]

In 1963, al-Hakim made a more deliberate attempt to engage and published *Al-Ta'am li kul Fam* (Food for every mouth). This play addressed the classic Third World topic of world hunger and unequal distribution of global wealth between the North and the South. Here he was publishing an involved, if not "committed," play about an acute world problem. Yet, committed writers were not impressed. Muruwwa, for instance, wrote that this play was a transparent response to the accusation that he was a disconnected ivory-tower writer.[135] It was another example of the existing gap between writers of different generations.

Equally painful was that former students and disciples also began to drift away from the cultural understanding of the udaba'. Such was the case of poet and literary critic Luwis 'Awad, a graduate of both Oxford and Princeton universities. In 1955 he became the literary editor of the daily *Al-Jumhuriyya* and immediately adopted the slogan "Al-Adab fi Sabil al-Hayat" (literature for life's sake). Positioning himself against the udaba' and looking back at the literary scene, his mission was to address the "dreadful vacuum in literary life in Egypt since 1936."[136] Like many other young intellectuals, he too supported the devastating attack of Mahmud Amin al-'Alim and 'Abd al-'Azim Anis on the udaba'. He continued to side with them even though he realized that the two unemployed academics were "too dogmatic and had gone, in fact, too far in their subordination of literature to life."[137] The best young minds, such as playwright, journalist, lawyer, and activist Lutfi al-Khuli, were also in the committed camp.

One of the last symbolic and most emotional acts in the gradual fall of the udaba' was Taha Husayn's hour-long eulogy of his longtime liberal colleague and cultural founding father, Muhammad Husayn Haykal, who passed away in December 1956. Crying publicly for the first time in his formidable career, Husayn bade farewell not only to Haykal but to their entire generation and its embattled notion of high culture.[138] In contrast, Mahmud Amin al-'Alim, expressed growing intellectual confidence in the scientific and revolutionary role of his generation's craft: "Today, [socialist] literary criticism is the most prominent intellectual activity in the Arab world and can possibly become the school from which all other intellectual streams can branch out, even those that have absolutely nothing to do with literature."[139] And so it happened, that one generation left the stage and another took over.

Oddly enough, both generations met one more time when, sometime in the early 1960s, TV hostess Layla Rustum invited Taha Husayn to debate the hegemonic intellectuals of iltizam, such as Yusuf al-Siba'i, 'Abd al-Rahman al-Sharqawi, Mahmud Amin al-'Alim, Anis Mansur, and others. He accepted and attended what was no doubt one of the most awkward, uncomfortable, and tense studio broadcasts that

Egyptian national television had seen since its establishment in 1960. To call it a debate would be misleading, as the format that Rustum chose allowed those in attendance (the "stars" as she called them) to ask Taha Husayn ("The Sun," in her words) questions and respond to his answers. She confidently began with writer and state intellectual Yusuf al-Siba'i, who presented a question about literary versus colloquial Arabic as a writer's language of choice. In plainly political terms, al-Siba'i asked Husayn, Should we direct culture toward the elite or the people? The conversation continued with Husayn's emphatic rejection of iltizam in which he expressed concerns over freedom of conscious and spelled out his dislike for state intellectuals and (as we shall see in the next chapter) for the authoritarian involvement of the state in cultural affairs.

Husayn was then asked about his loyalty to Descartes's school of thought and of the applicability of French Enlightenment to Egyptian cultural life. His questioners wanted to know if, considering the current socialist climate, he was still a committed follower of Descartes. "Of course, sir," Husayn answered and continued to talk about his experience at the Sorbonne and his Descartes class with Lucien Lévy-Bruhl. He then refused to acknowledge the literary contribution of the young generation when insultingly stating that he had never read al-Sharqawi's socialist novel *Al-Ard*, which, of course, everybody else had. Seated to his left, al-Sharqawi remained mortally silent. Probably as agreed before, Rustum asked Naguib Mahfouz to ask a question about the role of the writer in socialist society. Anticipating a hostile response, a tense Mahfouz declined to ask the question, while Husayn joked about his commitment to realism. Changing the subject, Mahmud Amin al-'Alim inquired about Husayn's opinion of the contribution of the young generation to the cultural heritage of the Arabs. Husayn hesitated and was asked once again to respond. With few minutes left to the program, Husayn gave in and opined that that the young generation wrote more than it read and that its superficial habit was to avoid examining any subject in depth. "Who of these new writers even read our old traditions? Who of them know any foreign language" he asked. "What they write does not indicate that they possess any width and cultural depth." Closing the broadcast, Rustum lamented that Husayn's final verdict was a bit too harsh, but he assured those present that it was all out of genuine love and concern.[140]

With that, the udaba' was silenced. The fall of the udaba' and the fact that Arab culture gravitated toward Beirut meant that the century-old *nahdawi* structure popularly known as "Egyptians write, Lebanese print, and Iraqis read," was gradually replaced by a diversified intellectual vanguard that, though situated in Beirut, included a mix of Iraqi, Syrian, Lebanese, and Palestinian intellectuals.[141] Besides publishing new influential journals and books, Beirut also emerged as a vibrant center for contemporary translation. As opposed to Cairo's elitist translations of Shakespeare, Beirut translated for the people, "thus closing a cultural gap in the lives of Arab readers."[142] This new burgeoning intellectual order could be summarized as "Arabs think, write, and publish in Beirut what they cannot think, write, and publish in Cairo and Baghdad."

Conclusion

The making of iltizam shows how a generational fault line transformed into a full-fledged struggle for cultural hegemony. This historical episode provides an opening—however limited—into seeing what happened inside decolonization. In this internal shift, not merely the literary field was rearranged but public presence as such, a development that had serious implications for the political arena as well. Once the new intellectual cadres began to blur the lines between politics and culture by self-describing themselves as "committed," the politicization process could move only forward. In their pursuit to politicize the act of thought itself, they narrowed down the act of writing to Sartre's basic questions: "What do we write? Why do we write? And to whom do we write?" In doing so they defined literature as the symbolic field in which cultural decolonization efforts would take place and literary criticism as the means by which they would purge their culture of colonial effects. Concomitantly, they abandoned the false universalism of colonial Enlightenment and the symbolic respect for Descartes. Instead, they drew meaning out of concrete local realities by extracting it vertically; that is, from the social bottom upward. Importantly enough, this was not a past-oriented fundamentalist project of "return" such as that of the literary-critic-turned-Islamist Sayyid Qutb (also a major disciple of Taha Husayn). Rather, by drawing on international intellectual models and a vocabulary whose immediate sources of inspiration derived from Paris and Moscow, the new critics stayed in the present and remained connected to the world. In that sense, and as we shall later see, intellectual decolonization was a globally oriented phenomenon.

As in other instances of radical transformation, the struggle over decolonization reopened the question of how to establish one's intellectual authority. From the perspective of a sociology of knowledge, it is important to note that, until the late 1950s, the new intelligentsia was largely outside the purview of state institutions, which included universities, publishing houses, the press, and professional associations. Indeed, this intellectual turn was informally organized around private journals, newspapers, cafés, and, more formally, around Marxist political circles and their parties. In this horizontal constellation, authority was based on quality of writing and thought, erudition, courage, and, especially, practical as well as theoretical commitment to autonomous politics. This moment of opportunity gave birth to an entire class of self-made and fairly independent intellectuals.

Parallel to this process and of equal importance was the corresponding rise of Beirut as the new and vibrant capital of Arab thought. In terms of its journals, publishing houses, progressive translation movement, intellectual diversity, freedom of thought, and sheer cultural energy, the intellectual process of decolonization shifted the balance away from Cairo toward Beirut. In that sense, new writers won much cultural space for their agendas as well as a concrete, safe, and supportive geographical location. This is just another example of the major intellectual dynamics that characterized this era and were hitherto invisible to students of decolonization and Cold War history.

Taking advantage of the abstract and real space that was left by the fall of the udaba', however, did not mean that the champions of iltizam could agree on what to do next. Quite the contrary. The rest of the decade saw an intense competition to influence public life in concrete political ways, with Pan-Arab existentialists like Suhayl Idris and communists like Mahmud Amin al-'Alim playing important roles in this struggle. As the once-engaged intellectuals acknowledged half a century later, the politicization of culture turned the act of iltizam into a subjective expression of revolutionary commitment. With extreme loyalty to one's own ideological position, social, cultural, and political truths became engaged situational truths. Locked in this subjective philosophical angle, precisely the situation that Taha Husayn foresaw when he introduced Sartre a decade earlier, the committed generation created a corrupt economy of truth that depleted the ability to create broad community consensus. This was the grave risk in the committed act of politicizing culture.[143]

Retrospectively, some of the risk was due to Sartre's reception in the region, which, by and large, excluded his philosophy. According to pioneering German historian Verena Klemm, since during this particular phase existentialism was reduced to iltizam, "the ontological basis of Sartre's theses was considered superfluous" and so was his distinction between involvement (*embarquement*) and engagement.[144] Consequently, even though all along they were very real, the ethical dangers of iltizam lurked unseen. Yet, in the context of decolonization, this risk was deemed insignificant, and the tradeoff of politicizing culture in return for new intellectual space was seen as an excellent strategy for change. Increasingly, however, this newly won space came under the purview of the state. We now turn to see how that came about and what it meant for the question of freedom.

FOUR

Meet the State

Nineteen fifty-eight was a year of many beginnings. Egypt and Syria merged into a united republic, the Iraqi monarchy was no more, and Lebanon and Jordan teetered on the brink of revolution. Trying to save its allies, the United States registered its first post–World War II military intervention in the region. Unapologetic and confident as ever, Nasser presided over an unprecedented revolutionary momentum. But there were also other beginnings, slower and less visible ones. Such was the case of the rise of the interventionist and patriotic Arab state. That too was supported by the *annus mirabilis* of 1958, which violently pitted "progressive" elements against so-called reactionary ones. Hailing from Beirut, the high priest of iltizam, Suhayl Idris, wrote in the language of "us" versus "them" about freedom versus slavery, revolution versus colonialism, revolutionary commitment and solidarity versus imperialist reaction, and of the betrayal of the old generations versus the revolutionary promise of the new generation (*al-jil al-jadid*). In particular, Idris singled out philosopher, diplomat, and politician Charles Malik, then acting minster of foreign affairs, for personally facilitating the Lebanese dependency on the American Eisenhower Doctrine, which brought the US Marines to Beirut's shores.[1] Equally engaged was Fayiz Sayigh, who lost his well-balanced temper and called to fight the communist movement, which he saw as antithetical to Pan-Arabism.[2] Everybody rooted for the liberating promise of Pan-Arabism, but only a few understood its inner workings and relation to the state.

What was Pan-Arabism? The overwhelming majority

of scholars view Pan-Arabism as a rational ideological system that, in both of its dominant manifestations, Nasserism and Ba'thism, strove mostly to achieve the project of Arab unity, whose goal was to replace the many existing Arab states with a unified political entity.[3] Departing from this narrow understanding, I consider Pan-Arabism not simply a rational political project but a theological system of political faith. How so? By formulating new notions of sovereignty, authenticity, and freedom, Pan-Arabism sacralized politics and offered a form of postcolonial salvation. To say that Pan-Arabism functioned as a political theology is to refer to the ways in which it created, promoted, and maintained a sacred political experience with its own institutions, norms, ethics, moral space, rituals, ethos, and distinct sense of history. This kind of sacred politics always points, strives, and aims toward the creation of popular sovereignty because it is there that the nation becomes alive, that the state emerges as the embodiment of popular sovereignty, and that docile subjects become willing and participating free citizens. Designed to compensate for the inherent weakness of semicolonial states that emerged after World War I, Pan-Arabism underwrote state authority and its effort to standardize, codify, centralize, and valorize the so-called scientific bureaucratic (objective, precise, and universally valid) procedures of the state in the service of the common good.

Appropriately to the era of decolonization, it was a system of faith that offered its followers much more than the Ba'th's signature ideological trinity of unity, socialism, and freedom. Offering full liberation, this theological formulation of the political gained traction and momentum only when it began to interplay with concrete politics of solidarity, sovereignty, and sacrifice, as in the Bandung Conference, the struggle over Algeria, and, above all, the Suez War. All three episodes, each in its way, served as a model for liberation. The working of the state was evident in all three of these, and the association between revolution, statism, and Pan-Arabism became common.

Becoming the generational choice of millions, the Pan-Arab project raised serious questions with regard to the well-being of basic liberal freedoms such as free speech and political association and, more generally, with regard to the ongoing problem of freedom: What was the place and role of the state in the promise of liberation? Can the Arab revolutionary project succeed without a state, and, by extension, can one be a revolutionary without a state? Is the state different than the Pan-Arab nation? How can one tell the two apart? What is the relationship between the cultural registrar of Arab nationalism and the state? What should it be? At a time in which the triumph of Pan-Arab iltizam and the hegemonic drive to rectify the individual in the body of the Pan-Arab state was there for all to see and celebrate, few people were willing to think critically about these questions. This chapter charts the rise of the interventionist and authoritarian state and focuses on the few intellectuals who, drawing on existentialist themes, were courageous enough to take a critical public position in defense of freedom, a position far outside the general consensus.

Who were these groups? Feminists who deployed radical individualism in order to rebel against patriarchy, Palestinian refugees who used existentialist themes such as "anxiety" and "facing death" to account for their traumatic expulsion from Palestine and their estrangement from fellow Arabs, and political dissidents who toyed with the notion of the "absurd" in order to contest the folly of an increasingly authoritarian state and zealous national politics. Alongside them one can find the wretched poor of the provinces who, though achieving intellectual mobility, felt the alienating impact of the city. At times working together, at others acting in complete separation from one another, by the early 1960s one could speak of an existentialist counterculture whose manifestations could be found all over the region but, especially, as the next chapter tells us, in Baghdad, the so-called capital of Arab existentialism.

Though freedom was on everyone's lips, even after a decade of debate, the basic question of what constituted freedom was still very relevant. "Don't think of freedom in terms of something you take from one and give to the other. It originates from within the subject toward others," wrote one cultural critic.[4] The relentless humanist Fayiz Sayigh, a sober Pan-Arabist, delivered a more alarming message: "[We need] a humanistic movement that believes in the freedom and dignity of the individual . . . [movement] that believes in the human being not in numerical terms, not as a building block, not as a sheep in a herd, and not as a tool in the hands of the state. But a movement that believes in the human being as the culmination and the ultimate subject of history."[5] Sayigh did not explicitly identify the Arab state, and Egypt more specifically, as a possible threat. Yet, he hinted that the interventionist patriotic state was already casting a menacing shadow. Later, Iraqi intellectuals coined the pejorative term "regime literati" (*muthaqqaf/ mufakkir al-sulta*), and over the decades this expression proliferated and became a common way of capturing an uncritical and sometimes immoral association between the thinker and the state.[6] Going beyond the metric parameters that signaled the rise of the state, this chapter examines some symbolic key moments that allowed the transregional

Pan-Arab state of Egypt to monopolize culture, appropriate the revolutionary project, buy the loyalty of intellectuals, and propagate a new notion of freedom as collective liberation from foreign rule.

State of Disguise

Taken by the promise of revolution to liberate Arabs, military officers and their civilian allies began promoting the state as the embodiment of the nation and the sole guarantor of its freedom. Steadily, the state occupied an ever-greater slice of the public sphere, and its revolutionary politics became a daily affair of exhibitionist spectacles and political narcissism. Nasser and his revolutionary state were there not simply to rule but to offer deep liberation and "make history." By orchestrating an endless stream of ecstatic revolutionary happenings and public holidays, they demonstrated, day in and day out, how the revolution develops the political body, engenders a history, and thus creates a new type of liberated human being.

They backed this ongoing revolutionary spectacle with an appropriate historical view that strung together a series of localized historical episodes of dissent and opposition to foreigners into the great epic chain of historic liberation and inevitable Pan-Arab triumph.[7] Nasserism, and later Ba'thism, presented this deterministic schematization of history in a manner that powerfully communicated the mystical and transformative force of the unified nation that safely nests in the robust body of the omnipotent state. Though this understanding permeated all spheres of Arab life, there was nothing distinctively Arab about this understanding.

The fact of the matter is that the Pan-Arab ethos of fantastic revolutionary continuum that collapsed past, present, and future into a single temporal unit was ubiquitous in the community of Bandung. Indeed, a new way of telling the story of struggle and sacrifice was gradually being canonized. According to anthropologist David Scott, "anticolonial stories about the past, present, and future have typically been emplotted in a distinctive narrative form, one with a distinctive story-potential: that of *Romance*. They have tended to be narratives of overcoming, often narratives of vindication; they have tended to enact a distinctive rhythm and pacing, a distinctive direction, and to tell stories of salvation and redemption. They have been largely dependent upon a certain (utopian) horizon toward which the emancipationist history is imagined to be moving."[8] The Ba'th doctrine of the Syrian ideologue and party founder, Michel ʿAflaq, is a classic example: "I will repeat what I already said before; our revolution [*inqilab*], is the axis of our movement and the element which distinguishes it from all other movements. It is necessary that Baʿthists will understand this revolutionary quality in the deepest possible way. . . . No other party is capable of calling for the same revolution that the Baʿth calls for. That is because *revolution is the secret of our new mentality* [*al-nafsiyya al-jadida*] *of Arab life*" (emphasis added).[9] This form of imaginary movement assumes that, beginning with individual mentality, the entire political body—that is, the nation and the citizenry—experiences epic transformation. But that was a dangerous illusion. It was not the Indonesian or Arab nation that was transforming but the state. And the two were by no means identical.

Undoubtedly, blurring the lines between the "nation" and the "state" was a staple of postcolonial governance. In India, for example, the state systematically monopolized the moral recourses of the civic community, or the nation, thus presenting itself as the ultimate embodiment of civic life.[10] With special focus on intellectuals, the state demanded full and total cooperation. As we shall see, in the Arab world, those who were willfully coopted by the state greatly benefited from it. But, for those intellectuals who hoped to tame the state and guide its actions in accordance with their own ideological designs, something else was in store. As it turned out, this arrangement rarely worked out to their advantage. Quite the contrary, by the mid-1950s, the Egyptian state showed little compassion for dissidents such as ʿAbd al-ʿAzim Anis and Mahmud Amin al-ʿAlim or free thinkers like Luwis ʿAwad. As already mentioned, along with dozens of other intellectuals, they were purged from their university positions, incarcerated, and tortured.[11] The fate of organized workers, Muslim Brotherhood activists, and radical thinkers such as Sayyid Qutb was much worse, and ranged from systematic torture to death. The presence of the state was therefore inscribed on the bodies of those who insistently upheld the difference between the political community and the state.

The Cause

The rise of the intolerant state as the culmination of the nation's existence was coupled with a corresponding fundamental shift in the intellectual field. In that respect, 1957 was an important year. Reinforced by the Suez War, Nasser's Egypt quickly "went on to set up the system of institutions through which it intended to control and mobilize the intellectuals, a system which in its essentials still exists today."[12] The person behind this state apparatus was Yusuf al-Siba'i, the forty-year-old "writer-general" who, until his assassination in 1978 at the hands of revolutionary Palestinians, worked tirelessly to achieve and maintain the state monopoly of culture. Functioning as the "general of the army of letters," he was the first secretary general of the newly established Higher Council for the Arts and Letters (1956) and presided over other state and quasi-state institutions, such the Association of Men of Letters (jam'iyyat al-udaba', founded in 1955), which operated as the Egyptian branch of the Congress of Arab Writers.[13] With such tight control over the levers of culture, "At the end of the 1950s when Nasser's prestige was at its height . . . , Egypt took over the direction, still through Yusuf al-Siba'i, of the Congress of Arab Writers and the Congress of Afro-Asian Writers."[14] Pan-Arab statism, therefore, was on the rise, and many Arab writers and institutions willfully submitted to the transregional Egyptian state, which was believed to stand for a cause greater than itself.

While the traces of this history could be found in the dozens of books and magazines all over the region, due to its canonical presence in Arab life it is particularly important to examine the fashion in which, during 1957, the influential community of *Al-Adab* went out of its way to champion the rise of the Pan-Arab state as the sole representative of the Arab Cause. What was the Cause? In the journal's fourth year, it seems that a classic cluster of postcolonial concerns, issues, and problems that were always on the mind of *Al-Adab*'s editors suddenly congealed into the single organizing concept of the Arab Cause (*al-qadiyya al-'Arabiyya*). It was not always the case. In early 1955, for example, a frustrated Arab diplomat, in private correspondence, rebuked the legendary editor Suhayl Idris for his editorial choices. Taking the letter to heart, Idris made the accusations public by publishing them on the front page of his journal: "While Arab destiny is being decided upon in the great capital cities (of the West) you are publishing a special issue on Arab poetry. Is this the only thing in Arab existence that concerns you, those who are regarded as the intellectuals of iltizam? Are you not interested in publishing a special issue on Arab destiny or on the Arabs and the world? . . . Is poetry all that we wish from God?"[15]

Two years later, after Bandung and Suez, and in the context of the war in Algeria, Suhayl Idris and the Arab world were quite transformed. Indeed, this era saw the emergence of the Arab Cause as a frame that went beyond the mere issue of political liberation to articulate a classic postcolonial platform that touched on multiple political, cultural, social, economic, and psychological aspects of Arab existence. Sovereignty, or what Sharabi described as a quest for "a sense of inner liberation and restoration of self-respect," was one of these important aspects.[16] Writing in *Al-Adab*, the Palestinian Naji 'Allush and the Syrian 'Abdallah 'Abd al-Da'im had much to say on the deep meaning of the Cause as well. To a degree, both men echoed 'Aflaq.[17]

Committed to this creed, *Al-Adab* actively participated in the making of Arab political theology; for instance, by embracing the image of the Arab *fida'i* or freedom fighter as the actual bearer and witness of revolutionary change. Whether it was the Palestinian fighter in the Gaza Strip, the Egyptian soldier in Port Said, or the rebel in the Kasbah of Algiers, all of these previously independent struggles were now siphoned into the great cause of Pan-Arabism, which itself was framed in the language of Bandung, Third Worldism, and the political theology of liberation. Against this background, the struggle in Algeria was internalized as an essentially Arab cause (*qadiyyat al-Jaza'ir al-'Arabiyya*) and not simply as an Algerian one.[18]

Slowly but surely revolution became a pressing daily concern, and a prevailing sense of daily communal struggle settled in.[19] As ideologue Ra'if Khuri wrote with respect to Egypt's revolutionary example: "If someone is an Arab, whether his specific country is Syria, Iraq, Saudi-Arabia, Palestine, Jordan, or North Africa, he is obliged to love Egypt. Lebanese, however, are asked much more than that. [We ask] that Egypt would flow in their blood and that her smile and wounds would be theirs to share. This is because [historically] Egypt is a complementary nation to Lebanon."[20] In its drive to militarize and subdue civic life to the demands of the Cause, the journal wrote that the "Lebanese writer is a soldier in the battle for Liberation."[21] Though the journal rejected the accusation regarding the "conscription of thought in the service of politics," two years after the fact, the anonymous diplomat who, in 1955, reprimanded Suhayl Idris for publishing detached "poetry" would have only praise for the young editor.[22]

Other dominant voices were on the same page. Published on the eve of the Third Congress of Arab Writers, Jurj Hanna's *Ma'na al-Qawmiyya al-'Arabiyya* (The meaning of Pan-Arabism), produced a statement about the responsibility (*mas'uliya*) of intellectuals to defend and advance the Arab Cause. Though being one of the most eloquent books published in 1957, Hanna also failed to distinguish between the cause of the nation and the workings of a state and, in a variation on a familiar communist theme, argued that because intellectuals are "engineers of the human soul . . . they are also the engineers of Pan-Arabism."[23] The idea of intellectual responsibility that Hanna promoted required intellectuals to use the "weapon of the word" (*silah al-kalima*) polemically, as in the effort to refute Western claims that Pan-Arabism was tantamount to fascism and Nazism but also constructively in the service of Pan-Arab culture.[24] As he put it, "At this current stage . . . , the mission of the responsible Arab intellectual is to fight the influence and designs of colonialism, battle reaction that trades in religion and sectarianism, expose conspiracies against the independence of all Arab countries, clarify the meaning of freedom and democracy, embody any progressive and liberationist movement, and actively participate in the construction of the nationalist and humanist edifice of Arab existence."[25] Elsewhere in the Arab republic of writing the message was quite the same. Few Arab intellectuals understood the true nature of state intellectual hegemony or anticipated that it would extend beyond Egypt to infect all Arab revolutionary regimes. In truth, most intellectuals were content enough with celebrating the state, not realizing that they would pay for it with their very own freedom.

Toward Intellectual Syndicalism

Historian Albert Hourani concluded his majestic history of Arab liberalism with a symbolic manifestation of its demise: the Third Congress of Arab Writers.[26] In December 1957 about a hundred Arab writers gathered in Cairo to discuss "literature and Arab nationalism." In contrast with the casual and highly intimate atmosphere of previous congresses, when the state was completely absent, the Third Congress was logistically as well as intellectually wrapped around the present and future of the Pan-Arab state. Convened under the patronage of the Egyptian government, the Third Congress was the place where committed intellectuals from all over the region (with the exception of Jordan and Saudi Arabia) lined up to pledge their allegiance to Pan-Arab statism.

Nasser welcomed them:

On behalf of the Egyptian people who believe in Arab unity, I am pleased to welcome you here in Egypt. On this occasion, the Congress of Arab Writers, the Arab people look up to you as an essential element of Arab nationalism. In order to support national unity and solidarity we are in need of unified thought. During an era of Cold War that deploys every possible weapon, the liberation of thought is a necessity. Literature and thought are two essential weapons in this war. You are the leaders of thought and have an essential task of clarifying affairs and establishing a future Arabic literature that is free. Free of foreign control and of foreign direction. In that, you could work for the sake of Arab solidarity and nationalism toward realizing our goals. May God be with you![27]

With this message as its guiding spirit, the Third Congress was to solidify the internal Arab front and celebrate the redemptive qualities of Pan-Arabism.[28] The unitary language was Nasserist, and to a certain extent Ba'thist. The general mood in the congress did not welcome disagreements and critical reflection. The guests came to celebrate the will to sacrifice or what Suhayl Idris described as "the right kind of iltizam."[29] And celebrate submission to the Pan-Arab state as the right kind of iltizam they did.

The Sudanese delegate spoke of a "new meaning of Pan-Arabism, which functions as a vital common interest and a shared fate that permeates Arab ontology."[30] Syrian poet Shawqi Baghdadi opined that "talking politics under the banner of Pan-Arabism is the same as talking about art and poetry."[31] Suhayl Idris wrote of "conscious and non-conscious writers" and called to support the former because their cultural instincts align iltizam with Pan-Arabism.[32] Writing of the "mission of Pan-Arabism," the Syrian writer Fu'ad Shayib maintained "that the human mission of Pan-Arabism constitutes the central arena of liberation in the heart of Africa and Asia."[33] Ra'if Khuri, who urged critics to "serve Pan-Arabism," wondered, "How can we manage to make Pan-Arabism an organic part of the literary work?"[34] Lastly, the congress concluded with two public statements. The first, which was sent directly to the UN, supported the Algerian resistance to colonialism. The second was addressed to the "the intellectuals of the world" and focused on reconnecting with other Third World intellectuals in the familiar language of Bandung.[35]

All in all, the congress accepted the state and nationalism as the ultimate object of intellectual labor and, as Ra'if Khuri put it, underscored the objective status of Pan-Arabism as one that lies beyond any intellectual system such as "Marxism, Sartrean existentialism, or any other ideology."[36] In speech after speech the communal ethos of faith in the Pan-Arab state and sacrifice on its behalf was reiterated, as was the theological expectation that this committed politics would liberate the people and, by extension, assist individuals in overcoming their limits. In hindsight, though the participants in the congress were all free and independent critical thinkers intellectually committed to freedom, they had submitted themselves to yet another form of domination whose exact nature was not at all clear. Only a few of the hundred or so participants begged to differ.

The president of the Tunisian delegation, the existentialist playwright and short-story teller, Mahmud al-Mas'adi, was one of those independent minds. In no uncertain terms, he urged his colleagues to fear the state. In his mature, confident, and critical address, "The Protection of the Writer and Pan-Arab Nationalism," al-Mas'adi argued that "the freedom of the writer is the most sacred human value that needs to be defended. It does not tolerate any limitation or restraint, as it is essentially either total or non-existent. . . . [The total freedom of the writer] is granted to the writer and the sphere of culture and thought which surround him. We should not try to siege the intellectual with any specific ideology."[37] Fearing the fragile status of the Arab intellectual, al-Mas'adi also warned that placing any political demands on intellectuals might result in a totalitarian-like system in which culture and thought are made by a central committee thus eliminating pluralism and free intellectual exchange. Culture and cultural exchange, he maintained, must be based on the freedom of the individual. "Essentially," al-Mas'adi wrote, "the human being is an individual. This is what he ought to be and this is the secret behind his dignity and human existence."[38] Driving his message toward conclusion, al-Mas'adi reiterated the concept of a sovereign writer, which most members of his generation found reactionary.[39]

Al-Mas'adi's strong public endorsement of radical individual freedom in times of sacred politics pitched against each other two competing notions of freedom. People like al-Mas'adi evoked the defeated liberal position of the udaba' who believed that any communitarian project must be derived from a conception of the individual as an autonomous and free subject. Though obviously noncommitted, it was also a Sartrean articulation of individual freedom of which al-Mas'adi had intimate knowledge from his many years of living and working in Paris. For the champions of Pan-Arabism, however, individual freedom was derivative of consensual collective action, which was embodied by the state.

Responding to al-Mas'adi's notion of the writer's freedom, the Syrian scholar of medieval Islamic pottery Dr. Jawdat al-Rikabi argued that "Arab nationalism creates only free writers who are worthy of their freedom. That is because Pan-Arabism and the individual self [al-dhat] are one and the same."[40] In other words, al-Rikabi's normative position placed the individual in the mold of state-run Pan-Arabism thus arguing for the existence of a unitary self. Overall, though the reaction to al-Masʿadi's minority voice was "vehemently hostile," as one scholar noted, al-Masʿadi stood tall and carried on.[41]

As soon as the congress was over, the embattled al-Masʿadi followed up with an antagonistic (and much cited) article, which took serious issue with the hegemonic articulation of politics and freedom: "The new fact in the East seems to me the hasty and systematic socialization of man. . . . Man, in his behavior, thinking, and even in his customs, is determined by society. Terms such as 'Mujtamaʿ' (society), 'Qawm' (community), 'Jamaʿa' (group) in opposition to the writer—the solitary person—were the obsessive leitmotifs of the conference."[42] The obsessions of the congress aside, al-Masʿadi also derided the public culture of Pan-Arabism and its intellectual superficiality: "What characterizes the aggressive anticolonialism of the 'Arab Qawmiyya' (Pan-Arabism) today is that it tends, more and more, to mix anticolonialism with an un-nuanced anti-Occidentalism. And this is perhaps the point—let's say it in passing—where the difference between the Tunisian position and the positions of the Arab East is most sensitive."[43]

Blasphemous as it was, al-Masʿadi's critique was not an impulsive knee-jerk reaction but a well-thought-through process of intellectual reflection. Given his dual upbringing as a bicultural Franco-Tunisian intellectual, who for two decades studied and then taught in Paris during the heyday of existentialism as a philosophy of freedom, al-Masʿadi developed an integrative vision of culture that was predicated on what he called Islamic humanism. Seeking to integrate the native and the authentic with metropolitan thought, he had almost an identical intellectual orientation to that of the Senegalese poet and politician Léopold Sédar Senghor. They were both influenced by the Parisian intellectual fermentation of the 1930s and then, in the late 1940s, founded major literary venues that sought to address the human condition in the colonies along the lines of Sartre's anticolonial humanism.

Famously, Senghor's Négritude movement was in conversation with Sartre's articulation of collective otherness and saw black humanism as a contribution, if not a correction, to European culture. Rejecting vociferous anticolonial nationalism, Senghor was impressed with al-Masʿadi's major existentialist work *Al-Sadd* (The dam, written in 1939 but published only in 1955), which, among other things, doubted the modernistic hubris of development and "belief in action." In due time, Senghor would preface the French translation of *Al-Sadd*, which he considered "a major model for the New African Literature."[44] Given

Senghor's notion of freedom that does not culminate in state sovereignty, the affinity between these two intellectuals was quite natural.[45]

In addition to the commonalities with Senghor, al-Mas'adi also shared the integrative worldview of 'Abd al-Rahman Badawi and, to a lesser extent, that of Egyptian philosopher Fu'ad Zakariyya. Like them, he also saw the individual as the elementary cultural unit and artistically experimented in blending Sufism with existentialism for the purpose of creating an authentic Arab subject. Committed to addressing the problem of authenticity, just like Badawi, al-Mas'adi believed in the revival of Islamic humanism (what he called the *real* Pan-Arabism) and cautioned "Magicians' apprentices of current politics in the Middle East" from the heavy and historic implications of their defeat, which would burden the Arab nation "with the heaviest responsibilities."[46]

Prophetically written a decade before the 1967 war, these words were shared by a few other, much shyer, attendees at the writers congress. Making a modest appearance, the indispensable Taha Husyan delivered a softened and almost hidden message about the independence of literature—despite literature's simultaneous commitment to Pan-Arabism.[47] It was one of his last public appearances in such a high-profile forum. His former student and loyal disciple Suhir Qalamwi was a bit more subversive. Being one of the few women to participate, she understood the destabilizing power of proper historical contextualization. By presenting an intellectual genealogy of Arab nationalism she paid tribute to this important contemporary phenomenon but, at the same time, cast doubt on its metaphysical claim to be the culmination of Arab history and its platform for collective deliverance. Exactly like al-Mas'adi, she saw Arab nationalism as a multilayered group dynamic that could point to several cultural directions beside state cooptation. Committed to her own sense of humanism, she lamented the way in which the exclusive Pan-Arab focus obscured the tragedy of Palestine.[48]

Another dissenting voice was that of the young and still largely unknown Palestinian scholar of Arab literature Dr. Muhammad Yusuf Najm. Taking issue with the unitary atmosphere of the congress, he used his relative anonymity to say that he "does not believe in the idea of iltizam in its current prevalent form" or in the politicized and artificial division between "committed writers and bourgeois or reactionary writers."[49] As we shall see, he was not the only Palestinian to protest the fact that, under the circumstances of Algeria and Suez, iltizam was reduced to the ethos of military sacrifice as a gateway to freedom.[50]

The Anti-magazine

Al-Mas'adi might have been one of the most experienced and educated intellectuals to cast doubt on the prevailing quality of freedom, but he was not alone. Outside the politicized editorial room and the prison cell—two spaces that housed an increasing number of intellectuals—a circle of Lebanese and Syrian poets published *Shi'r* (Poetry), a new journal and very soon a leading one. In the skilled hands of editors Yusuf al-Khal and Adonis ('Ali Ahmad Said), *Shi'r* followed an unapologetic anti-iltizam agenda centered on the entity of the individual. On the face of it, the two editors made an unlikely couple. At forty years old, al-Khal was already an experienced editor, an established poet, a professor of literature in AUB, a former UN press attaché on assignment in New York and then Libya, and, most controversially, an assistant to Charles Malik.[51] Fresh out of prison, Adonis was a twenty-seven-year-old nobody of humble rural origins with some experience in poetry and political troublemaking.[52] But, once cemented in 1957, their poetic alliance would prove to be both enduring and powerful. Both shared the not-so-popular belief that "society is built on individual life" and that the most essential element for the existence of society is the well-being of the individual. The journal's opening statement featured Archibald MacLeish's statement about the centrality of poetry in exploring the individualistic side of life.[53] As a product of its age, *Shi'r* too took as its subject matter the problems of authentic being, freedom, sovereignty, and self-determination. Yet, it treated them differently, with significant attention to notions such as alienation (*ghurba*), anxiety (*qalaq*), rejection (*rafd*), disintegration (*tamazzuq*), and loss of identity (*daya'*).[54]

As a pioneering platform and an ultimate home for avant-garde poetry, *Shi'r* promoted the prose poem which, in contrast with free verse and its gradual allegiance to mainstream iltizam, was unfamiliar, unestablished, and, most importantly, uncommitted. In fact, the character of the magazine was dictated by the objectives of prose poetry elsewhere, namely, experimentalism, liberal poetics, and universalism.[55] With these in mind, the dominant voice of the Pan-Arab state made little sense to the young poets of what was becoming the *Shi'r* movement. Indeed, in an environment that valorized sacrifice and martyrdom, Adonis's contribution to the first volume featured a traumatized soldier who spoke about the horrors of war.[56] Thus, rather than sink in the committed politics of the region, Adonis and al-Khal shifted their attention to addressing the world and participated in the creation of "a spiritual and intellectual humanist partnership."[57] There was much more to come from the noncommitted camp.

Writing from the Margins

Given the authoritarian nature of the state and the turmoil of decolonization, existentialist themes such as spiritual alienation, anticipation of death, absurdity, angst, estrangement, and revolt proved to be very effective in addressing the concerns of the time. Responding to these circumstances, existentialism became dominant in much of the poetry, prose, and theater of the late 1950s and 1960s. Thus, as mentioned, in 1955 the maverick Tunisian intellectual Mahmud al-Masʿadi published *Al-Sadd*, a work that cast doubt on the hubris of human economic and technological development.[58] Similar themes existed in Egyptian fiction, for instance, in the work of Naguib Mahfouz, Mustafa Mahmud, and, much later, in the work of Sonallah Ibrahim.[59] Heavily influenced by Camus's *The Stranger*, Ibrahim's experimental novel *Tilka al-Raʾiha* (The smell of it, 1966) famously launched into Arab literature the alienated ex-convict protagonist whose aimless life reduced the individual to a set of mechanical daily actions such as eating, getting dressed, smoking, and joyless sex. Crushed by the authoritarian state for his politics, the protagonist exists under the sway of an alienating regime and away from the authentic existence that decolonization promised.

In 1962, the Syrian short-story writer Jurj Salim published his one and only novel, *Fi-l-Manfa* (In exile), which explored the desperate search for meaning and salvation in the life of a protagonists who comes into life reluctantly, exiles himself to a remote village, and, eventually, faces execution. Likewise, the Syrian theater of the absurd dealt with themes of revolt and estrangement and expressed strong longing for the emergence of an authentic Arab subjectivity, in which everything would have its demonstrable place and value. Saʿd Allah Wannus, who was trained in France, was one of the most prolific existentialist playwrights of the 1960s. His 1965 play *Al-Maqha al-Zujaji* (Glass café), vividly depicts the tragedy of human existence with strong references to Arab reality. After the 1967 defeat, he used absurdity as a tool for sociopolitical criticism.[60]

Yet, beyond the general appeal of existentialism, some of the most interesting attempts of thinking critically with existentialism were those of minority groups such as the sharecropper's son who migrated to the city, the feminist who sought to overthrow patriarchy, the abandoned Palestinian refugee skeptical of an allegedly unifying Arab project, and the voices of alienated individuals who struggled to bridge the gap between the state's lofty rhetoric and their meager daily realities. Following are a few examples.

The Defeated

Hani al-Rahib lived the wretched life that characterized large swaths of the Arab countryside. A native of Syria, he grew up in the poor and mountainous coastal area around Latakiya. Being landless, his deaf father tirelessly worked the soil as a sharecropper and, on occasion, as a part-time tailor in the city. Food and security were scarce. It was 1939, and upon learning that she was pregnant with her ninth child Hani's illiterate mother desperately tried to abort him. She failed, and now there was another mouth to feed. In this kind of life, Hani recalled, cultural humiliation came with the territory, as being a poor peasant "meant being of lower worth, the object of ridicule and rejection."[61] It also meant very poor health. During the hard years of World War II, for example, three kids in the family perished, and then, in quick succession, Hani's father and mother departed as well. By virtue of excelling at school, Hani won a government scholarship to Damascus University and was thus saved from life in the gutters.

Living under a state with an inclusive national vision had its upside as well, and Hani, now a student of English literature, could begin imagining for himself something of a future. His moment came in 1960 when *Al-Adab* announced a regional competition for the best Arabic novel of the year. Putting pen to paper, thirty days later Hani had a draft, which, along with more than a hundred and fifty other aspiring writers, he sent to Beirut. Suhayl Idris took an immediate liking to it, and Hani grabbed the first prize. His debut novel, *Al-Mahzumun* (The defeated), was published that year. Hani al-Rahib was twenty-two years old, and he was already a famous writer.[62]

It is unclear how much existentialist literature Hani read, but, whatever its influences, *Al-Mahzumun* was immediately hailed as an existentialist novel par excellence. Written at the very peak of Pan-Arabism's bid for a spiritual refashioning of self and collective alike, the novel portrays an upcoming generation characterized by confusion, anxiety, mistrust, cynicism, an overbearing sense of disorientation, and an obsession with sex. Al-Rahib's somewhat autobiographical novel tells the story of Bashir, a poor student who migrates from the outskirts of

Latakiya to the campus of Damascus University. In a proudly modern era of state triumph over nature, both of his parents helplessly die of rheumatism. Losing faith in God, the protagonist charges: "I cannot recall a single time in which God intervened on my behalf or against it."[63] With God rendered useless, some of his friends believe in Arab unity and the struggle for Palestine and Algeria. Others, like Bashir, think that "Death for the sake of freedom, as in Algeria, is contemptuous" and that the United Arab Republic is an empty promise: "Get lost," shouts Bashir to one of his friends, "you live in the United Arab Republic and we live in prison."[64]

Burning time in cafés and dormitories, they read Camus's *Caligula*, *The Just Assassins*, and Sartre's *The Flies*, but the actual meaning of these plays do not seem to inform the aimless lives of Rahib's protagonists. As one of them readily admits, "I have no goal in life. Unity won't do it for me . . . hence, I continue to believe in nothing."[65] "We youth regard the world to be absurd. . . . We do many things with neither justification nor purpose."[66] Is this a problem? It is, and it isn't: "Our problem is that we do not have any problem."[67] At the same time, they deal with the burden of expectation and the specter of the state: "We must invent something new," they all say.[68]

Even an intimate attempt to form a relationship is articulated in terms of struggle (*kifah*) and sounds like a feverish speech by Nasser: "We are a new generation and we need to build our own morality."[69] Yet, the lofty ideals of Pan-Arabism do not translate to intimate life. Thus, though the protagonists are supposed to be liberated and united Arab citizens free of religious prejudices, the response to a romantic advance of a Muslim student exposes a different reality: "Oh, my God, are you dreaming? Do you think you are in the Latin Quarter? You should know that my father does not allow me to walk even a single step alongside a Muslim boy."[70] So much for the marriage of intimacy and political unity. The protagonists are constantly searching for sexual satisfaction, and in the aftermath of lovemaking the disoriented lover wonders if "it has anything to do with consciousness" and the self.[71]

In everyday life, Pan-Arab ideals and basic human solidarity repeatedly fail. When Bashir's pregnant lover is slowly bleeding to death on her hospital bed, her father refuses a Christian blood donation, and when hospital authorities fail to step in the poor girl dies. Family cohesion, social solidarity, and basic humanism are absent, and the individual is left exposed and vulnerable. All of this brings the protagonist to declare that "the revolution won't succeed . . . it would simply be another new defeat."[72] Writing these words in the midst of what most Arabs regarded as a successful collective era, there was no obvious defeat to speak of. Yet, focusing on existence, wherever the author turned his gaze he saw only defeat. Indeed, in future years, when defeats were as common as they were devastating, Hani al-Rahib would dedicate more novels to this topic, making him the foremost Arab novelist of cultural defeat. Indeed, the author reportedly said that "defeat lies in us, and my novels are an attempt to document this struggle between the elements of defeat and the opposite forces pushing to establish and elevate our humanity."[73]

Being a Woman

Though there was no established school of existential feminism with a visible public agenda, Simone de Beauvoir's call to decolonize womanhood did circulate. It is unclear whether Nazik al-Malaʾika ever read Beauvoir's *Le deuxième sexe*, which was fully translated to Arabic only in 1979.[74] Most likely she was exposed to it during her studies in the United States, as her analysis of the state of Arab society and of woman within it invokes Beauvoir's landmark composition. Al-Malaʾika's analytical starting point was emphatic: "If we were asked to accurately and clearly describe contemporary Arab culture in one word then we would say that it is an anxious [*qalaq*] society."[75] This anxiety results in an inability to synthesize reality into a coherent whole. Instead, Arab reality is one of fragments and splits that pit absolute "good" against an absolute "bad" and in which "thought" and "emotions" are entirely separated from each other. This fragmentation, she argued, extended to gender relation and fostered the belief that "woman have emotions but not ideas" and that, overall, "for a woman to be considered a woman she has to restrict herself to the domain of her home."[76] Lecturing and writing publicly about the unfortunate marginalization of women, al-Malaʾika warned against the serious social, ethical, and moral implications of this state of being.

Though a man, the influential Syrian poet and diplomat Nizar Qabbani saw eye to eye with al-Malaʾika and other feminists. A personal tragedy, the suicide of his beloved sister Wisal due to a so-called forbidden love affair, brought him to identify the plight of the Arab woman, the scarcity of her freedom, as well as her straightforward sexual repression, as a serious obstacle to Arab progress. Taking issue with Arab patriarchy and calling for a new relationship between men and women,

Qabbani wrote poems in a female voice and immersed himself in what he called "the feminine."[77] In "Pregnant" (*Hibla*) a woman reveals to her outraged lover that she is carrying his child:

Don't look so pale now, baby
Maybe I shouldn't have said it
But I really think I may be
Pregnant
You yelled like someone stung by a bee:
"No. NO! We'll rip that kid apart!"
You wanted to kick me out
To kick me hard
You started to swear at me
But there's no scaring me
I know what a cowardly bastard you really are.[78]

In another poem, "The despot," Qabbani attacks the double morality of prostitution:

What slavery! A woman lies under the [man] who bought her
For a few contemptible paper notes . . .
How despicable is the price of a human being,
Claimed to be an end, is made but a means
A woman is held responsible if she sins,
A man is not.
One bed joins them:
The woman is condemned, the man protected![79]

Qabbani's poems of the 1950s registered and gave voice and credence to the grave injustice done to women "by their fathers, brothers, husbands and other legal guardians, as well as by their illicit lovers. He told of the Arab male of his time who used women as a mere tool for pleasure, or as servants or slaves attending to his needs or whims, without the slightest consideration or concern for their feelings or respect for their persons as human beings."[80] He also bothered to portray the ideal image of what Arab women could become once liberated from the shackles of patriarchy. Qabbani was not a so-called Arab existentialist, but, like many others, he could not ignore its centrality and thus saw in existentialism a mode of female liberation. In *Al-wujudiyya* (The existentialist), Qabbani portrays Janine, an existentialist Parisian woman who exercises her freedom to the fullest extent, thus becoming a model for female liberation back in the Arab world.[81] In that, existentialism provided a language as well as an actual daily experience for what the freedom of Arab women could become.

Echoing this exact same voice, in 1958, the Lebanese writer Layla Ba'albaki continued where Qabbani left off and released her debut teen-angst novel *Ana Ahya* (I live!). Like Hani al-Rahib she too was twenty-two. Her novel tells the story of Lena, a nineteen-year-old girl-woman with a thirst for freedom. She does not share the Arab nationalist fever of her times: "Frankly, I do not have the mind to find a solution to the problems of Palestine, Kashmir, or Algeria. . . . What worries me . . . is how to walk for the first time with my high-heeled shoes that raise me seven centimeters above the ground. Will they break as I rush into the street?"[82] This is no simplistic teenage nihilism. The author's radical individualism has broad horizons, and what follows is an attack, an open revolt, against the Arab sociopolitical order, which is equated with a dominating male ethos. She rebukes her greedy and sexist male colleagues. She revolts against the prison-like institution of the Arab family with its authoritarian father figure and its double standards for the sexuality of men and women. She hates her father's authoritarianism and deplores her mother who "knows nothing of life except sharing a man's bed, cooking his food, and raising his children."[83] In revolt she finds her authenticity, her voice, and a hope for freedom. In her other published work as well, she talks only of her own freedom, sexuality, thoughts, needs, and wishes. Known at the time as the "Françoise Sagan of the Arabs,"[84] Ba'albaki was blamed for nihilism, radical individualism, and egoism. Eventually, her tirade against patriarchy and her call for sexual liberation became an all-encompassing Arab affair, when, for the first time in Lebanese history, the state brought charges against an author for "offending public morality."[85]

After lengthy proceedings and interrogations ("Why do you write in this sexually explicit fashion?" her interrogator asked), Ba'albaki was finally acquitted and, backed by her Arab colleagues, Lebanese intellectuals registered a modest triumph against the state.[86] Hegemonic forces in society may not have liked Ba'albaki, but they could not ignore her overall message: decolonization begins with the self, continues with the family unit, the institution of marriage, and domestic life. From there it directly extends toward society as a whole. As many other writers such as the Iraqi Fu'ad Takarli began to grasp, women were at the very center of this transformative process.[87]

Palestinian Destitute

Palestinians were another marginal group that was supposed to benefit from the Arab project of liberation. Yet, nothing of this sort happens in the fiction of Ghassan Kanafani, a Palestinian in exile. In 1963, at age twenty-seven, Kanafani published his much-acclaimed *Rijal fi-l-shams* (*Men in the Sun*), which tells the story of three Palestinian refugees who steal across the border from Iraq to the riches of Kuwait. The three men meet the elder Abu Khaizuran, a veteran political leader in the lost land of Palestine, and now a truck driver. He promises to smuggle them in his empty water-tank trunk and guide them safely to Kuwait. They agree, but the three men never make it to Kuwait. Succumbing to thirst, heat exhaustion, and suffocation they perish in the water tank while their guide passes his time joking with the Kuwaiti border police. Realizing the disaster, the driver closes the novella with the memorable cry: "Why didn't you knock on the sides of the tank? Why didn't you say anything? Why?"[88]

Being an allegory of the Palestinian tragedy of 1948 with the failure of its Palestinian leadership, the death of the omnipotent father figure, the collapse of the family as an existential sanctuary, and the betrayal of Arab allies, Kanafani's novella examined the question of individual control "with respect to the issue of national will, purpose and destiny."[89] As they face death in the desert, the true and authentic condition of the Palestinian people is revealed in a Heideggerian fashion that individualizes their situation in the world (*Dasein*): the Palestinian is alone.[90]

In a later novella, *'A'id ila Haifa* (*Returning to Haifa*), Kanafani's protagonists, Sa'id and Safiya, are Palestinians allowed for the first time since 1948 to briefly visit their hometown of Haifa. They return to confront the past they left so abruptly, a past that is not simply a distant abstract memory ready to be retrieved and claimed but a real person: during their escape from advancing Israeli forces, the couple had lost a newly born baby, Khaldun. Two decades later, Khaldun is a young Israeli man called Dov who had been adopted by the Jewish couple who came to live in Sa'id and Safiya's house. The dramatic encounter with Dov brings his perplexed parents to ponder the meaning of Palestinian existence and its contemporary possibilities. Here is Dov: "I did not know that Mariam and Evrat were not my parents until three or four years ago. Ever since I was a child I've been Jewish. . . . When they told me that I wasn't their son, nothing changed. And when they told me after that that my original parents were Arab, still nothing changed, nothing at all. That much is certain . . . in the end it's man who is the cause."[91]

If man is the cause, as Dov insists, then his Israeli existence surely precedes his Palestinian essence and, by implication, his life as a Jew takes total precedence over the fact that he is, essentially, a Palestinian passionately committed to the cause of Zionism. Facing destiny in this moment of clarity, Saʿid and Safiya's personal existence is suspended as it seems that nothing at all has been left of their life in Haifa, not even their most precious possession, their very own flesh and blood. Astounded by this understanding of their situation, the parents vow to commit Dov's Palestinian brother, Khalid, to the cause of Palestinian resistance, thus ushering in the possibility of a real Palestinian existence that is of the moment and directed toward the future—a future in which the alienated brothers could meet on opposing sides of the battlefield so as to test their respective commitments. The idea that armed resistance yields true existence was a staple of the 1960s and of Kanafani's own revolutionary life in the service of self-liberation through guerilla warfare. In July 1972 Israeli agents killed him in Beirut.

In sum, Arab writers of marginalized groups used existentialist themes in order to confront the ubiquity of patriarchal norms, sexual repression, political impasse, state authoritarianism, violence, and an overall absence of freedom and possibilities for self-liberation. The protagonists in these works are not sovereign, stable, and liberated characters as in the nationalist novel. Instead, they appear to be inconclusive and disoriented. Far from being sovereign and authentic subjects, they lack agency and repeatedly fail to shape the circumstances of their lives. Seeking true freedom and subjected to powerful statist and social forces, their anxious existence is repeatedly subjected to multiple interpretations. In its articulation in fiction, criticism of revolutionary subjectivity and of the Arab project of liberation more generally began and peaked with existentialism years before the 1967 defeat. In their words and deeds, these intellectuals issued a pressing reminder that internal decolonization remained a critical cultural task intimately tied to the issue of freedom and human dignity, without which the entire Arab endeavor of liberation was bound to fail.

Conclusion

Bringing the euphoric year of 1958 to a sad close, in October, the Egyptian *adib* Salama Musa passed away at age seventy-one. This was the man who had introduced Arabs to Freud, proliferated Darwinism, preached socialism, and served time in prison for his various political commitments. His death rekindled the conversation about the lost cultural space from which the udaba' had been evicted, and the possibility of a different kind of humanistic commitment.[92] Two months later, it would become impossible to deny the price of state monopoly over the generation and circulation of political meaning. On New Year's Day of 1959, just as it had with the Muslim Brotherhood, the United Arab Republic rounded up two hundred and eight leaders, activists, functionaries, and intellectuals of the Left. Most would remain in prison for years to come. Committed and aligned with the state as they all were, every now and then intellectuals received a reminder that their attachment came at a price.

As an eloquent Egyptian blogger reminds us, the roster of the accused reads like a who's who of the Egyptian activist intelligentsia, past and present: Fu'ad Mursi, 'Isma'il Sabri 'Abdallah, Muhammad Sa'id Ahmad, Mahmud Amin al-'Alim, 'Abd al-'Azim Anis, 'Adli Barsum, Yusuf Darwish, Sharif Hatata, Sonallah Ibrahim, 'Adil Hussain, Fu'ad Haddad, Rif'at al-Sa'id, Salah Hafiz, Fatma Zaki, Iryan Nasif, Nabil Zaki, Shuhudi 'Atiyya al-Shafi'i, and Lutfi al-Khuli.[93] Lutfi al-Khuli and his wife Liliane had a long-standing relationship with Sartre and Beauvoir and were part of a small circle of Egyptians in Paris, along with 'Adil Muntasir, who became close to the circle of *Les Temps Modernes*. This was how Sartre learned of the regime's crackdown against the Egyptian Left and of al-Khuli's fate. Monitoring freedom worldwide, such news quickly made it to the pages of *Les Temps Modernes*.[94] With the image of Nasserism as a repressive system burned into Sartre's mind, it would take years to persuade him to visit the country and meet its leader. Eventually, he would consent and, as we shall later see, once he and President Nasser finally got together, Sartre would petition him to release the last of the communist prisoners. This intervention came too late to Shuhudi 'Attiyya al-Shafi'i, the first martyr of the Left and a painful reminder of state brutality.

With the crisis slowly brewing, in 1961 the repressive measures of the Egyptian state resulted in the so-called crisis of the intellectuals, in which the creative forces in society were reluctant to contribute to a revolution that was thirsty for original thought. Indeed, "The intellectuals . . . worked in government posts, wrote books that had indeed to be published, even held high office in public agencies. What they refused to give the government was their hearts and, as a result, their ideas."[95] Lutfi al-Khuli, who was among the first to be released from prison and assume an important editorial position with the state, spoke of "a crisis of creativity and depth."[96] Poet and literary critic Luwis ʿAwad reported not having "any great creative capacity in the present period. As far as I am concerned, I feel in a state of receptivity face to face with such men as Sartre and [Bertrand] Russell."[97] The revolutionary state was literary short of ideas.

This state of affairs was anticipated by a few Jordanian, Lebanese, and Iraqi intellectuals who since 1956 had found themselves weary of Nasserism and Baʿthism. Thus, commenting on the unchecked march of Pan-Arab iltizam, a Jordanian critic wrote that "This new expression, iltizam, has thus far failed to create clear and real meaning." It functions mostly as "a mélange of social, political, national and international principle of struggle and revolution . . . [which] excel in violence . . . intellectual chaos and anarchy."[98] Another critic wrote that the champions of iltizam "are ignorant of the deep philosophical foundations of iltizam and imitate it without awareness and [true] knowledge."[99]

Continuing to publish the virtues of individual experience, in Beirut, home to the energetic, student-led Arab Nationalist Movement (harakat al-qawmiyun al-ʿArab), the most supportive Pan-Arab group outside of Egypt, the captains of Shiʿr fully agreed with this critique. Al-Masʿadi, as it turned out, was not completely alone in rejecting the idea that self-determination, human emancipation, and freedom must naturally lead to state sovereignty. Though traces of this minority position could be found all over the region, as the next chapter shows, skepticism toward the state was especially developed in Baghdad. It was there that Arab existentialism illuminated the difference between political emancipation and human emancipation and thus left a poignant commentary on the regional problem of freedom.

FIVE

Unfreedom's Counterculture

Against the backdrop of the successful revolutions of the 1950s, Mahmud Amin al-'Alim declared that "No noble citizen can remain a bystander in front of the current events that unfold in the Arab world" without becoming politically committed.[1] Perhaps that was true, but what kind of politics would these noble and committed citizens follow? Which ideas would inform their commitment to pressing public matters? Would they find Marxism, as he hoped, politically relevant? Or, as he feared, would they avoid this systematic ideology altogether and subscribe instead to something else? Alas, much to his dismay, with state culture setting the tone for what could be written, said, and thought, intellectuals in Beirut and Baghdad creatively engaged with the entire intellectual spectrum of existentialism to establish an oppositional posture or a counterculture that, at the very least, insisted on nonalignment with any collective cause. The existentialist counterculture that began to take form did so in relation to a growing state of estrangement, and, though the culture of alienation climaxed in the 1960s, its origins could easily be traced to an earlier time. For those who became associated with this counterculture the main issue at stake was the problem of unfreedom.

A state of unfreedom could be described as a condition of living passively in a world made by others and with which one, despite of repeated good-faith and meaningful attempts, cannot identify with. Characterized by a deep sense of alienation, it is a condition in which the ideal postcolonial unity between citizen, popular sovereign, and the state fails to realize. With basic sense of citizenship compromised, challenged too is the feeling of solidarity and the will to sacrifice for the sake of any collective endeavor such as a united Arab nation. Thus, operating as a form of dysfunctional social relationship, unfreedom "provides a point of entry into historically particular notions of rational agency, society, and human nature."[2] A sense of freedom is of course relative to one's power to meaningfully shape his or her life but, relativism aside, young people had quite a coherent sense of this collective condition and began reacting to it in creative and unexpected ways. They did so, working at times together and at times independently, by drawing on an existentialist repertoire that assisted them in finding their own place in the system. By the early 1960s one could speak of an existentialist counterculture whose manifestations could be found all over the region but, especially, in Baghdad, the so-called capital of Arab existentialism.

There, beginning in the late 1940s, a vibrant if small artistic scene of writers, poets, painters, students, and teachers began to address the problem of unfreedom in multiple terms, some of which were decidedly existentialist. In this environment, "existentialism competed with Marxism, and the two ways of thinking intersected. . . . Yet, the troubling awareness of freedom, the freedom of the body and of opinion, were associated here with the intellectual desire to achieve romantic isolation from society or the desire to confront society in words and deeds."[3] Feeling estranged, this young and diversified community insisted on "doing its own thing." Yes, in a time of collective regional awakening, revolution, national redemption, social justice, and all the rest were important points of reference, but Baghdad of the 1950s had a young-minded generation which asserted its right to do its own thing. Framed in Parisian terms, they were, so to speak, committed to their own freedom.[4]

The nebulous counterculture of Arab existentialism emerged as a critique of mass behaviors including the nationalist mob mentality, the narrow norms of mainstream society, and the growing power of the state. Casting themselves as social rebels, bohemians, misfits, and politically indifferent individuals whose lives were saturated with alcohol, tobacco, and sex, Baghdadi existentialists were alienated from the established order and exhibited a profound distaste for authoritarianism. Seeing society at large with its values, codes of behavior, and cultural expectations as the alienator, they mirrored this established order by spontaneously forming an amorphous community of alienation.

Especially in comparison with the discipline and passion of Iraqi communists, they were politically disengaged yet artistically active and innovative. Thus, withdrawing to the artistic, they insulated themselves from the prevailing moral climate and created something of a counterculture in which the prime emphasis was on performing existentialism in the service of everyday freedom. Undeniably, for this small and informal community of alienation, to be free meant to be determined neither by national causes nor by social norms but only by the ability think and act for oneself. This was Baghdad's spirit, and echoes of it could be found in the literature and conduct of intellectuals all over the region.

As some novelists later joked, Baghdad's carnivalesque allowed many of these disengaged artists and intellectuals to pretend that they were living in Paris. They could easily imagine themselves packed, along with hundreds of others, in a smoky cinema, listening to Sartre deliver his foundational lecture "Existentialism Is Humanism" (a text translated to Arabic in 1954 but that few Baghdadis had likely read). Sadly, as the political violence of the 1950s and early 1960s repeatedly and dramatically reminded them, they were not living in Paris. However, they owned the point about humanism and unfreedom, which they embraced, desperately, as strongly as they could.

Baghdad's Creative Mess

Iraq in the 1940s was a mess of a place. Inflation, the most critical index for the assessment of everyday economic well-being, was at an astonishing 500 percent. Radically destabilizing the social order, it contributed to a 50 percent decline in purchasing power and a sevenfold rise in the cost of living of living. This economic reality significantly complicated the development of a largely illiterate society in which half of the population was under the age of twenty. Despite growing revenues from oil, Iraq was still an agrarian society in which about 1 percent of landowners controlled 55 percent of all cultivable land, thus leaving landless peasants both economically and politically disenfranchised. Their flight en masse to the city further accentuated class divisions between urban notables, tribal leaders, effendis, peasants, workers, and the urban poor. However, as in the rest of the Arab world, "class" was second to generational experience as a factor that shapes politics.

Of course, all members of the urban postcolonial generation, as well as disenfranchised social groups as a whole, were anti-British. Notwithstanding the ubiquitous issue of indirect British control, the politics of the time revolved around questions such as universal education, labor rights, agrarian reforms, pro-fallah legislation, abolition of monopolies, progressive taxation, distribution of oil revenues and state wealth, and civic-military relations. These issues were on the minds— and animating the pens—of a burgeoning postcolonial generation determined to reform both state and society. As in Egypt, this generation felt outmaneuvered and manipulated in the theater of standard parliamentary politics and, therefore, resorted to radical change through street politics, often along violent lines. By means of strikes, sit-ins, and demonstrations, many of which were masterminded by the Iraqi Communist Party (ICP, the largest grassroots political party in the country and possibly in the Middle East), the political situation became volatile. Against this backdrop, in 1947, the government arrested and publicly executed the entire communist leadership. It was a gruesome act of state violence and a sign of things to come.[5]

Then came the 1948 war in Palestine and the defeat of the Iraqi forces there. For many politically involved Iraqis the establishment of an independent Israel reflected badly not only on the Iraqi army itself but also on the state as a whole and even on national politics as such. It was a fateful moment. Political disillusionment metastasized into mass violence. Known as the *wathba* (leap), a series of clashes with the government articulated the popular reaction to an Anglo-Iraqi treaty (the Portsmouth Treaty) that was perceived as national surrender. In terms of violence, the *wathba* was a serious tipping point that brought the government to indiscriminately kill its own citizens and push the opposition to further sacrifice its rank and file in the interest of sweeping regime change. As martyrs marked a path for others to follow, class affiliation took a second seat to a generational experience that called for struggle and sacrifice. The killing of communist student Ja'far al-Jawahiri, the brother of the famous poet Muhammad Mahdi al-Jawahiri, was a good example. In a memorable public appearance, in which he recited his freshly written poem "Akhi Ja'far" (My brother Ja'far), al-Jawahiri eulogized his slain brother and set the tone for an ongoing revolutionary struggle: "Do you not know that victims' wounds are but a mouth?" the poet asked.[6] The young generation knew that, but the government was yet to learn this lesson.

Iraq's winner-take-all politics further aggravated domestic affairs. Five different governments rose and fell between 1948 and 1952. That period also saw the complete collapse of the Jewish community, which, rather incorrectly, was seen as Zionist. With popular pressures mounting, this ancient minority began to depart for Israel, thus closing a glorious chapter in the history of the Mesopotamia.[7] Amid this tragic departure, violence once again erupted in a round of skirmishes known as the 1952 Intifada. This time it was a cross-country affair with multiple and diverse sites of protest, such as mosques, schools, cafés, and clubs, where the mobilization effort drew on cultural practices such as religious rituals, processions, demonstrations, sit-ins, assemblies, artistic performances, and the constant spread of rumors and gossip. As historian Hanna Batatu put it, the general atmosphere was that of "more and more extremism (and) less and less sense."[8] Especially senseless were the students who initiated and sustained the intifada and the state that reacted by purging from the education system "problematic" teachers, professors, and students, imposing martial law, and placing serious restrictions on freedom of expression and association. State informers or "spies of the Gestapo against the people," in the language of the communists, were now everywhere, and their presence began to be felt.[9] Senseless or not, the political establishment pushed back, and it did so effectively.

By mid-1954, the skillful politician and chief public manipulator Nuri al-Saʿid had succeeded in suppressing the opposition, arresting its leaders, and intimidating his opponents. From that point until the 1958 revolution, Nuri al-Saʿid and his allies blocked any chance of socioeconomic reform, rejected the political designs of Nasser's Pan-Arabism, and aligned Iraq squarely with British and American interests. Al-Saʿid's political success cost the freedom of hundreds of intellectuals, including leading professors, journalists, editors, and writers who were incarcerated in special camps under extremely harsh conditions. To avoid this form of state hospitality, some chose exile, and others succumbed to alienation.[10]

Fadil al-Jamali, a former director of the Ministry of Education, a foreign minister, and a prime minster—the professional pedagogue who held a PhD from Columbia University and delivered a vehement anticommunist speech in Bandung—supported these draconian measures. Seeing the phenomenon of "intellectual sabotage" as one that emerged from the specific generational experience of youth, the Iraqi government faced a similar problem to that of prerevolutionary Egypt. Anxious to control the youth, the government harnessed psychology and pedagogy to its goal. Yet, facing a ruthless Egyptian campaign that publicly sought to topple the Iraqi monarchy, no government program could tame the rebellious energy of the Iraqi youth who sided with Nasser's message. Angered and frustrated, al-Jamali snapped and half-seriously called the government "to provide a sufficient number of psychotherapists for the treatment of [political] critics who look at things through dark glasses."[11] In the midst of all of this political upheaval, the youth drove an unprecedented cultural renaissance, a genuine grassroots surge in artistic and literary creativity. Ironically, much of it was due to continuous government investment in education and, especially, due to the policies of Fadil al-Jamali.[12]

And so, though politically contested, from an educational and cultural standpoint Iraq became a land of opportunity hosting, for instance, scores of Palestinian intellectuals who, after 1948, took teaching positions there. The twenty-eight-year-old Jabra Ibrahim Jabra was one of these newly arrived individuals who, after losing his home in Jerusalem, settled in Baghdad and had much to offer to his new environment. "Palestinian teachers were everywhere," he recalled, and "we were offering whatever talent or knowledge we had, in return for a living, for survival. We were knowledge peddlers pausing at one more stop on our seemingly endless way."[13] A graduate of Cambridge University with an air of British aloofness, perfect English, and a properly matching necktie to complete his appearance, Jabra discovered the cultural fermentation of the late colonial era, and he liked it. Like many others, he felt that "the Arab imagination at the time was at the beginning of a wonderful awakening, possessing the desire to realize what was new and authentic."[14] Putting his skills to work, in no time at all Jabra befriended Iraq's small community of painters, writers, poets, sculptors, public intellectuals, and ideologues. As a teacher, novelist, poet, essayist, short-story writer, painter, art critic, and future translator of Shakespeare, he became an integral part of this milieu as well as one of its most admiring chroniclers. Yet, like other Palestinians, he was a guest, who was constantly reminded to shy away from politics so not to overstay his welcome.[15]

It was not that Palestinians had a direct political stake in Iraqi affairs. But, just like Fayiz Sayigh and Hisham Sharabi, because they had lost their homes and were forced to wander, Palestinian writers developed a unique perspective on the Arab state of being. "We lost Palestine," Jabra wrote, "because we had confronted a ruthless modern force with an outmoded tradition. Everything had to change. And change had to begin at the base, with a change of vision. A new way of looking at things. A new way of saying things. A new way of approaching and portraying man and the world."[16] The Palestinian quest for radical change was yet to make its mark in the Arab world; that would happen in the late 1960s. But, in the meantime, intellectuals like Jabra settled for the little stability that a modest teaching position could offer and the excitement of genuinely contributing to their immediate cultural environment. With its restless spirit of creativity and artistic experimentation in fields such as painting, sculpting, theater, creative writing, and especially poetry, Baghdad of the early 1950s perfectly fitted worldly wanderers like Jabra. All of those who penned, painted, directed, edited, played, or sculptured were in their twenties. It was a very impressive, young, and intimate scene.[17] Some quarters of it were also very political, while others visibly disengaged.

For instance, in 1953, the celebrated painter and sculptor Jawad Salim, cofounder of the Baghdad Modern Art Group, whose manifesto called for discovering the authentic national personality in art and securing historical continuity, won a prize at an international competition in Rome for his statue the *Unknown Political Prisoner*.[18] In it, he made his opinion about the state of freedom in Iraq perfectly clear. Trained by Polish artists who during World War II had been stationed as soldiers with the British army in Iraq, Salim later traveled to the art academies of Paris and Rome at the expense of the state. Upon his return he was a constant voice of artistic opposition to the monarchy. After the 1958 revolution, the new government commissioned him to create the gigantic *Monument to Liberty* (*Nusb al-hurriyya*).[19] Jawad is a fine example of young and politicized artists who used their talents to indirectly promote regime change. Among these, especially active were poets. That poetry could be a political form of speech was not new. Yet, starting in the most causal of ways, certain powerful changes in the structure and function of poetry made it particularly amenable to political usage.

The Prose of Counterculture

In late 1947 two Iraqi poets in their twenties, a man and a woman, independently of one another, published poems in a subversive new form that upset the traditional convention of the classic Islamic *qasida*, or poem. By doing so, Badr Shakir al-Sayyab and Nazik al-Mala'ika ushered into existence the Free Verse Movement.[20] Their poetic innovation is known in Arabic as *al-shi'r al-hurr*, which literally means free poetry. But free from what and for what? One can say that the goal of this new poetic form was to address a certain crisis of representation by which the standard *qasida* was unable to account for the disorienting experience of the postcolonial generation. Indeed, in an era of decolonization, intellectuals sought artistic means that could relate to the politics of the street, the so-called Iraqi people, and the struggles of the nation as a whole. Yet, though there were some exceptions, such as that of "Akhi Ja'far," from a poetic standpoint, the *qasida* could poorly do that. Its formulaic structure prescribed identical and regular line lengths as well as a singular rhyme scheme that could not accommodate, for example, the representation of multiple voices and shifting perspectives.

Free verse poetry, on the other hand, was characterized by irregular line lengths and irregular rhyme schemes, thus breaking down the mimetic convention of the *qasida* and allowing greater artistic flexibility and hence an improved freedom of expression.[21] "This greatly increased flexibility," al-Sayyab's biographer wrote, "made poets and their audiences perceive *al-shi'r al-hurr* as a 'freer' form when compared to the traditional form."[22] A major source of inspiration, in this regard, was the modernist poetry of T. S. Eliot, who rebelled against established poetical conventions in order to detach his generation from Victorian values and reflect critically on the carnage of the Great War.[23] This poetic reservoir spoke of a newly found freedom and of an internal emotional world that became handy also to al-Mala'ika's generation. Fully embraced, this new freedom was used in order to forcefully account for the troubles and hopes of the youth. Nazik al-Mala'ika, for instance, used it to identify with the victims of a cholera epidemic in Egypt. The poem was dotted with lines such as the following:

Even the gravedigger has succumbed,
the muezzin is dead,
and who will eulogize the dead?
. . . Death, death, death
O Egypt, my heart is torn by the ravages of death.[24]

She wrote "cholera" in less than an hour after hearing of the epidemic in a radio broadcast. Though the poem failed to gain the approval of her parents, both of whom were traditional poets and hence strongly disapproved of her new style, she did go ahead and publish it.[25] The poem was an instant success and, month by month, "This poetry spread fast in intellectual circles, whether it was published in the daily newspapers or not."[26] Becoming a regional phenomenon, free verse poetry found distinguished outlets in the progressive magazines of Beirut and Cairo. In Idris's *Al-Adab*, al-Sayyab's correspondence reveals the breadth and depth of these new regional literary networks and how they orchestrated literary circulation that extended all the way from Basra to North Africa.[27]

Carried by the fame of her poetry, fresh out of a year abroad at Princeton University and on her way to another advanced degree at the University of Wisconsin, Nazik al-Mala'ika was the only woman to whom Suhayl Idris gave the space and the role of a man as a board member of *Al-Adab*. She was thirty-three years old. In her new role, which included committed feminist poetry (for instance, against honor killing), she published front-page editorials and comprehensive analytical essays about the state of national Arab culture and the direction that Pan-Arabism should take.[28] Her belief in the politics and culture of Pan-Arab iltizam as the only viable solution to the realities of the Arabs, and especially Iraqis, served as a bridge between committed and disengaged youth.

Once established, both poets took time to reflect on their craft. The Pan-Arab al-Mala'ika wrote that "the truth is that it should be well within our capacity to consider the free verse movement as a purely social phenomenon, by which the Arab nation (*umma*) is seeking to rebuild its mentality (*dhihn*) upon a new foundation, in those deep and capacious recesses where so many treasures lie hidden."[29] In his assessment of the movement al-Sayyab echoed the ravaging struggle against the udaba': "Free verse is more than a variation of the number of similar feet in different verses. It is a new technical structure, a new realist trend that came to crush romantic limpness, the literature of ivory towers, and the rigidity of classicism; it likewise came to crush the oratorical poetry that political and social poets were accustomed to write."[30] Inspired by this new energy, which carried all the way to the post-1958 revolutionary court sessions where poetry was publicly recited, the Iraqi poem became a prime vehicle for political articulation for an era in which poetry truly ruled the streets. It was for that reason that Arab writers, who otherwise followed Sartre closely, emphatically rejected his exclusion of poetry from the list of committed arts.[31] This exclusion was especially unfortunate considering the fact that several poets, who differed from al-Mala'ika and al-Sayyab, saw themselves as counterculture existentialists.

Bohemian Existentialism

The creative energy, the spirit of experimentation, and the optimism about positive political change were not shared by everyone. Many felt alienated and subscribed to a corresponding lifestyle of bohemian or vagabond existentialism. It was an endemic Iraqi phenomenon that was closely associated with café life. Indeed, it is impossible to conceive of the transformation of Iraqi culture—and of the symbolic role of existentialism within it—without taking into consideration the unique role of Baghdad's cafés. As Sami Mahdi correctly observed, "It is not exaggerated to say that Iraqi cultural life was the extension of the cafés' life" and that these "cafés were the only alternative to cultural life which was devoid of institutions."[32]

The typical Baghdadi café was inhabited by circles of literati who had nowhere better to go as homes and apartments were too small, scarce, or simply unaffordable. Cultural institutions such as theaters, libraries, art studios, and, more generally, universities were also in demand. Many of these aspiring intellectuals, like Jabra Ibrahim Jabra, who was fortunate enough to hold a paying job, could afford only a tiny rented room in a downtown hotel. Others, like the impoverished newcomer to the capital, Husayn Mardan, could not even pay for that. So, instead of hosting salons in their cramped and poorly furnished rooms, and with no other public alternative, they inhabited the cafés, which, in turn, accommodated themselves to the idea that intellectuals "live there" by opening their doors at six o'clock in the morning and closing them as late as three-thirty in the morning.[33]

Crowded in a small urban space of less than half a square mile, mostly along al-Rashid street, cafés with names such as al-Baladiyya (city hall), al-Barlaman (the parliament), al-Jamahir (the masses), al-Aʿyan (the notables), Yassin, al-Shah Bandar, Khaydarkhane, al-Rashid, Umm Kulthum, Shatt al-ʿArab, al-Zahawi, and al-Bayruti served as the beating heart of Iraq's cultural and extraparliamentary political life. Each café had its own unique signature. Using record players, some featured only the music of the so-called Great Four, Egyptian singers and musicians Umm Kulthum, ʿAbd al-Halim Hafez, Muhammad ʿAbd al-Wahhab, and Farid al-ʿAtrash (originally a Syrian). Others, like Café Casino, were more versatile and dedicated each day of the week to a different singer.[34] The Swiss Café distinguished itself as a European space that welcomed women, thus being one of the few establishments in town to do so. Classic music, Jabra recalled, was its other big seller: "Off to one side in the café was the electric gramophone with recordings of Bach, Brahms, and Tchaikovsky for those who liked to listen to them. Next to the Swiss café was the famous Brazilian Café, which . . . was run by a highborn Syrian man, who liked to mix with his clientele, knew them by name and offered them the best Turkish coffee in town, which was made of Brazilian coffee beans, after which the coffee shop was named."[35]

Since cafés became cultural laboratories of sorts, some intellectuals decided to cut out the middleman and open their own establishment. Such was the case of poet Buland al-Haydari, whose artistic collective, Group of Lost Time, established Waq al-Waq café, so called after the mythical island of the great epic *The Arabian Nights*. Fearing communism, the police sent informers and eventually closed down this mythical island of the intellectuals "although not one of its owners or patrons was ever arrested."[36] It was such brushes with the secret police that prompted al-Sayyab to write a poem about the informers in the cafés.[37] A prime site for these informers was one of the most influential salons in town, the Hasan ʿAjami café, a famous hangout for leftists of all stripes and a "factory" for fine journalistic writing.[38]

But, beyond culture with a capital *C*, there was something else in the urban habitat of cafés, a phenomenon that was as nebulous as it was prevalent, and that came to be identified as existentialism. Indeed, in less than a decade, and for no apparent reason, Baghdad's existentialism swept the cafés and became a way of life and a vast intellectual category that allowed those who self-identified themselves as existentialists to talk about everything that transpired in Arab life. Baghdad's bohemian existentialism was not about issues such as commitment or the philosophical quest for authenticity. Instead, it was about nothing or, at least, nothing in particular. It was not anchored in the practice of reading, translating, and commenting on Sartre. Not even in writing like him or like Albert Camus. Though there were some "Sartre specialists," such as visiting professor, philosopher Dr. Albert Nasri Nadir, Baghdad's bohemian existentialism was a lifestyle choice wrapped up in endless talk about oneself. And, so, just as in postwar Paris, existentialism became a "word that everybody seemed to understand, a presumed philosophical movement that everybody seemed to know, a vague and nebulous daily behavior that everybody seemed to adopt."[39] In short, a scene.

Somewhat critical of this phenomenon, Jabra recalled:

The early 1950s for the young literati of Baghdad was the golden age of existentialism, whatever their understanding of it was from the translations of the writings of Jean-Paul Sartre and Albert Camus that reached them or from translated articles about them. Few of them could distinguish one from the other, and fewer still realized that Albert Camus was not an existentialist in the . . . sense that Sartre meant. Most of them liked to understand existentialism as a new bohemianism, philosophized this time in the cafés of Saint-Germain in Paris. For some it meant commitment as the Left in those days understood it. There were some who saw in its logic something exactly the opposite, namely, a sort of nihilism that allowed the individual to go beyond all values and all political philosophies. . . . Buland al-Haydari, who considered himself an existentialist in those days, was taken by this idea in his rebellious way.[40]

Other Arab observers were not as kind. Written with Baghdad's cafés in mind, one critic wrote of Sartre's followers in "cafés and bars who are influenced by the mentality of failure and disappointment" and are obsessed with "releasing the energy of the individual in order to pacify the self to the exclusion of any moral value or ideal." Consequently, "existentialism became . . . an intellectual opium for those who lost touch with real life."[41] Foreign inhabitants of the city, such as the British writer Desmond Stewart, were equally dismissive of "the young men who carried tired copies of Sartre and Camus into Hollywood films [but] rarely read more than a few pages."[42]

Visiting Baghdad on business, a former Cambridge classmate of Jabra was completely mystified by "the constant talk about existentialism . . . [and] could not find any explanations for this interest in Baghdad, where people read the French only in translation, yet they found something that dazzled them and nourished their aspirations for the new and the different."[43] Acting on their skepticism, one evening Jabra and his British friend penned "an existential" poem, which they then ascribed to Sartre by way of an Arabic translation from the influential magazine *Encounter*:

The claws of night mangle
The streets' torn-off fragments,
And the windows are bleeding
With eyes made of steel. . . .[44]

They then introduced Buland al-Haydari to "Sartre's" new poem and expected him to marvel at the prose and meaning of this new translation. But al-Haydari knew better. He found the poem's aesthetics similar to that of Jabra's own paintings and exposed the trick. It turned out that, at least for some, existentialism was not merely empty talk and a public pose but a meaningful aesthetic, if not intellectual, tradition. Yet, the image of Baghdad as a city with a silly existentialist scene persists to this day.

In his recent novel, *Papa Sartre*, ʿAli Badr revisits Iraqi existentialism and its veneration of Sartre. He too voices a skeptical comic take on it, which evokes Woody Allen's line, "I took a test in Existentialism. I left all the answers blank . . . I got a 100."[45] Because Iraqi existentialism was mostly an oral and performative tradition that left very little written record, reconstructing this era requires some investigative skill.[46] Indeed, Badr's novel is constructed around a ghostwriter who is hired to write the biography of ʿAbd al-Rahman, Iraq's greatest existentialist, now a forgotten figure. In addition to a careful reconstruction of ʿAbd al-Rahman's life and times, the ghostwriter is expected to clarify the murky circumstances of his death. Was it suicide due to existential angst, or a well-planned murder by the jealous lover of ʿAbd al-Rahman's own wife?

Though initially the ghostwriter met many obstacles, slowly but surely he began making progress. First he set out to reconstruct the image of ʿAbd al-Rahman as the "Sartre of the Arab world," and the person that Sartre sent "to save the nation and put an end to the life of banditry."[47] ʿAbd al-Rahman, we learn, was an "authentic existentialist . . . in soul and mind. His was not an acquired existentialism like that of his contemporaries . . . who had been influenced by Suhayl Idris or the existentialism transmitted by ʿAbd al-Rahman al-Badawi."[48] Studying in Paris, "ʿAbd al-Rahman had personally witnessed existentialism. He had touched it, felt it, and stuck to it like no one else."[49]

Upon his much-anticipated return to Baghdad, with a wife that he claimed was Sartre's cousin, he announced an ambitious mission: "Let's transform Baghdad into another Paris. Let's make it a second Paris, the capital of existentialism."[50] The idea was not simply to create a carbon copy of the French original. Not in the least: "We will establish an Arab existentialism with its own character. We want to promulgate it and distinguish it from Western existentialism as Sartre defined it."[51] People remembered that even Sartre took ʿAbd al-Rahman seriously and recalled how the Iraqi philosopher told them about his time with Sartre: "I was talking to my friend Sartre about some fundamental differences between us and suggested changes to include in his philosophy. He agreed with me on every single letter, in other words he agreed with me all the way."[52] Blessed by the French philosopher, "ʿAbd al-Rahman objected to Suhayl Idris's tendency to combine nationalism and existentialism (i.e., iltizam)."[53] Instead, he wanted pure and authentic Arab existentialism, and so committed was he to this project that he named his very own children Absurdity (ʿabath) and Nothingness (suda).[54]

As the ghostwriter's investigation matured, a different ʿAbd al-Rahman was gradually revealed: Though the young Iraqi philosopher studied at the Sorbonne toward "a doctorate in existential philosophy . . . he failed his studies and returned home without a degree in French existentialism. Instead, like all Iraqis who seek knowledge overseas but return without a degree, he brought back a blonde French wife," who was not at all Sartre's relative but a simple woman of humble origins.[55] Back home, ʿAbd al-Rahman declined Suhayl Idris's invitation to write for *Al-Adab*, explaining that his "philosophical thinking occurred in French and he was unable to translate it into Arabic. The truth was that ʿAbd al-Rahman was unable to write in French or Arabic. His thinking was disorganized, and he was unable to express his feelings in either language." Worse still, writes the mocking novelist, "his education was superficial and not derived from books. It was the same education that characterized most of the intellectuals of his generation; it consisted of hours in the morning spent talking, playing dominos, and smoking a water pipe in the café, going to the movies in the afternoon to stretch lazily on the comfortable chairs, and spending evenings drinking and gambling in bars. They only knew titles of books and what had been written in newspapers reviews. With words they built up kingdoms and knocked down others."[56] This shallowness, the ghostwriter revealed, applied also to ʿAbd al-Rahman's blind followers, who found his philosophy attractive because it "was clearer than Marxism. For example, whenever ʿAbd al-Rahman said 'nihilism' it meant that he wanted to get drunk, and whenever he said 'freedom' he was planning on sleeping with a woman, and 'commitment' meant an appointment at a bar or a nightclub." In short, his philosophy contained "pleasurable things" and these things, such as sex and drinking, might have been the direct cause of ʿAbd al-Rahman's untimely death.[57]

It turned out that his most loyal disciple became convinced that if he could only make love to ʿAbd al-Rahman's wife, "the Cousin of Sartre, the greatest French philosopher, it was as if he had slept with the whole of France."[58] Stereotypically, not much effort was needed to seduce the French lady, but, alas, the cheating couple was caught by the neighborhood's Imam, and a great scandal ensued. Was it this incident that drove ʿAbd al-Rahman to shoot himself? Or maybe the hand of his wife's lover was involved?

With the murder mystery unsolved, in the novel's final act, the ghostwriter was summoned to a meeting with the couple who had commissioned the biography. Though unpaid and robbed of the only two copies of his work, he was asked to forget about Sartre and existentialism and write a new book about a bold Iraqi philosopher named Michel. Present at the meeting, the Iraqi Michel explained, "I found

Sartre useless for Arabic culture, as nihilism and nausea didn't manage to solve our problems, but I read Michel Foucault and discovered that structuralism is the one approach that will work for us. I want to write a book [read: I want you to write the book] that explains this idea. What do you think?"[59]

Thus goes the parody of a vagabond pseudophilosopher and his circle of clownish followers. But regardless of this image, the historical question remains: Was Baghdad's existentialism simply a ridiculous, and perhaps meaningless, episode in Arab, and especially Iraqi, cultural life? Or is there a possibility that what appears to be a superficial scene had a deeper purpose and logic behind it? A historical look at a "real" Iraqi existentialist suggests some answers.

Committed to Himself

Though there was no real-life character resembling 'Ali Badr's protagonist, poet Husayn Mardan comes quite close to being that person. Known as the "number one existentialist in Iraq," whatever that meant, Mardan served as a fine example of what Baghdadi existentialism was all about.[60] He grew up on the banks of the Euphrates in the rural town of Hindiyya, where his father was a junior police officer. As a school dropout, Mardan's job was to carry clay and bricks at construction sites. In 1947, at age twenty, he had enough and escaped both his father and his job. An autodidact, he arrived to the capital with no possessions except, perhaps, his wild imagination, a gift for the written word, and a talent for scandal.[61] "In spite of his extreme poverty in those days," recalled Jabra, "and his vagabond and bankrupt life, he was greatly confident of his talent that no regular education had polished after he left his job in construction and clay."[62] In Baghdad he befriended Buland al-Haydari, the well-off son of a high-ranking Kurdish army officer, a scion to a venerable pedigree of clerics, and a man who could tell true existentialism from false. Though the two were of markedly different social backgrounds, they shared the same lifestyle of "loafing around . . . in the streets of Baghdad" and its many cafés and, more importantly, the same generational experience. And, of course, they also shared the long Baghdadi tradition that married vagabondage and vagrancy with poetry.[63]

After two years of wandering and getting by, in 1949, Mardan published his first poetry collection (diwan), Qasa'id 'Ariya (Naked poems). True to its title, the collection's subject matter was "libidinal desires, the pleasures of the body and the flesh, chaotic and inconsequential rebellion in the space of the brothel, an extreme antiromanticism which celebrates nihilistic and hedonistic pleasure, self-indulgence, anarchism and a rejection of religious orthodoxy," to name a few of its themes.[64] An "obscene" drawing of an amorous nude couple by the upcoming painter and sculptor Jawad Salim adorned its cover. Less than a year after its publication, in June 1950, counterculture and state collided when the government brought Mardan to justice for violating public morality. On the day of the trial, the courtroom was packed with supporters, some of whom, like the elder poet al-Jawahiri, testified on Mardan's behalf. Though his case could have gone either way, the defense attorney made a comparatively compelling argument about artistic freedom in which he cast Mardan as Iraq's Gustave Flaubert, whose freedom of expression, though shocking to the French bourgeoisie, was sacredly protected by his constitutional rights. The judge was impressed, and Mardan walked out of the courtroom a free man.[65]

Mardan's scandalous "obscenity" was just one element in a Baudelaire-like bohemianism that emphasized radical individualism and vehement anticommitment. Carrying on mostly about himself, he dedicated his first *diwan* to the great poet Husayn Mardan:

I did not love anything as I loved myself
The great rebel clothed in fog
The revolutionary poet and free thinker
To . . . Husayn Mardan
I lift these screams that originated
From his roots in ghastly moments
From his dreadful life.[66]

The dedication page of his second collection read: "To the giant wrapped in the fog of time, Husayn Mardan."[67] With this record in mind, it is indeed tempting to see Mardan as a "vagabond poet and a rebellious bohemian in the tradition of Baudelaire" whose poetry became "external to the politically engaged verse employed by other more celebrated, and canonized, modernist poets, in particular Badr Shakir al-Sayyab, Nazik al-Mala'ika, 'Abd al-Wahhab al-Bayyati and Buland al-Haydari."[68] That is true, but Mardan's retreat to the self and his attack on public morality was not merely an adolescent act of provocation.

Instead, it was a mature reaction to "the increasingly repressive bureaucratic state, the regulation and management of public life, the material transformation of its spaces, and the oppressive nature of social institutions (family, religion, the law, sexual morality)."[69] In an era that called for commitment and uniformity, Mardan emerged as a figure who brushed aside everything he was supposed to care deeply about, such as political liberation, progress, development, and the bourgeois objectives of the political urban class as a whole. Terrified of being lost in politics, he opted for an alternative intellectual space that was free of political partisanship and state oversight. Clarifying his position to supportive colleagues and critics alike, in August 1955, during the all-Arab debate about the role of the intellectual, Mardan joined the fray.

In an eloquent newspaper article (The artist between two responsibilities), Mardan acknowledged the value of iltizam's ethics of public responsibility. "However," he asked, "does that mean that I have to abandon and dissociate myself from my responsibility toward my own special existence?" His answer was an emphatic no. Though understanding the demand of Pan-Arab iltizam that the writer "would sacrifice his existence for the sake of collective existence," essentially, he still thought that there is something to be said on behalf of total freedom. Essentially, he saw the issue as a debate in which one group calls for "restricting the freedom of the artist by submitting him to collective social standards," whereas the other group calls for "lifting all the restrictions on the freedom of the artist." Elucidating the two prevalent notions of freedom, Mardan publicly chose to "keep the truth in his heart" and stay committed to himself.[70] This was classic counterculture existentialism.

Thus, in response to the onslaught of Pan-Arab iltizam on the one hand and pervasive Iraqi state authority on the other, Mardan's commitment to himself, that is, to his very own freedom and sense of truth and judgment, does not appear to be silly or meaningless even if he never read or understood anything of what Sartre and others were writing. As a so-called vagabond existentialist poet, Mardan and his ilk had a role to play: "The vagabond poet, as a model, is the exile's counterpart, whose wandering in Baghdad's streets, alleys, and centers, and his intrusions in pubs and cafés make him the unauthorized custodian of place. Overcome by despots and their gangs of every sort, the city needs these wanderers to inscribe its own agonies and ruptures."[71]

Murderous Politics

Like that of others before him, Mardan's heightened sensitivity to the increasingly zealous nature of committed politics and the possibility of violence was prescient. Indeed, in the aftermath of the 1958 revolution, communism and Baʿthism competed for total political hegemony. Both domestically and internationally, these two camps represented opposite approaches to the decolonization of Arab societies. While the early Baʿthists of Syria, like Michel ʿAflaq, sought to transform the Arab self and then unite the Arab world politically, the communists, in turn, paid little attention to the problem of the Arab self, refused unification, and focused instead on Iraq's unique socioeconomic problems. Dividing the cultural scene as well, some intellectuals, like al-Sayyab, famously switched sides, in his case from communism to Baʿthism.[72] Though seemingly of equal strength, the two camps were uneven. Lending their massive popular support to the new regime of General ʿAbd al-Karim Qasim, the communists dominated Iraqi politics and successfully blocked the pro-Egyptian and Pan-Arab camp of the Baʿth. With a total membership of a mere 895 in the entire Iraqi branch of the Baʿth, they were no match for the veteran communists.[73] Yet, what the Baʿthists lacked in numbers and organization they made up for with violence.

Indeed, between 1958 and 1963, the Baʿth's newly established National Guard launched multiple attempts to seize power and assassinate Qasim. Thus, the Iraqi Baʿth, which originally subscribed to ʿAflaq's idea of internal transformation and ontological revolution prior to seeking political office, abandoned that proposal and established a secret military wing whose sole goal was to capture power and eliminate opponents. At long last, after years of unsuccessful conspiracies, in February 1963 the Baʿth and its supporters in the army participated in a successful coup that terminated Qasim's rule (and his life). In the course of eliminating all forms of resistance, the Bath's National Guard systematically murdered close to ten thousand intellectuals, ideologues, and rank-and-file activists. Thousands more were imprisoned in makeshift detention centers erected in former cinemas and sports clubs. Equipped with detailed lists of communist activists allegedly supplied by the CIA, the Baʿth completely destroyed the political and cultural base of Iraqi communism.[74] Thereafter, massacres, torture, and systematic persecution in the name of ideology became so painfully common that the existential belief in "words as life" took on a particularly gruesome meaning. Arab decolonization indeed saw an unprecedented level of internal violence, much of which was now perpetuated on behalf of iltizam.

With the atmosphere of death and intimidation in Baghdad, even a cursory look reveals the depth of the divide separating its intellectual circles as well as the interesting role that existentialism played as an intellectual buffer between communists and Ba'thists. As a proponent of Ba'thi commitment, poet Sami Mahdi scorned the melodramatic and exhibitionist role-playing of existentialists and their meaningless language ornamented with inexplicable coded lines such as "existence does not exist for my sake but for its own."[75] He could not see it as a legitimate reaction to the intolerant politics of iltizam. But others could. In his memoirs, poet Fadil al-'Azzawi, a political prisoner at the time and hence a victim of the Ba'th, argued that ideologues had turned iltizam into a tool that produced bad politics as well as bad art. He branded it "Ba'thi iltizam."[76] On the ground, in the intimate setting of the cafés, Ba'thi iltizam looked something like this:

Secret Agent: Are you Communists, Ba'thists, or Nationalists?
Intellectuals: Write down that we are absurdists ['abathiyyun].
Secret Agent: What is this?
Intellectuals: We are neither Communists nor Ba'thists nor Nationalists.
Secret Agent: So in that case you are immoral.
Intellectuals: Exactly![77]

Since absurdists were not on the list of state enemies they were promptly released. But, of course, most encounters with secret-service agents did not end on a comic note but with prison and torture. As al-'Azzawi recalled, "Upon leaving prison in 1965 my older inhibitions were gone. I wanted to eliminate the holy justifications that were related to revolutions, morality, society, sex, regime, religion, poetry and writing. . . . I wanted to believe in a new revolution that would wash itself of the blood which always adhered to it."[78] This mission statement united some members of the Iraqi 1960s generation and their quest to destroy "the old world and its various institutions such as the state, society, family, gender and even poetry."[79] In a desperate effort to salvage their freedom, intellectuals like al-'Azzawi branded themselves "existentialists" and eclectically fused together the writings of Sartre, Camus, Simone de Beauvoir, Arthur Kostler, Che Guevara, and even Allen Ginsberg and the American beatniks.[80] In doing so, their urgent purpose was to critique political bigotry, militarism, social violence, and sexual repression.[81] In the words of Muhsin Musawi, "Iraqi writers have found themselves since the late 1940s more at home with Camus and Sartre. Resisting disciplinary commitment but opting for individual freedom, these intellectuals perhaps anticipated Adam Schaff in raising questions that were to accumulate at a later stage regarding the incompatibility between free choice and social and party politics and regulation."[82]

Notwithstanding the symbolic efforts of individuals, state repression on behalf of liberation was a growing trend that pushed not only Iraqi but also Egyptian writers such as Luwis ʿAwad and Muhammad Mandur to inquire about the fate of personal freedom, the fundamentals of human dignity, and the politics of iltizam.[83]

Conclusion

Bred in Baghdad but gradually extending westward toward Damascus, Beirut, and Cairo, existentialist counterculture constituted an everyday web of recreational, artistic, and literary practices, structures of meaning, forms of consciousness, networks of people, and modes of organization that pointed away from the culture of iltizam. Defined as a stance against unfreedom and an opposition to collective nationalism, state authority, and political rivalry, the existentialist hero took Baghdad as his domain and built a counterculture around it. At least ideally, those heroes lived in a state of total freedom from the constraints of social traditions and institutions, thus committing themselves unreservedly to the demands of inner, authentic being. By virtue of this position, existentialism was effective in exposing political bigotry, militarism, social violence, and sexual repression. Herein lies its value as the self-actualization of one's circumstances and the consequent refusal to conflate and erase the differences between individual and political freedoms.

However small, fragile, fragmented, and solipsist the existentialist counterculture appeared, by repeatedly questioning the flow of authority in society, it did offer a sustained political challenge that mainstream culture could not ignore. Indeed, forming something of a spectrum, the counterculture of existentialism ranged from the eccentric carnivalesque behavior of the café and the public scandal of vagabond poetry on the one hand, to more established and even mainstream forms of literary engagement on the other. All of these activities were anchored in alternative forms of self-realization that, within the context of decolonization, sought to reorganize the principal makeup of personal and collective consciousness. Remarkably, on the eve of the 1958 revolution, the Iraqi monarchy was quite detached from this grassroots intellectual commotion.[84]

Apathy aside, the push of existentialist counterculture against the pull of revolutionary commitment (iltizam) left its mark not only on devoted Marxists but also on committed revolutionaries. Outside Iraq, one of the young intellectuals who struggled with this existentialist tension was Syrian philosopher Muta' Safadi. Safadi was a Ba'thi revolutionary who wholeheartedly believed in the transformation of individuals into revolutionary heroes. These newborn heroes, he now observed, were conditioned by a "morality which is based in anxiety."[85] Why anxiety? Because the revolutionary self is torn between a commitment to a collective project and, simultaneously, a commitment to oneself. No Western philosophy, not even Heidegger, he argued, prepared his generation to deal with this tension. Safadi's solution was the creation of a new revolutionary hero who, while remaining an individual, "carries within himself a being which incites others to establish their own true individuality by recognizing the one precondition for the projected Arab selfhood, namely to be an Arab revolutionary."[86]

Furthermore, Safadi hoped that the new revolutionary hero would move from a position of "being an individual in revolt against something specific to a more generalized position of rebellion."[87] Thereafter, the Arab hero would emerge as a universal subject who opposed reactionary traditions, political fragmentation, imperialism, and feudalism wherever they appeared. "Only heroes," he concluded, "can assume the responsibility of victory, with its immense sadness and equally immense joy."[88] Put differently, Safadi asked that at the break of a new decade, that of the 1960s, the Arab revolutionary position should depart from its narrow adherence to Ba'thism and define itself with relation to a global project of liberation. In this new world, while the revolutionary concerns were local their cosmology was universal. Safadi was not the only one who began to develop a more universal vision. Already in 1954 al-Sayyab had raised the issue with Suhayl Idris: "Does the Arab intellectual [adib] need to become a global intellectual ['alamiyan] before he is a nationalist one, or should he begin with the nation and extend from it to humanity at large?"[89] Questions of priority aside, as the 1960s started in earnest, there was no question that the proper direction of Arab thought and action was to go global.

SIX

A Beachhead in the Sixties

From an Arab perspective, the global culture of the 1960s had many beginnings and multiple ideological godfathers. Communism, though constantly under attack, was still intellectually influential. Various forms of socialism and Marxism circulated widely as well. Liberalism and experimental avant-gardism, as in the case of magazines such as *Hiwar* (Dialogue) and *Shi'r*, held a very respectable place too. Though a neat intellectual genealogy could be constructed for each of these traditions, in everyday life they formed something of an ideological mélange that, regardless of the specificity of its individual parts, collectively pushed culture and politics leftward.[1] If there was ever a moment when the Arab Left was widely influential and had a real chance in politics, this was it. Practiced in several dominant states, including Iraq, Syria, and Egypt, as well as by much of the intelligentsia elsewhere, such as among Palestinians, the shift to the left was a decisive one. Yet, this general swing toward leftism did not automatically spell a position that aligned with the political goals of the Left in Europe and in much of the Third World. For this meeting of the minds, and perhaps even the guns, to happen, specific intellectual work was needed, and here too one can find multiple influences and pathways. Focusing on one, this chapter explores how Sartre's thought became instrumental to the process by which Arab publics became part of the global culture of the 1960s and how they used this new position as a passage toward universalism.

Undoubtedly, for the political elites of the region, establishing an intellectual beachhead in the 1960s was a crucial project. Yet, especially with regard to Sartre's contribution, this process was far from straightforward and ended up being quite circuitous. For instance, in October 1956, exactly a month after its publication in France, Sartre's "Colonialism Is a System" appeared in Arabic, translated by Suhayl Idris. He must have had some expectation that the text would usher in a new understanding of colonialism, one that perhaps would apply to his part of the Arab world as well. Alas, it did not happen. As we have already seen, the main focus in those days was on the question of freedom, commitment, and revolutionary rebirth. Other texts were placed on hold as well; for instance, texts that invoked Sartre's anticolonial humanism, a broad late 1940s to early 1950s critical engagement that, in coming years, would form the notional subfloor of the 1960s global culture of resistance. While, in and of itself, the nonlinear nature of Sartre's reception in the Arab world was not necessarily a problem, it did leave some gaps.

Here are a few of the lacunae that demand revisiting and further elaboration. First, the cumulative work of anticolonial humanism which began with Sartre but included writers such as Frantz Fanon, Aimé Césaire, and Léopold Sédar Senghor, needed to be recognized. The crux of this work was to expose the process by which epistemic racism dehumanized groups and pushed them into a hopeless zone of nonbeing where they were routinely suppressed, tortured, and violated. Second, to politically move forward as a united group, this body of thought needed to be reconciled with Marxism, as fears of an essential incompatibility between the two systems arose. Third, drawing on Sartre's politics, revolutionary theoreticians like the Syrian Muta' Safadi envisioned a new ethical subject of the Left whose horizons of action were global. This new subject was not a peaceful law-abiding bourgeois citizen but a revolutionary whose scope of analysis and action far surpassed the geographical limits of the Arab nation-state. As we shall continue to see in the following chapter, these three elements created an intellectual web that, in conjunction with concrete political engagements, allowed the inhabitants of the region to see themselves in a new light, not simply as Arab subjects but as universal citizens committed to a global struggle against injustice.

Repairing Missing Links

Occupied with internal concerns, Arab observers overlooked Sartre's early political stand against the French war in Indochina and even his early support for Zionist resistance against the British. All things considered, this oversight was small change. The more significant issue was the meaning of Sartre's anticolonial humanism, which was not so much about activism as about pure thought. This phase consisted of texts such as *Anti-Semite and Jew* (1946) and "Black Orpheus" (1948), which introduced key postcolonial notions such as otherness, authenticity, and alienation. (Another critical text, *Notebooks for an Ethics*, was written in 1947 and 1948 but only published posthumously and hence not available.) In the context of decolonization, these notions became critical to "spelling out the relationship between existential freedom and political freedom."[2]

"Black Orpheus," for example, "represents a clear shift in Sartre's politics in this period: in it, he synthesized ideas on freedom, collective otherness, and the concrete situation that had been brewing since *Being and Nothingness*."[3] This text was a result of his close collaboration with the Négritude movement of Aimé Césaire and Léopold Sédar Senghor as well as with the black American writer Richard Wright, who introduced Sartre to American racism and slavery. By virtue of this collaboration, the notion of otherness developed from being a problem that nests in outcast individuals (as Sartre theorized in *Anti-Semite and Jew*) to a problem that infects entire communities and is hence collective in nature, as in slavery. Mediated thorough his collaboration with Senghor, Sartre "tied the writers involved in the Négritude movement to his theory of intellectual engagement, first announced in *What Is Literature?* and began to address one of the key political questions of his day: Decolonization."[4]

Thus, whether the historical subject was the black slave, the colonized, the Jewish victim of anti-Semitism, or even Beauvoir's second sex, Sartre explored these subjects in equally sympathetic terms of collective otherness, alienation, and the denied freedom of the self. Influential writers like Fanon, Césaire, and Albert Memmi would then apply these insights to the state of the colonized subject and the project of decolonization, thus further theorizing as well as politicizing these conditions.[5] Indeed, following in quick succession, these writers published key anticolonial texts such as Fanon's *Black Skin, White Masks* (1952) and Césaire's *Discourse on Colonialism* (1955). These foundational ideas about the link between race, otherness, humanism, and decolonization had not yet been introduced to Arab audiences in any systematic fashion. Without their assimilation there would be no sixties, so to speak.

Cognizant of the fact that in Europe a new corpus of critical thought on colonialism and decolonization was in the making and that his audience had yet to catch up with it, Suhayl Idris put his faith in reading francophone thought against empire. It was a serious cultural commitment, and when, in the context of the Algerian struggle, some Iraqi intellectuals called to boycott French culture, francophone intellectuals in Beirut did the opposite. In June 1956, a month after its original date of publication in France, Suhayl Idris translated and prefaced Sartre's programmatic essay "Colonialism Is a System." Rather than boycotting French culture, Idris wrote, "We warmly greet Sartre and other free French intellectuals who are not deterred by French political pressure and terror. Our mind and hearts are nourished by their work, which assist us in continuing the struggle for freedom."[6]

This warm welcome aside, in the context of the Pan-Arab triumph in Suez that followed, Sartre's translated text was such an anomaly that it completely failed to affect the Arab conversation about colonialism. Foundational as the text was, for the time being, the struggle for Algeria was processed through the limited prism of sacrifice and martyrdom and not through key concepts such as race, alienation, alterity, and otherness. Occasionally, passing lecturers visiting from abroad alerted their audience to this intellectual gap. Such was the case, for example, when the famous French literary critic Picon Gaëtan pointed out Sartre's pivotal position with regard to decolonization. In April 1954, seven months before the Algerian war and a whole year before the Bandung Conference, Gaëtan visited Damascus and lectured on Sartre's political position vis-à-vis imperialism, Stalinism, and colonialism. Beyond explaining how Sartre took Bergson's place in philosophy and Gide's in literature, topics about which his audience already had heard enough, Gaëtan spoke of a set of ideas that presented Sartre as an emerging thinker of decolonization.[7] Yet, with the narrow intellectual focus on iltizam, the complexity of French colonialism and its impact on the colonized was lost.

In sharp contrast, the Arab world of the 1960s was ready to engage with these formulations, and their utility in conceptualizing Arabs' experience as the "others" of colonialism, imperialism, and even Zionism gained new appreciation. This was a natural move, but it should have raised some critical questions, such as what were the implications of the fact that the ontological foundations of the postcolonial other originated with the Holocaust and were therefore forever embedded in the specific trauma of the Jewish subject and its dialectical relationship with Europeans? Was otherness universal, or was it a particularly Jewish or even a Zionist condition? Do these historical links have any ethical meaning when applied to the Middle East? Partially aware of these challenges, in 1960, Suhayl Idris reintroduced Sartre's most important texts on Algeria, in which the insights of anticolonial humanism were put to work. Not for the first time Suhayl's wife, ʿAida, cotranslated them. They titled their collection *ʿAruna fi-l-Jazaʾir* (Our dishonor in Algeria). The "our" in the title related to the French.

Opening the new collection was Sartre's "Colonialism Is a System," which, given a second chance, was now likely to considerably substantiate the Arab understanding of colonialism through a case study they deeply cared about: Algeria. "I would like to show you," Sartre wrote, "the rigour of the colonial system, its internal necessity, how it was bound to lead us exactly where we are now, and how the purest of intentions, if conceived within this infernal circle, is corrupted at once. For it is not true that there are some good colons and others who are wicked. There are colons and that is it."[8] From there he embarked on "a thorough analysis of the mechanics of colonial economics that shows him fully immersed in the perspective developed by Marx, who argued that colonialism presented capitalism in naked form, stripped of the decorous clothing of European bourgeois society."[9] His historical narrative touched on the formation process of the colonial system and the interconnectedness of its effects with regard to land, labor, wealth accumulation and distribution, education, hygiene, urbanization, and political being.

Sartre's essay was very detailed, as "when we talk of the 'colonial system,' we must be clear about what we mean. It is not an abstract mechanism. The system exists, it functions; the infernal cycle of colonialism is a reality."[10] And here, after historicizing French Algeria, Sartre moved to reintroduce with greater clarity and political purpose some aspects of his "anti-colonial humanism." Claiming that colonialism is by definition a system of racial difference, he wrote that "one of the functions of racism is to compensate the latent universalism of bourgeois liberalism: since all human beings have the same rights, the Algerian (who does not enjoy the same universal rights) will be made a subhuman."[11]

What was the subhuman? Technically it was "those against whom people who dominate in a system of oppression make determinations concerning their own property and rights."[12] More to the core of the issue, the subhuman was the category that captured the complete erasure of indigenous subjectivity and any trace of its humanity; in short, an exceptional zone of nonbeing. Why was it important? As Sartre's anticolonial interventions in the 1950s made clear, this line of thought and "its vexed properties of agency and responsibility were indispensable if one wished to understand the dynamic world of colonial relations and the process of decolonization."[13] Thus, by elucidating the historical and ontological condition of the subhuman, Sartre—like no other intellectual—acknowledged and hence validated Third World subjectivity as well as that of victims of systemic racism and anti-Semitism. But this elucidation also did something else. It laid the foundations for the possibility of global ethics as a universal system in which the colonized claimed the higher moral ground, from which entire people could demand political change in universally recognized political terms. This was a major step toward their emancipation and metamorphosis into citizens.

Realizing its importance but unsure how to translate the concept of the subhuman to Arabic, ʿAida and Suhayl Idris used *"rajul asfal"* and *"rajul duni,"* which connote inferiority, wretchedness, poverty, low social status, as well as the sense of being dammed, as in Fanon's not-yet-translated text *Les damnés de la terre,* or *The Wretched of the Earth.* The emphasis in this translation was not on materiality but on the long-standing problem of human dignity (*karama*).[14] Writing five years earlier, Fayiz Sayigh also saw the problem of human dignity as central: "We believe in the Arab human not as a mere number in a greater statistic, not as a stone in a building, not as a king amongst his herd and not as a tool in the hands of the state. Instead, we believe that the human is the ultimate value in history and its very culmination."[15] In linking dignity, humanism, and decolonization Sayigh pushed the discussion forward, yet he, too, did not yet grasp the entire meaning and potential of the "other" (*al-akhar*) in the Arab context. (From a theoretical standpoint, this would begin to happen only with the Arab reception of Edward Said's *Orientalism*).

Such difficulties in fine theoretical adaptation aside, things got conceptually clearer when Sartre spoke of the right to resist colonialism: "This is the argument to which the leaders of the FLN have replied: even if we were happy under French bayonets we would fight. They are right. And indeed one must go further than them: under French bayonets they can only be unhappy."[16] And, in another place, "their liberation, and also that of France, can only be achieved through the shattering of colonization."[17] Sartre's final argument touched upon, but did not yet fully expose, the dialectic between colonized and colonizer and called for a committed fight against colonialism: "It is our shame; it mocks our laws or caricatures them. It infects us with its racism . . . it obliges our young men to fight despite themselves and die for the Nazi principles that we fought against ten years ago; it attempts to defend itself by arousing fascism even here in France. Our role is to help it to die. Not only in Algeria but wherever it exists."[18]

Building on Sartre's global engagement, other articles in *'Aruna fi-l-Jaza'ir* dealt with the testimonies of French soldiers in Algeria and, especially, the barbarity of French torture. Though here, too, some of the material had already been published in Arabic, it resonated differently now against the background of the 1960s. Commenting on the effort of French intellectuals to resist their government by making their experience of the war public, as in the testimonial French project of *Des rappelés témoignent* (1957), Suhayl Idris portrayed a close unity of mind and action between the French Left and the Arabs.[19] For their part, Arabs took full notice of Sartre's sacrifices on behalf of Algerians. Beginning with his public call for soldiers to disobey deployment to Algeria, through his participation in the September 1960 Manifesto of the 121, which forcefully condemned the war, continuing with his many statements on the war that exposed him to accusations of treason and, eventually, an attempt on his life. Undeterred, on behalf of himself and the entire noncommunist French Left, he continued to support the Algerian fight for freedom.[20]

Though many Arab intellectuals read Sartre in French, by the early 1960s, available material in Arabic showed the many ways in which Sartre "recognized outright the legitimate subjectivity of colonized peoples—not as a potential, but as a fact. His arguments in support of their right to self-determination were analogous to existentialist arguments concerning individual freedom."[21] With freedom in mind, at play too was the connection between dehumanization and torture. Illustrating how otherness, alienation, and race coalesce to make the subhuman, Sartre went on to show that, once stripped of its very humanity, the Algerian is subjected to the most inhumane forms of torture.

By far, the most famous case of the inhumanity of the Arabs, and hence of the free license to torture them, was that of the Algerian nationalist Djamila Boupacha. Her arrest and unbelievably horrific sexual torture and rape became a French national scandal when Simone de Beauvoir and legal activist Gisèle Halimi made her case public. Their 1962 book *Djamila Boupacha* offered a close reconstruction of her ordeal and, in addition to being an amazing example of scholarly and legal activism, it was, above all, an emotional act of recognition and human solidarity.[22] An Arabic version of the text was published immediately.

The fact that Sartre, Beauvoir, and the French Left committed themselves fully and publicly to an Arab struggle with universal implications made a huge and long-lasting impact on Arab readers.[23] It also encouraged the Arab Left, and with it the public, to move toward a more universal position in which the fight in Algeria constituted an important battle in the long war for Third World liberation. Thereafter, as for Aimé Césaire four years earlier, it would become quite clear that the global struggle against colonialism and racism were intertwined and could not be reduced to the dogmatism of class struggle or isolated cases of national liberation and "transfer of power."[24] A passage toward the universal was therefore called for and the 1962 Algerian triumph readily suggested itself as a bridge.

Is Existentialism Marxism?

In 1964 when Sartre was offered the Nobel Prize in Literature and quickly declined it, his project of global ethics was already well under way and "his perspective" had been liberally applied to multiple international struggles. But wherever his interventionist politics traveled, be it in his own neighborhood of Western Europe, behind the iron curtain of Eastern Europe, in socialist Cuba or, across the Mediterranean in the revolutionary Arab world, it had to reckon with what was already a well-entrenched system of thought among likeminded natural allies: Marxism. Even after substantial efforts to elucidate and resolve it, the nudging question that did not go away was to which degree existentialism and Marxism were compatible. It was a hotly debatable political question that at one point even CIA analysts of Eastern Europe were asked to address.[25]

The Middle East was no exception, and the dedicated efforts of Mahmud Amin al-ʿAlim to discredit existentialism and exhibit its profound incompatibility with Marxism are telling. Frustrated with the spread of an undefinable and nebulous form of Arab existentialism, al-ʿAlim called this trend "an intellectual weapon in the hands of reaction [rajʿiyya]" and maintained that marching under the irrational "banner of existentialism" and taking it as a "philosophical denomination" would result in total cultural collapse.[26] He explained,

When human actions and choices lose their social core and context, everything becomes excused and justified . . . and everything appears to be on the same plain as anything else . . . betrayal, crime, nationalism, justice, oppression, deviation, virtue, progress, backwardness, colonialism, liberation, monopoly, socialism . . . all of these emerge out of free action and choice. Sartre and his followers do not deny that their philosophy of freedom is irrational. . . . For us their philosophy is against reason, science and . . . the objective view of human beings.[27]

The Marxist Egyptian philosopher traced this problem to its core and argued that Sartre's "commitment has no defined content . . . it is not a commitment to a thing but to nothing . . . not a commitment to a value but to no value."[28] Commitment and freedom are of course very important but, as al-ʿAlim pointed out, "Social realties in our country are the reason for which these two concepts are so popular and for which the philosophy of existentialism became an important trend in the Arab world. . . . Yet, that does not mean that the social and political realities of the region can find their expression in existentialism."[29] In due time al-ʿAlim and Sartre would have a public exchange wherein Sartre would respond to his arguments. After all, Sartre was no stranger to this kind of critique. Nor were his followers in the region who took on the trouble to reconcile Marxism and existentialism.

Historically speaking, the effort to demolish the influence of existentialism and prove its incompatibility with Marxism was led by communists and Marxist theoreticians. Georg Lukács and George Novack, to give two examples, wrote systematic essays against an existentialism that they dismissively considered an egoistic philosophy of bourgeois intellectuals. They leveled the following criticisms: First, they rejected existentialism's individualism and considered it an ineffective method of sociopolitical action. Second, they contended that existentialism revolved around individual consciousness to the exclusion of any objective real-world parameter. Abandoning society, all that existentialism seemed to care about was authentic self-discovery and self-creation. Third, they argued that while for Marxists the world was lawful, ordained, and bound by clear cause-and-effect material processes that could be subjected to scientific analysis, for existentialists it was irrational, whimsical, and unpredictable. As a result, existentialists could elaborate no constructive plan for progressive social change. Fourth, as opposed to Marxists, existentialists experienced ambiguity as a predominant feature of life. Believing that everything was determined by ambiguity and chance, they disregarded any unambiguous perspective as deterministic and hence reductive of human experience. Fifth, because existentialists championed individual spontaneity and radically safeguarded individual freedom, they identified the masses, class action, and the state as threats to their sense of being. In consequence, they left no conceptual room for social relationships. Seventh, with these latter qualities in mind, Lukács and Novack deplored existentialists for nonconformism, which, they maintained, undermined any form of collective action.[30]

In response to this kind of criticism, and out of a will to liberate his philosophy and align it with Marxism, in 1960 Sartre published the tome *The Critique of Dialectical Reason*. This ambitious work was designed to theorize the kind of interventions that Sartre was already famous for in the Third World, such as his stance toward the ongoing war in Algeria. Indeed, it was the war in Algeria that truly separated him from communists and some other Marxists. Informed by colonized people in a state of revolution, *The Critique* paid close attention to group formation and action, thus moving away from the political unit of the individual to that of collectivities. Much of the book dealt with the experience of alienation and otherness as a collective condition that existentialism helped to reveal and account for. Much of it was based on his notion of the subhuman. However, though this new work was supposed to humanize Marxism and make it compatible with existentialism, few were convinced. For one thing, the book was not completed (a second volume was published posthumously only in 1985). But, more seriously, it was immediately criticized as being too long, too boring, too verbose, extremely technical, and quite idiosyncratic.[31] A far cry from the glorious reception of *Being and Nothingness*, in Europe it was mostly ridiculed or ignored. Yet, for people like Frantz Fanon, *The Critique* meant something completely different.

Here is what we know about Fanon and *The Critique*. Upon its publication in April 1960, Fanon got hold of the book and "read it with passion and enthusiasm." While in Tunisia, en route to cancer treatments in Moscow, he told Claude Lanzmann how impressed he was by the book. Curiously, he revealed to Lanzmann that *The Critique* already had arrived at the front lines in Algeria where the rank-and-file peasants-warriors-philosophers of the FLN, these "new men . . . in the inside" of the battle for liberation, had already begun reading and, as he insinuated, "applying it," so to speak.[32] That, as it later turned out, was utter nonsense, but it does speak volumes of the fact that "collective others" saw *The Critique* as instrumental to anticolonial liberation. Albeit on a small scale, similar enthusiasm was registered in other quarters of the Arab world.

In Cairo, the young philosopher Fu'ad Zakariyya, another up-and-coming icon of Arab thought, began working on the translation. Even though Suhayl Idris's kept promising readers that *The Critique* would soon be out and even placed newspaper ads to that effect, four years later, Zakariyya's two-volume translation was still in the making. As far as we know, though Zakariyya published some relevant articles, he never published the full translation.[33] But that probably mattered little, as those who could make sense of this inaccessible work had already read it in French. Even without the Arabic translation, the original colonial context of *The Critique* and its treatment of collective alterity were sufficient to convince Arab intellectuals that Sartre had reconciled existentialism and Marxism. In fact, like Fanon, Arab intellectuals could have justifiably felt that, even if they did not read it in Arabic, *The Critique* was addressed to them or, at the very least, was a very earnest attempt to theoretically include them in what was otherwise a European conversation from which they were customarily excluded. Granted, behind this ready belief in Sartre's alleged synthesis lay a deep local need.

As we have already seen in previous chapters, some of the Marxist European arguments against existentialism also resonated in the Middle East. Yet, what al-ʿAlim loathed in existentialism and what Lukács condemned as a "fetish of (abstract) freedom" younger intellectuals like the Syrians Jurj Tarabishi and Mutaʿ Safadi found extremely meaningful. Safadi, who was ten years older than Tarabishi, did appear to read *The Critique*. Rather than finding Sartre lost in individualistic passivity, as European communists charged, Tarabishi saw Sartre's global activism as Marxism with an added value. The value he had in mind Tarabishi called the total witnessing of existence in the world, or *al-shahada al-kamila*.[34] Bearing witness to the multiple struggles in Asia, Africa, and elsewhere, Sartre opened an important ethical possibility for mutual recognition and, ultimately, global justice.

For decolonized people, this effort was truly rehabilitating. But for European communists and many others on the continent, bearing witness to the violence of decolonization and the Cold War and thereby humanizing the inhabitants of the Third World carried little meaning. In hindsight, we can say that Sartre's witnessing would, in due course, become an important part of the human rights revolution during the 1970s, and, eventually, would open the door for transitional justice in places that witnessed major violations of human rights, such as South Africa.[35] Safadi, of course, could not foresee these developments but he did value Sartre's witnessing and interventionism, and he suggested that, from a Third World perspective, Sartre's ethical standpoint constituted a one-man political party that was more interventionist, and more effective, than all the communist parties combined.[36]

Jurj Tarabishi leveled a more systematic argument about how existentialism and Marxism complemented each other in Sartre's oeuvre.

In 1964, at the young age of twenty-five, Tarabishi, the high-school kid who years earlier had messed up the translation of Sartre's *What Is Literature?* sought to address the apparent discrepancy between Marxism and existentialism in a fashion that was organic to their Arab reception. Accounting for a substantial body of European thought, including Lukács's criticism, which he translated and published as a separate book, Tarabishi's impressive intellectual grasp foretold the immense influence that he was destined to have as one of the most prolific and powerful thinkers of the second half of the twentieth century. Once again, it also illustrated the significant role that young and unestablished thinkers had in the making of the global 1960s.

Tarabishi's effort emerged deep from within the Arab experience of both Marxism and existentialism and was designed to prepare the ground for a Third World socialist revolution that was itself informed by these two traditions. He began with a somewhat self-deprecating note on his generation's futile habit of pitting zealous socialist slogans against the hard realities of the postcolonial era. Curiously, he and his friends had absolutely no idea how they had become socialists. Did they read socialist theory? No, not really. Besides a few journalistic articles here and there, they did not intellectually engage with the foundations of their political faith. "We were rebels not revolutionaries," he assessed in hindsight.[37] Equipped with rampant temperament and not much else, they had only two political choices: communism or Ba'thism.

Most of them ended up joining the Ba'th Party but, still, could not tell the difference between "their socialism" and that of the communists. Under pressure to explain their position, they came up with an intellectual alibi that, as opposed to communism, their socialism was spiritual as well as materialist. They also said a few things against class struggle and the dire need for an inclusive view of the people. There was very little understanding of what this kind of class struggle actually meant in real political life and indeed, writes Tarabishi, "We felt that we were not standing on firm ground. That we actually do not have a theory."[38]

The obvious solution for this embarrassing state of affairs was to read extensively, as only such reading would allow them to own a theory and tell socialism from communism. They read whatever they could lay their hands on, mostly about Marx and Marxism. Though they believed that economic factors were paramount in human history, they took issue with Marxism for not addressing matters of culture, spirit, and existence.[39] Gradually, though, by way of this reading exercise, they moved from blind subscription to black-boxed "official ideologies" to discovering Sartre. That was a revelation: "Every revolutionary is in need of a theory . . . and the only possible revolutionary theory today is Marxism. But this does not at all mean that we need to understand Marxism as orthodox Marxists want. The contemporary Arab revolutionary needs to discover the living Marxism rather than the dogmatic and frozen one. The prime virtue of Sartrean existentialism is that it achieved this re-discovery of Marxism."[40]

The ground was now ready for a new translation of Sartre's *Materialism and Revolution* (1947), which was introduced under the title *Al-Marksiyya wa-l-Thawra* (Marxism and revolution). This misleading title gave the impression that Marxism, socialism, and Sartre's existentialism formed a seamless revolutionary cloth.[41] Thus, for *al-jil al-jadid*, Tarabishi's revolutionary generation, Sartre embodied the promise of a global humanistic Left, a movement that was to deliver them from the postcolonial state of being to that of global citizenship.

In order to be able to participate in this project from an Arab standpoint it was crucial to dispel any doubts about the incompatibility of Marxism and existentialism. Tarabishi's book did precisely that. Drawing on the tradition of Arab existentialism that the previous generation had begun, Tarabishi and his peers had much to rely on. And though he readily admitted that they often misunderstood Sartre, by and large, they got the big picture right and saw in him a thinker who addressed their cultural needs.[42] With this sensibility in mind, Tarabishi's analysis of European debates about Marxism and existentialism showed how the discredited features of existentialism (radical individualism, ambiguity, its fetish of freedom, its antideterminism, and so on) were precisely what made a Marxist-based Sartre relevant to the Arab generation of the sixties. Poet Fadil al-ʿAzzawi gladly admitted as much: "I liked Sartre for his attempt to unite the social with the individual; he made a difficult union between Marxism and Existentialism possible."[43] Reading Tarabishi's book one can understand why al-ʿAzzawi felt so.

With the idea of a universal Left in mind, Tarabishi argued that after a century of European socialism, capitalism had figured out how to subvert it. Hence, the "only real chance that socialism still has." was outside of Europe, in the Third World. "Will the people of the non-developed world know how to save themselves as well as socialism by means of revolution" asked Tarabishi?[44] As we shall shortly see, drawing on the Cuban experience and on the new Arabic translation of Fanon's *The Wretched of the Earth*, his answer was an emphatic yes; a new culture, a new humanism, and a new set of values would be the result of a regenerative Third World socialist revolution. The pre–May 1968 European generation also believed so.

Revolutionary Misreading

One of the curious intellectual legacies that passed from the 1950s into the 1960s was a tendency to blur the differences between Sartre and Camus and see both of them as committed existentialists in search of revolution. As a precursor of the 1960s global culture of resistance, the Iraqi poet ʿAbd al-Wahhab al-Bayyati was probably one of the most persistent writers who found in Camus and Sartre a justification and a source of moral support for a host of revolutionary virtues. Though eventually he moved to Moscow and played on an international stage alongside people like Pablo Neruda and Nâzim Hikmet, just like Nazik al-Malaʾika, his intellectual beginnings were very modest and very Iraqi.[45] A native of Baghdad, who was attracted from an early age to the written word, he was an integral part of the city's cultural renaissance. Being a specialist in fusing the poetic and the political, as one of the most respected Arab poets of the time, he too wrote in free verse. In his memoir, al-Bayyati traced the influences that shaped him back to the human landscape of his Baghdadi neighborhood, with its "wretched poor inhabitants, peddlers, workers, rural migrants and petite-bourgeoisie."[46] This popular background brought him to appreciate socialist realism and existentialism as two traditions that were preoccupied with freedom as well as with an intimate attention to the modern trials of ordinary human beings. Like others around him, he drew on Marxism-Leninism and existential commitment as intellectual traditions that point toward some kind of revolutionary solution to Iraq's problems. He added to this mix Camus's notion of metaphysical revolt, which he helped Arabize in a unique fashion.

Even though Camus's "I revolt therefore we exist" was an individual project that rejected any form of wholesale ideological solution such as socialism, Marxism, or, in the Arab context, ʿAflaq's style of revolutionary rebirth, al-Bayyati took it as a collective revolutionary project. Blurring the conceptual line between revolt and revolution, al-Bayyati seemed unaware of the fact that Camus's metaphysical rebellion was in opposition to collective revolution and that he publicly and famously washed his hands of any Marxist, communist, or socialist revolution. In fact, in France, where *The Rebel* became a major political event, Camus's readers "could hardly miss his description of how the impulse for [revolutionary] emancipation turned into organized, rational murder as the rebel-become-revolutionary attempted to order an absurd universe." Obviously, Camus offered a critique of Stalinism and its many French apologists. But, in addition, *The Rebel* was also a direct attack on Sartre's politics, whose devoted followers "had fallen victim to the idea that revolt should lead to revolution."[47] In what followed, Sartre and Camus embarked on a nasty and well-publicized quarrel that terminated their friendship.[48]

This episode, however, did not seem to influence the Arab reception of *The Rebel* as a fine example of Sartrean commitment. And, so, though Camus was a powerful critic of collective revolutionary projects, al-Bayyati and others understood his work as an endorsement of individual revolt that transformed into a collective effort, as in Pan-Arab and Ba'thi revolution. So much was clear in his poem "To Albert Camus" (*ila Albir Kamu*), which al-Bayyati dedicated to the French writer and in which, in the face of a Sisyphean state of being, an unstoppable revolutionary energy breeds existential liberation.[49] In 1966, when a respected group of Arab intellectuals came together to celebrate al-Bayyati's achievements, they all extolled this same understanding of existentialism and revolution.[50]

Granted, al-Bayyati was by no means alone in his revolutionary reading of Camus. In a lengthy and well-researched article about Camus's work, Iraqi literary critic Nahad al-Takarli argued that revolt is Camus's prescription against the absurdity of life and the quest to find meaning in it. This experience of revolt against life, he argued, is so fundamental to the making of the self that, as it confronts the injustices of the world, it extends from the individual to others (the "we"). Al-Takarli also took Camus's revolt to be a collective revolutionary enterprise that underlay important values such as solidarity, dignity, and the will to sacrifice. He even went as far as arguing that Camus had originally intended his work to be a subversive call for resistance (*muqawama*) against the Nazi occupation of France.[51] In line with the Arab project of decolonization, this was a common reading of Camus. Slightly lagging behind its reception in the Middle East, *The Rebel* was translated to Arabic only in 1963.[52]

Another example of the revolutionary translation of Camus into Arabic was evident in the case of his play *Les justes* (*The Just Assassins*, 1949). Translated to Arabic in January 1954, in this play Camus revisited the true story of a Russian revolutionary group that in 1905 assassinated a powerful, yet reactionary, grand duke. The play is set as a self-questioning moral drama about the political usage of revolutionary terrorism and the moral right to kill innocent people in the service of the revolutionary cause. Should the duke be assassinated at all costs, killing with him his wife and family, or should the revolutionaries wait for the rare opportunity of targeting the duke when he is alone? For young Arabs plotting a revolution, these were meaningful questions. When translator Imil Suwayri wrote to Camus telling him about the importance of the play for the Arab revolutionary project, Camus responded with a warm personal message about his affection for the Arab world, his birthplace. Other than that, he chose not to meaningfully influence the reception of his work by Arab readers and, unlike Sartre, evinced not real interest in the struggles of Arabs. That, however, did not deter the translator from telling his readers that *Les Justes* was a fine proof of Camus's revolutionary commitment.[53]

'Abd al-Mun'im al-Hifni, an Egyptian biographer and translator of Camus and Sartre, begged to differ with this reading. In his biography of Camus, al-Hifni correctly understood the message of *The Rebel* and refuted any possible revolutionary reading. As a translator of the two French intellectuals, he also alerted his readers to the fallout between Sartre and Camus as well as to the sharp ideological and personal divisions that now set them apart. This single voice, however, could hardly make a dent in the established understanding of Camus and Sartre as two likeminded revolutionary philosophers.[54]

That Camus's idea of revolt was appropriated by the revolutionary politics of iltizam illustrates once again the remarkable power of this concept in Arab thought. The fact that local intellectuals pledged allegiance to a notion of revolution that was entirely inconstant with that of Camus matters very little.[55] As al-Bayyati saw it, "The search for a poetic form which did not exist in our old poetry, and the metaphysical revolt against reality as a whole . . . brought (us) to discover the wretched reality in which the masses live."[56] With this in mind, "I felt that I was writing in defense of the freedom and justice of the wretched masses [al-jamahir al-ba'isa] and not in defense of myself. I understood iltizam as a request from the artist to deeply side with others and suffer as they do with them."[57] Hence the justification for al-Bayyati's habit of transitioning smoothly between poetry and revolutionary politics. And, like many others, he was ready to pay the price for his engagements. Indeed, by serving time in jail, living in poverty and under constant intimidation, pay he did. Losing his home and forced to leave his wife and children behind, al-Bayyati' gained a new Arab audience and a new appreciation for the emancipating potential of universal revolution.[58]

Once in exile, al-Bayyati transitioned from the standard anticolonial writings of his time to a more sophisticated postcolonial critique in which he exposed, for instance, the French hypocrisy of "liberty, justice, and equality" and celebrated liberation struggles in Egypt, Malaya, Kenya, and Algeria. Taking a cultural part in the metaphysical "battle for Arab destiny" (*ma'rakat al-masir*) and its core revolutionary values of sacrifice, resistance, and martyrdom, al-Bayyati's political horizons became truly global.[59] That these horizons were envisioned through a distorted prism that collapsed Camus and Sartre into a single image mattered little. Such reading opened new possibilities that brought al-Bayyati to embrace Che Guevara's conviction that "we create the man of the twenty-first century."[60] As we shall see, creating this man called not only for more intellectual work but also for concrete action.

Conclusion

The effort to articulate an Arab position that transcended the physical space of the Middle East but that remained organically connected to it rested on thought. This was why intellectuals began writing about the big ideas of the 1960s, such as racism, neocolonialism, settler colonialism, otherness, subhuman existence, human dignity, hegemony, justice, and the emancipating possibilities of guerilla warfare. Influenced by Sartre's reading of Fanon and by the kind of Marxism to which both thinkers subscribed, theoreticians were drawn to the emancipating power of anticolonial violence. But resistance was only part of the story. To effectively operate in the world as integrated and holistic revolutionaries, theoreticians had to address the long-standing differences between Marxism and existentialism. Fearing that this schism might fragment the unity of the Arab position and thus jeopardize its passage toward universalism, they invested considerable energy in shoring up any apparent theoretical differences between existentialism and Marxism.

Though this effort had its shortcomings—such as its inability to distinguish Camus and Sartre or, more seriously, to comprehend the destructive power of the state—it did produce a new sense of global belonging and responsibility. By adopting this global system of meaning making, the revolutionary Arab world acquired the ability to understand, connect with, and identify with distant and seemingly irrelevant events. Yet, as the next chapter shows, only when the state took serious interest in this left-wing project did its arcane ideas resonate more seriously, widely, and deeply, thus pushing the public closer than ever toward a universal Arab position.

SEVEN

Toward Universal Emancipation

At any given moment during the 1960s, multiplying liberation struggles and violent proxy wars for superpower hegemony dotted the globe. Assassinations of democratically elected leaders, massacres of political opponents, manipulations of democratic process, sponsorships of civil wars, theft of natural resources, systematic abuse of and discrimination against racial minorities, and so on—the playbook of the Cold War was red and ruthless. Whether we examine Latin America, Africa, Asia, or the Middle East, again and again a violent pattern repeated itself, in which a recently decolonized country was bullied into choosing sides and slowly sank into chronic civil war marked by foreign intervention. Quite amazingly, the task of exposing these events, creating awareness of their existence, and pronouncing clear rules of international behavior fell not on the UN, not on human rights organizations (which were not yet in existence), and not even on the international press. Exposing these destructive modes of global behavior fell to the victims from the Third World. Given this population's disenfranchisement and vulnerability, the burden was also assumed by a new type of Euro-American left-wing intellectual-activist whose moral compass pointed toward a set of universal values.

Cognizant of these dire global realities, Sartre situated himself at the forefront of an ethical battle to give a name to the nameless, a voice to the voiceless, and to publicly tell right from wrong. Armed with a major intellectual arsenal—not all of which was his own—comprising a theorization of racism and concepts such as neocolonialism, settler colonialism, otherness, subhuman existence, human dignity, hegemony, and injustice, he energetically stepped into the uncharted territory of the Cold War. By any measure, Sartre was probably the first true global intellectual, and his ethics, which were about pronouncing actual rules of behavior, dovetailed with his existential philosophy. The intellectual link between Sartre's anticolonial humanism and his attempt to intervene in all of the important causes of the 1960s beginning with Algeria and continuing with Cuba, Congo, Brazil, China, India, Angola, the Dominican Republic, Vietnam, and, eventually, Palestine, was not lost on the inhabitants of the Middle East.

Taken by the ideal of a universal ethical subject of the Left, a position that strove to mark and hold the moral high ground and call others to do the same, Arab intellectuals and associated political elites believed that by participating in this global movement the Arab person could make a successful passage into universalism, surpass its postcolonial condition, and emerge a liberated citizen. Put differently, the global struggle suggested itself as a vehicle that could transport its participants into a zone of being where they would be existentially liberated from their colonial burden simply by embodying a set of universal values regarding justice and freedom.

The ideas that underwrote this effort were of course important, but equally important and for many much more exciting, was the widespread emphasis on action. After all, without the willingness to fight on the ground and make real sacrifices, these ideas and ideals would indeed be worthless. Taking the interface between thought and action as its subject matter, this chapter begins with Che Guevara's visit to the Middle East; it continues with Egypt's intervention in Congo and Yemen and its competition with Israel for influence in Africa, and concludes with the effort to conceptualize the problem of Palestine in new terms. Applying the classic ideas of the global sixties to the field of struggle made it clear that the problems of Algeria, Congo, and Palestine shared striking similarities. That many of the ideas that allowed Arab intellectuals to discover these similarities originated with Sartre, or at the very least were associated with him, raised the expectation that Sartre, the icon of this global effort of the Left, would commit to Palestine just as he did to Algeria and Congo. More concretely, Arabs expected Sartre to follow the example of Che Guevara. Che's reception in the region, as we shall now see, was somewhat slow. Yet, after a bumpy start, his revolutionary politics were quickly embraced. Che reciprocated by strongly identifying with the Arab Cause. Sartre, it was hoped, would do the same.

Che Who?

Dressed in full army fatigues and accompanied by several Cuban comrades with an equally imposing revolutionary appearance, on June 18, 1959, Che Guevara landed in Gaza. With his current reputation as a roving ambassador of revolution in mind, one would have expected the thirty-one-year-old Che to teach guerilla warfare to the Palestinian resistance fighters (the Fedayeen), to tell them in detail about his grand *foco* tactics, and to take a note of their decade-long experience of resistance to Israel. Yet, nothing of that sort happened. The visit was a short, low-key event that was tightly controlled by Ahmad Sa'id, Gaza's Egyptian governor. The press contingent was kept to a minimum, no iconic photographs were published, and—so it seems—only a single image survived. Though Che and the Cubans had visited several refugee camps by day's end, they dined not with top leaders of the Palestinian Fedayeen, but with the Brazilian contingent of the UN Emergency Force. In fact, not a single member of the Fedayeen was present, and there was no talk of revolutionary theory, neocolonialism, Zionist imperialism, or any of the other 1960s subcategories of global resistance. Twenty-four hours after Che arrived in Gaza, he was back in Cairo. The next day the Egyptian newspapers buried the story.[1]

Truth be told, the Cubans were not taken very seriously. Che's name, for instance, never appeared in print as he was referred to as "head of the Cuban delegation." Earlier in the year, "when Fidel Castro and his victorious men marched into Havana in January 1959, slung round with guns and bandoliers and sporting their bushy beards, President Nasser tended to dismiss them as a bunch of Errol Flynns, theatrical brigands but not true revolutionaries."[2] So, with this Hollywood picture in mind, when Che first landed in Cairo, Nasser did not rush to the airport to greet him. Actually, Egyptian attention was entirely elsewhere with the more strategically important visit of Ethiopia's Emperor Haile Selassie. While Selassie received heavy press coverage and much attention, the Cubans, except for a few back-page reports on their whereabouts, got hardly any. Hosted in King Faruq's former summer palace, they waited for Nasser, who appeared the following day to officially greet Che and award him the United Arab Republic's Decoration of the First Order.[3] Quaint.

By that point, the Cubans had noticed the self-satisfied and paternalistic tone of their hosts who, believing that they had cracked the formula for successful revolution, were singing the praises of Nasserism to their allegedly inexperienced guests.[4] When Nasser and Che finally sat down to talk, their first meeting "was quite cool. Both sparred a little, sounding one another out. Che went so far as to question the extent of the Egyptian agrarian reform and thus provoked an argument."[5] "How many Egyptian refugees were obliged to leave the country?" asked Che. Nasser responded that not many had been. "That means," Che said, "that nothing much happened in your revolution." Nasser tried to explain that his aim was to liquidate privileges and not an entire class. Che was unimpressed, and the meeting ended on that sour note.[6] Thereafter, the Cubans left for Damascus, visited the tomb of Salah al-Din, a renewed symbol of resistance and sacrifice, and continued their tour to other members of the Bandung community. The historical truth is that "nothing much arose from the visit."[7]

This anecdotal episode tells us that the bearded, cigar-smoking Che was not yet an international icon of global resistance, and that the sixties, so to speak, had not yet started. In fact, the entire point of his

FIGURE 3   Che and Egyptian hosts in front of the mansion of Ahmad Sa'id, the Egyptian governor of Gaza

visit was to launch a three-month tour through the community of Bandung so that the Cubans could introduce themselves to the progressive elites of the Third World, kick-start the sixties in the process, and, they hoped, sell some sugar.[8] However modest, this was how Cuba began its search for a revolutionary role in world affairs. Acknowledgment was slow, but, in three years, its signature revolutionary rhetoric and resistance to imperialism would be globally recognized. Che himself would become a celebrated Third World icon and a model for a new type of revolutionary subject, one worthy of front-page coverage even in Egypt. Indeed, as we shall see, in Che's future dealings with Egyptians, Nasser would be respectful and attentive, as the Arab world by then had entered the struggle of the global South against the oppressive North.

The transformation of Che's image form an awkward nobody to an Arab role model captures the metamorphosis of the Arab revolutionary project as a whole. Fundamentally, the difference between the decolonization struggles of the 1950s and those of the 1960s was that, as opposed to the 1950s, which emphasized physical liberation of national territory, the 1960s ushered in the understanding that anticolonial struggles were about not simply reclaiming national space but, much more profoundly, the inner liberation of the human subject. Or, as Bob Marley later put it in his extraordinary "Redemption Song": "Emancipate yourself from mental slavery, none but ourselves can free our minds."

The frontiers of this existential struggle were to be found wherever unliberated people were living. Regardless of their racial, religious, and national affiliation, they were all brothers and sisters in arms. In this new age of solidarity, the unliberated subject of the 1960s would become emancipated by virtue of its global human bonds and the will of others to sacrifice on its behalf and vice versa. This was why the global culture of the 1960s saw no difference between the cases of Algeria, Vietnam, Congo, South Africa, the civil rights movement in the United States, and Palestine. It simply considered them variants of a single cause. This chapter show how certain intellectual connections and concrete state politics coalesced in the service of this new global vision.

A Better Revolutionary

Following Che, the Syrian thinker ʿAbdallah ʿAbd al-Daʾim wrote, "We must create the new Arab man."[9] Who is this new Arab man? asked

Lebanese critic Jurj Hanna: "The new Arab man," he answered, "is first and foremost he who knows himself and regards himself as sovereign and a maker of his destiny."[10] Al-Daʾim's quest for a new Arab man and Hanna's characterization of this male persona reflected an old understanding of Arab subjectivity that was completely devoid of the global horizons of the 1960s and of the possible contribution of women to it. Given the expanding intellectual universe of decolonization and the greater global connectivity of the age, the Arab revolutionary self was pressured to reorient.

At the time it was enough to switch on the radio or pick up a daily newspaper to hear, day in and day out, the bombastic rhetoric of revolution. Sometimes it seemed that, to invoke the limitless possibilities of thawra, all one needed was a microphone and a pen. Yet, of those with pens, only a few were serious thinkers worthy of the conceptual challenges that lie ahead. Two such significant individuals were the Syrians ʿAbdallah ʿAbd al-Daʾim and Mutaʿ Safadi. Both started their public careers as students of philosophy. Both joined the Baʿth enthusiastically but later parted ways with it in disgust. And both thinkers encountered a certain impasse in Arab revolutionary practice. Working through this difficulty, they ended up charting the new possibilities that the Arab revolution might open if it framed itself as a global endeavor.

Al-Daʾim began theorizing Arab nationalism in 1959 when he published a series of books on the emergence of a new Arab man, a new generation, and, eventually, a new revolutionary society. Matching theory to practice he joined the Baʿth. In 1962 he was appointed minister of information and four years later minister of education. According to contemporary Syrian philosopher Sadiq al-ʿAzm, al-Daʾim was a major influence on the younger generation. He was one of the most widely read thinkers of the time, and his texts circulated widely.[11]

Thinking almost exclusively within the intellectual parameters of Baʿthism, in his book *Al-Jil al-ʿArabi al-Jadid* (The new Arab generation, 1960), al-Daʾim drew a generational line between the older and corrupt generation and a young generation destined to be the vanguard that would deliver Arab society to a new revolutionary era. This transformation, he explained, was predicated on the psychological makeup of the new Arab man.[12] So far so good; there was not much new in this set of ideas. The elder Qustantin Zurayq, the intellectual godfather of Lebanese and Palestinian Pan-Arab students such as George Habash, already had popularized such designs and continued to do so during the 1960s.[13]

Aware of the momentum of Third World revolutionary thought, in

1963 al-Daʾim published *Al-Watan al-ʿArabi wa-l-Thawra* (The Arab nation and revolution) a book that captured, as well as significantly contributed to, the Arab turn toward global revolution. "The Arab revolutionary position," stated al-Daʾim, "is a human one" as it emerges out of the deep need to save the Arab self from the multiple forces that seek to curtail its freedom and fragment its existence.[14] Most dangerously, neocolonialism, he wrote, was a practice that destroyed society from within by nonmilitary and largely invisible means (see more below). Represented by the internal forces of reaction, it divided the social body economically and socially, robbed it of its autonomy, and thus subordinated it to external forces. The only way to defeat this new menace to Arab sovereignty, argued al-Daʾim, was by cultivating a new revolutionary subject who understood that, while neocolonialism was a local Arab reality, the fight against it was not.

By this time the Arab world had seen multiple political transformations that were locally called revolutions, including the ongoing Egyptian campaign in Yemen. Yet, when thinking about an ideal revolution, a model to be emulated, al-Daʾim had Cuba in mind.[15] In ʿAida Matraji Idris's new translation of Sartre's 1960 hagiographic and grossly overstated account of the Cuban revolution, *Ouragan sur le sucre* (Hurricane over sugar, published in English as *Sartre on Cuba*), al-Daʾim found his inspiration. "Revolution is a Strong Medicine," wrote Sartre in this Cuba booklet, and to properly administer it calls for strong doctors. Sartre celebrated Che as such a doctor and al-Daʾim too understood the necessity of creating many Arab "Ches."[16] Al-Daʾim was not the only one to be inspired by Che's "freedom or death." Thanks once again to ʿAida's quick translations, Arab audience could now read Sartre's fluent and energetic description of how the revolutionary consciousness of a select few can transform society and defeat neocolonialism. Slowly but surely a new revolutionary model had emerged, and the fact that it got the approval of the French Left was a bonus to the perceived domestic benefits.[17]

Al-Daʾim was not alone in taking the global revolutionary turn. In his capacity as an existentialist philosopher, novelist, playwright, and political commentator, Mutaʿ Safadi was probably the most prolific and versatile theoretician of revolution. Well versed in European philosophy, he coupled fiction with philosophy and published both in quick succession. In 1960, for instance, he published his classic novel *Jil al-Qadr* (The fate generation) about a group of philosophy students who, by way of articulating a new relationship between the self and the outside world, embark on a quest for self-creation, sovereignty, freedom, and political change. When their plot to assassinate the dictator fails, the group disintegrates, leaving its members with doubts about the fate of their generation and the meaning of revolution. This widely read novel was followed by close to five hundred pages of dense revolutionary theory:[18] published in 1961, *Al-Thawri wa-l-Thawri al-'Arabi* (*The Revolutionary and the Arab Revolutionary*) harnessed the canon of existentialist philosophy and Sartre's *Critique of Dialectical Reason* to spell out what Safadi considered to be the basic condition of "being revolutionary" and help his reader address the following questions: "Am I a revolutionary? Why am I rebelling and how?"[19]

Seeking to construct a humanistic and universal revolutionary self, Safadi hoped that fellow citizens would reach a higher level of being, not in relation to an abstract principle or social reform, but in relation to their disadvantaged beginnings.[20] Responding to the debates of the 1950s, Safadi had plenty to say about revolution in the context of iltizam and radical individualism, the role of the arts, the purpose of culture, and the nature of the nation. Concomitantly, he had nothing to say about the revolutionary usage of violence, the power of the state, and its tendency to coopt and manipulate revolution. This oversight, so characteristic of intellectuals of the time, would eventually prove very costly. As an engaged intellectual, Safadi's sphere of action was by no means restricted to self-searching novels and philosophy books about anxiety. He had very concrete political opinions about Arab unity that were supportive of Egypt's Nasser and highly critical toward the Ba'th Party. For this he spent part of 1963 in jail.

A year after his release, in 1964, Safadi moved to Beirut, an open city where freedom was more than an abstract principle and where local intellectuals knew they were lucky.[21] Protected by these freedoms, he published *Hizb al-Ba'th: Ma'sat al-Mawlid wa Ma'sat al-Nihaya* (The Ba'th party: The misfortunes of its beginning and its end). Passionately written, it was the most honest and scathing critique of the Ba'th's revolutionary endeavor to date. This one-of-a-kind book, which anticipated much of the post-1967 debates, engaged with the core issues of Arab political life and therefore merits a much more substantial discussion than that allowed here. The thrust of this sobering critique was to expose the revolutionary platform of the Ba'th as sheer state terror. Reaching power by means of army-party collusion in both Iraq and Syria, the means of this political feat included mass murder, incarceration, systematic torture, and statewide suspension of political rights.

With thousands of people dead, many more in prison, and countless others in exile, Safadi lamented these "ideological massacres" and mourned a noble revolutionary project that had turned against itself. He blamed Ba'thi intellectuals for betraying their ethical mission and for propagating an ideological emptiness that turned its back on the party's existentialist origins, which sanctified human freedom and total liberation. Its collective psychology of fear, he opined, would accomplish nothing except heartache and increased levels of violence. No theory of revolution guided these actions, he pressed on, and no humanism anchored them. Furthermore, argued Safadi, this murderous association with the army and the abuse of state power marked a clear divestment from international allies such as the noncommunist European Left. In doing so, the Arab revolutionary project of the Ba'th willingly removed itself from the universal fight for freedom, dignity, and liberation.[22] History would prove Safadi right, but for then, if the Ba'th was antithetical to the universal subject of the Left, an alternative revolutionary persona was needed.

At the same time that Safadi's accumulated work called for a renewed consideration of the Arab revolutionary project, the first translation and interpretations of Fanon's *The Wretched of the Earth* began circulating. Given the intellectual landscape of the time, Fanon was read with Sartre in mind. Arab intellectuals were not alone in finding the relationship between the two thinkers to be very suggestive, especially with regard to the link between violence and freedom.[23] Writing on this very issue, Jonathan Judaken maintained that "Fanon's seminal insight was to see racism interweaved with its institutionalized forms of colonialism, which meant that racism could be overcome only through a violent revolt against that system of oppression. In this Fanon and Sartre walked parallel roads to freedom."[24]

While we may question Fanon's actual commitment to violence, Sartre's hotheaded introduction to Fanon did sanctify the link between anticolonial violence and liberation. It was therefore instrumental in reducing Fanon's work to an essay about the emancipating virtues of anticolonial violence. Suhayl Idris translated and published Sartre's introduction to Fanon ahead of publishing Fanon's original text, which he called a "book-bomb."[25] And thus, from the very beginning, Arabic commentaries on Fanon were completely influenced by Sartre's take on the book. Their morality was clear: "Real independence is achieved only by revolutionary means. . . . Armed revolution is capable of raising the consciousness of the people for the sake of building its future and purging its ranks of reactionary and weak elements."[26] What was widely understood to be Fanon's purifying violence was absorbed in the region against the emerging crisis of state-run revolutionary culture. Yet, the implications of this encounter would become clear only after the 1967 war when the state would fail to liberate both people and land, and a new generation of Palestinians and left-wing associates would take Fanon's theory and Che's example as their model for a successful state-free liberation enterprise.

Beyond armed resistance, Arab critics took from Fanon the relatively new idea that "real independence" was, first and foremost, a struggle against a benighted human condition.[27] Fanon's famous words, now published in Arabic, fit together nicely with the Arab quest for a new revolutionary self: "Let us decide not to imitate Europe; let us combine our muscles and our brains in a new direction. Let us try to create the whole man, whom Europe has been incapable of bringing to triumphant birth."[28] For now, however, the project of revolutionary responsibility toward humanity was still under state hegemony. In this regard, Egypt was eager to provide a positive revolutionary example that eclipsed the corrupt practices of the Ba'th and illustrated that the state could act as a revolutionary force for global good.

Being on the Right Side of Things

During the 1960s, when the battle for postcolonial Africa was in full swing, the continent became one of the nastiest arenas of the Cold War. It was a war that had attracted the usual players but also new ones like Egypt, Israel, and Cuba. It also drew the unmitigated attention of the European Left. Competing for political and economic influence, the struggle in Africa added an unexpected international dimension to the already familiar dynamics of the Arab-Israeli conflict. In its self-appointed role as representative of the revolutionary Arab world, Nasser's Egypt cast a large shadow. In addition to broadcasting to Africa in at least thirty local languages, thus becoming the largest station on the continent, Egypt also conducted an ongoing diplomatic and military mission in support of African liberation.[29] Taking a leadership role in the cause of African liberation, the Egyptians enlisted on behalf of the fight against neocolonialism, thus aligning themselves with the anti-imperialist cause of the global Left.

On the other side of the ideological divide were the Israelis, whose mission in Africa, especially in its military and economic aspects, was quite developed. Israel too saw itself as a progressive socialist country that supported liberation, peace, and development. Needing to choose from multiple state actors, for African leaders in places like Ghana,

Congo, and Uganda, the question was not so much an ideological one, as in which entity was more socialist and progressive, but rather a simple business matter: which of the two sides could deliver more and better economic development for less? Which was willing to spend more money on education, healthcare, and basic infrastructure? Which was willing to offer military aid? On what terms?

Israel reached the continent ahead of Egypt. Alarmed by its exclusion at Bandung and fearing diplomatic and economic isolation as well as a general crisis of legitimacy, Israel prioritized the development of firm relationships with a host of newly liberated African nations. They started with Ghana, the first sub-Saharan colony to win independence. As soon as Ghana won its freedom, in March 1957 Israel opened an embassy in Accra, a full year ahead of Egypt. From that point until 1961, when the relationship stalled, the personal rapport between Kwame Nkrumah, his pro-Zionist advisers, and the Israelis developed quickly. Answering Nkrumah's plea for assistance in development, the Israelis sent dozens of experts to organize Ghana's health, agricultural, and educational sectors. They also assisted in developing Ghana's water resources, buttressing its construction sector, and establishing mutual trade networks and a joint shipping company. Though Israel was under severe financial strain, it extended several generous loans, thus offering a full-spectrum development package. Least talked about was the Israeli military's assistance in light arms sales and training a new cadre of captains and pilots. Much of these dealings boiled down to business, but there was also an ideological component.[30] As David Ben Gurion wrote to Nkrumah in January 1957, "Though of the white race, Jews have suffered . . . at the hand of white people."[31] He thus offered an intimate alliance of victims who intuitively understood each other.

Zionist idealism was also at play. Ideas regarding the liberation of other peoples brought Israel to promote itself as a natural friend of oppressed people and as a socialist example for development. At least part of its mission in Africa had a humanitarian aspect that was motivated by a strong belief in Israel's exceptionalism as a "light unto the nations."[32] Though Israel presented itself as an ideological ally of decolonized people, and though Nkrumah's advisers were close to Israel, increasingly, he had difficulty justifying Ghana's close rapport with Israel to Nasser and to the community of Bandung. At one point he even asked the Israelis to help Ghana articulate a postcolonial justification for their relationship. Though Nkrumah could clearly see that his natural camp was not that of Israel, he was initially concerned about Nasser's motives and his bid for African hegemony. He even relied on

Israeli intelligence reports in order to monitor Egypt's moves on the continent.[33] For a while everything went smoothly for the Israelis. During 1960 and 1961 about sixteen African countries won their independence. All but two established relations with Israel.[34] If the Egyptians were competing for influence they did not seem to be successful in branding Israel a racist protégé of imperialism. This would change, however.

In December 1957 Nkrumah sent a delegation to the Cairo conference of the Asian-African People's Solidarity Organization (AAPSO). Severing ties with Israel was not on the agenda, but the pressure was certainly there.[35] By the end of the month, Nkrumah had married Fathia, an Egyptian woman. "She spoke little English, while her groom spoke neither Arabic nor French." Though a private matter, Nasser briefed the woman on her responsibilities as a first lady. From a diplomatic standpoint, the marriage "disproved all rumors about competition for influence between the two men" or any other ideological disagreement.[36] In April 1958 Ghana hosted the Conference of Independent African States (CIAS). Known as the African Bandung, Ghanaian officials rejected Arab demands for a debate on Palestine. Two months later, in late June 1958, Nkrumah visited Cairo and this time agreed to issue a joint communique with Nasser advocating a "just solution to the Palestine question."[37] Shortly afterward Nkrumah's first son was born. He was named Gamal, as in the first name of the Egyptian president.[38]

The next time around, in January 1961, the Afro-Asian nations convened in Casablanca in order to address the brewing international crisis in Congo (see below). This time around the condemnation of Israel "as a tool of imperialism in Africa and elsewhere" got the support of Ghana, and the special relationship began to unravel. A month later, Nkrumah replaced the faculty at the flight school that Israel had established with British instructors. Several other programs were brought to a quiet close as well.[39] Apparently, the crisis in Congo had pushed everyone involved in Africa to choose sides. Nkrumah chose his and, returning to his academic roots as a graduate student of philosophy, coined the powerful concept of neocolonialism. It was immediately applied to the crisis in the Congo.

In debt to Marxism, neocolonialism imperfectly implied indirect continuation of colonialism and imperialism. Though quite vague, the Congo crisis allowed the general theory of neocolonialism a degree of specificity that went beyond economic penetration through a colonial-trained elite to emphasize political subversion, military pressures, and the heavy-handed politics of aid and development. Drawing on

Congo, in 1965 Nkrumah published *Neo-colonialism: The Last Stage of Imperialism*. This appreciative nod to Lenin theorized a relationship of nearly full economic and geopolitical dependency, thus explaining the involvement of former colonial powers in Africa as well as accounting for the imperial politics of the United States. Anecdotally, it is often mentioned that when the book was published an enraged US State Department canceled a $25 million loan to Ghana, thus making it the most expensive book ever published.[40] Interestingly, despite his many attacks on imperialism and finance capital, Nkrumah never wrote anything that established a link between Zionism and neocolonialism. Establishing this link was the job of Palestinians, Syrians, and Egyptians.

The Congo crisis was a classic Cold War affair, and as far as Africa and the Middle East were concerned a real watershed in the internationalization of the war. A remarkable moment of international clarity, the crisis became the ultimate litmus test for where one stood in the polarized global order of the early 1960s. It began like a classic case of decolonization. In 1960, as formal Belgian colonialism in one of the richest colonies in the world came to a slow close, Congo was far from being united. Comprising close to two hundred ethnic groups, it struggled to articulate a common ethos and a unified political strategy that could benefit everybody. Still, when elections were held in May, the veteran labor unionist and anticolonial firebrand Patrice Lumumba secured a solid win. Though immensely rich in minerals (such as copper as well as the uranium that was used to build the first US nuclear device) and hence of significant economic and strategic potential, Congo had no viable state institutions to speak of and was therefore extremely vulnerable.

Facing these challenges, Lumumba was inspired by the nonalignment movement of the 1950s and especially by Nkrumah. He therefore sought rapid economic development from which all ethnic groups and provinces would benefit equally. The vision was a noble one, but in July, struggling to establish his own legitimacy, Lumumba was confronted with a military mutiny and the secession of Congo's richest province, Katanga. Anxious to keep control over the multibillion-dollar mining business in Katanga, the Belgians actively supported Lumumba's enemies, thus furthering the fragmentation of the country. They were also the main culprits in cementing Lumumba's image as a communist puppet, a criminal, and a threat to regional peace. The United States subscribed to this political caricature and was eager to see, as well as to facilitate, his fall. To avoid a civil war, a UN peacekeeping force was sent in with a mission to secure Belgian withdrawal and assist the government in maintaining law and order. But the UN mandate had limitations. When Lumumba requested the UN to intervene militarily in Katanga and bring the rich province under the control of the central government, the UN refused. Isolated and under severe stress, Lumumba insinuated that in order to maintain the unity of his country he might seek Soviet help. Vindicated, Belgium and the United States now had solid proof that Lumumba was a Castro-like communist, and the proxy struggle for the control of Congo was set in motion.[41]

In desperation, Lumumba appealed to his progressive neighbors and natural allies from the nonaligned camp of the Left. Nkrumah, a mentor of sorts, agreed to send troops, and Egypt immediately stepped forward to transport them by air. In addition, Egypt had agreed to include its paratroopers in the UN peacekeeping mission and added to this aid package diplomatic, technical, and medical support. The stakes were high, Nasser observed: "When I hear what is happening in the Congo, I remember what happened in Egypt in 1956. . . . We support the question of freedom in the Congo because we consider it a matter that concerns us. If the Congolese issue is lost, freedom everywhere in the world will be threatened."[42] Understood in the immediate context of the struggle in Algeria, the Egyptians saw in the Congo affair a classic neocolonial case and responded by organizing the Casablanca Conference. Convened in January 1961, the meeting forged a united Afro-Asian front against neocolonialism and a commitment to the usage of force in order to resist it.[43] Though Lumumba's book on neocolonialism was not yet out his conceptual language was widely accepted as the standard political discourse to describe the reality of Congo.

Exactly ten days after this hopeful conference, the dire realties of the Congo left very few illusions as to who had the upper hand in the struggle. Following a military coup in the capital in September, General Joseph Mobutu, "a completely honest and dedicated man," according to the US ambassador, captured Lumumba and turned him over to his enemies in Katanga. They lost little time and, in the attendance of Belgian officers, tortured and executed him.[44] Film of his gruesome capture and torture circulated widely for all to see the real face of neocolonialism. By the standard of the time, it "went viral" so to speak. Vigilant Egyptian diplomats managed to evacuate Lumumba's children's and immediate family to Cairo. But the execution shook everybody.[45] Lumumba was not even thirty-six years old when he faced a firing squad under a big tree that had been reserved especially for him. With Lumumba's dismembered body drenched in acid and his skull crushed, Congo was now in secure hands, away from the alleged Soviet threat and its radical Third World allies.[46]

The cynicism of foreign economic domination, the divide-and-conquer strategy that fragmented the country, the American support for this hostile takeover, the helplessness of Lumumba's friends, and the brutal murder of a democratically elected head of state turned the Congo crisis into a rallying cry for freedom. In the wake of the assassination a diverse group of demonstrators took to the streets, and Belgian embassies in Cairo, Belgrade, Paris, London, and Moscow were attacked.[47] Taking the lead on this, Nasser nationalized some Belgian businesses and cut diplomatic ties.[48] The progressive Left in Europe was scandalized. Using Nkrumah's language, Sartre wrote an entire article on Lumumba and neocolonialism: "The African Nations have understood: . . . they will put in place a shared mechanism which will allow them to support revolutionary struggles in countries that have not yet gained independence. Unity is war; influenced by Algeria, some are understanding better and better that it is also a socialist revolution."[49] Among those who better understood the economic implications of neocolonialism was Nasser, who had just begun steering the Egyptian economy in a decidedly socialist direction known to the world as Arab Socialism. At least on paper, by the exhibitionist manifestations of ideology, Egypt was an exemplary Third World revolutionary state: an example even for Europeans whose capitalist governments were complacent with neocolonial domination and thrived on the relentless exploitation of their own working classes.

Israel was also involved in the Congo. Just as in Ghana it arrived well before independence in search of business and legitimacy and offered across-the-board civilian aid in return. Lumumba was interested, and so were the heads of the other political parties. Upon Congo's independence, Israel took notice of the political fragmentation and mediated, helping bring Lumumba and the opposition closer together. But, when local politics failed, the Israelis felt compelled to choose sides; seeing the emerging relationship between Lumumba, Egypt, and the Soviet Union, they decided to go with the West: the United States and its handpicked ruler, Mobuto Sese Seko. Lumumba was forgotten and was soon declared dead. At the behest of the Americans, Mobuto asked Israel for military assistance, and over the next few years he got plenty of it. The United States could now see that Israel was a useful Cold War ally and, with the United States' blessing, Israeli military assistance was extended to Western Angola as well. The camp of Egypt, Ghana, and Cuba now found itself supporting rebel groups that fought against

Israeli-trained troops. Entangled in a proxy war in Congo, the Arab side had a solid proof that Israel was nothing but a tool in the service of ugly imperialism.[50]

Squarely in the American camp and working with the guidance and funding of the State Department and the CIA, by 1966 Israel had military training programs and direct sales of weapons in at least seventeen newly liberated African states including Ethiopia, Uganda, and Tanzania. It also significantly outspent the Egyptians in extending financial support for new regimes.[51] The crisis in Congo would continue until 1965 when all the rebellions that Egypt, the Soviet Union, and Cuba actively supported failed, and Mobutu managed to secure his post as a leader of a unified Congo and a close US ally for decades to come.

Looking back at about a decade of Egypt's ideologically driven involvement in Africa and its competition with Israel over the hearts, minds, and evolving state apparatuses of newly liberated countries, many in the Arab world could feel that they were on the right side of things. Through its massive broadcasting program and military advisers, Egypt supported liberation movements in word as well as in deed. Its synchronized rhetoric and policies were framed by the new theoretical model of neocolonialism and the need to resist it by force. All of that became perfectly clear in many of Nasser's speeches as well as in several new books on neocolonialism.[52] The fact that in the Arab world neocolonialism was experienced through rivalry with Israel created a strong association between the evolving theory of neocolonialism and the Zionist nature of Israel.

The struggle in Africa also revealed that the Arab world shared potential ideological allies in Europe. The same people of the Left who supported the causes of Algeria and Cuba saw the Congo affair, as well as Vietnam, in similar terms.[53] Accounting for the emerging transnational consensus of the Left regarding such struggles, in 1964 Sartre published *Colonialism and Neocolonialism*. Suhayl and ʿAida immediately recognized the value of this work and quickly translated it. This collection of previously published essays connected the seemingly separate issues of torture, racism, authenticity, otherness, freedom, and liberation into a more or less coherent ethical statement around which the Left was building its consensus with regard to the international dynamics of the Cold War and decolonization. Once again, in the center of it all was the question of human freedom.

By republishing Sartre's preface to Fanon's *The Wretched of the Earth*, this collection emphasized the link between group formation and anticolonial violence, which Sartre first articulated in his *Dialectical*

Critique of Reason.[54] Naturally, this piece justified as well as valorized the use of anticolonial violence and the right to resist. Aided by the emerging consensus on anticolonial violence, it delineated the contours of the "just camp" and distinguished it from the "other camp" or, in the words of Josie Fanon, the widow of the deceased theoretician and freedom fighter, "our camp" versus "the camp of the assassins" (see chapter 9). Through the rhetoric and actions of Egypt, and by virtue of its alignment with Sartre's new work, the progressive Arab world could assure itself that it was squarely situated in the right camp. It was now about time to focus on the workings of neocolonialism back home.

Bringing the War Home

In 1962, against the backdrop of Syria's divestment from its short-lived political unification with Egypt (known as the United Arab Republic), Egypt's self-asserting shift toward socialism, and, most importantly, the success of the Algerian revolution, Nasser was ready for a "second Congo." Fighting in Africa to defeat neocolonialism, he discovered a similar reality in Yemen, Egypt's backyard. The southern tip of Yemen, or Southern Arabia, was under the British Colony of Aden. The busy port of Aden, the refineries that surrounded it, and the many military installations made the colony one of the last lucrative businesses that the British held in that part of the world. Just as in the Congo, the northern part of the country was torn along tribal lines between so-called royalists and republicans. The fragmented political realities of Yemen with its multiple tribal alliances and commitments made it hard to plan and predict any political move. Nevertheless, simplifying a complex reality and reducing it to a bipolar struggle between good and bad, the Egyptians supported the "revolutionary" regime of general ʿAbdullah al-Sallal in Sanaa against the "reactionary" Saudi-backed royalist camp in the north. It is an irony of Arab history that during this internal Arab struggle the presumably reactionary and pro-imperialist house of Saud presided over the establishment of OPEC (Organization of the Petroleum Exporting Countries), the single most important economic move against neocolonialism during the second half of the twentieth century.

Nonetheless, the political schism between the "revolutionary" republic in the south and the "reactionary" regime in the north was aligned with a regional political order in which the "progressive" regimes in Syria, Iraq, and Egypt attacked the "reactionary" monarchies of Jordan,

Kuwait, and Saudi Arabia. In what would become a long and bloody civil war, the Egyptians supported the "republican" Yemenis, and the Saudis backed their "royalist" brothers. While the geopolitical realities were those of Yemen, the rhetoric and the political imagination through which this civil war was articulated were those of the Spanish Civil War. Could Egypt resist answering the call of history and joining the fight on behalf of the progressive global Left? The answer was no.

Commenting on this conflict, in an elegant piece for the *New Republic*, Patrick Seale opined that "President Nasser's armed intervention in Yemen is the most ambitious and dangerous foreign adventure of his career."[55] It was true. Aware of the risks, at first, the Egyptian operation was quite modest. In 1963 it deployed only a fifteen-thousand-strong expeditionary force. But by 1965 that force had ballooned to more than sixty thousand. As Nasser bitterly pointed out to a fellow revolutionary historian: "I sent a company to Yemen and had to reinforce it with 70,000 soldiers."[56] These soldiers were involved in a classic counterinsurgent warfare of the kind that was intimately familiar to the British and the French. "It was a devilish enterprise, this Arabian adventure, consisting of grueling chases after perfidious tribesmen along winding goat paths in the mountains; interminable hours spent in the stifling rear of sluggish, unprotected armored carriers waiting for an ambush at the next bend; and long cold nights standing guard atop barren hilltops expecting an ever imminent onslaught from the dark."[57] Two years into the war "successive campaigns north and east of Sanna had won them nothing, their casualties had been large, the drain on Egypt's treasury was vast."[58] Beyond the military aspects of the campaign, the full scope of the Egyptian revolutionary project in Yemen ranged from the drafting of a republican constitution to the construction, almost ex nihilo, of modern state institutions including education and healthcare systems. As historian Jesse Ferris skillfully showed, this *mission civilisatrice* was well beyond Egypt's capacities.[59] Yet, committed as it was to the global fight, it pushed on.

In 1963 the Egyptian war effort was split between the war against the Saudi-backed royalists and the British in Aden. Nasser explained: "We cannot accept at all that Britain continues to colonize a part of the Arab nation."[60] Inflammatory as always, in May 1964, the *Voice of the Arabs* radio station translated Nasser's inability to accept the British presence in Aden into a threat: "Tomorrow the revolution will extend to each of the 14 states which form the South Arabian Federation. Tomorrow the volcano will erupt in the heart of Aden; the free will destroy the base of colonialism; the revolutionaries will burn down the oil refineries."[61] Doing their own postimperial calculation of cost versus benefit, in February 1966 the British declared their intention to withdraw from Aden by 1968 and to dismantle their huge military and economic instillations.[62] The fight in the south appeared to be over. But Nasser had something else in mind: "Some may ask, why we fight for independence when the British will grant it freely in 1968? Comrades, true independence is not given away but taken . . . the people must wage armed revolution against the enemy, in which they must pay the highest price in life and blood."[63] The sacrificial politics of Nasserism revealed themselves once again, and the poor people of Yemen paid the price.

Zealous by definition, the deeper Egypt sunk into the hopeless battle against the royalists, the greater was its commitment. Celebrating this commitment in 1964, the Egyptian Information Service published a special edition of Nasser's speeches against neocolonialism.[64] Arguing that "the road to Palestine ran through Sanaa," the Egyptians established a firm link between the fight against neocolonialism in Yemen and the fight against the Zionists in Palestine as two aspects of the same cause. In a 1963 speech to soldiers returning from a tour in Yemen, Nasser exhorted his troops: "Sailing [home] from the honorable battle in Yemen, you were crying Palestine!"[65] At least theoretically, what started in Yemen should eventually continue in Palestine.[66]

Che's Return

In February 1965, as the war in Yemen dragged on, Che arrived in the Egyptian capital, which he used as a base from which to travel to Algeria, Tanzania, and the Congo. High on his agenda was the mission of "Cubanizing Congo." To recall, this was his second visit to Egypt. His previous stopover in June 1959 had been something of a failure. But much had changed since then. Aware of the Cuban revolution's growing fame in leftist international circles and of the similarity of their causes, Nasser replaced his domineering attitude with true admiration. Famously, under the unique circumstances that surrounded Nikita Khrushchev's UN session in September 1960, Nasser met Castro. Once, in New York City, Nasser and Castro were both harassed by the local press, the US State Department, and various American pressure groups. Shortly after the Bay of Pigs, when Castro was forced to leave the luxurious Shelburne Hotel and had nowhere to stay the night, he took the advice of local black activists and moved to the popular Hotel Theresa in Harlem, then a black ghetto. Malcolm X, Nehru, Khrushchev, and Nasser all went to visit him there for what became a signature moment that, however briefly, aligned the human rights struggles of Third Worlders with that of African Americans.[67] In some odd fashion, it could be seen as a precursor to the Tricontinental Conference that was held in Havana the following year. Though, as we have seen, much of the intellectual nexus between these seemingly different human conditions was articulated more than a decade earlier in Paris, West Africa, and Bandung, actual political networking was slower to emerge.

So, with renewed appreciation for all things Cuban and given the situation in Congo, Vietnam, and Yemen, to name a few struggles, Che and Nasser had much to talk about. And there was other business, too, as "it was on this trip that he [Che] first encountered camels, and no one could make him come down from these newly discovered quadrupeds, on which he rode around the pyramids."[68] But even the delight of camels could not really improve Che's apparent somber mood. Obviously, he was quite disillusioned by the situation in Congo, but, much more seriously than that, he seemed entirely lost as a revolutionary. Feeling that the revolutionary cause was being hijacked by petty bureaucrats, Che could not reconcile the translation of lofty revolutionary ideals into the small deeds of everyday governance. This topic also dominated his long interview with the progressive magazine *Al-Tali'a*.

Fresh out of prison, Lutfi al-Khuli and University of Paris–trained developmental economist Sabri 'Abdallah were there to ask questions.[69] Touching on topics such as the mobilization of the masses, the organization of production, the division of labor between the party and the state, the function of unions, and the role of the revolutionary leader, the interview focused almost exclusively on the boring technicalities of the Cuban revolution. The doubtful Che found much to criticize in the Cuban experience, and all of a sudden its socialism appeared fragile and inconclusive, a far cry from Sartre's glorious account of a socialist miracle. Almost as an afterthought, Che was briefly asked about exporting the Cuban revolution to other parts of the world. With guerrilla warfare in mind, Che was quite confident about the prospects of global resistance. That was the only ray of light in an otherwise skeptical interview, the longest he had ever given to the Arab press.[70]

In his meeting with Nasser, Che made it clear that he much preferred being in the battlefield where he can face the forces of reaction with arms. He kept talking about sacrifice and death. Puzzled, Nasser focused on life and said that a successful revolution was built out of mundane and boring bureaucratic actions. Establishing and running factories in a proper socialist manner was indeed boring and hard but, ultimately, socially rewarding.[71] But Che had little patience for this kind of state-run revolution. He wanted to fight and confided in Nasser that, regardless of his bleak assessment of the situation in Congo, he was thinking of joining the battle there. Drawing on Hollywood once again, Nasser warned him that Africans didn't need another white Tarzan to help them and, if they cared to do so, they should fight the revolution on their own with logistical help from the outside.[72] He cautioned Che not to rush headlong on into another people's revolution. He had a powerful rationale:

I experienced this in Yemen when the revolution started there. I jumped to its help, and although I received reports that the situation was not right for revolution, I said, like you, that the mere fact that it had started was an important subjective element in itself, and it should be helped. But then I discovered, first, that it could not be helped from outside; second, that it would take a long time and much agony; and while we can accelerate the historical process of the revolution, we cannot jump over the natural and chemical process that creates the forces of the revolution.[73]

Equally problematic, Nasser saw no hope in the Congo and opined that "the revolutionary process in Africa was being aborted by neocolonialism."[74] Che listened carefully but nonetheless left for seven months of inglorious and unmitigated jungle disaster that resulted in the triumph of his Congolese adversaries.[75] He never returned to the Middle East but he didn't really need to. The once-anonymous Che was by this time a familiar face and an inspiration to a new cadre of Palestinians who, against Nasser's will, would soon follow his example.[76]

Universalizing Palestine

In protest against the British assault on Egypt in 1956, Palestinian historian Walid Khalidi resigned his teaching position at Oxford and embarked on an independent scholarly course in line with the destiny of his people. After years of planning, in December 1963, he and economist and political activist Burhan Dajani cofounded the Institute for Palestine Studies in Beirut. The urgent task they faced was to salvage Palestinian history from oblivion as well as to research and analyze the current realities in Palestine. Studying Israel fell under their purview, thus making the institute the first academic body in the Arab world to pay serious intellectual attention to Zionism. Though living in Palo

Alto, California, and periodically teaching philosophy in Stanford as a nontenured lecturer, Fayiz Sayigh was immediately drawn to this new intellectual possibility and directed the center during its first year. His first contribution, *Zionist Colonialism in Palestine* (1965), was the institute's first full-length monograph to be published. This thin, readable, and highly polemic essay was such a success that before the end of the decade it was translated to several languages, including French, Italian, German, and Spanish. More than any other publication at the time, it connected the cause of Palestine to the major intellectual debates of the 1960s. Though many other publications of this kind would follow, one can see in this particular booklet the birth moment of the global cause of Palestine.[77]

For Sayigh, "The fate of Palestine . . . represents an anomaly, a radical departure from the trend of contemporary world history." This is because whereas scores of nations around the world were liberated by the process of decolonization, "the Arab people of Palestine was finding itself helpless to prevent the culmination of a process of systemic colonization to which Palestine had been subjected for decades."[78] Given his former UN experience, Sayigh must have been aware that the United Nations' working definition of colonialism as "Western rule of non-metropolitan areas" did not cover the situation in Palestine. Indeed, Resolution 1514 from December 1960, the most important resolution to date for "Granting of Independence to Colonial Countries and Peoples" excluded indigenous minorities living under the majority rule of Europeans.[79]

How to explain this historical anomaly? Why, Sayigh asked, did the "separate existence" of Jews in Palestine override that of Palestinians? What was the ethical basis for this form of discrimination? What kind of philosophy justified it? What were the unique qualities of Zionist colonialism that formed this reality and distinguish it from classical European colonialism? The aim of his essay was to raise these questions, identify the cultural specificity of Zionism, and debunk its exceptional ethical basis.[80] Succinctly, Sayigh drew on the emerging notion of "settler colonialism" to argue that "the Zionist settler-state of Israel is characterized chiefly by three features: (1) its racial complexion and racist conduct pattern; (2) its addiction to violence; and (3) its expansionist stance."[81] Beginning with race, he argued that "Zionist racial identification produces three corollaries: racial self-segregation, racial exclusiveness, and racial supremacy. These principles constitute the core of the Zionist ideology."[82] Each of these came at the expense of native Palestinians and resulted in a situation that had no parallel in European colonialism: "Nowhere in Asia or Africa—not even in South Africa or Rhodesia—had European race-supremacism expressed itself in so passionate a zeal for thoroughgoing racial exclusiveness and for physical expulsion of native populations across the frontiers of the settler-state, as it has in Palestine, under the compulsion of Zionist doctrines."[83]

How should Palestinians respond? "Rights undefended," wrote Sayigh, "are rights surrendered."[84] In line with the emerging guerrilla ethos of the 1960s, Sayigh prescribed stiff resistance, thus subscribing to the political culture of decolonization and its belief that "the cause of anti-colonialism and liberation is one and indivisible."[85] Drawing on this indivisibility, Sayigh appealed to a broad-based leftist audience outside the Middle East and called upon them to reconsider their position on Palestine on sheer moral grounds: "the political systems erected by Zionist colonists in Palestine cannot fail to be recognized as a menace by all civilized men dedicated to the safeguarding and enhancement of the dignity of man. For whenever and wherever the dignity of but one single human being is violated, in pursuance of the creed of racism, a heinous sin is committed against the dignity of all men, everywhere."[86]

Passionate, lucid, and well argued, as a piece of intellectual activism Sayigh's *Zionist Colonialism in Palestine* hit all the major political categories of the 1960s, such as racial supremacy, segregation, exclusion, civil rights, emancipation, self-defense, and resistance. It invoked Algerian settler colonialism as well as the dire realities of black Americans with which he had a firsthand familiarity.[87] One can easily see the intellectual connection between his line of thought and the UN resolution from 1975 according to which Zionism is a type of racism. To no one's surprise, in due time he would be heavily involved in the making of this resolution.[88] Most interestingly to our discussion, in style as well as in its philosophical assumptions about race and otherness, Sayigh's book had Sartre's fingerprints all over it. That Sayigh agreed with Sartre was obvious, but would Sartre agree with Sayigh? That was an altogether different matter.

Sayigh's booklet is just one fine example of the kind of new writings about Zionism and Israel that some Arab intellectuals began to compose as they left behind the superficial characterization of Zionism as "imperialism" that prevailed during the 1950s. Seeking to universalize the problem of Palestine, Sayigh preceded even leftist European contributors such as Maxime Rodinson. Both writers, as we shall later see, eventually published their critiques of Israel in Sartre's special issue on the conflict. What brought them together was also what set them apart from the majority of writers in the Arab world. As an intellectual of the French Left, Rodinson had no problem critiquing Zionism and identifying with Palestinians. Yet, at the same time, as a Jew who had lost his parents in Auschwitz, he would not partner with a Palestinian cause that traded its universalism for anti-Semitism and Holocaust denial. Both Rodinson and Sayigh recognized that to universalize the cause of Palestine the cause had to purge and distance itself completely from anti-Semitism and, increasingly, to acknowledge the Holocaust and the suffering of the Jews. This, in a nutshell, was the main challenge that progressive intellectuals like Lutfi al-Khuli had to reckon with.

Even a brief and superficial review of Arab media and public conversation during the 1960s would immediately reveal that anti-Semitism was becoming more prevalent and that the denial and minimization of the Holocaust had become commonplace. The vicious broadcasting of Egyptian radio, which was helped by at least two former Nazi propaganda specialists, signaled the magnitude of the challenge of the Arab Left.[89] Arguing against a growing anti-Semitic tide that conflated Zionism with Judaism, even Sayigh and al-Khuli, two progressive voices who acknowledged the horrors of the Holocaust and drew on an Arab intellectual tradition that wholeheartedly resisted anti-Semitism, ended up drawing parallels between the Nazi extermination of the Jews and Zionist violence against Palestinians.[90]

Framed by the principled position against racism and neocolonialism, their basic observation was that since Israel was both racist and neocolonial it might have more in common with Nazi violence that it cared to admit. The point was not to belittle the Holocaust but to amplify and elevate the tragedy of Palestinians. Writing at the beginning of the Eichmann trial in Jerusalem, al-Khuli explained, "Our movement holds a distinction between Jews as people and the Zionist movement as a hostile colonial current."[91] With this in mind, and "given our revolutionary nature and our position against colonialism and racism, we cannot defend Eichmann and Nazism." For the same reason, "we [also] object to Ben Gurion's position as well as to that of international Zionism," which we consider "a hostile entity."[92] Taking the argument one step further and seeing racism as a common denominator between Zionism and Nazism, al-Khuli drew a false parallel between the racial violence of the Nazis and that of the Zionists. Seeing absolutely no philosophical and qualitative difference between the two, he wrote that "the crimes of Zionism are an extension of Nazi crimes."[93] Sayigh took this line of thought even further and equated the creation of a "Jew-free Germany" with that of an "Arab-free Palestine."[94]

What made the moral economy of al-Khuli's and Sayigh's position so problematic was that their strategy sought to universalize the realities of Palestine not only by developing justificatory universal terms (as indeed they did) but also by equating them with the terms of the Holocaust and insisting that, essentially, Zionists were a type of Nazi. Though even in Europe public consciousness of the exceptionality of the Holocaust took decades to develop and was by no means apparent during the 1960s, the analogy between Zionism and Nazism was, on a gut level, at odds with the unprocessed and unarticulated beliefs of many left-wing European intellectuals. Indeed, in the long run, especially after the 1970s, placing Zionism and Nazism on the same moral level did not assist in the effort to universalize Palestine as a just international cause. Quite the contrary.

Gradually, it appeared that the cause of Palestine hinged on acknowledging the exceptionality of the Holocaust. By that point, scholars of the Holocaust had developed an impressive interpretive grid and established practices of cultural coding and narration that transformed Nazism into a binding metaphor for extreme and unparalleled evil. The status of the Holocaust as a unique, exceptional, yet universal horror defied any equation with the Nakba.[95] Facing this process posed a huge challenge. If the leading intellectual and political forces of the Arab world dreamed of a successful passage to universalism, they would be asked to avow the historical exceptionality of the Holocaust and drop all parallels to Zionist actions in Palestine.

Having said that, as of 1965 it was probably hard to imagine that such nuances in arguments about racism would matter much, as the Holocaust had not yet been processed on an international level. As we shall shortly see, these unprocessed positions, beliefs, intuitions, and gut feelings still mattered greatly and eventually exploded in the most unexpected of circumstances. For instance, around the dining table when, in June 1967, Lutfi, Liliane, Sartre, and Beauvoir met as friends to discuss the recent war in Middle East. Whatever happened around that table, in the privacy of a Parisian apartment, would have huge implications for the Arab Left and the problem of Palestine as a universal cause.

Conclusion

After celebrating the Algerian revolution and hailing its historic achievement as a model for liberation struggles everywhere, including in the

United States, in June 1965 the legendary leader of the FLN Ahmed Ben Bella was ousted by a military coup and placed under house arrest. A similar fate awaited Nkrumah, who in February 1966 went into exile. A month later Indonesia's Sukarno was ousted. Against this background, the so-called second Bandung Conference, scheduled to take place in Algiers, was canceled.[96] The first generation of Third World regimes, a hopeful revolutionary experiment, inched closer to its end.[97] Yet, despite this sense of closure, the Arab revolutionary camp and Nasser's many followers could proudly say that they remained true to their ideals and committed to the global fight. To a degree, the January 1966 Tricontinental Conference in Havana, the movement's largest gathering, vindicated this position and illustrated that the revolutionary cause was still alive. As if to signal business as usual, Egypt opened a luxurious social club in downtown Havana.

By this point the notional infrastructure of the global 1960s was so well entrenched, and the revolutionary fervor so high, that many in the Middle East believed that, even in Europe, the future of socialism depended on the success of the revolution in the Third World. Not only Arabs felt that they were more revolutionary than the European Left, Europeans thought so too. In Charles de Gaulle's France, for instance, the Left was rumored to be in a coma. In an excellent book about the impact of Maoism in France, Richard Wolin illustrated how "many apostles of revolutionary struggle, like Sartre, Régis Debray and Herbert Marcuse, had flirted with Third Worldism. If the working class in advanced industrial societies seemed uninterested in revolution, in an era of decolonization, perhaps the 'wretched of the earth' would set in motion global capitalism's downfall."[98] This anticipation was widely shared by the pre–May 1968 European Left, who grew "accustomed to the idea that politically significant ideas always occurred elsewhere—in Eastern Europe, North Africa, Cuba and Asia. Thus in an era of global struggle to topple imperialism French radicals had been consigned to act as cheerleaders, demonstrating in support of Che, Arafat, Castro and Ho Chi Minh."[99]

Granted, Arab revolutionaries were not alone. Coming organically with the terrain of Third World internationalism were Sartre's ad hoc ethics of global responsibility. Undoubtedly, this project filled up an important lacuna that neither Bandung, with its preoccupation with the abstraction of identity, nor the many conferences and meetings that followed it could address. In order to be successful, the engagements of the 1960s needed an ethical framework that could later be developed into more general principles for political action. By traveling to multiple sites of struggle and writing about them Sartre did precisely that. Though the project would eventually be branded "unfinished," and his actions declared out of pace with his philosophy, his activism articulated and popularized a *codex universum* that both anchored and legitimized the cause. Furthermore, as a movement that preceded by a decade or two the rise of the human rights movement, the inability of mainstream international politics to identify and define colonialism as a human rights problem exposed a huge intellectual gap that Sartre tried to fill with his global activism.

Not only the people of the Middle East responded positively to Sartre's blend of existentialism and global ethics, so did intellectuals in war-torn Vietnam. There "existentialism offered Saigon intellectuals a way of explaining their chaotic and ambiguous wartime situation. It offered them the potential to believe that their good-faith actions might make meaning out of the seemingly random and occasionally unspeakable violent events of South Vietnam in the 1960s."[100] And still, unlike Vietnam, Sartre's legacy in the Arab world was so profound and constitutive of Arab liberation projects that it entailed a huge set of expectations. Probably the most important of these was that Sartre would be intellectually consistent and apply the conceptual language of existential humanism—which he had applied to the cases of Algeria, Cuba, and Congo—to Palestine.

EIGHT

High Hopes

At the start of 1967 Jean-Paul Sartre was an Arab hero. By its end, a traitor. In between, he visited the Middle East. This chapter tells the tale of that in-between. The major question that hovered over his visit was what Sartre would say. Would he take a clear position on any side's behalf? Would he name names and place blame with any of the parties? After wholeheartedly committing himself to the important causes of his time, intervening in what was called the Arab-Israeli conflict was a natural course of action. Indeed, given his connections and general appeal in the region, some believed a Sartrean intervention was long overdue.

Calls came not only from his Arab interlocutors but also from Sartre's own neighborhood. To recall one such example, upon Sartre's rejection of the Nobel Prize, the Jewish philosopher Emmanuel Levinas, then fifty-eight years of age, wrote Sartre to say that "by declining the prize you won the right to speak." Fearful of Israel's fate, Levinas urged Sartre to go to Egypt and meet Nasser: "He would listen only to you."[1] Eventually, in the weeks and days leading up to the 1967 war, Levinas's existential fear for the survival of Israel would take on a life of its own, and he would push the reluctant Sartre to take sides. But that would come later. For now, on the eve of Sartre's February 1967 visit to the Middle East, both Arabs and Israelis were anxious to illustrate their socialist and revolutionary credentials and hoped their display would entice the philosopher, and possibly the entire French Left, to their side.

Especially eager were the Egyptians, who had grounds to believe that their model of non-Soviet revolutionary socialism would appeal to Sartre in the same way that Cuba did.

But how did these respective expectations look on the ground—once the French group arrived in the Middle East? How were Sartre, Beauvoir, and Lanzmann received in the region? Whom did they meet and on what terms? What were their reactions to painful experiences, such as those of Palestinian refugees in Gaza and Holocaust survivors in Israel? Did Sartre, Beauvoir, and Lanzmann share the same views on the nature of the conflict? If not, how did these differences affect Sartre and his relationship with both Arabs and Jews? Before we turn to examine these questions, a word is in order about what scholars have made of Sartre's vision of conflict resolution.

As briefly mentioned in chapter 1, regarding Sartre's overall understanding of the Jewish question, Jonathan Judaken has provided the most serious analysis to date of Sartre's position on the conflict. Complemented by the work of Paige Arthur, Judaken's strategy has produced the best explanation to date for Sartre's inability to provide a clear ethical statement.[2] According to Judaken, Sartre subscribed to a protopostmodern position that saw conflicts such as that in the Middle East as fundamentally irreconcilable. With this, the only viable option for the engaged intellectual was to bear witness and register the divide with the understanding that "one side's legitimacy does not imply the other's lack of legitimacy."[3] Calling the Arab-Israeli conflict the *différend judéo-arabe*, Sartre anticipated Jean-François Lyotard's full-fledged argument about the *différend* as a "case of conflict, between [at least] two parties that cannot be equitably resolved for lack of a rule of judgment applicable to both arguments."[4]

Thus, given these irreconcilable differences, bearing witness was a position in which everything that Sartre wrote, said, and did would not and could not apply equally to both sides. In other words, because "no universal discourse . . . can provide a final arbitration of dispute," Sartre's legacy, and in particular its Arab reading, forfeited its alleged universality.[5] While this judgment still holds, the process by which Sartre came to embrace this position needs to be spelled out. After all, during the 1967 fallout between Sartre and the Arabs, even the forty-three-year-old Lyotard did not yet conceive of the Arab-Israeli conflict as a différend. Quite the opposite. Lyotard and many other intellectuals of the French Left had a clear position on the conflict, and it was not a pro-Arab one.

In Egypt

On February 25, 1967, Sartre, Beauvoir, and Lanzmann arrived in Cairo aboard a private airplane sent to pick them up. Flying in the opposite direction was another intellectual, ʿAbd al-Rahman Badawi, the leading existentialist philosopher and translator who, in despair, had given up on life in Egypt and soon took an academic position at the Sorbonne, where he stayed until his death.[6] But Badawi's departure by no means dampened Arab enthusiasm for the real thing and, indeed, "Egypt received Sartre not as a thinker but as an international organization."[7] Striking a positive note, Sartre published an open letter in Arabic to his hosts.

For a long time, and especially since the Algerian war of liberation, bonds of fraternity tie us together. . . . I am delighted to hear how you perceive your struggle against reaction. There are many paths that could lead to Socialism and I sense that your early experience is of benefit to many others and especially to those of us who come from the West. . . . All I hope is to hear from you about the path that associates socialism and freedom. . . . I know how much you are interested in the various revolutionary movements and your awareness of the global role of your revolution. I believe that it won't be a waste of time if we work together to understand how to make a better reconciliation between local specificity and globalism [ʿalamiyya]. Happily awaiting our conversation, I send you my brotherly regards.[8]

From Beirut, in the journal *Al-Adab*, Suhayl Idris warmly greeted Sartre and Beauvoir and thanked them for acknowledging the Arab struggle for "socialism, freedom, unity and peace." "However," he reminded readers, "this visit has another important side and that is to persuade Sartre to support the foremost just Arab cause of Palestine."[9] Idris felt that given Beauvoir and Sartre's record of unflinching support for progressive causes, a visit to the region would dispel what he called "Zionist propaganda." With this objective in mind, he called upon fellow Arab intellectuals to simplify and clarify the problem of Palestine so that the two luminaries could see the light.[10] By contrast, *Al-Ahram*'s welcoming editorial did not mention a word on the problem of Palestine.[11] These differences in emphasis were by no means a coincidence. Indeed, for *Al-Ahram*, it was an Egyptian moment, a celebration of their revolution and, as one popular magazine put it, a real "intellectual wedding" (*farah fikri*).[12]

FIGURE 4 Lanzmann, Beauvoir, and Sartre in an optimistic beginning.
Photo by Keystone-France/Gamma-Keystone via Getty Images.

And so, on that afternoon in late February, Husayn Fawzi, Luwis ʿAwad, Anis Mansur, and Lutfi al-Khuli, a representative circle of Egypt's foremost progressive intellectuals, greeted the couple at the airport. Though not a revolutionary intellectual, the beret-wearing playwright Tawfiq al-Hakim was also there. He was the only Egyptian intellectual whose work Beauvoir and Sartre had read and the only one to publish in *Les Temps Modernes*.[13] Taha Husayn was not invited and learned of the visit from the press. He told a reporter he had no hard feelings.[14] As agreed, ʿAli al-Samman assumed his responsibilities as a tour guide. The Egyptian press took pride in his role and viewed it as another indication that Sartre had been in concert with Egyptian intellectuals all along.[15] To celebrate as well as shed light on this special relationship,

Egypt's leading pundits and academics published a voluminous stream of commentary on Sartre's philosophy and Beauvoir's ideas. The most sophisticated philosophical coverage appeared in *Al-Fikr al-Muʿasir* and *Al-Taliʿa*, both of which also paid close attention to Beauvoir's feminism.[16] A special issue of the popular magazine *Al-Hilal* with Beauvoir, Sartre, and, of all choices, a seminaked Brigitte Bardot on the front and back covers, also offered serious coverage. Never in modern Arab history had a living foreign intellectual elicited so much interest. Local expectations ran very high.

Intellectually enthusiastic, Egyptians insisted on engaging Sartre at every occasion, even when time was pressing and the guest was visibly exhausted.[17] Whenever official business concluded the unofficial business began. One afternoon, al-Samman wrote, "a group of wives of leftist political prisoners surprised us with a visit at the Shepheard Hotel. They had sneaked into the hotel from a side terrace, located Sartre, and begged him to ask Nasser to release their husbands. . . . Most of the men had been in prison for two to three years, without even the formality of a trial."[18] But not all obligations were so serious, and having fun was definitely on the agenda.

Thus, occasionally, even when night fell and the day was over, Sartre, it seemed, could not get enough of Cairo. One midnight he dragged Tawfiq al-Hakim on a walk along the Nile.[19] On other occasions he got seriously drunk. Lanzmann recalled that "on more than one occasion al-Samman and I had to hold Sartre upright as he staggered back to his suite. He could not bear to be dependent on us and one night as we were carrying him back, even more drunk than usual, he started to insult us, his voice slurred, calling us 'queers,' insinuating that we were the prime example of how to resolve the conflict. ʿAli, who was unfamiliar with Sartre's cantankerous, drunken ravings, could not believe his eyes or ears. Since I was used to such behavior, I reassured al-Samman that everything would be fine in the morning and that the great man would not remember a thing."[20] And so it was, and the next morning, Sartre was back to business.

With Nasser

By the mid-1960s Sartre had visited, acknowledged, and hailed a whole gallery of revolutionary leaders. Nasser was not one of them. His 1960 book *Sartre on Cuba* was the most glaring example of how to celebrate a revolution and its leaders, and Egyptians, including their president, expected the same treatment.[21] In fact—misinformed about a forthcoming publication in *Les Temps Modernes*—in 1967 many Egyptians believed that Sartre was writing a book about Egypt, perhaps similar to his celebratory account of the Cuban revolution.[22] Finally, they thought, after years in which he refused to visit Egypt, the philosopher of freedom was ready to meet and acknowledge Nasser. Their meeting lasted three hours and included Sartre, Beauvoir, al-Samman, Lanzmann, and Haykal. Nasser reviewed the contours of the Arab-Israeli conflict and the difficulties in finding credible solutions to the refugee problem. He said that "war is a difficult thing" that Egypt would rather avoid. His tone was measured, reflective, and guarded. Beauvoir observed a certain "melancholy charm."[23] Nasser had excellent knowledge of who was in the room and took special interest in Lanzmann and his intimate understanding of Israel. The two had a long and frank conversation, one that left a very positive impression on Lanzmann. "One knows when one is in the presence of a statesman. Nasser was one, certainly," Lanzmann wrote. It was clear, he recalled again in 2012, that "Nasser did not want war."[24] Al-Samman also described a long and intimate exchange between Nasser and Lanzmann.[25]

Recalling his meeting with the wives of leftist prisoners in his hotel, Sartre asked Nasser to account for the systematic imprisonment of leftwing intellectuals. Nasser explained that the intellectuals were better off under administrative detention than they would be if they had to endure a formal prosecution, because in the former situation the judge would sentence them to long prison terms without the possibility of presidential parole. In administrative detention, so the argument went, the president could at least intervene.[26] Sartre did not argue with the idiosyncratic logic of the state, but pleaded with Nasser to release eighteen communist prisoners. Next came Beauvoir's interest in the state of the Egyptian women. Egyptian state feminism was at its zenith at the time, and Nasser was well versed in the cause of Arab women and supported their call to establish some form of gender equality. He explained to Beauvoir his campaign against female genital mutilation and its criminalization in 1958. Beauvoir later said about their conversation, "It is difficult to believe that he doesn't mean every word he says."[27] Sartre himself was also impressed by Nasser's global commitment; overall, an atmosphere of good faith and mutual understanding prevailed throughout the meeting.

To his guests' satisfaction, a few days later, Nasser released the communist prisoners.[28] Both sides regarded the meeting as a success (though, afterward, some journalists were ordered to destroy their film because Lanzmann allegedly had shown disrespect toward Nasser—Lanzmann's shirt was unbuttoned, and he put his hands in his pockets).[29] Even al-Samman got something out of this successful interaction: immediately after, Nasser held a private meeting with him and appointed him head of the Western European branch of the Middle East News Agency.[30] Al-Samman's bet had paid off.

With Students, Writers, and Women

Next on the schedule of the French triumvirate was an astonishing array of appointments with local intellectuals, writers, critics, artists, directors, poets, journalists, and activists. Most of these took place in Cairo, where Sartre shook hands with students in al-Azhar and attended a local production of *No Exit* ("The actors understood my play," he said).[31] But, without question, the cornerstone of their time in Cairo was the two public lectures that Sartre and Beauvoir delivered at Cairo University. Sartre spoke of the role of intellectuals in contemporary society and Beauvoir of the role of women in the modern era. Speaking on different nights, on both occasions the lecture hall was packed with thousands of ecstatic students and faculty members. More women than men attended Beauvoir's talk.

"Have you all read my work?" Sartre asked his audience. "I do not think so. I am nothing but a fashion to you."[32] He then delivered a long and somewhat hollow lecture in which he spoke in heroic yet general terms about intellectuals in bourgeois society.[33] At the urging of 'Ali al-Samman, he was careful to distinguish Western from Egyptian socialist intellectuals. But the speech had nothing of substance to say about intellectuals in the Arab world, let alone those in Egypt. At the end of the lecture students asked equally general questions about freedom, socialism, and, of course, existentialism. One student even asked Sartre to quit smoking as "service to humanity."[34] The only meaningful moment during the night came in response to a question about the current meaning of committed literature. Sartre's answer was sharp: "A few days ago I already told your colleagues that committed literature [*adab multazim*] is not purposive literature [*al-adab al-muwajja*]. If we can call it literature at all, purposive literature is in reality nothing but the writing of politically oriented texts. It might be good writing but it is not literature. In my mind committed literature is one in which the writer ponders the totality of his existence in the world."[35] Indeed, earlier that week, Sartre had told writers, "When I called for committed literature I did not mean propaganda."[36] These critical words echoed Tawfiq al-Hakim's and Taha Husayn's condemnations of iltizam, and it is very likely that al-Hakim and Sartre discussed the matter privately prior to this lecture.

In contrast to Sartre's bland lecture, which one foreign listener characterized as "a piece of crap," Simone de Beauvoir delivered before a mostly female crowd a passionate, courageous, and penetrating analysis of the female condition in Egypt.[37] Inspired by her meetings with supportive Egyptian feminists, Beauvoir's text was normative, universal, and, inevitably, judgmental: "When I examine the state of women in Egypt today I see a contradiction: On the one hand I face a society that successfully struggles to eradicate feudalism. At the same time your society still preserves feudal traditions such as the subordination of women."[38] Her mission that evening was to expose the typical cultural mechanism of subordination. She did so by explaining how societies create "a logic of difference" between men and women and utilize it to justify the social practice of inequality. She gave a powerful example: "The pattern of inequality which is based on (the logic of) difference is the very same one that white American racists employ in order to segregate the white from the black."[39] She then told her audience that she saw that very same mechanism at work in Egyptian society. Since racial segregation was something that educated Egyptians mentioned whenever the topic of America arose, the analogy to flawed gender relations was quite damning.

But Beauvoir was not simply being theoretical. She had witnessed this reality firsthand a few days earlier: "Women, if I am allowed to say so, are traditional entities that live a life of repetition: home making."[40] This tradition binds them and perpetuates their subordination. "In every opportunity I had to speak with women it became clear to me that they support [their] liberation strongly and that it is men who oppose it . . . they are obviously unhappy with subordination," which she called, "a problem of human dignity."[41] Beauvoir then argued that, far from being a natural condition, such inequality was a socially constructed phenomenon that extended to all spheres of life including the workplace.[42] Notably, during this lecture, Beauvoir's terms of discussion were the familiar terms of neocolonialism, applied to the state of women. Like black people and colonized subjects, women were deemed unfit and inferior, thus bearing internally the justification for their continued subjugation. And, as with decolonization at large, human dignity was at stake. It appears she had told Nasser the same.[43]

It was now the students' turn to ask her questions:

Mr. Fakhri: Since women are more emotionally sensitive than men it is dangerous for them to take political responsibilities. This observation obviously negates your opinion. I assume that you think that way because you never had any political responsibility. What do you think about that?[44]

Beauvoir: I am not interested in political responsibilities but in writing. . . . My method of inquiry into such matters is objective and hence truthful. I think that in my lecture I stated the truth when I told you that this is a world which is made by men (and for men) and I hope that it would change. . . . I said what I said because a large number of the women I encountered suffer from the condition that was imposed on them. I also said so because of the great loss which [your] society experiences when it deprives itself of the potential of women.[45]

Other questions followed:

Ms. al-Sharif: Has any fundamental shift in your perception of women's condition occurred since you published *The Second Sex*?

Beauvoir: No. My position did not change at all. What I told you today is basically a summary of what I presented in *The Second Sex*. . . .[46]

Ms. 'Ali: Isn't it necessary for men to participate in the duties of home keeping in order to have equality?

Beauvoir: Obviously. Labor should be (equally) divided. . . .[47]

Mr. Mahmud: What do you think about marriage?

Beauvoir: Well, I think that marriage should be a free partnership between men and women . . . and that each one of them should have the possibility to withdraw from this partnership if they so choose. However, in most cases, for women, marriage is a burden . . . a form of domination that men exercise.[48]

Beauvoir made it clear that she had not come to Egypt to make nice. Later she recalled, "I accused the Egyptian men of behaving like feudalists, colonialists and racists toward women . . . the very large number of women in the audience applauded frantically. . . . Other women came to thank me, sometimes behind their husbands' backs."[49] When the evening was over and the students turned to go home, they obviously had much to think about. Some men were unhappy, she recalled: "When I left an old gentlemen accosted me, he was carrying a paper he had written on the Koran. 'As for women's inequality, Madame, it forms part of religion—it is written in the Koran.'"[50] Beauvoir too thought of the problem in such terms: "the tradition of Islam is opposed to equality, and for the moment it is tradition that prevails."[51] In response, some journalists accused her of "not understanding that dissimilarities between men and women are derived of different psychological makeup."[52] Despite the controversy evoked by her words, in all of her public dealings in Egypt, Beauvoir took a critical position toward Arab men and the institution of patriarchy.

With Workers

The visit to Aswan was aimed at celebrating the technological miracle of the High Dam in Aswan, which for most Egyptians was not simply a hydroelectric and irrigation project but a vehicle for the total transformation of Egypt from an agrarian feudal society to an advanced industrialized one. Even before it was completed, and beyond the expected electrification of the Nile valley, the dam was already transforming the very essence of Egyptian men and women, turning them into new revolutionary beings. The most complete artistic manifestation of that radical metamorphosis was *The High Dam*, a painting by ʿAbd al-Hadi al-Jazzar (1925–1966). This work celebrated the mechanical, industrialized, and scientific anatomy of the new revolutionary man. In a kind of symbiotic relationship, a man in al-Jazzar's painting was building the dam and the dam was transforming the man. Indeed, Beauvoir remembered that Egyptians spoke of the dam as a powerful "civilizing force."[53] Both state and society took special pride in this revolutionary wonder, and the High Dam became a site of pilgrimage.

As the guardians of a national monument—a modern pyramid, if you will—Aswan's officials were accustomed to a steady stream of high-profile visits, as heads of state and dignitaries like Soviet Premier Nikita Khrushchev arrived throughout the year. So were the airport employees who, on the morning of Sartre and Beauvoir's arrival, discussed the usual business of the day.

Worker I: Who is coming today?
Worker II: They bring one named Sastro.
Worker III: Castro is coming not Sastro.[54]

Neither the former Indonesian Prime Minister Sastro (ʿAli Sastroamidjojo) nor Castro arrived that day, but Sartre and his company indeed did. Again, they had a busy schedule. They toured the dam where

Sartre was most interested in speaking to workers about their social benefits. The workers also had questions:

Worker: How is it possible to reconcile your previous position on Marxism with your current one?
Sartre: The simple answer is that I have changed my mind.
Worker: What do you think of racial segregation?
Sartre: The struggle against racial segregation turned violent and I maintain that the only way to confront this issue is through violence. Confronting violence with violence is the only solution.[55]

Female workers also had questions, not so much for Sartre about philosophy as for Beauvoir about marriage:

(Female) Worker: In some of your work you expressed skepticism [toward men] and a sense of being oppressed by them. Is that why you did not marry and have children?
Beauvoir: I decided not to marry and have children so I can write and think of these problems. The systematic class discrimination against women is not restricted to the workplace alone but extends into the domain of the house and the raising of the children.
(Male) Worker: Fine, but what do you think of marriage?
Beauvoir: It is an individual matter. Each person should decide for himself/herself. Men have more benefits in marriage. The important thing is that women should be able to divorce in mutual agreement and that one side would not impose his wishes on the other.[56]

It was probably for the best that the workers in Aswan had no knowledge of the fact that not only did Beauvoir not marry "her life-time partner" Sartre but, in fact, for much of the previous decade she was the lover of the man who stood next to him: Claude Lanzmann.

Intimate affairs aside, a horde of journalists were eager to discuss philosophy. Sartre replied that, to talk philosophy, he needed a minimum of three hours. He therefore asked Lutfi al-Khuli to arrange that time once they were back in Cairo. In place of philosophy, Sartre gave a fiery anti-imperial speech in which he denounced the crimes of the United States in Vietnam and endorsed the "rights of peoples."[57] He also reiterated his historical position on the question of national liberation: "Obviously I am emphatically against war. However, at the same time I stand firm on the side of national liberation movements. From the first instance I stood against American imperialism in Vietnam and sided with the Algerian struggle for liberation because I believed that freedom and peace would prevail in Algeria only with the triumph of the Algerian revolution."[58]

Eventually, the time arrived to discuss more substantial issues. Mahmud Amin al-ʿAlim was the right person to lead this discussion. Entering the lecture hall to attend al-ʿAlim's lecture, Sartre stopped by a display of his translated work. He was very pleased yet suddenly said in disbelief, "What is that? What is that?" His book *Existentialism Is Humanism* had a naked woman on its front cover. His hosts explained that "unfortunately, it's a commercial edition" published in the recent past, when the meaning of existentialism (previously associated in the popular imagination with sex) differed from what it had since become (serious philosophy).[59] Next came al-ʿAlim with a serious argument about philosophy.

Addressing Sartre's interest in understanding how Egyptian socialism furthers individual freedom, al-ʿAlim drew on his own work from the previous decade and argued that existentialism was external to the local notion of socialist freedom and, as such, largely irrelevant to Egyptian revolutionary efforts. Still hostile toward radical individualism, he stated that in Egypt the freedom of the individual was derived from the success of socialism's collective effort to create a just and egalitarian society. In this scheme, "the most important political challenge of our day is to share the responsibility of governing with the masses."[60] It was a defense of the Egyptian socialist understanding of individual freedom and a response to Sartre's open letter and the core of his intellectual agenda: individual freedom.

Not to undo the importance of al-ʿAlim's critique for an Arab audience, the truth was that Sartre had already faced this criticism two decades earlier, when French communists attacked existentialism as a "contemplative philosophy, philosophy *de luxe* and bourgeoisie philosophy." It had been maligned as a "metaphysical pathology" and a literature of "grave diggers."[61] Compared to this critique, al-ʿAlim was very polite. Sartre told him what he had told the dam worker a few hours earlier: "I have changed my mind." In a more substantial manner he then explained that his *Critique of Dialectical Reason* was a response to this criticism, and that his "new existentialism" successfully reconfigured the relationship between existentialism and Marxism. He therefore explained that "existentialism searches for solutions from within Marxism" and not outside it. According to Sartre, the only point of disagreement between existentialism and Marxism concerned "inevitability" and "determinism." He concluded by insisting that existentialism could also be Marxist and revolutionary.[62]

Yet, in contrast with Syrian intellectuals, many Egyptians were not persuaded by this explanation. Though al-'Alim seemed never to have read *Critique of Dialectical Reason*, Isma'il al-Mahdawi had published a review of that "difficult book" and was in an excellent position to judge it. He asked, "Did Sartre really become an existentialist Marxist?" "As far as philosophy is concerned, the answer is no" answered al-Mahdawi.[63] According to al-Mahdawi, while Marxism comprised three ideational branches—namely, dialectical materialism (philosophy), historical materialism (social science), and the scientific analysis of capitalism (economics)—Sartre addressed the second and third components but excluded philosophy. Given that limited focus, al-Mahdawi maintained that Sartre rejected everything that was external to the individual, such as "historical dialectic" and sought to replace it with unscientific "existential or individual dialectic." Al-Mahdawi's analysis led him to conclude that forces external to the individual, such as society at large, did not fare well in Sartre's philosophy, and that Sartre practically rejected dialectical Marxism, determinism, Marxist epistemology (*ma'rifa*) and, consequently, the entire objectivity of external reality (namely, society). In its place, Sartre envisioned an unspecified situation in which the truth of reality would be "transformed into the language of the individual."[64] Lucian Sayf published a similar critique in *Al-Hilal*.[65] Thus, in Aswan and elsewhere, Egyptian intellectual energies were directed against this particular issue, which seemed to undermine their understanding of socialist society and, by implication, their revolutionary achievements.

With Peasants

On the opposite side of the country another revolutionary achievement was waiting to be acknowledged: the village of Kamshish. Situated in al-Manufiya province at the heart of the delta, Egypt's agricultural center, Kamshish was the most recent example of how Egypt's revolutionary cadre was successfully fighting feudalism. As a symbol, Kamshish stood for the confiscation of land from oppressive landowners and the rehabilitation of peasants' rights. Truly, there were real heroes in the story of Kamshish, such as the slain rural teacher and social activist Salah Husayn and his widow Shahinda Maqlad.[66] Salah confronted the largest landowning family in the village and paid with his life. Sartre

FIGURE 5 In Kamshish: from right, Shahinda Maqlad, Sartre, al-Samman, Beauvoir, Liliane al-Khuli, and an unidentified official. Courtesy of 'Ali al-Samman.

heard the heroic story of Kamshish and the struggle of its poor inhabitants for dignity and land. The role of women in bringing down that bastion of feudalism through street activism and by leading the masses was self-evident. Beyond that, the French knew little of the rural politics that were unfolding at the moment of their visit.

Sometime in February, rumors had circulated in Kamshish about a forthcoming high-profile visit. The villagers were still in a struggle with the governorate over development plans when Shahinda Maqlad got hold of Lutfi al-Khuli, who confirmed the rumors. But as soon as the villagers started planning the details of the visit, they ran into opposition from the governorate, which wished to select and train a delegation of twenty peasants to meet with the guests. The locals, who requested an open meeting, were warned that "Egypt's reputation is at stake."[67] Refusing the governor's plan, they met to discuss what to ask Sartre. They struggled a bit and then decided to ask questions that expressed a "high level of political consciousness."[68] They thought they had an agenda in hand. However, when the day of Sartre's visit came, the governorate marched three long columns of peasants from neighboring villages to Kamshish. In response, the locals cordoned off the lecture hall and denied entrance to the governor's peasants. Mayhem ensued.

Muhammad Abu al-Ghar, then a young medical teaching assistant from Cairo University, who in 2013 headed the Egyptian Socialist Democratic Party, wrote a tragicomic account of what happened in Kamshish that day. Disappointed by his inability to attend Sartre's full-house lecture at Cairo University a few days earlier, Abu al-Ghar pulled some strings in al-Manufiya province and secured a front-row seat in Sartre's town-hall meeting at Kamshish. Heading toward Kamshish in his private car, a luxury in those days, he noticed lines of uniformed students waiving the flags of Egypt and France and calling enthusiastically "Long Live Sartre, Long Live Simone!"[69] Arriving at the over-packed town hall, Abu al-Ghar witnessed a soccer-match-style skirmish between the peasants of Kamshish, the governors' peasants, and the police force. As usual, the police won, and the meeting then started, to the governor's satisfaction.[70]

Rather than giving a lecture, Sartre insisted on an open town-hall-style dialogue with Lutfi al-Khuli serving as a moderator and translator. Sartre opened and invited the peasants to share their experiences. Much to al-Khuli's surprise, one by one the peasants stood up and read sophisticated philosophical queries from a piece of paper about the various forms of existentialism and about the differences between Sartre and early existentialist writers. Then came the turn of rural "existentialist" women to ask Beauvoir similar questions. It was unclear how many of these peasants were from Kamshish. Much to his disappointment, the stunned al-Khuli realized that the governorate had staged the entire event.[71] As the guests were about to leave, "the peasants asked . . . about the theater play, the music and the drinks" that the governor had promised in return for their participation.[72] Beauvoir later wrote, "We had an uninteresting conversation with the audience. . . . The visit did not tell us anything about the condition of the fellahin."[73]

With Palestinian Refugees

After touring Egypt south to north and back, the organizers finally made time for what was obviously a sideshow: the trip to Gaza. Though al-Khuli deeply cared about the plight of Palestinians, the government's priority was to receive high-profile acknowledgment for Egypt's revolution. Honoring Sartre's insistence on maintaining an ambiguous stance toward Palestine, al-Khuli created a buffer around the issue: he asked fellow Egyptians to respect that "[our guests] . . . would like to study the facts of the conflict before they would express their opinions."[74] Though al-Khuli would eventually feel cheated by Sartre, at the time, he urged his countryman to be patient.

A noteworthy exception to this orchestrated patience was registered a few days earlier when Suhayl Idris landed in Cairo with the goal of getting Sartre to speak clearly about Palestine and visit Beirut next.[75] He was one of the few intellectuals who refused to accept the condition of ambiguity. On one occasion, Idris chased Sartre to his car and demanded an unequivocal statement on Palestine. The door was slammed on Idris's hand before the vehicle drove away. The trip to Gaza, therefore, took place under circumstances that allowed Sartre and the Egyptian state ample room for ambivalence. Indeed, even when they were finally heading by airplane northward toward Gaza, their hosts decided to divert the flight and first bring the group to al-ʿArish where Egyptian jet pilots drilled their MiG-21 fighter jets in preparation for war. Finally, toward the day's end, they continued to their original destination, Gaza.[76]

By all accounts, the visit to Gaza was a disaster. Walking through the refugee camps of Jibalya and Dir al-Balah, the French were enthusiastically greeted with ululation. They witnessed the poverty and humiliation of refugees, a painful reality that was difficult to ignore. On several occasions, Sartre stopped to converse with refugees. Their stories were heartbreaking. Sartre asked if they were waiting for Arab armies to liberate Palestine or if they planned to do it themselves. They insisted on self-liberation.[77] He then took time to make some important statements: "Thanks to your help, I was able to witness Palestinian reality and to better understand what the men, women and children who live in the camps, away from their land, feel. I also understand their deep desire to return to this land. I know that you are currently getting organized in order to accomplish this goal and since I understand [your situation] I would like to express my sympathy to you. . . . I would like to assure you that *I wholly acknowledge the national right of all Palestinian refugees to return to their country*" (emphasis added).[78]

Whether or not he fully realized the meaning of his words, Sartre had publicly embraced the Palestinian right of return. He did so without explaining how to reconcile this right with the right of Israel to exist, which he also supported. But until a return was possible, Sartre could not understand why rich Arab states refused to rehabilitate the refugees. He expected Arab solidarity to salvage Palestinian dignity instead of leaving them forever dependent on the United Nations Relief and Works Agency (UNRWA), which he considered a classic creation of US imperialism. Beauvoir thought the same: "Why had the refugees not been encouraged to build houses like those put up by the peasants of Kamshish, for example?"[79] The two were in agreement that the refugees could be aided regardless of the ultimate solution to the conflict. We know that Sartre shared this opinion with his hosts.[80]

But just when a sacred Palestinian right was finally being publicly acknowledged, things took a turn for the worse. It is unclear what precisely triggered the anger of some of the refugees, but at some point the tour broke into a fight. According to one account, journalists took a picture of Sartre with a child carrying the Palestinian flag. Allegedly, Lanzmann intervened and informed Sartre that this was the flag of Palestinian resistance, implying that he was "taking sides." Thereafter, Lanzmann insisted that the photographer expose the film and destroy the image.[81] This might have been the trigger for the fight. Whatever the truth, 'Ali al-Samman remembered that eventually the refugees "attacked the guests, as they failed to distinguish between Jews and Israelis."[82] Beauvoir's recollection of the meeting was very negative and, quite amazingly, she ended up blaming the refugees for their own condition.[83] Lanzmann too recorded a painful exchange in which "Each Palestinian phrase was a chant of war" that carried echoes of anti-Semitism and hinted at no prospects for a nonviolent resolution to the conflict.[84]

For the refugees of Gaza, Zionists were always Jews, and the possibility that there might be some other kind of a non-Zionist Jews was purely theoretical. Indeed, the Zionists of Israel were called al-Yahud: the Jews. Especially painful was a personal attack on Claude Lanzmann and the refugees' failure to comprehend that he was a Jew who had staunchly supported the cause of Algeria and, along with his late sister Évelyne, hosted FLN activists in his home.[85] The Egyptians hosts were also disappointed. Lutfi al-Khuli insisted time and again that Jews and Zionists are not synonymous. A month earlier, in anticipation of Sartre's visit, his journal explained Sartre's position on anti-Semitism and once again reminded—perhaps even cautioned—his readers to be wary of the differences between Jews and Zionists.[86] Al-Samman also acknowledged the problem: "Some of the Palestinian leaders in the camps," he wrote, "were not politically suitable for this kind of a meeting."[87]

In stark contrast to the wretchedness of the refugee camps, a luxurious banquet given by the Egyptian governor of Gaza revealed that the political and economic leadership of the Gaza Strip was living in circumstances entirely divorced from those of the refugees. Shocked by the disparity between the poor refuges and the wealthy Egyptian leadership, Beauvoir whispered to Liliane al-Khuli, "I cannot swallow even one bite."[88] "At dinner time, another lavish banquet," Liliane answered back, "and all of this while the people outside are starving!"[89]

After dinner, an acrimonious exchange took place between Sartre and the official Palestinian leadership, Ahmad al-Shuqayri, head of the PLO and a follower of Nasser. "The conversation was tense," recalled Beauvoir, "because Sartre hoped that a means might be found of reconciling the right of the Palestinians to go back to their country and Israel's right to existence. . . . But the Palestinians insisted that the Jews should be expelled from occupied Palestine."[90] Sartre said that he would communicate their opinions to his circle in Paris. "That's not enough!" said one of the Palestinians angrily. "We should have liked you to share them."[91] The evening ended awkwardly. According to Beauvoir, "Liliane and Lutfi had felt most uneasy at the Palestinian leaders' violence and lack of logic. They too found the atmosphere in Gaza stifling."[92] At the same time, however, Liliane did not lose sight of her beliefs and told Beauvoir that "the Jews should have stayed in their 'own countries' after the war." That made Beauvoir think that Liliane "knew nothing whatsoever about the Jewish question as it existed in the West."[93] For the time being, such differences were suppressed, and ambiguity was allowed to do its job—though not for long; three months later, their relationship would break down in the most agonizing way.

Distressed by the events in Gaza, but also still mourning the tragic suicide three months earlier of his sister, the actress Évelyne Rey, Lanzmann could not sleep that night.[94] He approached al-Samman and told him how disturbed he was by the popular display of hatred toward Jews. It was the second time during the visit that Arabs had viewed Lanzmann as the Jewish friend of their enemies.[95] Again, al-Samman acknowledged the problem but explained that hatred could be found on both sides of the border, and that the French party was particularly unlucky in meeting these Palestinians and not those of Beirut who had a much "higher level of political consciousness."[96] Given that the outstanding Palestinian intellectual Walid al-Khalidi was reportedly among those present, as were fifteen other thinkers and writers including Latifa al-Zayyat, it is unclear why a more serious conversation did not take place.[97] All we know is that the day ended in disappointment, and that everyone involved, including the Egyptian hosts, was depressed.[98]

Lanzmann, however, was doubly depressed. In addition to being personally targeted, he also felt that Sartre was drifting away from the cause of Israel and closer and closer to the cause of the Arabs. On several occasions, he confronted Sartre and pressured him to "be balanced." Beauvoir, who had the exact same impression, confronted Sartre as well. Yet to no avail.[99] Even though Sartre said nothing concrete, he appeared to be siding with his hosts, immersing himself in their cause and publicly appearing to sympathize with them. Worse still, in preparation for the Israeli leg of the tour, Lanzmann noticed that Sartre was immersed in Georges Philippe Friedmann's *Fin du peuple juif?* (*The End of the Jewish People?*) Having concluded an investigative tour of Israel similar to the tour Sartre was about to take, Friedmann, an anti-Zionist Jewish sociologist, had argued that the state of Israel threatened to eliminate the Jewish people as a whole.[100] Of all the books Sartre could have picked up in preparation for his visit to Israel, he had settled on one of the most extreme anti-Israel texts. Disappointed, Lanzmann believed that Sartre had left for Israel with a "hostile and prejudiced" opinion.[101] Now a rift between them was imminent.

Sartre himself continued to walk a fine line. Though, by invoking the Palestinian "right of return," he gave the impression that he was squarely on the Arab side, the unsuccessful visit to Gaza, and the philosopher's reluctance to state his position vis-à-vis Zionism, Israel, and the conflict in conclusive and unambiguous terms troubled Arab pundits. Outside Egypt, intellectuals wanted to hear from Sartre that Israel was nothing but a neocolonial entity. Had Sartre said so, all other issues relating to the conflict would have reached their obvious resolution. Yet, he refused to go that far.

In this context, Ahmad ʿAbbas Salih, a progressive revolutionary intellectual, addressed Sartre publicly:

The writing and public positions of you and the great Simone de Beauvoir were decisive, clear and unambiguous. However, your vague and yet undefined position on Israel diminishes your reputation as, for us, Israel is nothing but a colonial base for international imperialism whose goal is to defeat the cultural efforts of the new Arab man.[102]

Undoubtedly, you were aware of the position of our revolution against anti-freedom forces around the world. Clearly, we did not disagree with you on Cuba, Vietnam, Algeria as well as the general cause of freedom. However, [with so much in common], how is it that we disagree with you on such a clear tragedy [such as Palestine]? How do you, the protector of freedom, disagree with Israel on its position toward Vietnam, Cuba, Algeria and Africa yet, at the same time, agree that the abusive Israeli entity is legitimate?[103]

Driving his point to its natural conclusion, Salih surmised, "It is obvious for us that there is a certain gap here. A mistake, whose unclear cause brought you to fundamentally contradict yourself. Is your knowledge of us inaccurate? Is your perception of the revolutionary transformation that we are undergoing not based on proper knowledge?"[104]

Also unsatisfied, the pro-Palestinian Arab press was scandalized by the visit and blamed Egypt for marginalizing the issue of Palestine. The anti-Nasserite Jordanian radio station was very clear in this regard: "The Arab Socialist camp headed by Gamal Abdel Nasser has always tried to sow dissention between Arabs and blur the problem of Palestine. Whereas the Arabs have always had one single problem—the problem of Palestine, the [socialist] camp has created a wealth of new problems, such as the problem of socialist change, the problem of alignment, and non-alignment, the problem of Congo, Vietnam, etc."[105]

Unlike the Jordanians, the Syrians supported the cause of liberation struggles in the decolonized world and expected Sartre to visit Syria and see that "we are not anti-Semites and anti-Jewish and that the armed struggle for the liberation of Palestine is not a racist movement but a liberationist one."[106] Inasmuch as he was aware of them, Sartre did not answer his critics. He had already heard much of this from Liliane al-Khuli, the most eloquent and effective critic of Israel on the entire tour.[107]

As the visit drew to a close, Sartre condemned once again neo-colonial propaganda against Nasser and said that Nasser was a serious political leader and a deep thinker.[108] In one of his last interviews, he told the Lebanese daily *Al-Nahar*, "One day I will tell you what I think of the Palestine problem."[109] On March 13, Sartre, Beauvoir, and Lanzmann packed their suitcases and flew to Athens. They would now have to deal with equally demanding and oversensitive Israelis.

In Israel

The next day the French party boarded El Al flight 222 to Tel Aviv. MAPAM and the Left were filled with anticipation. The Israeli government and much of the public, on the other hand, saw Sartre as a threat. Though they had no evidence, at least none yet, they believed that in addition to being a pro-Arab and anti-American intellectual, Sartre had an issue with Zionism. Many ordinary Israelis believed so: "Nothing good can come out of this visit . . . as already while visiting Egypt Sartre declared his position on the refugees without even hearing our view" declared one popular newspaper.[110] To further complicate matters, Sartre's visit overlapped with that of Günter Grass. Given that, for the first time since the Holocaust, a famous German writer—one who claimed that Israel had normalized its relationship with former Nazis for the sake of money—was visiting the country, the Israelis felt defensive, confused, and, mostly, divided over the legitimacy of and need for the two visits. The Writers Association, for instance, decided to boycott Grass and endorse Sartre. Others rejected both. In this context, some satirists joked that the Israeli psyche was already so burdened that it could not process the two visits without unleashing at its esteemed guests.[111] And unleash it did. Also acting out was the French embassy, which officially boycotted the visit and the notorious antiambassador "who did not bother to inform us or the Quai d'Orsay of his arrival."[112]

Yet, Israeli leftist circles ignored all of that, and among those who had a stake in the visit, expectations were high. Perhaps too high. Lanzmann was so beside himself that immediately upon their arrival he approached Flapan and unequivocally informed him that "the fate of the Jewish people is dependent on the success of this visit."[113]

FIGURE 6   Arrival in Israel. Photo by Moshe Milner, Government Press Office (Israel).

If so, then from the very beginning, it did not go very well for the team of "the Jews." The head of the hosting committee, the elder poet Avraham Shlonski, a contemporary of Tawfiq al-Hakim, appeared to be unfocused and out of touch. Against all expectations, he refused to let journalists at the airport present questions and insisted that the tired and unsmiling guests be taken to their hotel at once. The press retaliated with negative reports on "an awkward atmosphere" that "felt like a dreary meeting of third-rank party activists."[114] It was clear to everybody that Sartre's arrival was a public-relations disaster. Only two highly enthusiastic eleven-year-old boys, who had hitchhiked from a nearby town to see the philosopher, were content with what they saw and heard.[115]

Far more problematic than public-opinion management, however, was the growing tension between Sartre and Lanzmann. For Lanzmann, Zionism was a just and historically inevitable correction to the Holocaust. As his lifelong emotional engagement with Israel illustrates, his own identity was tightly wrapped up in the experience of the Jewish state.[116] Sartre, on the other hand, thought and wrote of Judaism and anti-Semitism, maintained that Israel had a right to exist, but, at least publicly, had not yet made up his mind about Zionism.[117] Just like the Israelis around him, Lanzmann sensed Sartre's unspoken ambiguity toward Zionism and took personal issue with it. A fall out between them was inevitable.

It happened on the second day of the tour. During a visit to the Weitzman Institute, Israel's leading scientific academy, Sartre met with the best and brightest of Israel's scientists. Perceiving their "too-perfect American accent, as a clear sign of consubstantial American imperialism," Sartre gave them the cold shoulder.[118] When Lanzmann saw Sartre view Zionism through such neocolonial lens, he angrily accused him of being "biased against Israel." The next day Lanzmann boarded a flight to Paris and left the tour he had worked so hard to produce.[119] Beauvoir sided with Lanzmann but did not abandon the visit. She, Sartre, Ely Ben Gal, their French-Israeli translator, and Monique Neimark, their French-Israeli hostess, continued alone, driving a small private car. Unlike in Egypt, the Israeli government was nowhere to be seen, and the role of the public committee that hosted them became purely symbolic. Flapan and his men took care of everything. For better or for worse, it was MAPAM's show.

Quite appropriately, therefore, their first official meeting was with MAPAM's iconic leader Meir Ya'ari. The meeting was a disappointment. As he had done repeatedly throughout the visit, Sartre began the conversation by asking his interlocutor to accept the Palestinian right of return.

Ya'ari: How can one imagine the return of a million Arabs to such a small state?

Sartre: I speak only about the right of return as a principle that is a preliminary condition for their eventual renouncing of its application. You must understand that it is impossible to justify the Jewish right of return after two thousand years and to deny the same right to the Arabs after only twenty years.

Ya'ari: It would be irresponsible on my part to affirm a theoretical right which one knows is inapplicable. . . . I am not a philosopher but a man of politics.

Sartre: You know better than me where politics that is not based on principle could lead.

Ya'ari: After World War I we Jews got a state in principle (from the British) and twenty-five years later we got Auschwitz. Here [you have] some principles that are not supported by reality.

Sartre: The refugee camps that I just saw in Gaza last week are realities that weigh heavily on the future of Israel.

Ya'ari: All the more reason why not to suggest an abstract solution!

Sartre: . . . It is the nature of the principle to be anything but abstract.[120]

On this note, the meeting came to an end. Ya'ari immediately understood the debacle and, later, when he was asked by the party's daily newspaper, *Al Ha-Mishmar*, to transcribe their conversation for print, he omitted the above exchange and several other statements that he thought might reflect badly on MAPAM. He wrote Flapan to say that "Sartre was not 'in shape' and told me a few things that would not be healthy to publish."[121]

What brought Ya'ari to silence this exchange had nothing to do with Sartre's "shape" and everything to do with his rejection of the politics of victimization. Indeed, Sartre refused to accept the particularity of Jewish victimhood as the only grounding of an ethical framework that would inform and guide the political. Instead, he adhered to a universal position where rights should be acknowledged in the abstract, thus opening a space for the potentiality of otherness, regardless of its eventual political actuality. Such a position rejected the exclusivity of ethics based on competitive victimization and insisted instead on submitting the ethical to the realpolitik of the Arab-Israeli conflict. To make his point clear, Sartre extended Ya'ari's logic to the extreme and said that, based on the logic of competitive victimization, the Palestinians might have a higher claim as victims because their tragedy had happened only twenty years ago and persisted in the refugee camps. Clear as he

FIGURE 7 With Meir Ya'ari in his kibbutz. Courtesy of the Yad Ya'ari Archive.

was with Ya'ari, however, Sartre did not leave a philosophical text or a more organized statement on the subject that could substantiate his position.

After Ya'ari, Sartre met with former general and present minister Yigal Alon in his kibbutz house on a beautiful shore of the Sea of Galilee. Alon was another iconic Zionist. Again, Sartre inquired about the refugees' right of return. A French-speaking friend of Alon who was present that evening answered that the Palestinians were already in Israel as Jordan, the West Bank, and the Triangle area were all part of historic Israel. "How can one speak of their return? It is as if I would have demanded of you to return the inhabitants of Marseilles to Paris. But why to Paris? I have learned something from you," responded Sartre enigmatically.[122] He heard similar things from Alon. They parted ways on friendly terms. Beauvoir said she had "a lovely evening," and Sartre, a bit more introspective, said that "[General Alon] is the most sympathetic Fascist I ever met."[123]

The tour continued along these same crooked lines. Though rejecting the proposition that Zionist society "solved the problem of women," Beauvoir had a great time. Sartre, on the other hand, continued to be suspicious, guarded, critical, and generally unimpressed.[124] Such was the case when he met the director of the Histadrut, the General Federation of Laborers and a socialist point of Israeli pride. In response to the director's proud account of the revolutionary role of the federation in protecting workers and increasing productivity, Sartre dismissively exclaimed "Your Histadrut is a sacred monster."[125] On a different occasion, Sartre declined an invitation to visit a military installation and abruptly canceled a meeting with the army's chief of staff, General Yitzhak Rabin. "I came to meet the people, the Left and Civil Society, not the military," he said. "Besides, I had already spent an excellent evening with this Fascist general!"[126] While the Syrian press took proud note of this incident, Sartre's unexpected position angered even his closest Israeli allies who knew of his visit to Egypt's airbase the previous week.[127] One journalist would later wonder if Israeli militarism was worse than Egyptian.[128] As Lanzmann had beforehand, they tried to explain that Israel lacked a civic-military divide, and that this unity was a salient characteristic of Zionism without which one could not make sense of it.[129] Sartre was unconvinced, and more cancellations followed.

In the following days, he canceled a parliamentary meeting with political leaders of the nonsocialist Left as he was uninterested in the opinions of the political Center and the Right. He also canceled a public meeting in the southern city of Beer Sheva as well as one with the ideologically minded staff of New Outlook. Apparently, he feared that their questions about the conflict would unsettle his ambiguity. Yet, most offensively, he canceled the meeting with the mythical founder of the Israeli state, David Ben Gurion, who waited for Sartre in vain in his pioneer desert cabin. In contrast, there were no cancellations of his meetings with Arab citizens of Israel.

To the contrary, Sartre requested additional meetings with various fringe groups. As guests of the Israeli Communist Party, the only joint Jewish-Arab political partnership, Sartre and Beauvoir were welcomed by a vibrant intellectual milieu that was committed to their agenda without reservation. Taking their cues from the likes of Lutfi al-Khuli and the global progressive Left that Sartre led, Arab intellectuals in Israel saw great opportunity for peace. Poet and upcoming politician Tawfiq Ziyad was quick to declare that the "new Sartre" who recently had resolved his differences with Marxism and communism was now in a position to propose a regional agenda that "would cast new light on the cause of our people."[130] This message was echoed in meetings in several Arab towns and villages where residents spoke at length about systematic discrimination against Arab citizens. Sartre listened and sympathized with "the suffering of the Arab population," thus implying that Zionists were discriminating against the Palestinian citizens of Israel.[131] The hosts received Sartre enthusiastically and, on occasion, perhaps too much so. Thus, while visiting Nazareth, the contingent was nearly crushed by an ecstatic crowd. Sartre braved the popular pressure, but Beauvoir did not and reportedly had some very offensive things to say to her translator about the Arabs who celebrated their arrival.[132]

Comparing what seemed to look like two very separate visits to Israel, Israeli Jews were baffled: "Sartre is a morally courageous person," wrote *Yediot Ahronot*, "and it is unclear what scares him so much in Israel" that he refuses to meet openly and talk. How can he learn anything?[133] Indeed, as understood from the fall out with Lanzmann, Sartre resisted Zionism, and, though he never left a text or even a sentence explaining this resistance, his behavior spoke volumes. In fact, in as much as he engaged with the identity of Israelis, he always approached it from the angle of Judaism, anti-Semitism, and the Holocaust. Thus, when he met with a group of prominent academics in the house of the legendary German-Jewish scholar Gershom Scholem, a pioneer in the study of Jewish mysticism, he asked them, "What does being Jewish signify to you?" and not, What does it mean to be an Israeli?[134] This encounter, however, was intellectually meaningful, delightful, and lengthy. Past midnight, when everybody was already exhausted, and it was time to bring the day to a close, Sartre was still fully engaged. Fatigued, Beauvoir sarcastically asked Sartre if he had "dropped anchor." They finally left.[135] At another, more personal encounter, he questioned Ely Ben Gal, the translator who in the wake of the Holocaust left France to become a Zionist kibbutz member, about his identity:

Sartre: Why did you become a Zionist?
Ely: For three thousand years . . .
Sartre [interrupting him]: No! Why are you a Zionist?
Ely: Because of the experience of emancipation . . .
Sartre: Forget emancipation.
Ely: All national minorities . . .
Sartre [interrupting again]: I ask why you are a Zionist.
Ely: . . . This is the direction to which Jewish history points.
Sartre: History does not indicate anything!
Ely: You cannot ignore the lessons of history.
Sartre [frustrated]: But I ask why are YOU a Zionist.
Ely: [Because] France is a country of bastards.[136]

Again, more than any official statement, it was pedestrian exchanges such as this that exposed Sartre's unease with the Zionist ethics of vic-

נידונו לסיור מודרך היטב

FIGURE 8 "Sentenced to a well-guided tour." Caricature published in *Haolam Hazeh*. Reproduction of original by Gaby Kasan.

timization. Of course, nothing was personal; Ely would later move back to Paris to do his PhD work under Sartre.

Yet, it was an attitude to which the already suspicious and highly sensitive Israeli public reacted immediately. Beyond disappointed, angry, and ultranationalistic letters to the editor ("Who needs Sartre? We have our own Jewish prophets, judges, and philosophers!"), MAPAM was blamed for orchestrating an unpatriotic and highly partisan tour.[137] Especially due to the various cancellations, they were blamed for closely controlling access to Sartre and for engaging Sartre from a "provincial" and self-deprecating standpoint.[138] One caricaturist captured the general mood when he portrayed Sartre, Beauvoir, and Lanzmann as MAPAM's prisoners. Sartre saw the caricature and asked to meet the publisher-turned-politician Uri Avneri and his editor Shalom Cohen. It was a cordial meeting over cigarettes, whiskey, and ice cubes.[139]

Resistance to Zionism aside, there was also much high-profile business as Sartre met the prime minster (Levi Eshkol), the president (Zalman Shazar), chairman of the Kneset (Kadish Luz), and a few other captains of Israeli society. Minster of education Zalman Aran was well equipped for his meeting with Sartre. His assistants prepared a portfolio with a sophisticated summary of Sartre's key ideas with special attention given to Sartre's notion of the "other." They explained to their minister that Sartre viewed "otherness" as an alienating existential and situational condition from which, as they put it, the "Jews, Black and Yellow" races suffered. Though the executive briefing did not list Palestinians living in Israel as the "others" of Zionists, Aran thought that Sartre might see them as such and asked his assistants to prepare a report on the efforts of his office in promoting education among Israel's Arab minority. His assistants warned Aran that that Sartre and Beauvoir were "Aggressive anti-conformists" and that the lady was "Very Egocentric."[140] Aran survived the meeting, which produced no headlines. In all of these encounters, Sartre never communicated any form of identification with Zionism. Undoubtedly, he felt more comfortable among opposition circles, which made no effort to defend Zionism and even critiqued it. According to Beauvoir, they "got on very badly with members of (the ruling party) MAPAI and generally speaking with all right-wing Israelis."[141]

Though previously "cold and reserved," a more sympathetic, open, and engaged Sartre suddenly appeared when visiting the kibbutz and encountering the so-called peasant-intellectual. Both he and Beauvoir tended to romanticize some aspects of kibbutz life, in which shepherds read philosophy books while tending to their flocks. Apparently, both spoke of Sartre's translator Ely Ben Gal, who allegedly read Sartre's *Critique of Dialectical Reason* while he was on duty with his sheep.[142] They began by visiting Ya'ari's home, Kibbutz Merhavia. Luckily, the visit did not follow the negative pattern of earlier days, and the clash with Ya'ari did not cloud the visit. Poet Tuvia Rivner welcomed the French duo and offered a few opening comments. A tour of the place followed. Though Rivner, and others, recalled a friendly and dynamic conversation about socialism and the life of the kibbutz, the visit was quite uneventful.[143]

The next stop promised more. Visiting Lehavot Ha-Bashan, a frontline kibbutz "under the cannons of the Syrian army," they were greeted by the kibbutz secretary Heini Bornstein, a familiar face.[144] Originally a Swiss Jew from Basel, Bornstein had befriended Sartre and Beauvoir two years earlier while serving as a representative of the kibbutz movement in Paris. Heini and his wife, Hasia, hosted the guests in their modest room. They had much to talk about and they could do so in French. Hasia was a heroine of the Grodno underground. Losing her entire family in Treblinka, she had moved to the Aryan side of Białystok, where she lived undercover, worked for the resistance, and took an active part in the ghetto uprising. In a conversation that stretched long into the night, the guests, and Beauvoir in particular, asked detailed questions about Hasia's previous life and about the metamorphosis of their hosts from ordinary middle-class Europeans into Zionist socialists of the frontier. Sartre asked to be woken the next morning in time to meet the kibbutz members on their way to work. Taken by the spirit of solidarity, after breakfast Sartre and Beauvoir cleared their own table. Later, attending collective meetings, both Sartre and Beauvoir shared their impressions from Egypt and China and compared the various socialist experiments.[145]

After hours of conversations with French, Swiss, and Belgian Jews who had survived the Holocaust, Sartre and Beauvoir said they were ashamed of the fate of Jews in Europe and happy to see that they were building a new socialist life for themselves. "I see here family members of our friends who were murdered create a world of joy . . . you are an example for the entire world," said Beauvoir. Sartre added, "You have a right to be proud."[146] If any encounter in Israel deeply influenced the French couple, this was it. The missing-in-action Lanzmann would have been proud too, as the visit validated his own life story, as well as the reason he chose Zionism. Indeed, Sartre revered the survivors and saw in their experience a universal moral lesson, which the Voice of Israel radio station was quick to echo.[147] This was why, during the visit and in the following months, Sartre insisted that Hasia's friend, the legendary partisan and participant in the Białystok Ghetto uprising in Poland, Haika Grossman, sit as a juror on the Russell Tribunal for crimes in Vietnam. No matter how much pressure the Algerian government (which was supposed to host the tribunal) exerted against her nomination, Sartre would not budge and insisted on her participation.[148]

Bidding farewell to the kibbutz, they returned to Tel Aviv. The key event of the visit was organized by a committee of Israeli intellectuals who opposed the war in Vietnam. It took place on March 24 in Tel Aviv, where Sartre gave a public lecture about Vietnam, American imperialism, and the Third World. The entire Israeli intelligentsia attended the event and, somewhat awkwardly, sang "Le Marseillaise." Even Israel's celebrated warrior General Moshe Dayan was in the audience. Dayan and Sartre, however, did not meet.[149] As an emerging ally of the United States still pursuing its patronage, the Israeli government feared this event the most, and though Sartre communicated his point loud and clear he was cautious in his choice of words and delivered only his standard anti-imperial message.

As the visit drew to an end, Sartre convened a final press conference. Much to the surprise of all, "a new Sartre" reported to the podium. The reserved and unsmiling philosopher now appeared relaxed, engaged, and pleasant. He even joked. Perhaps he was happy to finally go home. Whatever the reason, for the first time since his arrival, he left behind a sympathetic impression of Israel. He spoke warmly of the diversity of opinions in Israel and of its contradictions that made the "new Jewish Israelis" one of the richest people in history.[150] He also said that, on first impression, "Israel is the only place where a non-Jew can say about someone else 'this is a Jew' without being anti-Semite."[151] As in Egypt, he refused to take a position with regard to the Arab-Israeli conflict, citing his position as that of "absence." On March 29, Sartre, Beauvoir, and Arlette Elkaim, Sartre's adopted Jewish daughter who had joined the tour a week earlier, returned home. Little did Sartre know that his warm farewell message was about to unleash a storm that would once again put the entire project in jeopardy.

Conclusion

Ambiguity, therefore, was the name of the game. For one Israeli journalist, Sartre's political art summoned an anecdote that resonated with Israelis, and that neighboring Arabs would have surely appreciated as well. Appearing in an Israeli newspaper a day after Sartre's departure, the story goes that a rabbi was asked to judge between two quarreling parties. The old rabbi listened carefully to the first person and told him he was right. He then listened to the second person and told him he was right, too. When the rabbi's wife intervened and pointed out the impossibility of the rabbi's position, he assured her that she was also right.[152] As the story of the visit shows, however, Sartre's ambiguity was not simply his own but that of everyone else who was willfully involved in producing this project, especially Simha Flapan, Lutfi al-Khuli, and ʿAli al-Samman. Most importantly, it was not an ambiguity that was born on the spot but one that had taken two years to evolve. The absence of a Sartrean text, therefore, was somewhat of a joint project. Though uncomfortable at being forcefully maneuvered by Sartre, Lanzmann, and Beauvoir toward this particular choice, both Israelis and Arabs believed that, following the visit, Sartre's introduction to the special issue of Les Temps Modernes would vindicate their position and thus win them the support of the entire French Left and, perhaps, even that of the world as a whole.

Curiously, though the three French intellectuals presented themselves as a unified group, they failed to hide their differences. All three members pursued individual agendas that in one way or another became quite apparent. Lanzmann wanted Sartre to discover and embrace Zionism in the very same way in which he had as a post-Holocaust French Jew. In his memoir, Lanzmann left a beautiful and honest account of his slow, yet powerful, discovery of Zionism.[153] We can assume that he expected Sartre to undergo the same epiphany. Sartre's refusal to do so, must have felt like a personal rejection of his identity, and it resulted in a temporary breakdown between the two as well as Lanzmann's abandonment of the tour. From that point onward Lanzmann followed only his conscience and took an independent political line that openly asked the French Left to side with Israel.

On her part, Beauvoir was primarily interested in the life of women and the conditions for their emancipation. This was the main prism through which she experienced the region. And since state feminism, whether Israeli or Arab, failed to impress her, she developed a very negative view of patriarchy and was especially critical of the attitude of Arab men. Seeing Israel through the experience of the Holocaust, she did not mind Zionism as a civic-military unit. Her one and only critique of Israel was a certain skepticism of the Zionist claim that it liberated women. Concomitantly, she had little sympathy for the cause of Palestine and found herself in the same camp as Lanzmann.

As for Sartre, though he took pains not to say or write anything conclusive, his gestures, body language, and overall condescending attitude betrayed a profound aversion to Zionism. He deplored militarism and rejected anything that was identified with the Israeli state, its symbols, rituals, and narratives. The only exception was his deep sympathy with Holocaust survivors, but here too he chose to frame their experience in terms of Jewish authenticity and not, as Lanzmann insisted, as part of the revolutionary effort of Zionism to create a new type of Israeli man and woman. In sharp contrast with his gloomy appearance in Israel, Sartre's vivacious exploits in Egypt suggested a level of appreciation for the fact that his thought informed the postcolonial Arab project as a whole. Indeed, the degree to which his plays, novels, philosophy, and political tracts were enthusiastically and meaningfully embraced was impossible to miss. Since nothing of that sort happened in Israel, by that point Sartre should have surely understood how central his work was to the Arab project of liberation.

Divided as they were and with the spectacle of ambiguity in full swing, everybody was free to draw their own conclusions as to who stood where and why. And, so, in the heat of the visit, the Israelis saw Sartre as a committed Arab philosopher and as a dangerous antagonist. They had no clue of the anxiety that this visit evoked across the border and of the desperate hope that the Arab position would be acknowledged by the man who most informed its constitution. Arabs too were oblivious. Feeling vulnerable, they had no idea that the relation of Sartre to Zionism was anything but a love story. This mutual ignorance solidified the respective positions of the parties and prompted both to increase the pressure on Sartre. In April 1967, as winds of war began blowing in the region, the otherwise obscure visit of an idiosyncratic philosopher became entangled in a dynamic that assumed a life of its own and that even the lubricated political machine of *Les Temps Modernes* and its many committed associates could neither foresee nor control. So much was at stake on the eve of the war that a failure of any kind would deal a mortal blow to the universal aspirations of an entire generation.

NINE

Fiasco

Did Sartre betray the Arabs? And, if so, why, how, and in what sense? What were the reactions to this alleged betrayal, and how did it affect the legacy of Arab existentialism, the ongoing quest for postcolonial freedom, and the belief in the liberating power of the universal Left and its ability to serve as an alternative political community? Against the backdrop of the June 1967 war, this chapter continues the story of Sartre's effort to ethically intervene in the Arab-Israeli conflict. In so doing, it takes note of the actions of not only Middle Eastern actors but also the Third World intelligentsia, the French Left, and the Jews of France. Almost without exception, during the tumultuous months of May and June 1967, all of these parties became intensely involved in what they simplistically saw as an epic battle between good and evil. With multiple new actors joining the fray—and forcefully questioning Sartre the person as well as Sartre the ethical institution— the philosopher's shaky edifice of ambiguity and political absence began to crumble. When it finally gave in, its collapse suggested that the Arab project of postcolonial universality was, after all, not supported by Sartre ethics of global liberation.

Is Sartre Sartrean?

It was a curious coincidence that, while Sartre was wrapping up his tour in Israel, the Third Congress of Afro-Asian Writers was concluding its weeklong session in Beirut. Unlike the congress of the 1950s, this diverse group of hundred and fifty writers representing forty countries did not come to Beirut to discuss arcane matters of literary form and technique. They came for politics, and they had a message:

[First,] we consider the Zionist movement to be colonialist in nature, expansionist in its goals, racist in its logic and Fascist in its means. Second, we consider Israel to be . . . a colonial bridgehead that assists neocolonialism to preserve its influence in Asia and Africa. Third, we consider the violent Israeli presence in Palestine to be settler colonialism [isti'mar iskani] . . . and therefore see in its liquidation a proper liberationist cause. Fourth, we maintain that the revolutionary solution to the problems of the Arab nation . . . is fundamentally connected to the goal of destroying Israel. . . . Fifth, we consider Israel to be fascist, racist and a cultural setback to human progress.[1]

Turning Palestine, rather than Vietnam, into the central topic of the congress was the joint work of the Syrian and Palestinian delegations, which threatened to split the congress unless their cause was embraced. The North Vietnamese delegation agreed, and even Egypt went along with this plan.[2]

But that was not all. With so many other just global causes, the congress condemned the "great cultural conspiracy" against the value of the written word. They referred to the recent revelation that the CIA had funded various cultural venues around the world and, most shockingly, that Tawfiq Sayigh's beloved journal, *Hiwar*, was on the list of beneficiaries.[3] Expectedly, the congress issued strong words in support of liberation struggles against neocolonial and imperial powers such as the one in Yemen but, especially, that in Vietnam.[4] Discussing Vietnam in Beirut, the writers used language and terms of analysis identical to those Sartre used in his Vietnam lecture in Tel Aviv. Yet, the distance between Sartre in Tel Aviv and the Afro-Asian writers in Beirut was greater than the mere 131 miles that separated the two coastal cities. For the first time since Sartre's engagement with Third World liberation, his followers seemed to be charting their own independent path. Granted, he was instrumental in developing and propagating a Third World language of liberation, with all its attendant concepts, terms, and lines of argumentation, but by no means was he in control of its usage. As the gathering in Beirut made perfectly clear, nowhere was the gap between Sartre and Third World intellectuals more apparent than in the case of Israel/Palestine.[5]

As Sartre's ideas about neocolonialism and racism began to be liberally applied to Israel, there was an expectation that Sartre would understand that "the existence of Israel is not an integral part of the Jewish problem and hence not a solution to it."[6] A Syrian pundit expected Sartre to realize this, return to his roots, draw the obvious conclusions, and justify the right for armed struggle: "Sartre is undecided about the usage of armed struggle as a way of settling the problem of Palestine. . . . The joint struggle of Palestinians and Arabs to remove what is known as Israel, is predicated on all the elements of a revolutionary position, especially in its Sartrean sense."[7] To accuse Sartre of not being Sartrean—and of turning his back on the corpus of thought that justified Fanon-style liberation violence—emerged as the new line of argumentation in the struggle to sway the philosopher to the Arab side.[8] Thereafter, his stand on Palestine emerged as the ultimate litmus test for Sartre's progressive revolutionary position. The conundrum remained though: Why did Sartre fail to understand that "the Arab struggle in Palestine is an existential act . . . the only act to justify Palestinian existence . . . and assure its freedom"?[9]

The Jewish Question: A Last Call

Sartre's visit to the region prompted his Arab followers to engage in a final attempt to decipher Sartre's position on the Jewish question and, by implication, on the problem of Palestine. Inevitably, Sartre's yet untranslated *Anti-Semite and Jew* became relevant to the discussion. "The innovation in Sartre's study of the Jews," wrote a Syrian critic, "is that he presents the Jewish Question as a problem of those who oppress the Jews more than that of the Jews themselves. The anti-Semite is a fearful person who projects the problems of the world, as well as his own troubles onto the Jews. From that standpoint Sartre analyzes the relationship between the Jew and the Anti-Semite but also that between the black person and those that hate him, the worker and the capitalist and between woman and man."[10]

Though Sartre's phenomenological and hence relational and existential perspective was properly understood, it was immediately rejected in favor of the traditional philosophical understanding that essence, or the core and unchanging nature of a thing, overrides the importance of its existence. In that regard, Marx was a good antidote to Sartre, and indeed the Syrian author points the reader to Marx's "successful" study of the Jewish question in which he seeks to uncover the "objective" religious essence of the Jewish character as a main cause for the misfortune of the Jews. Thus, the author summarized, "The difference between Sartre and Marx is that while the former views the Jewish Question as a relational problem between the 'I' and the 'other,' the latter explores the socio-economic system of the Jews."[11] As Badawi had already explained in the late 1940s, the reason for engaging the world from an existentialist standpoint was that "existence precedes essence." This key element of existentialism, a mainstay of the entire intellectual system, was precisely what allowed the intellectual breakthrough of postcolonial thought and applied equally to European Jews as it did to black people, women, workers, the colonized, and, of course, Palestinians.

Another Syrian writer who addressed Sartre's *Anti-Semite and Jew* was not so much interested in philosophy as in practical affairs, namely, advising fellow Arabs on how to deal with Sartre's ambiguity. The author argued that "Sartre's involvement in contemporary affairs is [conducted] vis-à-vis oneself but also toward others" and for that reason he has a deep "identification with Jews as the victims of the Nazis." At the same time, the anonymous author maintained that, though the Holocaust brought Sartre to search for a solution to the Jewish problem, he "always distanced himself from the claims of Zionism to represent all Jewish victims." As Sartre told one of the many students who approached him in Egypt, "I cannot hide my support for the Arabs who suffered from colonialism. However, I also identify with the Jews who were suppressed for a very long time by Europeans." Given Sartre's admittedly perplexed position, "the role of Arab writers," the article advised, "is to differentiate between Zionism and Judaism and between the Palestinian problem and the Jewish problem in Europe. . . . Arab writers also need to insist on the racist nature of Zionism and its connection to colonialism and capitalism. [Viewed from this perspective], the Palestinian problem would appear as the struggle of a people for liberation and independence."[12] This was practical advice in the spirit of ʿAli al-Samman, Fayiz Sayigh, and Lutfi al-Khuli, who, like this Syrian writer, saw in Sartre's cautious involvement "simply a first step in positioning the Palestinian problem globally."[13]

All of these belated interventions with regard to "major disagreements with Sartre about how to understand the Jewish Question" were reasonable and measured, but they did little by way of interrogating Sartre's unfinished ethics.[14] Indeed, a long list of questions waited to be addressed. Given Sartre's notion of the other, why wouldn't he treat the otherness of Jews and Palestinians equally? Was there a deep ethical reason for that? Did he have in mind a hierarchy of otherness in which one particular other deserved more recognition than another? What happens in complex historical situations such as the one in Palestine when Europe's other takes for itself a Palestinian other? What kind of ethics can serve as a political compass for navigating this conflict humanely? How does Sartre's philosophy help us in telling right from wrong? As is usually the case with unaddressed intellectual problems, they have a way of presenting themselves even when uninvited. This happened exactly one day after Sartre's return from his Middle East tour.

L'affaire Scemama

Summarizing his impression of Sartre's last press conference in Tel Aviv, André Scemama, *Le Monde*'s correspondent in Israel, cabled his office what he thought was a standard and fair-minded journalistic report. As he later told an Israeli colleague, he expected no trouble.[15] On March 31 the newspaper published Scemama's piece in which he claimed that Sartre subscribed to the classic thesis of Theodor Herzl's Zionism about the birth of an authentic and liberated Jew in Israel. Most dramatically, the piece quoted Sartre as saying that such a liberated Jew could exist only in Israel. While the report mentioned Sartre's disagreement with the Israeli position about the Palestinian right of return, for all intents and purposes, the implication of Scemama's article was that the Israelis had won Sartre over.[16]

In an instant, Scemama's article unleashed a storm on both sides of the Arab-Israeli divide and within each side internally. It also brought considerable pressure from multiple Jewish intellectuals in Sartre's own circle who demanded that Scemama correct his assessment. Sartre too was furious and considered Scemama's article "an obvious act of sabotage whose sole purpose is to create a crisis of trust between himself and the Arabs to whom he personally promised to stay neutral."[17] Under pressure to respond quickly, and unsure of himself, Scemama asked an Israeli colleague to provide him with the actual transcript of Sartre's press conference.[18] Once again, Sartre found himself in the middle of a vicious cycle with multiple conflicting demands upon him. Even playwright Samuel Beckett, a lifelong resident of Paris, joined the fray mocking "Mr. Sartre for allowing Israelis to exist," as if they needed approval for their existence from a Left Bank intellectual.[19] Yet, the real problem was not the off-the-cuff dinner comment from Beckett but that the Arabs now felt betrayed.

The hotheaded Ahmad al-Shuqayri, chairman of the PLO, insisted on the immediate withdrawal of all Arab writers from Sartre's special issue of *Les Temps Modernes* and began pressuring them to do so. Already highly suspicious of Sartre after his disappointing visit to Gaza, al-Shuqayri believed Scemama's piece provided the ultimate justification for disengaging from Sartre. Highly attentive to the Israeli media, the Jerusalem-based Palestinian daily *Al-Quds* was first to break the news with the headline "Sartre Says in Tel Aviv What He Avoided in Cairo."[20] On behalf of a unified Palestinian-Syrian position, the influential Syrian daily *Al-Thawra* launched an attack:

Is it possible that every tragedy that Europe inflicted on the Jews would become a justification for the occupation and deportation of another people? Sartre had scandalously forgotten that Israel is an occupying state. . . . What does Sartre think about the application of his logic on Israel to Rhodesia and South Africa? . . . How does he deal with all these contradictions? And what does Sartre have to say about the fact that, economically speaking, Israel is siding with imperialism? If Sartre will not change his mind about Zionism . . . then he is surely going to fall down as a liberationist thinker for all the struggling peoples and not only for Arabs. That is because the contradiction between liberation and Zionism is deep and comprehensive. Sartre should be capable of understanding that.[21]

With the scandal over Sartre's declaration in Tel Aviv came a certain reevaluation of his role in Algeria as well. "Sartre's position in support of Algeria," argued the Jordanian daily *Al-Dustur*, "was more due to his concern for the spilling of French blood than his worry for the Algerian right for freedom and liberation."[22] Though untrue, this statement reveals the mood in the pro-Palestinian camp and their suspicion— still unarticulated—that Sartre might be a traitor to their cause. Many of these concerns and accusations appeared in the pages of *Le Monde*, thus putting further pressure on Sartre.[23]

Egyptians, however, flatly rejected the Syrian and Palestinian effort to delegitimize Sartre. As ʿAli al-Samman explained to Flapan during these stormy days, overall, the Egyptians had a positive experience with Sartre and saw no reason for calling Sartre's special issue off.[24] Instead, they wanted Sartre to publish in the Egyptian press a clarification of, or correction to, his alleged endorsement of Zionism. The result was the beginning of back and forth negotiations between Sartre, the Palestinians, and the Egyptians on the wording of a new statement about Sartre's position on Palestine. Sartre's Palestinian interlocutors wanted him to replace his usage of "the right of Palestinians to return" with "the national right of the refugees for the entire land of Palestine."[25] With mounting pressures accumulating daily, in early April Sartre gave in to Arab demands and composed the following statement: "I insist on Israel's right to exist and on the recognition of its sovereignty. The state of Israel must remain open to any Jew who would like to live in it *but it cannot request all the Jews to settle there. I therefore reject Ben Gurion's approach of 'maximum Zionism'"* (emphasis added).[26]

Though Sartre's statement did not address the ethical contradictions that *Al-Thawra* pointed out and that everyone in Paris, including Flapan, read in translation, the Egyptians were content with the text.[27] Lanzmann, however, strongly objected and called Flapan to alert him of Sartre's inability to face Arab pressures. As he had done time and again during the course of this affair, Lanzmann provided Flapan with inside information and assessment of Arab positions, thus practically violating *Les Temps'* neutrality and, by extension, Sartre's. Flapan acknowledged this problematic practice: "Kudos to Lanzmann who is taking care of our interests" he wrote to Yaʻari.[28] No one in Sartre's inner circle was looking after Palestinian interests.

Fearing an anti-Israeli declaration, Lanzmann and Flapan decided to dissuade Sartre from publishing a statement and met with him to make their case. They argued that since he had never made any public statement about Zionism it would be wrong to do so for the first time in the Arab press. Besides, since he had yet to write the introduction to the special issue, any statement about Zionism to an Arab newspaper would severely compromise his position of neutrality/absence and would therefore be self-defeating.[29] Sartre agreed, but had a condition. He asked Flapan to write to *Le Monde* and say that "Sartre did not express any opinion about Zionism which he sees as an internal business of the Jewish people."[30] Sartre explained that such a move would keep the Arabs engaged. Flapan quickly agreed, and on April 8 *Le Monde* published his firsthand testimony, which exonerated Sartre of the accusation of supporting Zionism during his visit to Israel. It also published a short reply by André Scemama in which he firmly held his ground.[31]

Upon reading Flapan's piece in *Le Monde* the Israelis were flabbergasted. What caused Flapan to publish such a text? An Israeli journalist referred the question to Lanzmann, who was believed to be behind Flapan's fluent French text. He got a classic Lanzmann response: "I cannot tell you anything, I do not want to tell you anything and I don't know anything either."[32] He thus left them free to draw their own conclusions. *Yediot Ahronot* argued that the "affair has nothing to do with Sartre and *Le Monde* and is, in fact, a classic Jewish affair . . . a tempest in a teapot by sick Jews who cannot forgive the world and themselves for being born Jews."[33] By "Jews" the newspaper meant not only Flapan and "a few other Israelis" in Paris but what it called "Sartre's Jewish circle"—namely, Lanzmann, Maxime Rodinson, Claude Estier, and Jean Daniel (contributing editor to *Le Nouvel Observateur*). These "self-hating Jews," the familiar argument went, signed multiple petitions on behalf of "Kurds, Viet Cong fighters and communist spies but refused to sign on behalf of Elie Cohen," the Israeli spy who recently had been executed in Syria.[34]

As for Flapan, his service to Sartre was seen in Israel as a traitorous rebuke of Zionism. He was therefore singled out as a traitor who for two long years in Paris had done nothing but criticize his own government.[35] His party's newspaper *Al Ha-Mishmar* and some of his best friends also endorsed Scemama's interpretation of Sartre's press conference. To make things worse, Flapan heard from Eric Rouleau that his career in Paris was about to be over as his furious colleagues back home had demanded his immediate suspension.[36] His agonizing letters to bosses, colleagues, newspaper editors, and friends reveal a person under siege whose good intentions and multiple efforts on behalf of a historic Arab-Israeli understanding had gone wrong. He frantically wrote home, correcting factual mistakes in newspapers reports, rebuking them for their cheap scandalous behavior, lack of critical spirit, and for "aiding Ahmad al-Shuqayri and Syria."[37] Flapan saw the whole affair as nothing but one big conspiracy by right-wing Israelis and Jews like Scemama whose goal was the destruction of Sartre's project.[38]

Writing to Amnon Kapeliuk, a close friend and a fellow journalist, Flapan explained once again the meaning of Sartre's "neutrality to the point of absence" and said that "notwithstanding Sartre's positive experience in Israel, he is neither a Zionist nor an anti-Zionist. I am sorry, but this is the difficult and unpleasant truth. All we can hope for is an action on behalf of peace."[39] Amnon responded: "Indeed, for better or for worse, Sartre did not mention Zionism. . . . However, some of his articulations evoked Zionist language. Read his speech again and you will see for yourself that his words trigger Zionist associations." In addition, "I think that you should not have signed the letter to *Le Monde*. We in Israel did not receive very well the fact that a Zionist declares publicly that Sartre is not a Zionist. It would have been better if Lanzmann had signed it."[40]

A month later, by early May, the affair was no more. With a total Arab-Israeli war impending, pressing questions about the actual, rather than the philosophical, right of Israel to exist became concrete. Sartre's ambivalence left Israelis second-guessing their standing in the world. Worse still, the renowned pro-Palestinian British historian Arnold Toynbee contributed his fair share to Israeli anxiety when he told, of all venues, *Playboy Magazine* that "The Zionists seem to be obsessed with the idea that having their own country will somehow prevent the Germans or someone else from doing what has been done to the Jews in Europe in the past. I think they are thereby exposing their descendants to the risk of suffering the same sort of thing in the Arab world." Summarizing this statement, *Yediot Ahronot* bluntly wrote, "The inhabitants of Israel believe that by forming a state they will avoid the fate of European Jews. They are wrong."[41]

Sartre's Betrayal

With the full mobilization of Arab publics and armies, Israel's destruction now seemed to be around the corner. For Arabs this was not simply a single battle against Israel but, as a Syrian writer later put it, part of "a Third World campaign" against neocolonialism.[42] Indeed, in one way or another, the entire intellectual course of the 1960s pointed in this direction, and once this reservoir was activated, so to speak, there was no going back. Indeed, already in April, the Arab belligerent rhetoric of annihilation as liberation had taken on a life of its own, and unilateral political and military action followed suit. Arabs saw the crisis as an opportunity to undo the historical injustice of Palestine by way of a classic 1960s project of self-liberation. From the bottom up, a popular zeal for action manifested in daily demonstrations, marches, and an endless loop of political speechmaking. On the macro level, defense treaties were signed, and a joint Arab command was established. On the micro level, a group of Palestinian students wrote to the Syrian president to say how much they wished for the liberation of Palestine. To make the point, they inscribed their petition with their own blood.[43] For Israelis, but also for many Jews around the world, the Arab enthusiasm for total war triggered a deep existential crisis and fear of a second Holocaust. Though the month of May was already pregnant with a mesmerizing Arab defeat, almost everyone believed the exact opposite outcome was inevitable. And thus, on May 22, when Nasser closed the Tiran Straits to Israeli shipping, many felt that Israel's end was imminent.

Especially dramatic was the situation in France, where "Jews felt the shock of the Holocaust abandonment" and relived the traumatic moment in which the French government handed over French Jews to the Nazis.[44] In response, Jews took to the streets of France's major cities in unprecedented numbers. This communal moment came on the heels of the Treblinka Affair, which, since the publication of Jean-François Steiner's *Treblinka* the previous year, had forced the French public as well as the Jewish community to abandon its silence over the Holocaust and debate the realities of extermination as well as the passive conduct of many of the victims who were controversially blamed for going to the slaughter like sheep.[45] Was another Holocaust coming the way of their loved ones in Israel? Would they be led like sheep to the slaughter once again?

Many of the public intellectuals who originally weighed in on the Treblinka Affair, such as Beauvoir (who prefaced Steiner's book), Lanzmann, and Pierre Vidal-Naquet, were once again engaged in what they saw as a last-ditch effort to save Israel. Urgent action was needed, and members of the community began to speak "publicly and with emotionally charged rhetoric to the rest of the French nation about the Holocaust, which they presented as trauma: singular, incorporable and incomprehensible."[46] This was a radical departure from the subdued conversational culture of the preceding twenty years as, until May 1967, French Jews had been reluctant to challenge a nation that was not yet ready for critical self-examination. Debating Steiner's book about the realities of the camps was one thing, but insinuating that the French turned over their Jews to the Nazis and were about to do so again was a different kind of argument. As Lanzmann, a leading voice on this issue, told *Le Monde*, "If Israel were destroyed, it would be far more serious than the Nazi Holocaust."[47] And, so, the hitherto unprocessed trauma of the Holocaust found in the Arab-Israeli conflict a vehicle for its articulation, with the guiding theme being an acute existential crisis over its impeding repetition. Though the Arab public had no connection to France's so-called Vichy syndrome and to the "return of the repressed," it too was going to be influenced by it.

In a near hysteric prewar atmosphere that marked the actual "beginning of a certain Holocaust consciousness in French public discourse," public opinion took a decidedly pro-Israeli turn.[48] The popular weekly the *Nouvel Observateur* asked on its cover "Must Israel Be Destroyed?" Beauvoir recalled, "I lived through those days in a state of extreme anxiety. . . . I felt a friendship for both countries (Egypt and Israel) and the idea that their armies were about to start killing each other . . . was hateful to me. Above all, I was afraid for Israel. . . . All my Jewish friends were overwhelmed."[49] Arlette Elkaim was also anxious. She wrote Ely Ben Gal to say that "not a day passes by without me and Sartre thinking about Israel. Sartre speculates about Nasser's intentions and he is very worried. Without having any illusions he thinks of sending Nasser a telegram."[50]

Against this dramatic background, on Friday, May 27, Sartre sat down to write the introduction to the special issue of *Les Temps Modernes*. He reiterated the editorial line of "We promised neutrality—or if you will—absence" but, nonetheless, the tension in the streets and the anxiety of his adopted Jewish daughter infiltrated the text.[51] Verbal acrobatics could not mask the fact that Sartre too was petrified by the specter of a second Holocaust in which, as he put it, "the state of Israel will be ruined and the Jews would be thrown to the sea."[52] He, too, could not escape the threat of repetition in which once again France would betray its Jews. He asked Arabs to understand this unique historical context and reiterated his experience of "the Arab-Israeli conflict as a personal tragedy."[53] On the same day, he wrote to Ely Ben Gal in Israel: "We think of you all the time with anxiety and profound [feelings] of friendship. Here, we do what we can with poor means to make sure that the worst is avoided."[54] As he wrote these words, Sartre knew that he had taken a public step from which there was no easy return.

Growing day by day, the commotion in the Jewish community led to the establishment of advocacy groups such as Comité de Solidarité Français avec Israël. A mass rally of thirty-thousand people was organized in support of Israel. In no uncertain terms the Jews asked their French compatriots to side with them against "Arab Nazism" and a second annihilation.[55] The efforts to mobilize public opinion in support of Israel were successful, and multiple appeals for peace appeared in the daily press.[56] Finally, on May 30, *Le Monde* published the following statement:

The undersigned French Intellectuals believe that they have shown that they are friends of the Arab peoples and opponents of American imperialism. Without adopting all the policies of the Israeli leaders, we affirm that the state of Israel is now proving a clear desire for peace and calm. It is incomprehensible, whatever the moves of the great powers, that part of public opinion considers as self-evident Israel's identification with an imperialist and aggressive camp, and the Arabs with a socialist and pacifist camp; that it forgets at the same time that Israel is the only country whose very existence is in question; that everyday threatening proclamations are coming from the Arab leaders. Under these circumstances, we call upon democratic public opinion in France vigorously to refrain:

1. That Israel's security and sovereignty, obviously including free passage in international waters, is a necessary condition and starting point for peace.

2. That this peace is possible and must be assured and affirmed by direct negotiations between sovereign states in the mutual interest of the people concerned.[57]

Who signed it? Sixty-eight writers, artists, politicians, journalists, professors, students, and public intellectuals including Marguerite Duras, Arthur Koestler, Pablo Picasso, Vladimir Jankélévitch, Pierre Vidal-Naquet, Claude Roy, Daniel Mayer, and, last but not least, the champion of the différend, Jean-François Lyotard.[58] In short, Paris's intellectual elite took sides in an act that even today still reminds Arab intellectuals of Julien Benda's "betrayal of the intellectuals."[59] Some signatories, like philosopher Robert Misrahi, were former students of Sartre and staunch Zionists. Misrahi believed that the United Arab Republic was fascist, that the Arab Left was nonexistent, and that Palestinian refugees constituted "a small imperial problem" and no more.[60] Others, like former socialist minister and acting president of the Human Rights League (*Ligue des droits de l'homme*), Daniel Mayer, were not at all committed to Zionism.[61] Many of these intellectuals, like Pierre Vidal-Naquet, were veterans of the struggle for free Algeria and former signatories of the courageous Manifesto of the 121.[62] There were also a few on the left who refused to sign the statement, such as professors Jacques Berque and Maxime Rodinson, himself a Jew.

When some of the signatories and other leftist activists met in the Philosophy Department of the Collège de France to discuss recent developments, bitter disagreements and harsh language polarized the group.[63] Can one support Israel and still be an anti-imperialist socialist? Does standing with Israel mean finding yourself on the same side as the United States? Under pressure, Lanzmann cried, "Should we be forced to shout Long Live Johnson because America is the only force that can save Israel? I am ready to do it!"[64] His willingness to side with imperialism to save Israel exposed the divisions in the French Left between a minority coalition of pro-Arab communists, Maoists, and Trotskyites who spoke out in *L'Humanité*, and all the rest who supported Israel in the mainstream media.[65] Also joining the fray in those tumultuous days was Georges Friedmann, the writer of *Fin du peuple juif?*, which Sartre had read avidly while touring Gaza. Friedmann believed that Israel had a historic debt to settle Palestinian refugees.[66] He too was a minority voice.

What did Sartre and Beauvoir do? With the special issue of *Les Temps*

Modernes only a week away from publication, both signed the May 30 statement thus publicly abandoning their committed position to "neutrality and absence." Beauvoir signed immediately, but Sartre was torn and tried to avoid the issue. Lanzmann went looking for him. He waited for Sartre on the doorstep of his apartment, and had the reluctant philosopher sign the declaration.[67] A different version has it that Sartre was already involved in the drafting of the declaration, insisting on making it more palatable to Arabs.[68] In Jerusalem, over the podium of the Israeli Kneset, the new parliament member Uri Avneri publicly read the French public declaration and took pride in Sartre's support of Israel.[69] Members of Sartre's Arab circle were devastated. Sartre, an Arab hero, had betrayed them. They had already been frustrated with his ambiguity, but a signature on behalf of Israel was a different matter altogether.

Et Tu, Sartre?

Finely tuned to Paris, upon the circulation of the public statement, Suhayl Idris promptly cabled Sartre: "Your position in support of a country [Israel] that raped a land and expelled its people betrays your earlier support for struggles in Algeria, Cuba and Africa. . . . Arab intellectuals, many of whom are your friends, are saddened by your surrender to Zionist propaganda."[70] Until that point, and especially since the tour in Egypt, Idris had been convinced that Sartre identified with the Arab Cause. He was also sure that, following this telegram, Sartre would publicly reverse his position. It never happened, and, in the following days, an avalanche of anti-Sartre condemnation descended on the region. The Palestinian poet Muʿin Basisu compared Sartre's reactionary position on Palestine to that of John Steinbeck, once a progressive writer and now a staunch supporter of the Vietnam War; he nicknamed Sartre "Jean-Paul Steinbeck."[71] The Iraqi minister of culture was less conversational and issued a sweeping ban on the entire corpus of Beauvoir and Sartre's writing. Baghdad, the so-called capital of Arab existentialism, abruptly cut itself off from its great source of inspiration. Somewhat surprisingly, Idris, the great propagator of Sartre in the Arab lands, supported the ban and cabled the Iraqi minister to say so.[72] In Algiers, a large bonfire of Sartre's books registered the popular anger over his betrayal.[73] In Cairo, an emergency meeting of intellectuals condemned Sartre in the strongest possible terms. A quick CIA field officer cabled his superiors a brief note on Sartre's fall as a "victim to the current Middle East crisis."[74]

Liliane and Lutfi al-Khuli read the pro-Israeli statement on June 1, on their way from Algiers to Paris. When they arrived, Jacques Berque and Maxime Rodinson, two of the most prominent pro-Arab voices throughout the crisis, asked Lutfi if he intended to meet Sartre.[75] He answered in the negative and said that he did not understand "How a person who is famous for his position on behalf of freedom can take an opposite stance simply because of Israel?"[76] Though eventually the 1967 war would drive a wedge between Rodinson, Berque, and Sartre, the two academics told al-Khuli that he should meet Sartre.[77] They said that Sartre was deeply distressed and that without him the declaration could have been even more hostile to Arabs.[78] Al-Khuli ignored that friendly advice.

Also infuriated by Sartre's position was Fanon's widow, Josie. She saw his signature as a traitorous act that exposed the true character of the entire French Left. In a furious op-ed in the Algerian *El Moudjahid*, a French-language newspaper that historically represented the cause of the FLN, she strongly condemned the racist anti-Arab position of the French Left that thought that "all Arabs are Fascists, that the there is no Arab Left and that [since] only the United States can oppose the destruction of Israel, we should all shout 'Long Live Johnson!'"[79] She wrote that Sartre had switched sides from Fanon's camp to this "other camp. The camp of murderers. The camp that kills in Vietnam, the Middle East, Africa and Latin America."[80] Unable to recognize the legacy of her late husband in this "other camp" she said that it represented the old white European colonizer who could not humanize the otherness of the Arabs. Given Sartre's colossal betrayal, she symbolically asked the progressive publishing house Maspero to remove Sartre's iconic preface to Fanon's *Wretched of the Earth*. Maspero complied, and the next edition appeared without the canonical preface.[81]

Meanwhile, the special issue of *Les Temps Modernes* featuring no less than forty-five articles and holding 991 erudite pages was ready for distribution. It reached the vendors on June 4, on the eve of war in the Middle East. It was a poignant coincidence. "Addressed to the [French] Left" the issue was an excellent guide to a serious understanding of the conflict.[82] From a political standpoint, it called for dialogue, although by that time no one harbored any illusions about peace.[83] The contribution of ʿAli al-Samman, who rejected any kind of direct dialogue, foresaw the official policy of the Arab world for the next decade.[84] Palestinian intellectuals like Anis Sayigh found much interest in the volume and decided to publish the "Israeli section" in translation.[85] In a powerful piece that would later appear as a separate book Maxime Rodinson's "Israel: a Colonial Fact?" conceptualized Israel as an entity that embodied the very idea of "settler colonialism." It was a sophisticated and pioneering critique and one of the most enduring contributions to the issue. The Syrian press immediately translated it.[86] Understanding the destructive potential of Rodinson's piece, Lanzmann initially refused to publish it. He was overruled by Sartre.[87] Sartre may have signed the public statement that could be read as pro-Israeli, but he was unwilling to restrict the meaning of neocolonialism and its possible application to Zionism.

Isolated in Paris, Lutfi al-Khuli had no details of the war. He heard that the Americans and British were fighting for Israel and that the CIA was planning regime changes in Syria and Egypt.[88] Though this claim had come from the mouth of Nasser and was quoted in the French press, it was completely untrue, but given the experience of the 1956 Suez War and the general dynamics of the global Cold War, it sounded to al-Khuli quite probable.[89] Day in and day out, he witnessed the popular French celebration of Israel's victory and eventually heard the shocking news of Nasser's resignation. He found the anti-Arab atmosphere in Paris hysteric and distasteful.[90] Beauvoir also remembered "an outburst of anti-Arab racism" of the kind that was prevalent during the war in Algeria.[91] In desperation, Arab students in France petitioned de Gaulle to urgently address the situation as a serious international conflict and reaffirm France's commitment to the Arabs in a clear and lucid voice.[92] But to no avail; the anti-Arab sentiment was as strong as it was prevalent. Sad, angry, and disillusioned al-Khuli thought of confronting Sartre with a single sentence: "This is the result of your statement!"[93] Instead he published the sentiment in an op-ed.[94]

Shortly after the piece's publication Lutfi received a phone call from Sartre who invited him for lunch. He reluctantly accepted. Once again, Liliane, Lutfi, Sartre, and Beauvoir were seated around the same table. "How come you are in Paris since June first without calling me?" Sartre asked. "Because you positioned yourself against the struggle of the Arab people!" answered Lutfi. "What are you saying? And which position?" asked Sartre. "All I did was to take a principled position against war. I did not change my support for the Arab and Palestinian struggle for freedom and progress."[95] A heated conversation followed during which the two couples found little in common. According to Beauvoir, Liliane and Lutfi were in a poor state: "They had no news of their family and their friends and they were consumed with anxiety. They had seen anti-Arab demonstrations and they had been the object of hostile remarks themselves. 'If Egypt had won, we should have been

torn to pieces,' said Liliane. Their reaction took the form of a feverish exasperation . . . and [they] found our skepticism intolerable. They
blamed us angrily for not having loudly and publicly taken Egypt's side
against Israel. It was a painful interview."[96] The truth of the matter,
however, was that Beauvoir took sides in the conflict: "When the moment of the cease-fire came I rejoiced that Israel had been spared."[97]
And she also had a rationale: "I did not consider Israel an aggressor. . . .
I also denied that Israel was colonialist; the country did not exploit
a native labor-force that would sell the manufactured products of the
colonies at a high price—there was no mother country. I did not look
upon Israel as a bridgehead of imperialism. . . . It is not true that Israel's
existence hindered the development of Arab countries. . . . For my part,
I find the idea that Israel might vanish from the map of the world perfectly hateful."[98]

Indeed, for complex intellectual reasons, such as the identification
of Jews as suffering from the same existential circumstances as women,
Beauvoir sided with Israel.[99] Though Lutfi and Liliane heard only a
softened version of Beauvoir's true position, the meeting disappointed
them profoundly. Lutfi was especially reluctant to accept Sartre's apol-
ogetic explanation for signing the statement. "Listen!" Sartre finally
said, "how about we schedule a comprehensive dialogue? I am anxious
to explain my position to [my] Arab friends."[100] The next day they met
again in Sartre's home.

Al-Khuli left a detailed account of that second meeting. A trial lawyer by training with an imposing posture, piercing eyes, and a strong
sense of conviction, al-Khuli confronted Sartre on an array of issues.
Striking a conciliatory tone, Sartre was quick to dispel any suspicion:
"I insist," he said, "that I was, still am, and will always be an ally to
the Arab peoples."[101] Al-Khuli then asked how the French could fail to
see that this was not a conflict between Muslims and Jews but between
Zionists and Arabs.[102] Sartre answered, "I agree . . . this is not a religious
problem. Even Nasser had asked me how could we be anti-Semites when
we ourselves are Semites?"[103] Al-Khuli pressed on, asking how the establishment of Israel as a response to European anti-Semitism "could be
considered a human and democratic solution to the Jewish problem?"[104]

Responding, Sartre went on a long and evasive review of the various
forms of Zionism and their objectives. Al-Khuli interjected, urging a
more concrete response, but Sartre continued to meander. Al-Khuli cut
him off again: "You are not answering my question. I want to know if
Israeli Zionism is the solution to the Jewish problem. Based on your
visit to Israel, is it an objective, human and peaceful solution?"[105]

Sartre: I understand why many of my Jewish friends are connected to Israel. . . .
However (given that 12.5 million Jews live in the West), Israel is not the solution
to the Jewish Problem . . . and is not a solution to Anti-Semitism. [Furthermore,]
if I concur with the existence of Israel, it is not because it is a solution to the
Jewish Problem but because it is an existing human fact which includes men,
women and children . . . and these children have no understanding of this problem. From this perspective the talk about the destruction of Israel generates
nothing but pain. Once again I do not think that Israel is the solution to the
Jewish Problem.[106]

Al-Khuli: But Israel was established with the force of arms as a solution the Jewish
Problem and not simply as a human reality for a few Jews who fled oppression.[107]

Sartre: By the standards of that era, Herzl's nineteenth-century idea of creating a
state in Jerusalem was not a crime. . . . Why so? Because it was a colonial solution like all the other solutions in that era. No one thought at that time about
the right of colonized people to define themselves.[108]

Al-Khuli: But can't you see that Zionism strives to perpetually expend the borders of
Israel on the expense of the Arabs in order to absorb more immigrants?[109]

Sartre: Yes, I agree that this is indeed a dangerous direction that should not be
accommodated. . . . I know many Jews here in Paris who support Zionism but,
though conflicted with themselves, would rather not live in Israel. . . . For instance, [Robert] Mizrahi who defends Israel vigorously . . . but nonetheless stays
here . . . many other European Jews want Israel but refuse to live there.[110]

Al-Khuli then moved to discuss the criminal Israeli usage of napalm
bombs during the war. Sartre agreed that whether in Vietnam or in
the Middle East, it was indeed a crime to use such weapon. "Are you
saying that General Dayan is a war criminal?" asked al-Khuli. "Yes," replied Sartre, "General Dayan is a war criminal because he used Napalm
and because of his expansionist motivation."[111] Toward the end of the
dialogue, Sartre tried to explain the situation of French Jews and the
activation of the Holocaust trauma in conjunction with the war. "It is
important," Sartre said, "to look at the tragedy [of the Holocaust] also
from the other (Jewish) side" and not only from the perspective of Europeans sending their victims to Palestine.[112] The meeting ended with
Sartre's message to the Arabs: "I beg you to communicate to the Egyptian people and all of the Arab peoples my solidarity with them. . . . I
also want to wish Nasser to continue to enjoy, as we have just recently
seen, the support of the masses in order to further his struggle and
achievements."[113]

They parted ways on friendly terms, but Sartre had more explaining
to do. Shortly after the war he called 'Ali al-Samman. "You avoid me,"

charged Sartre. Al-Samman answered whatever he answered, and Sartre said back: "It might have been that I was misled as a person but surely you understand the independence of the man in front of you. . . . You should accept in him the side you like and ignore what you do not like."[114] Al-Samman chose to ignore the whole thing, and their relationship came to an end.

Upon his return to Egypt, Lutfi al-Khuli published the dialogue in *Al-Ahram*.[115] He felt that he finally had got Sartre to say concrete things, such as that Israel was not the solution to the Jewish problem, that its foundational logic was purely colonial, and that Dayan was a war criminal. In a meeting with Suhayl Idris, al-Khuli assured him that "Sartre had changed his position."[116] Idris answered, "Arab intellectuals expect Sartre to publish a new statement. . . . They are not content with what he said privately to you."[117] Al-Khuli said that Sartre had indeed committed to publish such a statement soon. The two might have had in mind the pro-Arab statement that Bertrand Russell had just published in response to a plea from the Arab League. Independently of Sartre, his partner in the tribunal, Russell, accused Israel of aggression and of violating a cease-fire.[118] But Sartre published no similar statement. Concluding the unfortunate saga of Sartre's de facto defection, Idris wrote in his magazine, "We hope to win this great intellectual once again to our ranks."[119]

On his part, Lutfi was no longer in a position to pursue the affair. One of the several Egyptian security services had secretly recorded him and Liliane criticizing Nasser. His office had been wiretapped all along, and reports of his business were communicated all the way to the top. Both were sent to prison, leaving their five-year-old daughter without her parents. Nasser, who was apparently angered by Lutfi's "arrogant and disrespectful manner," agreed to release Liliane but kept Lutfi in jail. He endured the hardship of prison but refused to apologize and was released only after Nasser's death in 1970.[120] There is no record of Sartre and Beauvoir campaigning for his release.

Conclusion

In the weeks and months after the war, the intellectual process of disowning Sartre's work continued in full swing. Writing in the Egyptian popular cultural magazine *Al-Hilal*, Ibrahim ʿAmr declared the coming of a "Post-Sartre" era. His article was not a petty knee-jerk reaction to Sartre's disappointing position but a serious call for replacing existen-

Michel Foucault, Jacques Lacan, Claude Lévi-Strauss et Roland Barthes.

FIGURE 9 "Better Than Sartre": Michel Foucault, Jacques Lacan, Claude Lévi-Strauss, and Roland Barthes. Cartoon by Maurice Henry.

tialism with a better intellectual system. To make the point, *Al-Hilal* featured a cartoon by Maurice Henry recently published in *La Quinzaine Litteraire*. The cartoon, which has since been canonized as an accurate snapshot of France's intellectual transformation, featured Michel Foucault, Jacques Lacan, Claude Lévi-Strauss, and Roland Barthes as they returned to the visceral and concrete realities of nature at the expense of the abstract qualities of existentialism.

'Amr explained that, unlike the fashion of existentialism, structuralism offered a new mode of comprehension in the humanities and, taking after Foucault, opined that Sartre was "a thinker of the 19th century who (unsuccessfully) tries to tackle the issues and concerns of the 20th century."[121] For Arab readers, the literature of structuralism was new and completely unfamiliar. Yet, the point was not so much about structuralism itself as about replacing Sartre's dysfunctional ethics with a better system. Quite simply, they felt that by betraying his own ethical commitments to support the oppressed, Sartre had failed them.

Originally, the core idea of this engagement was the following: "He [Sartre] posited a politics of universal emancipation in which the intellectual mediates social and political conflicts by relating the particular situation to the universal conditions of human liberation."[122] Reviewing the historical record, there was nothing that Arab writers missed about the applicability of this formulation to their own condition. In their minds they were engaged all along in the project of universal emancipation, and their writers-martyrs-prophets did their best to manage a long list of cultural tensions in order to further the prospects of human liberation worldwide.

Though they were reluctant to process the fact that Sartre's notion of otherness was informed by Jewish experience, they did account for his ethical engagements, which are scattered all over his oeuvre in a rather free-floating fashion. Some of his relevant works, such as *Notebooks for an Ethics*, were published posthumously and others, such as his so-called 1964 Rome Lecture and the 1965 Cornell Notes, are still in manuscript form and hence were never consulted. In fact, only in recent years have philosophers and intellectual historians managed to assemble a more or less complete record of Sartre's unfinished ethics.[123] But even had the Rome Lecture been available, its announcement that "the historical moment has come for socialism to rediscover its ethical structure, or rather, to unveil it," would have been in complete alignment with Arab thoughts and actions.[124] As we have seen in previous chapters, the reconciliation of socialism, nationalism, and antiimperialism was a keystone of this ethical structure. Not only Arabs were eager to contribute to this end, the Third World as a whole was onboard. Indeed, it was the Third World that set an example for how daily revolutionary actions by regular people contributed most significantly to the emergence, or rediscovery as Sartre would have it, of global socialist ethics. Arab intellectuals in particular approached this universal project as a vocation of daily intellectual and political work.

In so doing, they did what everybody else who was committed to this project did: follow Sartre's politics. Since Sartre's ethics were intimately bound up with his political activism, Arab intellectuals developed a robust habit of reading, decoding, venerating, and emulating his example. As we have seen in the previous chapters, especially during the high sixties, they found a strong association between freedom and revolt in which both serve as a conduit toward a more universal position. The justification for anticolonial violence emerged from this very link. The expectation from Sartre to be true to his politics and be Sartrean was therefore a natural response to his position of total absence with regard to the conflict.

In the context of this conflict, there is no doubt that Sartre failed to entertain ahead of time the ethical need for a hierarchy of otherness. In an international environment in which colonizer and colonized differed from one another in so many ways (racially, religiously, economically, culturally, and politically), there was no actual need for an ethical hierarchy of otherness, and the possibility of two others locked in a struggle for life and death was purely theoretical. Palestine was such a reality.

The Arab world did not understand this impasse as a philosophical problem but as a political issue. Sartre's signature on behalf of Israel was taken to be more than a mere few drops of ink against war, the kind of act that could later be reframed, repackaged, or even retracted as Lutfi al-Khuli had hoped. Instead, the signature became psychologically associated not only with the devastating political, military, and even cultural defeat of the war but also, and as seriously, with a divestment from a shared left-wing project whose horizons were universal and whose creed was freedom. Hence the Arab world received Sartre's signature as an iconic act of betrayal, not only by Sartre himself but also by his coterie, the city of Paris, the French Left and, in particularly somber moments, Europe in its entirety. This form of colossal betrayal, therefore, was not simply a personal issue regarding a specific individual who, at the moment of truth, shifted his alliances. Rather, it was the betrayal of the universal promise of liberation and its unfortunate failure to include and recognize the Arab experience. We will return to this notion of colossal betrayal in the epilogue.

Epilogue: A Cosmic No Exit

Paris, winter, 2002. An old man walks slowly up the street. He breathes heavily and struggles to walk. He falls down. A French doctor rushes to help him. He is taken to a local hospital where he is diagnosed as having had a stroke. The old man speaks incoherently about being an Egyptian philosopher. No one misses him. He has neither family nor relatives. Finally, the Egyptian embassy is contacted and ʿAbd al-Rahman Badawi is flown to Cairo, where he will pass away a few months later, on July 25. Upon his death, the headline of the daily international newspaper *Al-Hayat* reads, "The Pioneer of Modern Arabic Philosophy Passed Away as a Stranger."[1] The headline was not quite accurate, but it did capture the sense of an unfulfilled hope. He had been the "first Arab existentialist" and the young hope of an entire generation. An intellectually sensitive man, he was also famous for being an extremely difficult one. Exactly two years before his death he boasted, "Due to what I wrote existentialism became a major stream in the makeup of most Arab intellectuals." Arrogant, but true. He also complained that "Arab intellectuals constantly misunderstood existentialism and mixed it up with irrelevant intellectual traditions."[2] Disappointed by the course that public culture took and by the atmosphere of bigotry and authoritarianism in his home country, in February 1967 Badawi had left for a life of exile in Paris where, in a strange case of continuity, he took residence in the Hotel Lutetia, the same hotel in which Taha Husayn had once resided.[3] He lived there for most of his life, until the day he fell down.

The *annus horribilis* of 1967 forced Badawi to rethink the ongoing riddle of Arab existence. He was hardly alone. Gradually, he gave up the synthesis of Western and Islamic philosophy and returned—some say escaped—to the warm bosom of religious heritage, or turath, where he longed for a different kind of homecoming.[4] Needless to say, this form of return was not just a personal journey but a generational move away from the universal culture of the 1960s and deeper into the familiar and safer domains of religiosity. Whether Badawi escaped universalism or confidently marched toward the collective cul-de-sac of autochthonous particularism, his death was surely a symbolic one, as it evoked melancholic thoughts of the life and sudden death of an entire intellectual tradition and the proud generation that had believed in it and had carried it forward.

Arab existentialism was an extended exercise in intellectual *bricolage*. There were several dead ends and, yes, also battles of philosophical speculation whose ultimate influence on actual life was nil. However, within the immense cultural effort of decolonization, Arab existentialism held a central place as a variation on the influential postcolonial theme of self-liberation. Serving as a tool for individual and communal introspection and self-fashioning, the ethos of Arab existentialism revolved around the issues of authenticity, sovereignty, and freedom. In that, and unlike, for example, the reception of existentialism in the United States, Sartre's work was constitutive of the new Arab self.[5] In this, it registers the intellectual specificity of Arab decolonization, showing how diverse, multilayered, and even contradictory that self-fashioning process really was.

Authenticity was the first order of the day. Quite urgently, there was a fragmented cultural self to heal, and because the colonial Arab self also contained within it the European other, the potential of existentialism was immediately recognized as a possible bridge between these two badly coordinated lobes. The project of authenticity was always, and still is, on the minds of Arab intellectuals. But, during the 1950s and 1960s, it was also the first aspect of decolonization to be exclusively relegated to Pan-Arabism. Concomitantly, in its deeper and more culturally substantial Islamic form, authenticity became the business of experimental Marxists, imprisoned mavericks, an ossified clerical establishment, and embattled members of the Muslim Brotherhood. Against this background, a new brand of Islamic fundamentalism was born in Egyptian prison cells. It rarely featured in any of the hegemonic cultural or intellectual venues of the time but, as it turned out, it would own the future.[6]

Instead, the intelligentsia believed that addressing the challenges of sovereignty and freedom would suffice to rehabilitate Arab life. The hegemonic notion of commitment, or iltizam, was foundational to this dual effort. No other concept during the era proved so versatile and applicable to a host of situations and political constellations as that of iltizam. Its tasks were significant. The Arab revolutionary scene of the 1960s was a young one. And if no men of the nineteenth century were calling the shots, it was partially because the politics of iltizam aggressively retired these men. The phasing out of the udaba', against their will, was the work of young intellectuals who invoked iltizam to expose the degree to which the udaba' relied on colonial humanism, especially in its French version.

Iltizam was also implicated in the battle for and against radical individualism. To whom is the new Arab man committed, to society or to itself? Because it was entangled in the question of freedom and sovereignty this became a major question of the day. With the rise of the authoritarian Arab state and its sacrificial politics, iltizam became associated with sacrifice on behalf of the nation as means of regaining collective sovereignty. Being an existential effort that sought to alter Arab ontology, the state defined the notion of iltizam as commitment to the sacred politics of collective sacrifice and rebirth. In this way, iltizam became the subject of Pan-Arabism. Emptied of its original meaning of intellectual commitment to freedom as such, it gradually slipped into the traitorous trap of self-referential commitment to commitment. In this new role, it was used to justify horrendous acts of political terror against a long list of real and imagined internal enemies. Though existentialism equipped the authoritarian nation-state with an effective tool for the suppression of freedom, it also endowed the opponents of this state with a rich intellectual repertoire with which to resist this oppression. In this role, it was especially useful for marginal groups and individuals who opposed the reduction of decolonization to state sovereignty and imagined alternative venues of freedom.

Another notable aspect of Arab existentialism was its smooth interface with Third Worldism and the revolutionary culture of the 1960s. If until the 1950s the main Arab perspective on world order was that of East versus West, the 1960s vertically reconfigured this order as one that pitted the South against the North. Via the prevalence of existentialism, an actual political link was made to Sartre and his ethics of global action. Here what mattered was not lofty philosophy but on-the-ground political action against racism, settler colonialism, neocolonialism, imperialism, and so on. The ethics that followed from global political action were all-encompassing as they pertained to state, society, and the self. Most importantly, they pointed toward humanity at large and hence toward a new form of universality. Subscribing to the idea that Middle Eastern battles were merely one front in a global war, the Arab Left developed an expectation that the difficult heritage of colonialism would find its resolution via its attachment to a universal framework.

Somewhat less conclusively, though time and again Arab existentialism brought intellectuals to question the governing norms of sexuality, rebel against them, or simply experiment on their own, these pages fall short of addressing the issue of sexuality in a thorough manner. Granted, the material is very suggestive in showing how the liberation of the self cannot be divorced from the broader issue of sexual liberation. Yet, a serious reconsideration of this topic should extend its mandate to systematically question the shifting meaning of sexuality during decolonization and the current historiography of gender and decolonization as a whole. My impression is that the Arab Cause of liberation was constructed as an exclusive domain of male activity whose gendered identity has yet to be explored in detail.

Taken as a whole, this era was characterized by the intimacy of politics and the belief in real emancipation. For the politically involved Arab citizen of the 1960s, the great "isms" of the time, such as socialism, Marxism, communism, and anti-imperialism, were experienced not as rigid and impersonal ideological dogmas but as meaningful personal choices. In addition to functioning as intimate intellectual companions and guides to culture, politics, and everyday dilemmas of life, these ideologies also operated as an ethical compass that assisted in navigating the labyrinth of decolonization. But even within the safe and validating domain of ideology the line between the assuring calmness of certainty and doubtful anxiety proved to be very thin. As the late Samir Kassir readily acknowledged, there was no self-reflection on the postcolonial condition that was not anxiety producing. This destructive form of anxiety was as prevalent as it was amorphous. Indeed, it was an anxiety that had no object. It was not about this or that political, cultural, or social choice but about the very meaning of being Arab in a modern world made by others.[7] Within this uncertain space, existentialism offered a theoretical opening, or a possibility of exit toward a more complete form of being. As it turned out, by way of Sartre, it also offered membership in a false universal. So much became clear in 1967.

A Genealogy of Betrayal

The culture of the sixties encompassed too many characteristics to name in detail, but a list of its most striking features might resemble this inventory compiled by Arthur Marwick:

> Black civil rights, youth culture and trend setting by young people; idealism, protest, and rebellion; the triumph of popular music based on Afro-American models and the emergence of this music as universal language, with the Beatles as the heroes of the age; the search for inspiration in the religions of the Orient; massive changes in personal relationship and sexual behavior, a general audacity and frankness in books and in the media, and in ordinary behavior, relaxation of censorship, the new feminism, gay liberation; the emergence of "the underground" and the "counter culture"; optimism and genuine faith in the drawing of a better world.[8]

Converging toward the revolutionary events of May 1968 in Mexico, in the United States, France, Czechoslovakia, and much of Europe, a sense of idealism merged with a propensity toward protest and rebellion, both of which were wrapped in universal language. Marking the cultural dominance of young people, the global culture of the sixties rejected rigid social hierarchies and docile deference to authority of any kind. Young people had much to say about rampant racism and the subordination of women to men. For many, as Marwick noted, this long list was topped with the utter rejection of Cold War hysteria and empty forms of patriotism.[9]

Not all of these characteristics manifested themselves in the Arab world, most of them certainly not. One obvious omission, for example, was the popular will to systematically emancipate women and subaltern groups. But, regardless of their differences, when young people of the Left spoke about revolution, the general impression was that they collectively worked together toward a global revolution with Third Worlders as respected equal partners. While in the Euro-American world the bustling energy of the sixties would abruptly explode in May 1968 and then slowly metamorphose into something quite different, with few avant-garde exceptions, the Arab sixties ended abruptly. In fact, we can put a date on it: June 5, 1967.

Though many intellectuals saw the defeat coming and were by no means surprised, for most observers, the war's impact was so shockingly deep and so sharply painful that it was initially met with denial and rejection. Some of the early responses cast the blame entirely on outsiders and even called for a complete ban on Western culture due to its culpability.[10] But as weeks turned into months it became obvious that the war was radically reconfiguring what was known and thought in the Arab world. It was inscribed into people's subjectivities as a foundational moment following which "everything" would have to change. Granted, the war was experienced very differently across the region, and answers to the question of what had actually been defeated and who and what were to be held responsible varied greatly.[11] To say that the ethos of Arab existentialism was defeated is of course very superficial. Yet, to claim that the story of Arab existentialism is a sensitive barometer for the subject of defeat is a different kind of argument. Indeed, as we have seen, tragically, Arab existentialism accounted for roughly three busy decades during which Arab publics and their influential elites and intellectuals constructively toiled for the sake of freedom, sovereignty, and authenticity.

In that context, the close relationship with Sartre was a living testimony to the centrality of existentialism in Arab thought as well as a constant reminder of the power of an enduring intellectual alliance and the shared goal of liberation. At least that was the impression. As the Middle East inched closer and closer toward war, the common front began to unravel. When the finality of Sartre's position became clear, there was only one way of interpreting it: as an iconic betrayal. That the most devastating defeat in modern Arab history also saw the breakdown of the relationship with Sartre and the questioning of existentialism was not simply a wicked coincidence. The two, as we have seen here, were closely intertwined.

Then came May 1968. Though the impact of this moment on the Arab world remains unexplored, it is probably safe to say that, with the exception of Palestinians, who began to chart an independent course of action, its impact was rather negligible.[12] True, in November 1968 Egyptian students violently rebelled against the state, but their effort was quickly contained and shared very little with what their colleagues were doing elsewhere in the world. In many quarters, there was a sense of disinterest, even rejection. Indeed, perhaps ironically, after years of Third World revolutionary experiments, everything that the Arab Left had dreamed and fought for suddenly erupted in Paris, a faraway metropolis that had only recently rejected Arabs in the most racist of ways. Worse, the alleged allies from the European Left, now branded the New Left, were busy doing their own "new" thing. Their focus was at home. Indeed, the vector of May 1968 pointed elsewhere, away from the revolutionary Third World and into the new frontiers of human rights and antitotalitarianism.

While in the short run the radicals of 1968 campaigned for revolution, a cause that they intimately shared with the Third World, in the long run they settled for ethics. Concern over the general question of human rights called attention to the cultural dynamics by which gays, immigrants, prisoners, workers, and women are constantly marginalized. It also brought attention to the institutional side of social marginalization; for instance, with regard to the realities of psychiatric asylums. It gave birth to a philosophy of desire. Taking the cause of human rights to the global level, members of this generation created new models for international civic action such as Médecins Sans Frontières (MSF). Such organizations fashioned an entirely new relationship to the Third World, one that replaced the politics of revolution with disdain for authoritarianism and an ethical concern for human well-being. Since then, these issues have dominated the public agenda. "Nowhere in the West," wrote one historian, "was the collapse of the revolutionary identity of the Left more spectacular than in its original homeland, France."[13] Revolution was out, ethics was in, and save for a fraction of the European Left that was radicalized anew and sought to bring about a defeat of capitalism by forging violent international alliances with Japanese, Palestinians, Venezuelans, the Italian Brigate Rosse (Red Brigades), and the German Rote Armee Fraktion (Red Army Faction, or RAF), the cause of revolution in Europe was over and done with.[14]

With these developments, gone too was the enchanting power of the Third World to serve as an example and inspiration. Amid massive violations of human rights, as in Pol Pot's Cambodia or Idi Amin's Uganda, the sixties generation and the emerging New Left quickly lost "some of the more naive illusions about the Third World's potential for spearheading world revolution."[15] No work was more vicious in its sweeping condemnation of Third Worldism than Pascal Bruckner's diatribe *The Tears of the White Man*.[16] As the Third World was divested from, the notion of globalization was becoming ever more prominent. "For theorists of this phenomenon there was only one world—the Third World was neither the problem nor the solution. If Third Worldism had undermined a Eurocentric view of the planet, a concept of globalization was able to both integrate and replace its insights."[17] For good or ill, these were the 1970s.

And what about the Arab-Israeli conflict? For the most part, with the collapse of the "Arab Cause" due to its Third World provenance, the conflict was reduced to the problem of Palestine. The separate Israeli-Egyptian peace deal of 1979 did further damage to the idea of a united Arab Cause and basically rendered it obsolete. If non-Palestinian Arabs still had troubles that decolonization failed to address, they were welcome to hold their own governments accountable. Left to their own fate, Palestinians forged their own project of self-liberation. Quickly abandoning any dreams about liberation by proxy, as in Nasserism, they followed the example of popular guerrilla campaign of the kind Chairman Mao, Ho Chi Minh, and Che Guevara had prescribed. To do so, Palestinians such as Ghassan Kanafani gave up the concept of iltizam and coined the new term of *muqawama* (resistance). Just like its predecessor, *muqawama* sought to inscribe the political onto the cultural and proliferate a new form of literature to match the effort on the battlefront. It became known as *adab al-muqawama* (resistance literature).[18] Importantly though, unlike the defeated concept of iltizam, *muqawama* prided itself on the complete absence of the overbearing authoritarian state and claimed for itself the Zionist enemy as a well-defined object. Placing the responsibility for liberation on individual actors and demanding they literally take their destiny into their hands does, of course, invoke some existentialist themes.

Back to France, with Palestine as the core of the conflict, one would have anticipated that the intense 1970s focus on the moral rights of marginalized groups would bring about a clarification of Sartre's ethical impasse and would push people to take sides. By and large, that did not happen. Sartre himself continued to zigzag between support for Zionism and sympathy for Palestinians. True to his relational and phenomenological approach to the conflict, he continued to resist any thought about the essence of Zionism or Palestinian resistance. However bloody and terrible, it was still a relationship.

Thus, in August 1972, when the Palestinian terrorist organization Black September murdered in cold blood members of the Israeli delegation to the Munich Olympics, Sartre, then in the midst of a Maoist phase, supported their actions as a legitimate form of resistance. Facing the rage of Israelis and Jews worldwide, two years later, in 1974, he joined dozens of intellectuals from around the world, including Beauvoir, in condemning UNESCO for its decision to withhold assistance from Israel in the fields of education, science, and culture because of its archeological excavations in Jerusalem and their influence on Palestinian heritage.[19] By that point Palestinians of the liberation movement saw Sartre as an enemy, and Palestinian poet Mu'in Basisu comically featured Sartre as a secret agent who travels to Beirut in order to attack Palestinian cultural institutions.[20] Continuing the pattern, following Raymond Aron and Marc Chagall, in 1976 the man who refused the Nobel Prize accepted an honorary PhD in philosophy from the Hebrew University.[21] As Ely Ben Gal, Sartre's former student and tour guide in Israel, put it, "Sartre was very pro-Israeli and also very pro-Palestinian."[22]

Although, in the very long run, an ethical reading of regional conflicts including Israel's siege of Beirut and its destruction, the First Intifada, the daily oppression of the occupation, and so on would forever tarnish the moral standing of Israel, Sartre's legacy of ambiguity still casts a large shadow on the question of Palestine and on the willingness of key European intellectuals to publicly side with it. Over the years, Sartre's ethical impasse assumed a larger dimension as the origination point of an entrenched genealogy of absence that, though it began with him, continues to this day. The public position of Pierre Bourdieu is a good case in point. When the bloodbath of the Second Intifada was in full swing, Bourdieu was quite forthcoming about the sense of paralysis that afflicts him in confronting the problem of Palestine. Offering an explanation for his difficulty, he repeated Sartre's formulation verbatim: "How to choose between the victims of racist violence par excellence and the victims of these victims?"[23]

The frustration that many observers and pro-Palestinian activists have with this genealogy of absence is immense. Most obviously, they register displeasure with an entire cadre of French intellectuals who penned bookshelves of influential critical theory whose implications for Zionism are clearly damning, but whose authors refuse to spell out these implications politically and stand by them. Just as was the case with Sartre, they are being asked how they can deny the obvious political implications of their ideas. Why the contradiction? In that sense, many thinkers still feel that, regardless of what happens in Palestine/Israel, Sartre's ethical impasse and his genealogy of absence, or betrayal, is still at play. Here is one eloquent example of this frustration:

What is it about the nature of Zionism, its racism, and its colonial policies that continues to escape the understanding of many European intellectuals on the Left? Why have the Palestinians received so little sympathy from prominent leftist intellectuals such as Jean-Paul Sartre and Michel Foucault or only contingent sympathy from others like Jacques Derrida, Pierre Bourdieu, Etienne Balibar, and Slavoj Zizek? . . .

While most of these intellectuals have taken public stances against racism and white supremacy, have opposed Nazism and apartheid South Africa, seem to oppose colonialism, old and new, most of them partake of *a Sartrian legacy* which refuses to see a change in the status of European Jews, who are still represented only as holocaust survivors in Europe [emphasis added]. The status of the European Jew as a coloniser who has used racist colonial violence for the last century against the Palestinian people is a status they refuse to recognise and continue to resist vehemently.[24]

Mutatis mutandis, this is the very same argument that Lutfi and Liliane al-Khuli, Suhayl Idris, Fayiz Sayigh, and countless of others, including, most recently, Farouk Mardam-Bey, have repeatedly raised since the mid-1960s.[25] Though far less pessimistic, Edward Said made a similar point following a somber 1979 meeting with Sartre in which the philosopher once again failed to deliver an unambiguous statement about Palestine.[26] While much, of course, has changed since the 1970s, the specter of Sartre's iconic betrayal and the genealogy of absence that it created still haunt the Palestinian quest for freedom and human dignity.

Yet, however haunting the memory of Sartre's position on Palestine remains, it would be historically wrong to reduce the legacy of Arab existentialism to the soured relationship with Sartre and equally wrong to reduce Sartre's Arab legacy to the question of Palestine and his genealogy of absence. True, sometimes it seems as if with the exception of a neighborhood grocery store in Cairo that still operates under the suggestive name al-Wujud wa-l-'Adam, or *Being and Nothingness* (yes, there is such a place), not much is left of the once-hopeful era of existentialism. But intellectual legacies such as these never simply disappear into thin air. Indeed, recently, exactly seventy years after its original date of publication, a local scholar finally translated Sartre's *Réflexions sur la question juive* (*Anti-Semite and Jew*) and, however briefly, rekindled an inter-Arab interest in Sartre's Arab legacy (and in his betrayal).[27] Clearly, the legacy of an entire generation who worked tirelessly to change their reality and take responsibility for it—just as classical existentialism instructed them to do—still lives on, and the trauma of 1967 should not be allowed to eclipse this story and consign its memory to oblivion.[28]

No one understood this better than Suhayl Idris. In April 1980, on the occasion of Sartre's death, he edited a special commemorative issue, titled "Sartre's Absence"; he did not mean it as a pun. He began by saying, "Even though Sartre supported the existence of Israel and defended it," and even though his position on Palestine was not what Arab intellectuals had hoped for, his major influence on the Arab world squarely stands to his credit.[29] A sentimental retrospective followed. Everything that was fit to print about Sartre and Arab existentialism since *Al-Adab*'s first day in circulation appeared in this issue.[30] It featured virtually everything of importance and touched on the entire spectrum of this legacy. Learned discussions of ontology, freedom, responsibility, authenticity, and angst. Assessments and reassessments of Sartre's shifting politics, the open political letters that Suhayl Idris periodically addressed to Sartre, articles that celebrated the Arab bond to Sartre, more scholarly analysis of his literature, philosophy, and plays. An obvious appreciation of committed literature and translations of his critical articles on torture in Algeria and the fate of the subhuman, the nature of colonialism and neocolonialism, his violent introduction to Fanon, his writing on Cuba, and a selection of Simone de Beauvoir's autobiographical writing, as she, too, was part of this legacy. It concluded with a few freshly written French obituaries about the first global intellectual, the imperfectly committed man who inspired millions to seriously think about the meaning of everyday freedom.

Publishing this special issue in the midst of the murderous Lebanese civil war, the divestment of Egypt from the cause of Palestine, the deepening grip of the Israeli occupation, the triumph of the authoritarian state, the ubiquitous crushing of freedoms, the depressing Iranian revolution, the superficial reinvention of Islam as the "solution for everything," the rise of violent fundamentalism, the related cultural divestment from universalism, and the suffocating sense that the Arab world was trapped in a permeant state of crisis (*azma*), Suhayl Idris reminded his readers of a bygone era. He retold an almost-forgotten tale about the political journey of his generation, and how it constructively embraced existentialism as a vehicle for postcolonial liberation. Bravely writing a chapter in the existential struggle for a postcolonial exit, in the wake of 1967, the realities of the region spelled something else. It reads: No Exit.

Notes

INTRODUCTION

1. Ahmad 'Abbas Salih, "Risala ila Sartar," *Al-Katib*, March 1967, 25. On Salih's life see his obituary in *Al-Sharq al-Awsat*, http://archive.aawsat.com/details.asp?issueno=9896 &article=366494#.VT_oVZNQB_A, accessed April 28, 2015.
2. I could not verify the historical truthfulness of this claim. See advertisement for the Arabic translation of *Les Mots* in *Al-Adab*, December 1964, 66.
3. Andre Bercoff, "Une inéluctable et difficile repersonnalisation," *Le Monde*, April 15, 1967, vii.
4. Mujahid 'Abd al-Mun'im Mujahid, *'Asifa 'ala al-'asr* (Beirut: Dar al-Adab, 1965), 5; "Hal yumkin 'an yatrah Sartar qadiya Filastiniyya fi uruba?," *Al-Thawra*, March 11, 1967, 7–8.
5. Malek Bennabi, *Fikra al-Ifriqiyya al-Asyawiyya fi daw' mu'tamar Bandunj*, trans. 'Abd al-Sabur Shahin (Cairo: Maktabat Dar al-'Uruba, 1957), 255.
6. For Iran, see Ali Gheissari, *Iranian Intellectuals in the Twentieth Century* (Austin: University of Texas Press, 1998), 97–98; Hamid Dabashi, *Theology of Discontent: The Ideological Foundation of the Islamic Revolution in Iran* (New York: New York University Press, 1993), 115–35; Ali Rahnema, *An Islamic Utopian: A Political Biography of Ali Shari'ati* (London: I. B. Tauris, 1998), 117–30.
7. Edward Said, "Diary," *London Review of Books* 22, no. 11 (June 1, 2000): 42–43, http://www.lrb.co.uk/v22/n11/edward-said/diary, accessed September 28, 2015.
8. Mark Greif, *The Age of the Crisis of Man: Thought and Fiction in America, 1933–1973* (Princeton, NJ: Princeton University Press, 2015).

9. Paige Arthur, *Unfinished Projects: Decolonization and the Philosophy of Jean-Paul Sartre* (New York: Verso, 2010), 41, 53.
10. Storm Heter, *Sartre's Ethics of Engagement: Authenticity and Civic Virtue* (London: Continuum, 2006), 1.
11. Arthur, *Unfinished Projects*, 78.
12. Charles Taylor, *The Ethics of Authenticity: Malaise of Modernity* (Cambridge, MA: Harvard University Press, 1991), 101.
13. Heter, *Sartre's Ethics*, 3.
14. Ibid.
15. Ibid., 102–3.
16. "Africana thought refers to an area of thought that focuses on theoretical questions raised by struggles over ideas in African cultures and their hybrid and creolized forms in Europe, North American, Central America and South America and the Caribbean." Lewis Gordon, *Existentia Africana: Understanding Africana Existential Thought* (London: Routledge, 2000), 1.
17. Magnus Bassey, "What Is Africana Critical Theory or Black Existential Philosophy?," *Journal of Black Studies* 37, no. 6 (July 2007): 914–35.
18. For a recent example see Pankaj Mishra, *From the Ruins of Empire: The Intellectuals Who Remade Asia* (New York: Farrar, Straus and Giroux, 2012).
19. Gary Wilder, *Freedom Time: Negritude, Decolonization, and the Future of the World* (Durham, NC: Duke University Press, 2015); Aishwary Kumar, *Radical Equality: Ambedkar, Gandhi, and the Risk of Democracy* (Stanford, CA: Stanford University Press, 2015).
20. On this see chapter 6 and Arthur, *Unfinished Projects*, xiii; Robert Young, *White Mythologies: Writing History and the West* (London: Routledge, 1990), 28; Robert Flynn, *Sartre: A Philosophical Biography* (Cambridge: Cambridge University Press, 2014), 314–54.
21. Mahmud Amin al-'Alim, "Al-Hurriyya wa-l-iltizam 'inda Sartar," in *Ma'arik fikriyya* (Cairo: Dar al-Hilal, 1970), 228.
22. V. Y. Mudimbe, *The Invention of Africa: Gnosis, Philosophy, and the Order of Knowledge* (Bloomington: Indiana University Press, 1988), 83–87; Robert Young, "Sartre: The African Philosopher," in Jean-Paul Sartre, *Colonialism and Neocolonialism* (London: Routledge, 2006), ix–xxvii.
23. I have published a more comprehensive critique of this field elsewhere: Yoav Di-Capua, "Arab Existentialism: A Lost Chapter in the Intellectual History of Decolonization," *American Historical Review* 17, no. 4 (October 2012): 1061–91.
24. Marc Matera, *Black London: The Imperial Metropolis and Decolonization in the Twentieth Century* (Berkeley: University of California Press, 2015); John Lonsdale, "Anti-colonial Nationalism and Patriotism in Sub-Saharan Africa," in *The Oxford Handbook of the History of Nationalism*, ed. John Breuilly (Oxford: Oxford University Press, 2013), 318–37; Elizabeth Schmidt, "Top Down or Bottom Up? Nationalist Mobilization Reconsid-

ered, with Special Reference to Guinea (French West Africa)," *American Historical Review* 110, no. 4 (2005): 975–1014.

25. Frederick Cooper, *Citizenship between Empire and Nation: Remaking France and French Africa, 1945–1960* (Princeton, NJ: Princeton University Press, 2014), 4.

26. This critique applies in the otherwise outstanding work of Richard Immerman and Petra Goedde, eds., *The Oxford Handbook of the Cold War* (Oxford: Oxford University Press, 2013) and Odd Arne Westad, *The Global Cold War: Third World Intervention and the Making of Our Times* (Cambridge: Cambridge University Press, 2007).

27. For similar critique see Dane Kennedy, "Imperial History and Post-colonial Theory," in *The Decolonization Reader*, ed. James D. Le Sueur (New York: Routledge, 2003), 1–22; Neil Lazarus, *The Postcolonial Unconscious* (Cambridge: Cambridge University Press, 2011), 1–21. Having said that, the Subaltern Studies Group tried to rehabilitate local thought and capture the mental/spiritual world of the subaltern. Their consequent claim was that the subaltern did not behave as a colonized subject and retained his or her own notions of community, politics, and culture. Hence their argument that colonialism involved dominance without hegemony. Ranajit Guha, *Dominance without Hegemony: History and Power in Colonial India* (Cambridge, MA: Harvard University Press, 1997).

28. Tackling some of the same problems, Frederick Cooper observed that "colonial history in the era of decolonization suffered a double form of occlusion. From the 1950s into the 1970s, the idea of modernization occluded the colonial. In the 1980s and 1990s the idea of modernity occluded history." *Colonialism in Question: Theory, Knowledge, History* (Berkeley: University of California Press, 2005), 53. Relevant scholarship includes Jeffrey Byrne, *Mecca of Revolution: Algeria, Decolonization, and the Third World Order* (New York: Oxford University Press, 2016); Piero Gleijeses, *Conflicting Missions: Havana, Washington, and Africa, 1959–1976* (Chapel Hill: University of North Carolina Press, 2002); Matthew Connelly, *A Diplomatic Revolution: Algeria's Fight for Independence and the Origins of the Post–Cold War Era* (Oxford: Oxford University Press, 2002); Todd Shepard, *The Invention of Decolonization: The Algerian War and the Remaking of France* (Ithaca, NY: Cornell University Press, 2006); Frederick Cooper, *Decolonization and African Society: The Labor Question in French and British Africa* (Cambridge: Cambridge University Press, 1996); Gary Wilder, *The French Imperial Nation-State: Negritude and Colonial Humanism between the Two World Wars* (Chicago: University of Chicago Press, 2005); and Karen Bouwer, *Gender and Decolonization in the Congo: The Legacy of Patrice Lumumba* (New York: Palgrave, 2010).

29. See, for instance, Ilham Khuri-Makdisi, *The Eastern Mediterranean and the Making of Global Radicalism, 1860–1914* (Berkeley: University of California

Press, 2010); Marwa Elshakry, *Reading Darwin in Arabic, 1860–1950* (Chicago: The University of Chicago Press, 2013).

30. For a review of the nationalist bookshelf, see the bibliography of Adeed Dawisha, *Arab Nationalism in the Twentieth Century: From Triumph to Despair* (Princeton, NJ: Princeton University Press, 2003); Malik Mufti, *Sovereign Creations: Pan-Arabism and Political Order in Syria and Iraq* (Ithaca, NY: Cornell University Press, 1996).

31. See, for instance, the important studies of Albert Hourani, *Arabic Thought in the Liberal Age* (Cambridge: Cambridge University Press, 1983) and Elizabeth Suzanne Kassab, *Contemporary Arab Thought: Cultural Critique in Comparative Perspectives* (New York: Columbia University Press, 2009). In a different category of public history, one can find Fuad Ajami, *The Arab Predicament: Arab Political Thought and Practice since 1967* (Cambridge: Cambridge University Press, 1981). Scholars of Arabic literature are the only ones who systematically identified modes of thought and experiences in this era that transcend state-led nationalism; see, for instance, Margaret Litvin, *Hamlet's Arab Journey: Shakespeare's Prince and Nasser's Ghost* (Princeton, NJ: Princeton University Press, 2011).

32. Israel Gershoni and Amy Singer, "Introduction: Intellectual History in Middle Eastern Studies," *Comparative Studies of South Asia, Africa and the Middle East* 28, no. 3 (2008): 383–84.

33. For Sartre's reception in China see Chi Zhang, *Sartre en Chine, 1939–1976: Histoire de sa réception et de son influence* (Paris: Éditions Le Manuscrit, 2008).

34. For an evaluation of this trend see Michael Scott Christofferson, *French Intellectuals against the Left: The Antitotalitarian Moment of the 1970s* (New York: Berghahn, 2004); Julian Bourg, *From Revolution to Ethics: May 1968 and Contemporary French Thought* (Montreal: McGill-Queen's University Press, 2007); Kristin Ross, *May '68 and Its Afterlives* (Chicago: University of Chicago Press, 2002); see also Bernard-Henri Lévy, *Sartre: The Philosopher of the Twentieth Century* (Cambridge: Polity Press, 2003).

35. Sunil Khilnani, *Arguing Revolution: The Intellectual Left in Postwar France* (New Haven, CT: Yale University Press, 1993); Tony Judt, *Past Imperfect: French Intellectuals, 1944–1956* (Berkeley: University of California Press, 1992). See also Judt's magisterial narrative of European history, in which he places Sartre's moral blindness and acceptance of violence within a larger historical context: *Postwar: A History of Europe since 1945* (New York: Penguin, 2005), 210–11, 216.

36. Ronald Santorini, *Sartre on Violence: Curiously Ambivalent* (University Park: Pennsylvania State University Press, 2003); Jennifer Ang Mei Sze, *Sartre and the Moral Limits of War and Terrorism* (New York: Routledge, 2010); Michael Fleming, "Sartre on Violence: Not So Ambivalent?," *Sartre Studies International* 17, no. 1 (2011): 20–40.

37. Alexander Zevin, "Critique of Neo-Colonial Reason," *New Left Review* 70 (July–August 2011): 141–42.

38. Marnia Lazreg, *Torture and the Twilight of Empire: From Algiers to Baghdad* (Princeton, NJ: Princeton University Press, 2007), 213–36; James Le Sueur, *Uncivil War: Intellectuals and Identity Politics during the Decolonization of Algeria* (Philadelphia: University of Pennsylvania Press, 2001). On reducing Sartre to the cause of Algeria, see Denis Bertholet, *Sartre* (Paris: Plon, 2000), 421–43; Annie Cohen-Solal, *Sartre: A Life*, trans. Anna Cancogni (New York: Pantheon, 1987), 415–35.

39. Robert Young argues that Sartre's contribution to postcolonial thought was neglected and its intellectual origins are usually traced back to other people like Fanon; Young, "Sartre," ix–xxvii.

40. Jonathan Judaken and Robert Bernasconi, eds., *Situating Existentialism: Key Texts in Context* (New York: Columbia University Press, 2012).

41. For typical case studies from Ghana and Algeria, see Jean Allman, "Phantoms of the Archive: Kwame Nkrumah, a Nazi Pilot Named Hanna, and the Contingencies of Postcolonial History-Writing," *American Historical Review* 118, no. 1 (2013): 104–29. Todd Shepard, "Of Sovereignty: Disputed Archives, 'Wholly Modern' Archives, and the Post-decolonization French and Algerian Republics, 1962–2012," *American Historical Review* 120, no. 3 (2015): 869–83.

42. Jordanna Bailkin, "Where Did the Empire Go? Archives and Decolonization in Britain," *American Historical Review* 120, no. 3 (2015): 885.

43. Omnia El Shakry, "History without Documents: The Vexed Archives of Decolonization in the Middle East," *American Historical Review* 120, no. 3 (2015): 921.

44. For a fuller appreciation of this problem, see Lewis Gordon, "The Problem of Biography in the Study of the Thought of Black Intellectuals," *Small Axe: A Caribbean Journal of Criticism* 2, no. 2 (September 1998): 47–63.

45. David Armitage, "The International Turn in Intellectual History," in *Rethinking Modern European Intellectual History*, ed. Darrin McMahon and Samuel Moyn (New York: Oxford University Press, 2014), 232–33.

46. The journal in question is *Modern Intellectual History*. Almost every issue draws attention to the global context of non-European thought. See, for example, the special issue Shruti Kapila and Faisal Devji, eds., "An Intellectual History for India," *Modern Intellectual History* 4, no. 1 (2007).

47. Samuel Moyn and Andrew Sartori, "Approaches to Global Intellectual History," in *Global Intellectual History*, ed. Samuel Moyn and Andrew Sartori (New York: Columbia University Press, 2015), 9.

48. See, for instance, Kris Manjapra, *Age of Entanglement: German and Indian Intellectuals across Empire* (Cambridge, MA: Harvard University Press, 2014); Christopher Bayly, *Recovering Liberties: Indian Thought in the Age of Liberalism and Empire* (Cambridge: Cambridge University Press, 2011); and

Kepa Artaraz, *Cuba and Western Intellectuals Since 1959* (New York: Palgrave Macmillan, 2009).

49. Timely and eye opening as global intellectual history might be, essentially, it functions only as an inclusive historiographical perspective and not as a methodology. While featuring excellent ad hoc studies, it has no ambition, for instance, to address major theoretical questions relating to intellectual translation, agency, structure, contingency, and context. The tacit assumption is that, while we transition into a more global consideration of our subjects, the standard procedures of intellectual history and the accumulated methods of this discipline will stay the same. For an unsympathetic critique of global intellectual history and a response to it, see Sanjay Subrahmanyam, "Global Intellectual History beyond Hegel and Marx," *History and Theory* 54, no. 1 (February 2015): 126–37; see also Samuel Moyn and Andrew Sartori, "What Is Global Intellectual History—If It Should Exist at All?," *Imperial and Global Forum* [blog], University of Exeter, February 23, 2015, http://imperialglobalexeter.com/2015/02/23/what-is-global-intellectual-history-if-it-should-exist-at-all/#more-1964, accessed October 15, 2015.

50. Hanna Meretoja, *The Narrative Turn in Fiction and Theory: The Crisis and Return of Storytelling from Robbe-Grillet to Tournier* (London: Palgrave, 2014), 9.

51. Ibid., 22.

52. There is also an aesthetic domain (concerned with questions such as what narrative fiction and art in general are about), which is less relevant here; ibid., 7.

53. Deirdre Bair, *Simone de Beauvoir: A Biography* (New York: Touchstone, 1990), 519.

54. Wilder, *Freedom Time*, 12–13; Lewis Gordon, *What Fanon Said: A Philosophical Introduction to His Life and Thought* (New York: Fordham University Press, 2015).

CHAPTER ONE

1. Said, "Diary."

2. 'Aida al-Sharif, "Sartar fi-l-Qahira," in *Sartar wa-l-fikr al-'Arabi al-mu'asir*, ed. Ahmad 'Abd al-Halim 'Atiya (Beirut: Dar al-Farabi, 2011), 152.

3. 'Ali al-Samman, interviewed by the author, April 18, 2016.

4. 'Azmi 'Abd al-Wahhab, "Ziyara li-misr afsadaha al-yahudi Lanzmann: Sartar bayna fallahin kamshish wa 'Abd al-Nasir," *Al-Ahram al-'Arabi*, June 4, 2005, 59–60; al-Sharif, "Sartar fi-l-Qahira," 152.

5. Al-Sharif, "Sartar fi-l-Qahira," 179.

6. Ibid., 153–55, 158–61.

7. Ibid., 61.

8. Lamuchi, "Sartar wa-l-sira'"; al-Khatibi, "Dumuʿ Sartar."

9. Al-Samman, *Awraq ʿumri: Min al-malik ila ʾAbd al-Nasir wa-l-Sadat* (Cairo: Al-Maktab al-Misri al Hadith, 2005), 37–55.

10. Ibid., 64–66.

11. Ibid., 59–63.

12. Al-Samman, interview; Aly El-Samman, *Egypt: From One Revolution to Another; Memoir of a Committed Citizen under Nasser, Sadat, and Mubarak* (London: Gilgamesh, 2012), 38.

13. "Asifa pumbit shel studentim ʿAravim," December 14, 1966, Ministry of Foreign Affairs, "Paris: Hasbara be kerev studentim ʿAravim," folder 1708/8—ꞩn. 93.2/6-136, ISA, Jerusalem.

14. Al-Samman, *Awraq ʿumri*, 69–71.

15. Ibid., 61–63; *Al-Ahram*, January 16, 1965.

16. During the 1960s the Israeli Ministry of Foreign Affairs asked Israeli students in Paris to associate with Arab students and write detailed reports on their activities. This amateur spying program, in which some Israeli students of Arab origins passed as Arabs, yielded numerous reports on individuals, groups, and the overall political climate among the growing body of Arab students. On July 19, 1966, a top-secret cable sent from Paris to Jerusalem announced the immediate suspension of the program due to an unspecified "severe incident" and several other minor accidents. In addition, the Israeli security services commissioned at least two top-secret studies about all Arab students in Europe. See "Studentim," July 19, 1966, Ministry of Foreign Affairs, "Paris: Hasbara be kerev studentim ʿAravim," folder 1708/8—ꞩn. 93.2/6-136, ISA, Jerusalem.

17. The Middle East News Agency was established in Cairo in 1955 and was nationalized by the state in 1960. On al-Samman's friendship with Aron, see al-Samman, *Awraq ʿumri*, 90.

18. Ibid., 69–84.

19. The request was delivered through Louis Joxe, minister of Algerian affairs and chief French negotiator for the Evian talks that terminated the Algerian war. Al-Samman was personally acquainted with Joxe. El-Samman, *Egypt: From One Revolution to Another*, 41–42.

20. Ibid., 101, 104.

21. Ibid., 104–5.

22. Ibid., 104.

23. Al-Samman, interview.

24. On the Treblinka Affair, see chapter 8.

25. "Asifa pumbit shel studentim ʿAravim," December 14, 1966, Ministry of Foreign Affairs, "Paris: Hasbara be kerev studentim ʿAravim," folder 1708/8—ꞩn. 93.2/6-136, ISA, Jerusalem.

26. Al-Samman, *Awraq ʿumri*, 105.

27. Dawud Talhami, "ʿAla dawʾ liqaʾ maʿa al-faylasuf al-Faransi: Sartar wa-l-masʾala al-Filastıniyya," *Shuʾun Filastıniyya* 12 (1972): 66.

28. Al-Samman delivered the news to 'Izz al-Din Sharaf, a secretary in the embassy and the brother of Sami Sharaf, Nasser's secretary; al-Samman, *Awraq 'umri*, 105–7.

29. For the unenthusiastic view of Flapan's predecessor, Buma, and on Paul Ricoeur's interests in Israel's socialist achievements, see Buma to Ya'ari, March 23 and November 10, 1965, folder 2, 20.7-95, YY, Givat Haviva, Israel.

30. Flapan's diary, folder 2, 20.7-95, YY, Givat Haviva, Israel.

31. Ya'ari to Flapan, December 28, 1965, folder 2, 20.7-95, YY, Givat Haviva, Israel.

32. Flapan to Ya'ari, January 5, 1966, folder 2, 20.7-95, YY, Givat Haviva, Israel.

33. Flapan to Ya'ari, January 13, 1966, folder 2, 20.7-95, YY, Givat Haviva, Israel.

34. See the back-and-forth correspondence between Flapan and Ya'ari, January 13 and 21, 1966, folder 2, 20.7-95, YY, Givat Haviva, Israel.

35. Yishayahu Ben Porat, "Ish sodo shel Sarter megia ha-erev le Israel," *Yediot Haronot*, February 22, 1966, 3.

36. See correspondence between Flapan and Ya'ari, March 2, 19, and 24, 1966, folder 2, 20.7-95, YY, Givat Haviva, Israel.

37. Ra'nan to Flapan, April 7, 1966, folder 7, 5:22, YY, Givat Haviva, Israel.

38. See correspondence between Flapan and Ya'ari, January 13 and 21, 1966, folder 2, 20.7-95, YY, Givat Haviva, Israel.

39. It is unclear who represented Palestinians and Syrians at this point. See Flapan's diary no. 2, December 17, 1965, folder 2, 20.7-95, YY, Givat Haviva, Israel.

40. 'Ali al-Samman, "Ana atadaman ma' Misr mundhu Harb al-Suiz," *Al-Ahram*, December 1965, 7.

41. Ibid.

42. Ibid.

43. Ibid., 7, 11.

44. Ibid., 11.

45. See chapter 7.

46. "Reayon im Sarter," *Al Ha-Mishmar*, March 29, 1967, 1.

47. Al-Samman, "Ana atadaman," 11.

48. "Jean-Paul Sartre be reayon meyuhad," *Al Ha-Mishmar*, January 18, 1966, 1, 4.

49. Claude Lanzmann, interviewed by the author in San Francisco, February 27, 2012.

50. During his lifetime, al-Khuli was imprisoned no less than twelve times, serving seven of his sentences under the republic.

51. On Lutfi al-Khuli's political engagements, see Ginat, *Egypt's Incomplete Revolution*.

52. In a similar fashion, two years earlier Russell had corresponded with the

editors of the Israeli magazine *New Outlook*. For the letter see Bartrand Rasil, "Khitab maftuh min Bartrand Rasil ila al-muthaqqafun al-'Arab," *Al-Tali'a*, April 1965, 8–10; also quoted in al-Khuli, *Hiwar ma'a Bartrand Rasil wa Jan-Bul Sartar* (Cairo: Dar al-Ma'arif, 1968), 116–25.

53. Al-Khuli, *Hiwar ma'a Bartrand Rasil wa Jan-Bul Sartar*, 57.

54. Russell, *Yours Faithfully*, 411–12.

55. Lutfi al-Khuli, "Hawla bidayat al-hiwar ma' Sartar," *Al-Ahram*, December 26, 1965, 7.

56. Ibid., 9.

57. Ibid.

58. Ibid.

59. Ibid.

60. "By 1964, Egypt transmitted 766 hours per week, second in the world only to the United States, and in March 1965 opened the world's largest and most powerful broadcasting station." James Brennan, "Radio Cairo and the Decolonization of East Africa, 1953–1964," in *Making a World after Empire: The Bandung Moment and Its Political Afterlives*, ed. Christopher Lee (Athens: Ohio University Press, 2010), 187.

61. Sadiq Jalal al-'Azm, interviewed by the author in Berlin, July 3, 2013.

62. Box 205, folder 7, and box 281, folder 1, FSC, J. Willard Marriott Library's Aziz A. Atiya Library, University of Utah, Salt Lake City, Utah, USA.

63. Sayigh, *Anis Sayigh*, 187; Flapan's diary no. 4, February 1966, folder 2, 20.7-95, YY, Givat Haviva, Israel.

64. Flapan's diary no. 5, March–April 1966, folder 2, 20.7-95, YY, Givat Haviva, Israel.

65. Ibid.

66. Ibid.

67. Ibid.

68. "Sarter al Israel," *Al Ha-Mishmar*, April 22 1966, 2.

69. Ibid.

70. Ibid.

71. "Sakana la Yehudim," *Yediot Ahronot*, April 22, 1966, n.p.

72. Flapan's diary no. 5, "Meetings with Arabs: Top Secret," March–April 1966, folder 2, 20.7-95, YY, Givat Haviva, Israel.

73. See discussion of the Scemama affair in chapter 8 and in Flapan's diary no. 7, October 9, 1966, folder 2, 20.7-95, YY, Givat Haviva, Israel. See also Uri Avneri's autobiography, in which he explains why Flapan was disliked; Uri Avneri, *Optimi* (Tel Aviv: Yediot Ahronot, 2014), 545–47.

74. Flapan learned of these details from Lanzmann; Flapan's diary no. 7, October 9, 1966, folder 2, 20.7-95, YY, Givat Haviva, Israel.

75. Flapan's diary no. 7, October 9, 1966, folder 2, 20.7-95, YY, Givat Haviva, Israel.

76. Al-Samman, *Awraq 'umri*, 106.

77. See, for instance, Davies, *Sartre and "Les Temps Modernes."*

CHAPTER TWO

1. "Duktura fi-l-falsafa," *Al-Ahram*, May 30, 1944, 2.
2. ʿAbd al-Rahman Badawi, *Sirat hayati* (Beirut: al-Muʾassasa al-ʿArabiyya li-l-Dirasat wa-l-Nashr, 2000), 1:150–51.
3. Fayiz Sayigh, "Self-Examination and Arab Youth" (address given at the fourth Annual Convention of the Organization of Arab Students in the United States, University of Wisconsin, Madison, September 6, 1955), 9–10, box 267, folder 6 It1, FSC, J. Willard Marriott Library's Aziz A. Atiya Library, University of Utah, Salt Lake City, Utah, USA.
4. Omnia El Shakry, "The Arabic Freud: The Unconscious and the Modern Subject," *Modern Intellectual History* 11, no. 1 (April 2014): 89–118.
5. ʿAbd al-Rahman Badawi, *Humum al-shabab* (Cairo: Maktabat al-Nahda al-Misriyya, 1946), 132.
6. Ibid., 134.
7. Ibid., 135.
8. Like other "unfulfilled Enlightenments" (Indian, Asian, Latin American, and even Russian), the Arab project of Enlightenment, the Nahda, was trapped in the classic paradoxes of colonial modernity. For more on the predicament of colonial Enlightenment, see David Scott, *Conscripts of Modernity: The Tragedy of Colonial Enlightenment* (Durham, NC: Duke University Press, 2004).
9. Badawi, *Humum al-shabab*, 140.
10. Badawi, *Sirat hayati*, 1:213–23.
11. On youth and attraction to fascism and Nazism, see Israel Gershoni and James Jankowski, *Confronting Fascism in Egypt: Dictatorship versus Democracy in the 1930s* (Stanford, CA: Stanford University Press, 2009); Israel Gershoni, *Arab Responses to Fascism and Nazism: Attraction and Repulsion* (Austin: University of Texas Press, 2014).
12. Omnia El Shakry, "Youth as Peril and Promise: The Emergence of Adolescent Psychology in Postwar Egypt," *International Journal of Middle East Studies* 43, no. 4 (November 2011): 591.
13. Ibid.
14. Ibid., 164–65.
15. Badawi, *Humum al-shabab*, 142.
16. For the trials and tribulations of this generation, see Haggai Erlich, *Youth and Revolution in the Changing Middle East, 1908–2014* (Boulder, CO: Lynne Rienner, 2015); Christoph Schumann, "The Generation of Broad Expectations: Nationalism, Education, and Autobiography in Syria and Lebanon, 1930–1958," *Die Welt des Islams* 41, no. 2 (July 2001): 174–205.
17. Jean Hering, "In Memoriam: Alexander Koyré," in *Philosophy and Phenomenological Research* 25, no. 3 (March 1965), 454.
18. Given his status as a foreign intellectual whose major academic degrees were from Germany, it was difficult for Koyré to find a permanent

position at a major French university. Overall, this was the third time Koyré had been invited to teach in Fu'ad University's Department of Philosophy. While in Egypt he worked for the *Comité national d'Égypte de la France libre*; Badawi, *Sirat hayati*, 1:62. For Koyré's biography, see the online archive of the Centre Alexander Koyré in *l'École des Hautes Études en Sciences Sociales*, http://www.koyre.cnrs.fr, accessed April 2, 2012; Ethan Kleinberg, *Generation Existential: Heidegger's Philosophy in France, 1927–1961* (Ithaca, NY: Cornell University Press, 2005), 59.

19. Lalande moved to Fu'ad University in October 1937, where he joined an already established cohort of French scholars, such as Emile Bréhier and Louis Rougier. Lalande taught in Cairo between 1926 and 1930 and from 1937 through 1940; Badawi, *Sirat hayati*, 1:61–62; Muhammad Mubarak, *Al-Jabiri: Bayna turuhat Lalande wa Jan-Biyajih* (Beirut: al-Mu'assasa al-'Arabiyya li-l-Dirasat wa-l-Nashr, 2000). On Fu'ad University, see Donald Reid, *Cairo University and the Making of Modern Egypt* (Cambridge: Cambridge University Press, 1990).

20. The phenomenologist's open-ended manner of thinking departed significantly from the theoretical cognition of knowledge and moved toward the practical concerns of everyday life. This shift was entirely new to French philosophy of the 1930s, which was still focused on Bergson. Indeed, aspiring intellectuals like Maurice Merleau-Ponty and Raymond Aron felt bored by Bergsonian philosophy and ill prepared, philosophically speaking, to deal with the realities of the 1930s. As Raymond Aron succinctly put it, "[In German philosophy] I found everything I could not find in France"; Kleinberg, *Generation Existential*, 89; Joseph J. Kockelmans, "Phenomenology," in *The Cambridge Dictionary of Philosophy*, ed. Robert Audi (Cambridge: Cambridge University Press, 1999), 664–66.

21. Koyré later held a position in the *École Pratiques des Hautes Études*; Kleinberg, *Generation Existential*, 59.

22. Quoted in Tom Rockmore, *Heidegger and French Philosophy: Humanism, Antihumanism and Being* (London: Routledge, 1995), xii.

23. The seminar focused on Heidegger but also offered a new reading of Hegel, who, until that point, was seen in France as an outdated romantic philosopher. Koyré's journal covered the same terrain. He was aided by other graduates of Husserl's circle, such as Jean Hering, and by Emile Bréhier, who also taught in Cairo. Michael Roth, *Knowing and History: Appropriations of Hegel in Twentieth-Century France* (Ithaca, NY: Cornell University Press, 1988), 2–9, 97.

24. On Alexandre Kojève, see Vincent Descombes, *Modern French Philosophy*, trans. L. Scott-Fox and J. M. Harding (Cambridge: Cambridge University Press, 1998), 9–48; Roth, *Knowing and History*, 83–146.

25. Other participating members during the 1930s would become a who's who in French thought of the 1950s and 1960s: Georges Bataille, Jacques Lacan, Raymond Queneau, Maurice Merleau-Ponty, Eric Weil, André

Breton, and Emmanuel Levinas. Granted, "what happened in the seminar between 1933 and 1939 changed the face of modern French philosophy"; Kleinberg, *Generation Existential*, 65–66, 69.

26. For 'Abd al-Raziq's biography, see Ahmad Zakariyya al-Shilaq, *Al-Shaykh Mustafa 'Abd al-Raziq wa mudhakaratihi: 'Aql mustanir tahta al-'amama* (Cairo: Al-Hay'a al-Misriyya al-'Amma li-l-Kitab, 2006), 13–56; Ibrahim Madkur, "Mustafa 'Abd al-Raziq: Ra'is Madrasa," in *Al-Shaykh al-Akbar Mustafa 'Abd al-Raziq: mufakkiran wa adiban wa muslihan* (Cairo: Al-Hay'a al-Misriyya al-'Amma li-l-Kitab, 1982), 8; Badawi, *Sirat hayati*, 1:58–59.

27. Given the status of philosophical knowledge in the university at that time, Lalande understood that the most important thing was to teach methodology. By teaching his *Les Théories de l'induction et de l'expérimentation* (1929), Lalande hoped to steer the scholarly habits and intellectual orientation of students toward a pre–World War I French philosophical tradition. Originally, Badawi worked with Lalande, who instructed Badawi to shy away from the *moda* of Heidegger and Karl Jaspers and settle for a more canonical topic. After some negotiation, Lalande reluctantly agreed on "Death in Contemporary Philosophy." Yet, with war raging in Europe, Lalande decided to leave for France, and Alexander Koyré took over his post; Badawi, *Sirat hayati*, 1:63.

28. Hasan Hanafi, "Phenomenology and Islamic Philosophy," in *Phenomenology World-Wide: Foundations, Expanding Dynamisms, Life-Engagements; A Guide for Research and Study*, ed. Anna-Teresa Tymieniecka (Dordrecht: Kluwer Academic, 2002), 318–21.

29. Yet, Badawi's master's thesis was what works of this kind often are: an exercise. Written in French, it was eventually published in Paris in 1964; Abdurahman Badawi, *Le Problème de la Mort dans la Philosophie Existentielle* (Cairo: Institute Français d'archéologie Orientale, 1964).

30. Though Badawi's notion of time is reminiscent of Bergson's notion of *durée* as an exploration of "real" time that eludes mathematics and science as a kind of duration, the two differ markedly in terms of their understanding of human subjectivity as the vessel of time. Characteristically immodest, Badawi preferred to think of his work as "complementary to that of Heidegger"; Badawi, *Sirat hayati*, 1:179–80; see Badawi, *Le Problème de la Mort*, 1–7.

31. Koyré later held a one-year position in the Institute for Advanced Study at Princeton. He never returned to teach in the Middle East; Bernard Cohen, "Alexandre Koyré (1892–1964)," *Isis* 57, no. 2 (Summer 1966): 157–66; John Herivel, "Alexandre Koyré (1892–1964)," *British Journal for the History of Science* 2, no. 3 (June 1965): 257–59; Alexandre John Murdoch, "Koyré 1892–1964," *Proceedings and Addresses of the American Philosophical Association* 38 (1964–1965): 98–99.

32. Some of Koyré's colleagues, such as Heidegger's translator Henry Corbin, were Orientalists, and the possibility of making such intellectual connections was viewed with excitement; Badawi, *Sirat hayati*, 1:63–65.

33. Ibid., 1:153–55.
34. This 1944 lecture was published as "Khulasat Madhhabina al-wujudi: al-zaman al-wujudi" in ʿAbd al-Rahman Badawi, *Dirasat fi-l-falsafa al-wujudiyya* (Cairo: Maktabat al-Nahda al-Misriyya, 1966), 236.
35. "In which relationship is not that of one subject to another or between the subject and things but a relationship between the subject and itself"; ibid., 239. See also ʿAbd al-Rahman Badawi, *Al-Zaman al-wujudi* (Cairo: Maktabat al-Nahda al-Misriyya, 1955), 153–239.
36. Quite interestingly, with the approval of Taha Husayn, Badawi used the medieval Islamic term *Aniya* to Arabize Heidegger's *Dasein*. For a full technical explanation, see Badawi, *Al-Zaman al-wujudi.*
37. ʿAbd al-Rahman Badawi, *Al-Insaniyya wa-l-wujudiyya fi-l-fikr al-ʿArabi* (Cairo: Maktabat al-Nahda al-Misriyya, 1947), 68, 94–95; Charles Smith, *Islam and the Search for Social Order in Modern Egypt: A Biography of Muhammad Husayn Haykal* (Albany: State University of New York Press, 1983), especially chapter 6.
38. In Badawi's words, "[The goal is to] establish a comprehensive philosophy for our generation." Badawi, *Al-Insaniyya wa-l-wujudiyya*, 103.
39. R. Arnaldez, "Al-Insān al-Kāmil," in *Encyclopaedia of Islam*, 2nd ed., ed. P. Bearman, T. Bianquis, C. E. Bosworth, E. van Donzel, and W. P. Heinrichs (Leiden: Brill, 2011). Consulted online on April 5, 2017, http://dx.doi.org.ezproxy.lib.utexas.edu/10.1163/1573-3912_islam_COM_0375.
40. From this standpoint, Sufism was not merely an exercise in individual self-awareness but a full-fledged analysis of subjectivity. Badawi, *Al-Insaniyya wa-l-wujudiyya*, 68–71, 96–97, 103–4, 107–40; see also his exploration of the Perfect Man doctrine in ʿAbd al-Rahman Badawi, *Al-Insan al-kamil fi-l-Islam* (Cairo: Maktabat al-Nahda al-Misriyya, 1950).
41. The first substantial commentary in any language on Heidegger was written in Japan. For a revisionist assessment of the relationship between Heidegger, East Asian thought, and comparative philosophy, see Stella Sandford, "Going Back: Heidegger, East Asia and 'The West,'" *Radical Philosophy* 120 (July/August 2003): 11–22. For influence in Vietnam, see Wynn Gadkar-Wilcox, "Existentialism and Intellectual Culture in South Vietnam," *Journal of Asian Studies* 73, no. 2 (May 2014): 377–95.
42. Philosophical and legal synthesis had been on the minds of Arab intellectuals since the 1890s. Friedrich Nietzsche, *The Use and Abuse of History* (New York: Bobbs-Merrill, 1957), 21–22.
43. Mahmud Amin al-ʿAlim, "Hiwar," *Adab wa Naqd*, no. 21 (May 1986): 102.
44. Habib Malik, "The Reception of Kierkegaard in the Arab World," in *Kierkegaard's International Reception*, ed. Jon Stewart (Farnham, UK: Ashgate, 2009), 41–49; Glen Mitoma, "Charles H. Malik and Human Rights: Notes on a Biography," *Biography: An Interdisciplinary Quarterly* 33, no. 1 (Winter 2010): 222–41. For discussion of other young Arab phenomenologists, see Hanafi, "Phenomenology," 318–21.

45. El Shakry, "The Arabic Freud," 91.
46. El Shakry, "Youth as Peril," 596.
47. Ibid., 597.
48. Ibid., 596–98.
49. Ibid., 595.
50. Yusuf Murad, review of *Al-Zaman al-wujudi*, by ʿAbd al-Rahman Badawi, *Majallat ʿilm al-nafs* 1, no. 1 (June 1945): 80.
51. By 1950 Badawi had published fourteen short books on philosophy.
52. "Man lives between despair and anxiety and the only meaningful thing is his efforts and commitments," explained Shaʿban Barakat. Barakat, "Al-Wujudiyya," *Al-Adib*, July 1948, 42; Barakat, "Al-Wujudiyya," *Al-Adib*, March 1948, 24–25.
53. ʿAbd al-Rahman Badawi, "Al-Qisa al-wujudiyya ʿinda Sartar," *Al-Adib*, July 1947, 3–5.
54. See his series of imaginary dispatched from Paris in *Al-Adib*: Badawi, "Min Paris ila Salwa," *Al-Adib*, August 1946, 12–14; September 1946, 8–10; September 1947, 3–4; September 1948, 3–5; November 1948, 3–5.
55. See, for instance, an accusation that an article from *Al-Adib* was plagiarized from the May 1947 issue of *Al-Katib al-Misri*: ʿAbd al-Satar Shams al-Din, "Hawla majalay al-wujudiyya fi falsafat Nietzsche," *Al-Adib*, July 1949, 63.
56. Mourad Wahba, "Contemporary Moslem Philosophies in North Africa," in *African Philosophy: An Anthology*, ed. Emmanuel Chukwudi Eze (Oxford: Blackwell, 2000), 50–55.
57. Badawi deplored commitment and, later in life, claimed that Sartre had nothing to offer by way of philosophy. Badawi, *Sirat hayati*, 1:183.
58. However, in a series of critical essays on Sartre's existential philosophy, Najib Baladi accounted also for *Being and Nothingness*. Baladi, "Jan-Bul Sartar wa mawaqifuhu," *Al-Katib al-Misri*, April 1946, 427–34; see also *Al-Katib al-Misri* follow-ups in June and July 1946, 50–59 and 277–83 respectively.
59. Taha Husayn, *Mustaqbal al-thaqafa fi Misr* (Cairo: Matbaʿat al-Maʿarif, 1938), 1:30–39, 45–70, 71–124 and 2:263–74, 496–501.
60. See Roel Meijer, *Secular Liberal and Left-Wing Political Thought in Egypt 1945–1958* (London: Routledge, 2002); Amy Johnson, *Reconstructing Rural Egypt: Ahmed Hussein and the History of Egyptian Development* (Syracuse, NY: Syracuse University Press, 2004).
61. For an early example of a ubiquitous trope, see Salama Musa, *Ma hiya al-nahda?* (Cairo: al-Hayʾa al-Misriyya al-ʿAmma li-l-Kitab, 1993).
62. Rami Ginat and Meir Noema, "Al-Fajr al-Jadid: A Breeding Ground for the Emergence of Revolutionary Ideas in the Immediate Post–Second World War," *Middle Eastern Studies* 44, no. 6 (November 2008): 867–93.
63. "The seated scribe is no idle symbol: it was not only *Al-Katib al-Misri*'s title and masthead, but also later the logo of the General Egyptian Book Orga-

nization, an Egyptian state-funded publishing enterprise, indisputably the most prolific institution of literary publishing in modern Egypt, if not the whole Arab world. The amanuensis figure recalls the image of the twenty-seventh-century B.C.E. genius Imhotep, Pharaoh Djoser's semi-sacred scribe, chancellor, architect and medical doctor." *The Seated Scribe* (2620–2500 BCE) is on display in the Louvre museum in Paris. Christopher Dwight Micklethwait, "*Faits Divers*: National Culture and Modernism in Third World Literary Magazines" (PhD diss., University of Texas at Austin, 2011), 175–76. Retrieved from http://catalog.lib.utexas.edu/search/ t?SEARCH=Faits+Divers%3A+National+Culture+and+Modernism+. For Harari Brothers, the Jewish publisher of *Al-Katib al-Misri*, see Joel Beinin, *The Dispersion of Egyptian Jewry: Culture, Politics and the Formation of a Modern Diaspora* (Berkeley: University of California Press, 1998), 247.

64. On Gide and Taha Husayn, see Michael Allan, *In the Shadow of World Literature: Sites of Reading in Colonial Egypt* (Princeton, NJ: Princeton University Press, 2016), 115–30.

65. "Barnamij," *Al-Katib al-Misri*, October 1945, 1–3.

66. Muhammad ʿAwd Muhammad, "Al-Intidab wa-l-wisaya wa-l-istiʿmar," *Al-Katib al-Misri*, March 1946, 199–213; and April 1946, 401–13.

67. Najib al-Miʿri, "Jan-Bul Sartar," *Al-Katib al-Misri*, April 1946, 426–34; Baladi, "Jan-Bul Sartar wa mawaqifihi al-falsafiya," *Al-Katib al-Misri*, June 1946, 50–59; for a translation from French, see Rujir Arnaldiz, "Usul al-Wujudiyya," *Al-Katib al-Misri*, March 1947, 294–305.

68. Taha Husayn, "fi-l-Adab al-Amriki—Richard Wright," *Al-Katib al-Misri*, October 1947, 3–22.

69. Didier Anzieu, "Al-Wujudiyya," *Al-Katib al-Misri*, October 1946, 119–48.

70. David Cooper, *Existentialism: A Reconstruction* (Oxford: Blackwell, 1990), 172–77.

71. Taha Husayn, "Al-Adab bayna al-ittisal wa-l-infisal," *Al-Katib al-Misri*, August 1946, 373–88.

72. Husayn Mahmud, "Al-Fann min ajl al-fann," *Al-Katib al-Misri*, January 1947, 66–73.

73. Taha Husayn, "Mulahazat," *Al-Katib al-Misri*, June 1947, 10, 9–21.

74. For a variety of reasons, Sartre excluded poetry (as well as other non-representational arts like music) from the list of committed modes of expression. Though he later reversed his position, Arab critics of all stripes found the exclusion of poetry—a historically major form of committed expression in Islamic culture—incomprehensible; Anwar al-Maʿdawi, "Al-Adab al-multazim," *Al-Adab*, February 1953, 14–15; Muhammad Barada, "Tahawwulat mafhum al-iltizam fi-l-adab al-ʿArabi al-hadith" in *Tahawwulat mafhum al-iltizam fi-l-adab al-ʿArabi al-hadith*, ed. Muhammad Barada (Beirut: Dar al-Fikr al-Muʿasir, 2003), 37; ʿAbd al-Wahhab al-Bayyati, *Tajribati al-shiʿriyya* (Beirut: Manshurat Nizar Qabbani, 1968), 37.

75. He also equated commitment with communism and socialism; Husayn, "Mulahazat," 9–21.

76. Jean-Paul Sartre, *What Is Literature?* (New York: Harper and Row, 1965), 126, see also 28, 65, 122, 161, 239, 267.

77. Cohen-Solal, *Sartre: A Life*, 257–58.

78. Husayn, "Al-Adab bayna al-ittisal wa-l-infisal," 373–88; Husayn, "Mulahazat," 9–21.

79. See Arabic translation of *Prometheus Misbound*. André Gide, "Prometheus dhu al-daw' al-muhmal," *Al-Katib al-Misr*, January 1948, 511–46. For their correspondence, see table of contents of *Valors* as published in *Al-Katib al-Misri*, March 1946.

80. While some sources state that Gide nominated Husayn for the Nobel Prize in Literature, the archive of the Nobel Prize Committee lists Ahmad Lutfi al-Sayyid and Professor Bernard Guyon of Fu'ad University as Husayn's official nominators. Pierre Cachia, "Husayn Taha (1889–1973)," in *Routledge Encyclopedia of Arabic Literature*, ed. Julie Scott Meisami and Paul Starkey (New York: Routledge, 2010), 297. See also Husayn's entries in the nominations database at Nobelprize.org, http://www.nobelprize.org/nobel_prizes/literature/nomination/nomination.php?action=show&showid=1043 and http://www.nobelprize.org/nobel_prizes/literature/nomination/nomination.php?action=show&showid=1156.

81. Salama Musa, *Hu'ula' 'allamuni* (Cairo: Dar al-jil li-l-tiba'a, 1966), 271–80; Musa, *Al-Adab li-l-sha'b* (Cairo: Mu'assasat al-Khanji, 1961), 12–13.

82. 'Abbas Mahmud al-'Aqqad, *'Aqa'id al-mufakkirin fi-l-qarn al-'ishrin* (Cairo: Maktabat Gharib, 1968), 141–55. See a reprint of two essays from the late 1940s: al-'Aqqad, *Bayna al-kutub wa-l-nas* (Beirut: Dar al-Kutub al-'Arabi, 1966), 15–33.

83. Coining the Arabic term *iltizam* for the French *engagement*, it ultimately prevailed at the expense of the term *indiwa*. Taha Husayn, "Al-Adab bayna al-ittisal wa-l-infisal," *Al-Katib al-Misri*, August 1946, 373–88.

84. For a discussion of café existentialism, see Cooper, *Existentialism*, 2, 12, 96, 170, 171.

85. Cohen-Solal, *Sartre: A Life*, 266.

86. 'Abd al-Rahman Badawi, "Salwa," *Al-Adib*, August 1947, 3–5.

87. Ibid.

88. David Tresilian, "Isma'il Sabri 'Abdullah: Mapping the Arab Future," *Al-Ahram Weekly*, July 4, 1991.

89. Others included, from Tunisia, al-Shadhli al-Qalibi (future minister of culture), Ahmad bin Salif (future minister of finance), and, from Morocco, 'Abdallah Ibrahim (future prime minister). 'Abd al-Rahman Badawi, *Sirat hayati*, 2:195.

90. For the postcolonial generation and the Third World, see Samir Amin, *Mudhakarati* (Beirut: Dar Saqi, 2006), 75–89.

91. Ahmad Muhammad 'Atiyya, *Anwar al-Ma'dawi: Asrihihu al-adabi wa asrar*

ma'satihi (Riyad: Dar al-Mirrikh, 1988), 190; see also Suhayl Idris, *Dhikrayat al-adab wa-l-hubb* (Beirut: Dar al-Adab, 2002), 86.

92. Ibid., 103.
93. Ibid., 107.
94. M. M. Badawi, *A Short History of Modern Arabic Literature* (Oxford: Clarendon, 1993).
95. Mustafa Hamil, "Mohamed Zafzaf's Al-Mar'a wa-l-Warda or the Voyage North in the Postcolonial Era," *International Journal of Middle East Studies* 38, no. 3 (August 2006): 420, 421.
96. El Shakry, "Youth as Peril," 599.
97. Ahmad Muhammad 'Atiyya, *Anwar al-Ma'dawi*, 193, 209; see also Idris, *Dhikrayat al-Adab*, 86–87.
98. 'Abd al-Rahman Badawi, *Sirat hayati*, 1:198.
99. Ibid., 2:194.
100. For a debate of this issue, see *Al-Adab*, November 1955, 72–73.
101. Simone de Beauvoir, *All Said and Done* (New York, Putnam, 1974), 378.
102. 'Abd al-Rahman Badawi, *Sirat hayati*, 1:184.
103. Ahmad Muhammad 'Atiyya, *Anwar al-Ma'dawi*, 209.
104. Idris, *Dhikrayat al-adab*, 109.
105. Ibid., 112.
106. 'Abdallah al-Mashnuq, "Mawja adabiyya," *Al-Adib*, July 1946, 4–5. Idris took some issue with this characterization; Suhayl Idris, "Ay mawja adabiyya hunaka?," *Al-Adib*, August 1946, 14–19, 65; Ahmad Muhammad 'Atiyya, *Anwar al-Ma'dawi*, 36.
107. Ibid., 231–32.
108. Anwar al-Ma'dawi, "fi-l-Adab, wa-l-fann, wa-l-haya," *Al-Adib*, February 1948, 23–25.
109. Fu'ad Windawi, "Al-Adib bayna al-hurriyya wa-l-iltizam," *Al-Adib*, April 1948, 58.
110. Ahmad Muhammad 'Atiyya, *Anwar al-Ma'dawi*, 159.
111. Ibid.
112. Ibid., 231, 234.
113. Ibid., 212.
114. Quoted in M. M. Badawi, "Commitment in Contemporary Arabic Literature," *Cahiers d'histoire mondiale* 14, no. 4 (1972), 868.
115. Though Cairo received the first thousand copies, its reception in Egypt was slower than in Baghdad. Ahmad Muhammad 'Atiyya, *Anwar al-Ma'dawi*, 243, 249.
116. "Mihnat al-adab," *Al-Adab*, April 1953, 70–71; "Shakawa al-adab al-'Arabi al-hadith," *Al-Adab*, May 1953, 1–5; "Azmat al-majalla al-adabiyya fi-l-'alam al-'Arabi," *Al-Adab*, October 1953, 12–16; Raja' al-Naqqash, "fi Azmat al-naqd al-'Arabi al-mu'asir," *Al-Adab*, November 1954, 8–10, 63–66.
117. The two other children were Munir (b. 1930) and Mary (b. 1929); box 189, folder 3, FSC, J. Willard Marriott Library's Aziz A. Atiya Library, Univer-

sity of Utah, Salt Lake City, Utah, USA; Sayigh, *Anis Sayigh*, especially, 10–78; see also Saqr Abu Fakhr, "Fayiz Sayigh: intisar al-hurriyya ʿala al-idiyulujiya," published in *Filastin*, March 2012, http://palestine.assafir .com/article.asp?aid=980, accessed April 10, 2013.

118. Hisham Sharabi, *Embers and Ashes: Memoir of an Arab Intellectual* (Northampton, MA: Olive Branch Press, 2008), 8.

119. Ibid., 24.

120. See box 189, folders 4, 5, FSC, J. Willard Marriott Library's Aziz A. Atiya Library, University of Utah, Salt Lake City, Utah, USA.

121. Fayiz Sayigh, "Personal Existence: An Essay" (master's thesis, American University of Beirut, 1945).

122. Sharabi, *Embers and Ashes*, 28.

123. Jonathan Judaken, "Sisyphus's Progeny: Existentialism in France," in *Situating Existentialism*, 98.

124. Sharabi, *Embers and Ashes*, 23.

125. Ibid., 16, 25.

126. Ibid., 49.

127. Ibid., 9.

128. For the history of the SSNP, see Zuwiyya Yamak Labib, *The Syrian Social Nationalist Party: An Ideological Analysis* (Cambridge, MA: Center for Middle Eastern Studies of Harvard University, 1966); Adel Beshara, *Lebanon: The Politics of Frustration—the Failed Coup of 1961* (New York: Routledge, 2005), 29–47; Beshara, *Syrian Nationalism: An Inquiry into the Political Philosophy of Antun Saʿadeh* (Beirut: Bissan, 1995); on youth revolt, see Erlich, *Youth and Revolution*, chapters 3–4.

129. Sharabi, *Embers and Ashes*, 11.

130. Abu Fakhr, "Fayiz Sayigh."

131. Fayiz ʿAbdullah Sayigh, *Ila ayna? Bahth tahlili naqdi fi mawqif al-hizb al-Suri al-qawmi al-ijtimaʿi min al-fikr wa-l-din wa-hurriyyatuhu* (Beirut: Dar al-Kitab, 1947), 7–21.

132. Sharabi, *Embers and Ashes*, 59.

133. Ibid., 60.

134. Ibid., 56.

135. Ibid., 2.

136. Ibid., 3–4.

137. Ibid., 80–81.

138. Fayiz Sayigh, "Existential Philosophy: A Formal Examination" (PhD diss., Georgetown University, 1950), 306, 308. Retrieved from http://ezproxy.lib .utexas.edu/login?url=http://search.proquest.com.ezproxy.lib.utexas.edu/ docview/301812305?accountid=7118.

139. For Malik's important role in drafting the Declaration, see Samuel Moyn, *The Last Utopia* (Cambridge, MA: Harvard University Press, 2012), 65–66; Mitoma, "Charles H. Malik," 222–41.

140. Sayigh's official title was chief of research, delegation counselor, and member of the Yemen delegation to the UN; box 375, folder 1, FSC, J. Willard Marriott Library's Aziz A. Atiya Library, University of Utah, Salt Lake City, Utah, USA.

141. Fayiz Sayigh, *Understanding the Arab Mind* (New York: Organization of Arab Students in the United States, 1953), 29–30.

142. Fayiz Sayigh, "Self Examination and Arab Youth," 10–11.

143. Ahmad Muhammad 'Atiyya, *Anwar al-Ma'dawi*, 196, 207, 210; Idris, *Dhikrayat al-adab*, 106.

144. David Lloyd, "Colonial Trauma/Postcolonial Recovery?," *Interventions: International Journal of Postcolonial Studies* 2, no. 2 (2000): 212–28; Stef Craps and Gert Buelens, "Introduction: Postcolonial Trauma Novels," *Studies in the Novel* 40, nos. 1–2 (Spring/Summer 2008): 1–12.

CHAPTER THREE

1. Ishaq Husayni, *Azmat al-fikr al-'Arabi* (Beirut: Dar Bayrut, 1954), 8–21; for a critical review of the book, see Husayn Muruwwa, "*Azmat al-fikr al-'Arabi*," *Al-Thaqafa al-Wataniyya*, March 1954, 55.

2. Fayiz Sayigh, *Risalat al-mufakkir al-'Arabi* (Beirut: Manshurat Majallat al-Akhad, 1955), 5–80.

3. Raja' al-Naqqash was a disciple of Anwar al-Ma'dawi and *Al-Adab*'s correspondent in Cairo; Raja' al-Naqqash, "Fi azmat al-naqd al-'Arabi al-mu'asir," *Al-Adab*, November 1954, 8–10, 63–66.

4. Indeed, Iraqi writers who published in Beirut around the same time confirm this diagnosis. See, for instance, the commentaries of Iraqi literary critic Nahad al-Takarli: "Al-nitaj al-jadid," *Al-Adab*, August 1954, 33–39; "Al-Masrah al-wujudi," *Al-Adib*, January 1953, 3–6; "Simun di Bufwar wa mushkilat al-mawt," *Al-Adib*, July 1953, 33–34; see also 'Awad Majid al-'Azmi, "Al-Nuzha al-wujudiyya," *Al-Adib*, January 1952, 27–31.

5. On Luwis 'Awad and this debate, see 'Abbud Hanna, *Al-Madrasa al-waqi'iyya fi-l-naqd al-'Arabi al-hadith* (Damascus: Wizarat al-Thaqafa wa-l-Irshad al-Qawmi, 1978), 157–67, 195–207.

6. "Surat al-Adab," the original *Al-Jumhuriyya* article, was republished in Taha Husayn, *Khisam wa naqd* (Beirut: Dar al-'Ilm li-l-Malayin, 1977), 72–89.

7. For a coverage of the Egyptian controversy, see "Al-sura al-l-madmun fi-l-adab," *Al-Adab*, April 1954, 73–74.

8. For a sketch of Muruwwa's life, see 'Abbas Baydun, "Husayn Muruwwa," *Al-Safir*, September 18–24, 1985, 10.

9. Husayn Muruwwa, "Min al-Najf dakhala hayati Marx," *Al-Tariq* 43, nos. 2–3 (June 1984): 180.

10. Taha Husayn, "Yunani fa la yaqra," in *Khisam wa naqd*, 90–107.

11. "Al-Adab bayna al-sigha wa-l-madmun," *Al-Thaqafa al-Wataniyya*, March 1954, 57.

12. Ibid.

13. Ibid., 57–58.

14. "Sada maʿrakat al-adab," *Al-Thaqafa al-Wataniyya*, April 1954, 56–57.

15. Ibid., 57.

16. *Al-Ahram*, January 23, 1953, 13.

17. Pierre Cachia, *An Overview of Modern Arabic Literature* (Edinburgh: Edinburgh University Press, 1990), 18–19.

18. "Maʿarik al-adab wa-l-haya," *Al-Adab*, February 1954, 69–70.

19. "Li-Man wa li-madha naktub?," *Al-Adab*, November 1954, 4–7.

20. Ibrahim Fathi, "Al-Sira al-dhatiyya al-siyasiyya li-ʿAbd al-ʿAzim Anis," *Alif: Journal of Comparative Poetics*, no. 22 (2002): 90–91.

21. For Muruwwa's account of his time in Moscow, see Muruwwa, *Qadaya adabiyya* (Cairo: Dar al-Fikr, 1956), 66–85.

22. Mahmud Amin al-ʿAlim met Muruwwa for the first time only in 1956, during the inaugural meeting of the Arab Writers Association in Bludan, Syria. Mahmud Amin al-ʿAlim, "Husayn Muruwwa fi rihlatihi al-thalath," in *Husayn Muruwwa: Fi masiratihi al-nidaliyya fikran wa mumarsa* (Beirut: Dar al-Farabi, 1997), 38.

23. Fathi, "Al-Sira al-dhatiyya," 90–91.

24. For Lebanese involvement in the publication process, see Mahmud Amin al-ʿAlim and ʿAbd al-ʿAzim Anis, *Fi-l-Thaqafa al-Misriyya* (Cairo: Dar al-Thaqafa al-Jadida, 1989), 15–34.

25. Ibid., 5–15.

26. See a letter from Mahmud Amin al-ʿAlim to Muhamd Dakrub thanking Muruwwa and others for their critical contribution; Muhamd Dakrub, "Kalimat ʿan Husayn Muruwwa wa ʿan al-farah bi jadid al-akhirun," in *Husayn Muruwwa shahadat fi fikrihi wa nidalihi* (Beirut: Dar al-Farabi, 1981), 153–54.

27. Al-ʿAlim and ʿAbd al-ʿAzim, *Fi-l-Thaqafa al-Misriyya*, 20.

28. Ibid., 19.

29. Ibid., 21.

30. Ibid., 19.

31. ʿAbd al-Wahhab al-Bayyati, *Tajribati al-shiʿriyya* (Beirut: Manshurat Nizar Qabbani, 1968), 20.

32. Al-ʿAlim and ʿAbd al-ʿAzim, *Fi-l-Thaqafa al-Misriyya*, 49–51, 95–104.

33. Ibid., 17–18.

34. Ibid., 63.

35. Ibid., 63–64.

36. Ibid., 67.

37. Cooper, *Existentialism*, 72.

38. The cause for this misreading was that, whereas for Sartre *Dasein* was a conscious subject, for Badawi (and of course for Heidegger himself) *Dasein* was an unconscious subject but a way of being. In his 1947 *Letter on Hu-*

manism, Heidegger strongly criticized Sartre's reading of *Dasein*; Kleinberg, *Generation Existential*, 18.

39. Muhammad Dakrub, "Tawhij al-munadil/tawhij al-kitaba," *Adab wa Naqd*, no. 145 (September 1997): 110–111; Verena Klemm, "Different Notions," 56.

40. See influence on Nabil Sulayman, *Al-Idiyulujiya wa-l-adab fi Suriyya, 1967–1973* (Beirut: Dar Khaldun, 1974).

41. In his preface Muruwwa alluded to both problems; Mahmud Amin al-'Alim and 'Abd al-'Azim Anis, *Fi-l-Thaqafa al-Misriyya*, 5–15.

42. For instance, "Muhimat al-adab wa wajib al-adib," *Al-Adab*, January 1953, 74; Ra'if Khuri, "Al-Adab: Naqid al-dawla," *Al-Adab*, March 1953, 5–7; Suhayl Idris, "Shakawa al-adab al-'Arabi al-hadith," *Al-Adab*, May 1953, 1–9; Suhayl Idris, "Al-Naqd aladhi nurid," *Al-Adab*, August 1953, 1–2. For a self-promoting article on *Al-Adab*'s own achievements, see "*Al-Adab* fi 'amiha al-thani," *Al-Adab*, January 1954, 1.

43. Idris, "Al-Naqd alladhi nurid," 2.

44. Ibid., 1.

45. Anwar al-Ma'dawi, "Al-Adab al-multazim," *Al-Adab*, February 1953, 12.

46. Ibid.

47. 'Abdallah 'Abd al-Da'im, "Al-Ibda' alladhi nahtaj ilayhi," *Al-Adab*, February 1954, 1.

48. Ibid., 2.

49. Ibid., 3.

50. Ibid., 3–6.

51. 'Ali Baddur, "Fi risalat al-adab," *Al-Adab*, May 1954, 54–55.

52. On the Syrian scene, see Alexa Firat, "Cultural Battles on the Literary Field: From the Syrian Writers Collective to the Last Days of Socialist Realism in Syria," *Middle Eastern Literatures* 18, no. 2 (2015): 153–76.

53. Muta' Safadi, "Iltizam al-adab al-hadasi," *Al-Adab*, June 1954, 53–56.

54. Ahmad Kamal Zaki, "Al-Mas'uliyya fi-l-adab," *Al-Adab*, August 1954, 17–19.

55. Ra'if Khuri's interest in Palestine dates to the 1930; see also Samah Idris, *Ra'if Khuri wa turath al-'arab* (Beirut: Dar al-Adab, 1986), 59–66.

56. Ra'if Khuri, "Al-Insan: Al-qima al-ijtima'iyya al-'ulya," *Al-Adab*, January 1953, 49–50.

57. Ra'if Khuri, "Al-Adab: Naqid al-dawla," *Al-Adab*, March 1953, 5–7.

58. Ra'if Khuri, "Ayyuha al-adab, man anta?," *Al-Adab*, November 1954, 1–3.

59. Da'ud Jirjis Darwish, "Nuzu' al-adab: Bayna al-indiwa' wa-l-iltizam," *Al-Adab*, July 1953, 42–45.

60. Radwan al-Shahal, "Al-Hayy al-Latini," *Al-Thaqafa al-Wataniyya*, March 1954, 51–53.

61. "Ma'rakat al-wujudiyya," *Al-Adab*, November 1955, 73.

62. Khuri Shahada, *Al-Adab fi-l-maydan* (Damascus: Matba'at Dimashq, 1950), 143.

63. Ibid., 161.
64. Ibid., 177.
65. Ibid., 66–67.
66. Ibid., 162.
67. Ibid., 146, 159.
68. Jurj Hanna, "Handasat al-insaniyya," *Al-Thaqafa al-Wataniyya*, March 1954, 8–11, 6.
69. Ibid.
70. Husayn Muruwwa, "Khitab Husayn Muruwwa fi majlis al-silm al-ʿilmi," *Al-Thaqafa al-Wataniyya*, July 1954, 3–5.
71. Husayn Muruwwa, "Maʿ udabaʾ al-silm fi Barlin," *Al-Thaqafa al-Wataniyya*, August 1954, 1.
72. Ibid., 1–4, 64.
73. ʿAbbas Baydun, "Husayn Muruwwa: Wulidtu shaykhan wa amutu tiflan," *Al-Safir*, September 18–24, 1985, 10.
74. Muruwwa, *Qadaya adabiyya*, 66–67.
75. Ibid., 70.
76. Ibid., 72–73.
77. Ibid., 74.
78. In Muruwwa's words, "Soviet writers found mistakes in the application of Socialist Realism which they duly discussed"; ibid., 79–80.
79. Ibid., 98.
80. Ibid., 81, 85.
81. Cynthia Ruder, "Socialist Realism," in *Encyclopedia of Russian History*, ed. James Millar (New York: Macmillan, 2004), 4:1415–19.
82. For Zhdanov speech, "Soviet Literature—The Richest in Ideas, the Most Advanced Literature," http://www.marxists.org/subject/art/lit_crit/sovietwritercongress/zdhanov.htm, accessed June 15, 2012.
83. On their contribution, see Hanna, *Al-Madrasa al-waqiʿiyya*, 77–155.
84. Muruwwa, *Qadaya adabiyya*, 8. For an intellectual biography of Muruwwa, see Yoav Di-Capua, "Homeward Bound: Husayn Muruwwah's Integrative Quest for Authenticity," *Journal of Arabic Literature* 44, no. 1 (2013): 21–52.
85. Husayn Muruwwa, *Dirasat naqdiyya fi dawʾ al-manhaj al-waqiʿi* (Beirut: Maktabat al-Maʿarif, 1965), 5.
86. Muruwwa, *Qadaya adabiyya*, 5.
87. Ibid.
88. See, for instance, Mahmud Amin al-ʿAlim, *Maʿarik fikriyya*; Muhammad ʿAbd al-Halim ʿAbdallah, *Qadaya wa maʿarik adabiyya* (Cairo: Dar al-Shaʿb, 1974); Muruwwa, *Qadaya adabiyya*, 6–7; Muhammad Dakrub, "Malamih min al-masira al-fikriyya li-munadil," *Al-Tariq* 47 (2–3), June 1988, 24–26.
89. "Hikayat adabuna fi ʿamina al-thani," in *Al-Thaqafa al-Wataniyya*, January 1955, 1.
90. Sabry Hafez, *The Quest for Identities: The Development of the Modern Arabic Short Story* (London: Saqi, 2007), 243.

91. Muruwwa, *Qadaya adabiyya*, 6–7.
92. Ibid., 31.
93. Ibid., 17–18.
94. Ibid., 18–19.
95. Ibid., 17–18.
96. Mahdi ʿAmil, "Husayn Muruwwa: Al-Mawqif wa-l-fikr," *Al-Tariq* 47, nos. 2–3 (June 1988): 14–15.
97. Muruwwa, *Qadaya adabiyya*, 35.
98. Ibid., 37.
99. Baydun, "Husayn Muruwwa," September 24, 1985, 10.
100. Muruwwa, *Qadaya adabiyya*, 24–25, 87–88.
101. Dakrub, "Malamih," 36.
102. Tayib Tizini, "Husayn Muruwwa," *Al-Tariq* 47, nos. 2–3 (June 1988): 66.
103. Mahdi ʿAmil, "Husayn Muruwwa: Al-Mawqif wa-l-fikr," *Al-Tariq* 47, nos. 2–3 (June 1988): 16–17; Muhammad al-Misbahi, "Muttasil min ajl munfasil," *Al-Tariq* 47, nos. 2–3 (June 1988): 110.
104. Dakrub, "Malamih," 36.
105. Hanna Mina, "Shayʾ min al-dhikra wa shayʾ min al-damʿ," *Al-Tariq* 4, nos. 2–3 (June 1988): 50; Muruwwa, *Qadaya adabiyya*, 48.
106. N. A. "Marhalatuna al-Jadida," *Al-Thaqafa al-Wataniyya*, April 10, 1954, 2.
107. Muruwwa, *Qadaya adabiyya*, 40.
108. Muhammad Sabr ʿArab and Ahmad Zakariyya al-Shalaq, eds., *Awraq Taha Husayn wa murasalatahu* (Cairo: Dar al-Kutub wa-l-Wathaʾiq al-Qawmiyya, 2007), 1:266; "Al-Adab wa-l-hayat," *Al-Adab*, May 1955, 1.
109. Raʾif Khuri, "Al-Adib yaktubu li-l-kaffa," *Al-Adab*, May 1955, 2.
110. Ibid., 5.
111. Ibid., 8.
112. Ibid., 8.
113. Taha Husayn, "Al-Adib yaktabu li-l-khassa," *Al-Adab*, May 1955, 9.
114. Ibid.
115. Ibid., 12.
116. Ibid., 9.
117. Ibid., 10.
118. Ibid., 13.
119. Ibid., 11.
120. Ibid., 14.
121. Ibid., 16.
122. ʿAbdallah ʿAbd al-Daʾim, "Hawla munazarat Taha Husayn wa Raʾif Khuri," *Al-Adab*, June 1955, 4–6; Ahmad Kamal Zaki, Shaʿban Barakat, and Buland al-Haydari, "Liman yaktubu al-adib?," *Al-Adab*, July 1955, 17–22, 77; ʿAbdallah ʿAbd al-Jabbar, "Liman yaktubu al-adib?," *Al-Adab*, September 1955, 47–48, 77.
123. The editor Ahmad Hasan al-Zayyat announced the closing, and *Al-Adab* registered it as an end of an era; N. A. "Al-Nashat al-thaqafi: Misr,"

Al-Adab, April 1953, 70–71; see also N. A. "Ma'arik al-adab wa-l-haya," *Al-Adab*, February 1954, 70. Concomitantly, in place of the old journals, new journals such as the *Al-Thaqafa al-Jadida* (Iraq), *Al-Tali'a, Al-Tariq* (Lebanon), and *Al-Ghad* (Egypt) began making their local marks.

124. "Al-Za'ama al-adabiyya bayna Bayrut wa-l-Qahira," *Al-Adab*, February 1954, 69–70; Anwar al-Ma'dawi, "Zawaya wa liqatat," *Al-Adab*, October 1955, 11–14.

125. Mina, "Shay' min al-dhikra," 45–60. While the full history of Arab literary criticism is yet to be written, the following describe some of the aesthetics and personal shifts during the 1950s: David Simah, *Four Egyptian Literary Critics* (Leiden: Brill, 1974) and Pierre Cachia, "The Critics," in *The Cambridge History of Arabic Literature*, ed. M. M. Badawi (Cambridge: Cambridge University Press, 1992), 417–42.

126. Husayn was especially critical of Camus and the notion of the absurd. Taha Husayn, *Naqd wa islah* (Beirut: Dar al-'Ilm li-l-Malayin, 1977), 5–16.

127. Ra'if Khuri, "Nurid naqdan 'aqa'idiyyan," *Al-Adab*, July 1955, 2–3, 74; Ra'if Khuri, "Al-adab al-hurriyya wa-l-mas'uliyya," *Al-Adab*, October 1956, 8–11. In 1968 Ra'if Khuri summarized his position on art, aesthetics, and politics in the book *Al-Adab al-mas'ul*.

128. Ra'if Khuri, "Hakadha 'allamna 'Umar Fakhuri," *Al-Adab*, June–August 1959, 2–3.

129. Salama Musa, "Nahnu nufakkir bi afwahina," *Al-Adib*, July 1955, 73–74.

130. Musa, *Ha'ula' 'alamuni*, 271–280; Musa, *Al-Adab li-l-sha'b*, 12–13.

131. Verena Klemm, "Different Notions of Commitment," 56.

132. Quoted in Ibrahim Fathi, "Al-Sira al-dhatiyya al-siyasiyya li-'Abd al-'Azim Anis," 90.

133. Tawfiq al-Hakim, *Al-Ta'duliyya: Madhhabi fi-l-haya wa-l-fann* (Cairo: Maktabat al-Adab, 1955), 121.

134. For a new study of this text, see Shereen Hamed Shaw, "A Study of Tawfiq al-Hakim's Equilibrium Doctrine and Philosophical Narratives" (PhD diss., University of Liverpool, 2015). Retrieved from http://ezproxy.lib .utexas.edu/login?url=http://search.proquest.com.ezproxy.lib.utexas.edu/ docview/1780172044?accountid=7118.

135. Muruwwa, *Dirasat naqdiyya*, 33.

136. Abdul-Nabi Isstaif, "Going beyond Socialist Realism, Getting Nowhere: Luwis 'Awad's Cross-Cultural Encounter with the Other," in *Tradition, Modernity, and Postmodernity in Arabic Literature: Essays in Honor of Professor Issa J. Boullata*, ed. Kamal Abdel-Malek and Wael Hallaq (Leiden: Brill, 2000), 116.

137. Ibid.

138. Taha Husayn, "Muhammad Husayn Haykal," *Al-Adib*, April 1957, 71–73.

139. Salah 'Atiya, ed., *Taha Husayn wa ma'raktuhu al-adabiyya* (Cairo: Dar al-Jumhuriyya li-l-Sahafa, 2008), 2:129.

140. Unfortunately, I cannot precisely date this broadcast. Layla Rustum's show, "Najmak al-Mufaddal," aired for three years. "Liqa' Taha Husayn ma'

Layla Rustum wa nujum al-adab," https://www.youtube.com/watch?v=sU
-ULahGxKA, accessed December 4, 2015.

141. Ma'dawi acknowledges shifts in the traditional Arab division of intellectual labor. Anwar al-Ma'dawi, "Zawaya wa liqatat," 11–14.

142. Anwar al-Ma'dawi, "Harakat al-tarjama bayna Misr wa Lubnan," *Al-Adab*,
June 1955, 5–7.

143. For a postmortem reassessment of iltizam, see Barada, "Tahawwulat
mafhum al-iltizam."

144. Klemm is the first historian to study and identify iltizam as a major cultural moment. Unfortunately, I was unable to read her German-language
study and relied instead on her publications in English; Verena Klemm,
"Different Notions of Commitment (*Iltizam*) and Committed Literature
(*al-adab al-multazim*) in the Literary Circles of the Mashriq" in *Middle East-
ern Literatures* 3, no. 1 (January 2000): 55; see Verena Klemm, *Literarisches
Engagement im arabischen Nahen Osten: Konzepte und Debatten* (Würzburg:
Ergon, 1998); Rhiannon Goldthorpe, "Understanding the Committed
Writer," in *The Cambridge Companion to Sartre*, ed. Christina Howells
(Cambridge: Cambridge University Press, 1992), 142.

CHAPTER FOUR

1. Suhayl Idris, "Yawmiyyat al-thawra fi-Lubnan," *Al-Adab*, September 1958,
2–8, 81–83.

2. Fayiz Sayigh, "Ma'rakatuna ma' al-shuyu'iyya," *Al-Adab*, June 1959, 1–3.

3. For a standard review of Pan-Arabism, see Dawisha, *Arab Nationalism*, and
Mufti, *Sovereign Creations*.

4. Kamal Yusuf al-Hajj, "Al-Hurriyya," *Al-Adib*, January 1958, 2.

5. Sayigh, *Risalat al-mufakkir al-'Arabi*, 119.

6. Fatima Mohsen, "Debating Iraqi Culture: Intellectuals between the Inside
and the Outside," in *Conflicting Narratives: War, Trauma and Memory in Iraqi
Culture*, ed. Stephan Milich, Friederike Pannewick, and Leslie Tramontini
(Wiesbaden, Germany: Reichert, 2012), 13; Yasmeen Hanoosh, "Contempt: State Literati vs. Street Literati in Modern Iraq," *Journal of Arabic
Literature* 43, no. 2/3 (2012), 387. There are at least twenty Arabic books
on the subject, including 'Azza Badr, *Al-Muthaqqaf wa-l-sulta* (Cairo: Dar
al-Jumhuriyya li-l-Sahafa, 2014); Muhammad Zuhayr and Jamil al-Kutbi,
Al-Muthaqqaf al-'Arabi wa-l-sulta (Cairo: Matabi' al-Ahram, 1995); Ahmad Balkhayri, *Al-Muthaqqaf wa-l-sulta: Mawaqif wa rihanat* (Rabat: Dar
al-Tawhidi li-l-Nashr wa-l-Tawzi', 2013); and 'Abd al-Husayn Salih al-Ta'i,
Jadaliyat al-'alaqa bayna al-muthaqqaf wa-l-Sulta (London: Dar al-Hikma,
2013).

7. On the epic historical imagination of Nasserism, see Yoav Di-Capua, *Gatekeepers of the Arab Past: Historians and History Writing in Twentieth-Century
Egypt* (Berkeley: University of California Press, 2009), 248–81.

8. Scott, *Conscripts of Modernity*, 8.

9. Michel 'Aflaq, "Al-Ba'th al-'Arabi haraka tarikhiyya," in *Fi Sabil al-ba'th*, 4th ed. (Beirut: Dar al-Tiba'a wa-l-Nashr, 1970), 37–39.

10. Arjun Appadurai, *Modernity at Large: Cultural Dimensions of Globalization* (Minneapolis: University of Minnesota Press, 1996), 39.

11. Richard Jacquemond, *Conscience of the Nation: Writers, State, and Society in Modern Egypt*, trans. David Tresilian (Cairo: AUC Press, 2008), 15.

12. Ibid., 15.

13. Taha Husayn held a symbolic role in the association, which was de facto run by al-Siba'i; ibid., 19.

14. Ibid.

15. Suhayl Idris, "Al-Shi'r wa-l-masir al-'Arabi," *Al-Adab*, April 1955, 1.

16. Hisham Sharabi, *Nationalism and Revolution in the Arab World: The Middle East and North Africa* (Princeton, NJ: Van Nostrand, 1966), 101.

17. Naji 'Allush, "Ma'na al-taharrur al-'Arabi," *Al-Adab*, November 1957, 49–53; Naji 'Allush, "Al-Thawra bayna al-nazariya wa-l-irtijal," *Al-Adab*, August 1957, 44–45; see also 'Abdallah 'Abd al-Da'im, "Al-Jil al-'Arabi al-jadid amama mustaqbalihi," *Al-Adab*, June 1957, 9–13, 91–95; "Thawriyyat al-qadiyya al-'Arabiyya," May 1956, in Michel 'Aflaq, *Ma'rakat al-masir al-wahid* (Beirut: Dar al-Adab, 1963), 71–75.

18. Ra'if Khuri, "Durus min Bur Sa'id," *Al-Adab*, December 1957, 3–4; 'Ali Baddur, "Al-Thawra bayna al-nazriya wa-l-waqi'," *Al-Adab*, September 1957, 61–64; Muhammad al-Naqqash, "Tha'irun fi kul makan," *Al-Adab*, September 1957, 1–3. For 'Aflaq's understanding of the Arab Cause, see "Mustaqbaluna min khilal al-azma al-hadira," 88–90 (September 1956), "La Ruju' wa la taraju'," 91–95 (September 1956), "Thawratuna fi tariq al-nudj," 96–98 (October 1956), "Mustawa jadid li-nidaluna," 99–102 (October 1956) in 'Aflaq, *Ma'rakat al-masir al-wahid*.

19. Naji 'Allush, "Thawrat al-Jaza'ir," *Al-Adab*, March 1957, 10, 78–79; 'Abdallah 'Abd al-Da'im, "Ma'sat al-Jaza'ir," *Al-Adab*, September 1957, 4; Ra'if Khuri, "Al-Hall al-wahid li-qadiyyat al-jaza'ir," *Al-Adab*, March 1957, 2–3.

20. Ra'if Khuri, "'A'id min Misr," *Al-Adab*, June 1957, 1.

21. "Hawla ma'rad al-kharif al-Lubnani," *Al-Adab*, February 1957, 73.

22. "Al-Iltizam," *Al-Adab*, April 1957, 85.

23. Jurj Hanna, *Ma'na al-thawra* (Beirut: Dar Bayrut, 1957), 101.

24. Ibid., 101–3.

25. Ibid., 110.

26. Hourani, *Arabic Thought*, 355–56.

27. Jamal 'Abd al-Nasir, "Hajatuna ila al-taharrur al-fikri," *Al-Adab*, January 1958, 3.

28. Suhayl Idris, "Mu'tamaruna al-adabi al-thalith," *Al-Adab*, January 1958, 1.

29. Ibid., 2.

30. Quoted in "Waqai' al-mu'tamar al-thalith li-l-udaba' al-'Arab," *Al-Adab*, January 1958, 101.

31. Ibid., 102.
32. Idris, "Mu'tamaruna al-adabi," 1–2.
33. Fu'ad Shayib, "Risalat al-qawmiyya al-'Arabiya," *Al-Adab*, January 1958, 13.
34. Ra'if Khuri, "Wajibat al-naqid fi khidmat al-qawmiyya al-'Arabiyya," *Al-Adab*, January 1958, 14.
35. "Waqai' al-mu'tamar," 119; "Nida' ila udaba' al-'alam," *Al-Adab*, January 1958, 4.
36. Ra'if Khuri, "Aajibat al-naqid," 107.
37. Mahmud al-Mas'adi, "Himayat al-adib," *Al-Adab*, January 1958, 27.
38. Ibid., 28.
39. Quoted in Badawi, "Commitment," 858–59, originally in Mahmud al-Mas'adi, "Himayat al-adib," 28.
40. Jawdat al-Rikabi, "Hawla himayat al-adib: Al-Hurriyya fi khidmat al-qawmiyya al-'Arabiyya," *Al-Adab*, January 1958, 30.
41. Quoted in M. M. Badawi, "Commitment," 858–59.
42. Mohamed-Salah Omri, *Nationalism, Islam and World Literature: Sites of Confluence in the Writings of Mahmud al-Mas'adī* (Abingdon, UK: Routledge, 2006), 42.
43. Ibid., 41.
44. Omri, *Nationalism, Islam and World Literature*, 44; Robin Ostle, "Mahmūd al-Mas'adī and Tunisia's 'Lost Generation,'" *Journal of Arabic Literature* 8 (1977): 153–66.
45. On this see Wilder, *Freedom Time*.
46. Cited in Omri, *Nationalism, Islam and World Literature*, 43.
47. Taha Husayn, "Al-Udaba' hum bunna' al-qawmiyya al-'Arabiyya," *Al-Adab*, January 1958, 7–11.
48. Suhir Qalamwi, "Qadaya al-naqd al-hadith," *Al-Adab*, January 1958, 17–19.
49. Quoted in "Waqai' al-mu'tamar," 117.
50. For a discussion of fluctuations in the meaning of *iltizam*, see "Al-Iltizam," *Al-Adab*, April 1957, 85.
51. "Yusuf al-Khal, Poet, Critic," in *Crosshatching in Global Culture*, ed. John Donohue and Leslie Tramontini (Beirut: Orient-Institut der DMG, 2004), 2:606–9.
52. Similar to Fayiz Sayigh and Hisham Sharabi, Adonis also joined Antun's Sa'ada's Syrian Socialist Nationalist Party but left it in 1958.
53. Archibald MacLeish, *Shi'r* 1 (Winter 1957), 3.
54. See, for instance, Khalida Sa'id, "Bawadir al-rafd fi-l-shi'r al-'Arabi al-jadid," *Shi'r* 19 (July 1961), 88–95; René Habashi, "Al-Shi'r fi ma'rakat al-wujud," *Shi'r* 1 (January 1957), 88–95. For an outstanding take on *Shi'r*'s enterprise, see Robyn Creswell, "Tradition and Translation: Poetic Modernism in Beirut" (PhD diss., New York University, 2012). Retrieved from http://ezproxy.lib.utexas.edu/login?url=http://search.proquest.com.ezproxy.lib.utexas.edu/docview/992988836?accountid=7118. See also Angela Giordani, "*Shi'r*

and the Other Revolution of the Arab Fifties" (unpublished manuscript, 2010, University of Texas at Austin).

55. Otared Haidar, *The Prose Poem and the Journal Shi'r: A Comparative Study of Literature, Literary Theory and Journalism* (Reading, UK: Ithaca Press, 2008), 93.

56. Adonis, "Majnun bayna al-mawta: Ma'sat fi arba' ma'arik," *Shi'r* 1 (Winter 1957), 26–37. See also René Habashi, "Al-Shi'r fi ma'rakat al-wujud," *Shi'r* 1 (January 1957), 88–95.

57. "Ila al-qari'," *Shi'r* 15 (July 1960), 5–9; Haidar, *Prose Poem*, 99.

58. Ostle, "Mahmūd al-Mas'adī," 153–66.

59. A sense of metaphysical revolt underlies 1959's *Awlad Haritna* (translated as Children of Gabalawi), which is an allegory of mankind's religious struggle to achieve harmony and justice. Absurdist themes characterize much of Mahfouz's writing during the 1960s, when the promise of rational national politics reached its dramatic limitations. Mustafa Mahmud's 1961 *Al-Mustahil* (The impossibility) is a novel that deals with an estranged protagonist whose father suppressed the emergence of his selfhood. Striving to find meaning in life he ultimately revolts against societal conventions, especially those related to sex. Another relevant novel of the time was Mahmud Diyab's *Al-Zilal* (The shadow, 1964); Hayim Gordon, *Naguib Mahfouz's Egypt: Existential Themes in His Writings* (New York: Greenwood Press, 1990); Ali Jad, *Form and Technique in the Egyptian Novel, 1912–1971* (London: Ithaca Press, 1983), 295–307; Samia Mehrez, *Egyptian Writers between History and Fiction* (Cairo: American University Press, 1994), 39–57; Stefan Meyer, *The Experimental Arabic Novel* (Albany: State University of New York Press, 2001), 16; Muhsin al-Musawi, "The Socio-Political Context of the Iraqi Short Story, 1908–1968," in *Statecraft and Popular Culture in the Middle East*, ed. Eric Davis and Nicholas Gaverieldes (Gainesville: University Press of Florida, 1991), 202–27.

60. Other important playwrights were Walid Ihlasi, Farah Bulbul, and 'Ali 'Uqla 'Ursan; Ewa Machut-Mendecka, *Studies in Arabic Theatre and Literature* (Warsaw: Dialog, 2000), 86–96; Nadim Ma'alla Muhammad, *Al-Adab al-masrahi fi Suriyya: Nash'atuhu, tatawwuruhu* (Damascus: s.n., 1982), 62–165.

61. "Hani al-Rahib," in *Crosshatching in Global Culture*, ed. John Donohue and Leslie Tramontini (Beirut: Orient-Institut der DMG, 2004), 2:928–30.

62. Khalil Suwaylih, "Sira ishkaliyya nafira," *Al-Wasat*, February 28, 2000, 54–55; Mahmoud Saeed, "Remembering Hani al-Rahib: Death Ends Novelist's Portrayal of Arab World in Crisis," *Al-Jadid* 6, no. 31 (Spring 2000), http://www.aljadid.com/content/remembering-hani-al-rahib-death-ends-novelists-portrayal-arab-world-crisis#sthash.BBsABqvE.dpuf, accessed April 5, 2017; Bassam Frangieh, "Hani al-Raheb and Writing in the Sands," *Banipal* (Autumn 2000): 36–37, http://www.banipal.co.uk/back_issues/47/issue-9/, accessed April 5, 2017; see also *Al-Adab*'s review: Falih al-Tawil,

"Dirasa wa naqd li-riwayat Hani al-Rahib 'al-mahzumun,'" *Al-Adab*, July 1961, 7–10; Ahmad Sulayman al-Tawil, "Al-Mahzumun Aydan," *Al-Adab*, October 1961, 36–39; see also Shakir Farid Husayn, "Kira'a fi-l-riwa'i al-Suri Hani al-Rahib," in *al-Hiwar Al-Mutamaddin*, March 25, 2010, http://www.ahewar.org/debat/show.art.asp?aid=209062, accessed October 20, 2014.

63. Hani al-Rahib, *Al-Mahzumun* (Beirut: Dar al-Adab, 1961), 23.

64. Ibid., 61, 151.

65. Ibid., 24.

66. Ibid., 33.

67. Ibid., 63.

68. Ibid., 80.

69. Ibid., 148.

70. Ibid., 157.

71. Ibid., 225.

72. Ibid., 249.

73. Saeed, "Remembering Hani al-Rahib."

74. Simun di Bufwar, *Al-Jins al-akhar*, trans. ʿAli Sharaf al-Din (Beirut: al-Maktaba al-Haditha li-l-Tibaʿa wa-l-Nashr, 1979). Partial translations circulated since the 1950s, including a version jointly translated by a committee of university professors and released in Beirut by al-Maktabah al-Ahliyah.

75. Nazik al-Malaʾika, "Al-Tajziʾiyya," *Al-Adab*, May 1954, 1.

76. Ibid., 6.

77. "Nizar Qabbani," in *Crosshatching in Global Culture*, ed. John Donohue and Leslie Tramontini (Beirut: Orient-Institut der DMG, 2004), 2:883.

78. Translated by A. Z. Forman in his blog *Poems Found in Translation*, http://poemsintranslation.blogspot.com/search/label/Qabbani, accessed October 20, 2014. See also translation by M. A. Khouri and H. Algar in *Journal of Arabic Literature* 1 (1970): 86–87.

79. Arieh Loya, "Poetry as a Social Document: The Social Position of the Arab Woman as Reflected in the Poetry of Nizar Qabbani," *International Journal of Middle East Studies* 6, no. 4 (October 1975): 487.

80. In his erotic and love poems Qabbani also took issue with the religious establishment. Writing of a beautiful woman, he says, "In the form of your face I read / The glorious form of Allah." Loya, "Poetry as a Social Document," 484, 487; see also Wisam Mansour, "Arab Women in Nizar Kabbani's Poetry," *Comparative Studies of South Asia, Africa and the Middle East* 25, no. 2 (2005): 480–86.

81. Nizar Qabbani, "*Al-Wujudiyya*," http://www.aldiwan.net/poem5823.html, accessed October 20, 2014.

82. Layla Baʿalbaki, *Ana ahya* (Beirut: Dar Majallat Shiʿr, 1963), 45.

83. She calls her father an opportunist war profiteer and a "shadow of a human being." Ibid., 5, 19–20, 112–13.

84. Anis Sayigh, "Ana ahya," *Al-Adab*, May 1958. 59. The Arabic translation of Sagan's *Aimez-vous Brahms* was published by *Al-Adab* in 1961.

85. Samira Aghacy, "Lebanese Women's Fiction: Urban Identity and the Tyranny of the Past," *International Journal of Middle East Studies* 33 no. 4 (2001): 503–23.

86. Editors, "Difaʿan ʿan al-hurriyya: Layla Baʿalbaki," *Hiwar*, September–October 1964, 176–82.

87. Fuʾad al-Takarli's 1960 novel *Al-Wajh al-akhar* (The other face) raised the same concerns albeit in a more digestible language.

88. Ghassan Kanafani, *Men in the Sun*, trans. Hilary Kilpatrick (Cairo: American University Press, 1991), 56.

89. Meyer, *The Experimental Arabic Novel*, 28.

90. Barbara Harlow, "Reading of National Identity in the Palestinian Novel," in *The Arabic Novel Since 1950: Critical Essays, Interviews, and Bibliography*, ed. Issa J. Boullata and Roger Allen (Cambridge, MA: Dar Mahjar, 1992), 89–106; Orit Bashkin, "Nationalism as a Cause: Arab Nationalism in the Writings of Ghassan Kanafani," in *Nationalism and Liberal Thought in the Arab East Ideology and Practice*, ed. Christoph Schumann (London: Routledge, 2010), 92–112.

91. I replaced the original translation of the Arabic word *qadiya* to signify "the cause" rather than "an issue." Translated by Barbara Harlow in "Return to Haifa: 'Opening the Borders' in Palestinian Literature," *Social Text*, nos. 13/14 (Winter–Spring 1986): 19.

92. Hatir ʿAbbas al-Salihi, "Salama Musa al-mufakkir al-hurr," *Al-Adib*, October 1958, 10–12.

93. "Requiem," *Baheyya: Egypt Analysis and Whimsy* [blog], June 20, 2006, http://baheyya.blogspot.com/2006/06/requiem.html, accessed November 15, 2014; Anouar Abdel-Malek, *Egypt: Military Society; The Army Regime, the Left, and Social Change under Nasser* (New York: Random House, 1968), 125–29.

94. Adel Montasser, "La Répression Anti-Démocratique en Égypte," *Les Temps Modernes*, nos. 173–77 (August–September 1960): 418–41. This piece was later expanded and published as a book; Adel Montasser, *La Répression anti-démocratique en République Arabe Unie* (Paris: Temps modernes, 1961).

95. Abdel-Malek, *Egypt*, 190.

96. Ibid., 191.

97. Ibid., 194.

98. ʿIsa al-Nuri, "Al-Adab wa-l-iltizam," *Al-Adib*, August 1958, 5–8.

99. Radwan Ibrahim, "Al-Iltizam wa-l-asala," *Al-Adib*, October 1958, 49.

CHAPTER FIVE

1. Al-ʿAlim, "Al-Hurriyya," 226.
2. Andrew Levine, "Foundations of Unfreedom," *Ethics* 88, no. 2 (January 1978): 162. The notion of "collective unfreedom" has a venerable Marxist pedigree; see, for instance, G. A. Cohen, "The Structure of Proletarian Unfreedom," *Philosophy and Public Affairs* 12, no. 1 (Winter 1983): 3–33. Furthermore, in 1964 Herbert Marcuse used the term "unfreedom" to describe the democratic condition in industrialized societies.
3. Fatima Mohsen, "Debating Iraqi Culture: Intellectuals between the Inside and the Outside," in *Conflicting Narratives: War, Trauma and Memory in Iraqi Culture*, ed. Stephan Milich, Friederike Pannewick, and Leslie Tramontini (Wiesbaden, Germany: Reichert, 2012), 12.
4. For other treatments of this theme, see Yasmeen Hanoosh, "Contempt: State Literati vs. Street Literati in Modern Iraq," *Journal of Arabic Literature* 43, nos. 2–3 (2012): 372–408; Eric Davis, *Memories of State: Politics, History and Collective Identity in Modern Iraq* (Berkeley: University of California Press, 2005), 82–147.
5. For socioeconomic analysis, see Marion Farouk-Sluglett and Peter Sluglett, "The Transformation of Land Tenure and Rural Social Structure in Central and Southern Iraq, c. 1870–1958," *International Journal of Middle East Studies* 15, no. 4 (November 1983): 491–505; Hanna Batatu, *The Old Social Classes and the Revolutionary Movements of Iraq: A Study of Iraq's Old Landed and Commercial Classes and of Its Communists, Baʿthists, and Free Officers* (London: Saqi Books, 2004), 465–536, 1185; Phebe Marr, *The Modern History of Iraq* (Boulder, CO: Westview, 2004), 61–80; Samira Haj, *The Making of Iraq, 1900–1963: Capital, Power, and Ideology* (Albany: State University of New York Press, 1997), 79–109.
6. For the emotional public commemoration ceremony and the recitation of the poem, see Orit Bashkin, *The Other Iraq: Pluralism and Culture in Hashemite Iraq* (Stanford, CA: Stanford University Press, 116). For the poem see the complete works of al-Jawahiri, available online at http://www.jwahri.net/#top, accessed April 6, 2017.
7. On Jewish Iraq, see Orit Bashkin, *The New Babylonians: A History of Jews in Modern Iraq* (Stanford, CA: Stanford University Press, 2012).
8. Batatu, *The Old Social Classes*, 666–78.
9. The best guide to the life and times of Baghdadi intellectuals is Bashkin, *The Other Iraq*, 105; see also Tareq Ismael, *The Rise and Fall of the Communist Party in Iraq* (New York: Cambridge University Press, 2008), 42.
10. For a partial list of high-profile detainees, see Anonymous, "Uslub jadid li-itihad al-fikri fi-l-ʿIraq," *Al-Thaqafa al-Wataniyya*, March 1955, 57.
11. Quoted in Khaldun al-Husry, "The Iraqi Revolution of July 14, 1958," *Middle East Forum* 41, no. 1 (1965): 28. On the generational experience of Iraqi youth, see Sarah Pursley, "A Race against Time: Governing Femininity

and Reproducing the Future in Revolutionary Iraq, 1945–63" (PhD diss., City University of New York, 2012), 202–52. Retrieved from http://ezproxy .lib.utexas.edu/login?url=http://search.proquest.com.ezproxy.lib.utexas .edu/docview/1018426654?accountid=7118. See also Yousif Abdul-Salaam Yacoob, "Vanguardist Cultural Practices: The Formation of an Alternative Cultural Hegemony in Iraq and Chile, 1930s–1970s" (PhD diss., University of Iowa, 1988). Retrieved from http://ezproxy.lib.utexas.edu/login?url= http://search.proquest.com.ezproxy.lib.utexas.edu/docview/303695333 ?accountid=7118.

12. The number of secondary and college students rose steadily during this period, reaching 135,658 at the time of the 1958 revolution, about half of which resided in eight-hundred-thousand-person-strong Baghdad; Batatu, *The Old Social Classes*, 35, 481–82, 1120; Muhsin Musawi, *Reading Iraq: Culture and Power in Conflict* (London: I. B. Tauris, 2006), 42.

13. Jabra Ibrahim Jabra, "The Palestinian Exile as Writer," *Journal of Palestine Studies* 8, no. 2 (Winter 1979): 77, 80.

14. Jabra Ibrahim Jabra, *Princess Street: Baghdad Memories*, trans. Issa Boullata (Fayetteville: University of Arkansas Press, 2005), 80.

15. Ibid., 136–37.

16. Jabra, "The Palestinian Exile," 82.

17. Musawi, *Reading Iraq*, 113; Nada Shabout, *Modern Arab Art: Formation of Arab Aesthetics* (Gainesville: University Press of Florida, 2007), 23–31; SARTEC, ed., *Iraq Contemporary Art* (Lausanne: SARTEC, 1977), 99–116; Jabra, *Princess Street*, 62–63.

18. Hassan Shakir al-Said, "With Jawad Salim: The Unknown Political Prisoner," *Modern Art Iraq Archive*, item no. 221, http://artiraq.org/maia/items/ show/221, accessed June 5, 2014.

19. Shabout, *Modern Arab Art*, 28; Sarah Pursley, "A Race against Time," chapter 1.

20. Previous Egyptian attempts at free verse were less influential; Shmuel Moreh, "Free Verse," in *Encyclopedia of Arabic Literature*, ed. Julie Scott Meisami and Paul Stakey (Oxford: Routledge, 2010), 236–37.

21. Ibid.

22. Terri DeYoung, *Placing the Poet: Badr Shakir al-Sayyab and Postcolonial Iraq* (Albany: State University of New York Press, 1998), 193.

23. On these influences, see Shmuel Moreh, *Ha ilan ve ha ʿanaf: Ha sifrut ha ʿaravit ha hadashs ve yetziratam ha sifrutit shel yotzei Iraq* (Jerusalem: Magnes, 1997), 65–103.

24. Nathalie Handal, ed., *The Poetry of Arab Women: A Contemporary Anthology*, trans. Husain Haddawy (New York: Interlink Books, 2001), 177.

25. Simone Stevens, "Nazik al-Malaika (1923–2007): Iraqi Woman's Journey Changes Map of Arabic Poetry," *Al-Jadid* 13/14, nos. 58/59 (2007/2008), http://www.aljadid.com/content/nazik-al-malaika-1923-2007-iraqi-woman

%E2%80%99s-journey-changes-map-arabic-poetry, accessed May 10, 2014.

26. Jabra, *Princess Street*, 73.

27. See correspondence with Suhayl Idris, Yusuf al-Khal, Adonis, and many others in *Rasaʾil al-Sayyab*, ed. Majid al-Samarraʾi (Beirut: al-Muʾassasa al-ʿArabiyya li-l-Dirasat, 1994).

28. On one occasion, for instance, she argued that the quintessential characteristic of Arab society was a deep sense of anxiety that, in turn, led to social fragmentation and lack of unity. Nazik al-Malaʾika, "Al-Tajziʾiyya fi-l-mujtamaʿ al-ʿArabi," *Al-Adab*, May 1954, 1–6. On her feminist poetry and interventions and their context, see Noga Efrati, *Women in Iraq: Past Meets Present* (New York: Columbia University Press, 2012), 42–43, 72, 140; Orit Bashkin, "Representations of Women in the Writings of the Intelligentsia in Hashemite Iraq, 1921–1958," *Journal of Middle East Women's Studies* 4, no. 1 (2007): 53–82.

29. Quoted in Terri DeYoung, *Placing the Poet*, 196.

30. Quoted in Issa J. Boullata, "Badr Shakir al-Sayyab and the Free Verse Movement," *International Journal of Middle East Studies* 1, no. 3 (July 1970): 253.

31. Al-Bayyati, *Tajribati al-shiʿriyya*, 37.

32. Sami Mahdi, *Al-Mawja al-sakhiba: Shiʿr al-sittiniyat fi-l-ʿIraq* (Baghdad: Dar al-Shuʾun al-Thaqafiyya al-ʿAmma, Wizarat al-Thaqafa wa-l-Iʿlam, 1994), 37.

33. Khalid Zahra, "Al-Madina wa-l-nas: Maqahi Baghdad al-qadima," Zoomin.TV, YouTube video, 5:32, https://www.youtube.com/watch?v=i3NGLFDdxS0, accessed May 4, 2017.

34. Fayiz al-Haidar, "Ahyaʾ Baghdad wa maqahiha al-shaʿbiyya manbaʿ al-adab wa-l-thaqafa," in *al-Hiwar al-Mutamaddin*, http://www.ahewar.org/debat/show.art.asp?aid=153743, accessed May 4, 2017.

35. Jabra, *Princess Street*, 63.

36. Ibid., 122.

37. Moreh, *Ha Ilan ve Ha ʿAnaf*, 108–9; Yousif Abdul-Salaam Yacoob, "Vanguardist Cultural Practices," 126–27.

38. Zahra, "Al-madina wa-l-nas."

39. Cohen-Solal, *Sartre: A Life*, 264.

40. Jabra, *Princess Street*, 83.

41. Shahada, *Al-Adab fi-l-maydan*, 63–64.

42. Desmond Stewart, "Contacts with Arab Writers," *Middle East Forum* 37, no. 1 (January 1981): 19.

43. Jabra, *Princess Street*, 88.

44. Ibid., 88–89.

45. "Woody Allen Existentialism," YouTube video, 0:27, https://www.youtube.com/watch?v=RB9afLhro3M.

46. For a review of the novel and discussion of Baghdad's oral existentialism, see "Sartar wa-l-wujudiyya fi Baghdad al-sittinat," http://www.aawsat

.com/details.asp?issueno=8070&article=80132#.U4kaN3Z40xE, accessed May 15, 2014.

47. Ali Badr, *Papa Sartre*, trans. Aida Bamia (Cairo: American University Press, 2009), 22.
48. Ibid., 111.
49. Ibid., 79.
50. Ibid., 42.
51. Ibid., 53.
52. Ibid., 78.
53. Ibid., 79.
54. Ibid., 47.
55. Ibid., 29.
56. Ibid., 34.
57. Ibid., 70.
58. Ibid., 81.
59. Ibid., 176.
60. Fadil al-ʿAzzawi, *Al-Ruh al-hayya: Jil al-sittinat fi-l-ʿIraq* (Damascus: Dar al-Thaqafa li-l-Nashr, 1997), 103.
61. Haytham Bahoora, "Baudelaire in Baghdad: Modernism, the Body, and Husayn Mardan's Poetics of the Self," *International Journal of Middle East Studies* 45, no. 2 (May 2013): 318.
62. Jabra, *Princess Street*, 83–84.
63. Ibid., 82; Musawi, *Reading Iraq*, 132.
64. Bahoora, "Baudelaire in Baghdad," 316–17.
65. Ibid., 313–16; Jabra, *Princess Street*, 83–84.
66. Translation by Haytham Bahoora, "Baudelaire in Baghdad," 318; see also Husayn Mardan, "Al-Ihdaʾ," in *Al-Aʿmal al-nashriyya* (Baghdad: Dar al-Shuʾun al-Thaqafiyya al-ʿAmma, 2009), 1:11.
67. Jabra, *Princess Street*, 83–84.
68. Bahoora, "Baudelaire in Baghdad," 313–16; Mardan, "Al-Mafhum al-haqiqi li-l-falsafa al-wujudiyya," in *Al-Aʿmal al-nashriyya*, 2:149–50.
69. Haytham Bahoora, "Baudelaire in Baghdad," 317.
70. Mardan, "Al-Fanan bayna masʾuliyatayn," in *Al-Aʿmal al-nashriyya*, 2:98–99. See also Mardan's rejoinder to an Iraqi debate about existentialism and humanism, "Al-Mafhum al-haqiqi," 2:149–50 and "Al-Ihdaʾ," 1:11.
71. Musawi, *Reading Iraq*, 132.
72. Badr Shakir al-Sayyab, *Kuntu shuyuʿiyyan* (Cologne: Manshurat al-Jamal, 2007). For Elliott Colla's fascinating account of al-Sayyab's divestment from communism, see Elliott Colla, "Badr Shākir al-Sayyāb, Cold War Poet," *Middle Eastern Literatures* 18, no. 3 (2015): 247–63.
73. Batatu, *The Old Social Classes*, 966–73; Michael Eppel, *Iraq from Monarchy to Tyranny: From the Hashemites to the Rise of Saddam* (Gainesville: University Press of Florida, 2004), 198–204.

74. Batatu, *The Old Social Classes*, 966–73; Eppel, *Iraq from Monarchy to Tyranny*, 206.
75. Mahdi, *Al-Mawja al-sakhiba*, 149, 170–71, 221.
76. Al-'Azzawi, *Al-Ruh al-hayya*, 168, 312, 356; Mahdi, *Al-Mawja al-sakhiba*, 100.
77. Al-'Azzawi, *Al-Ruh al-hayya*, 155.
78. Ibid., 90.
79. Mahdi, *Al-Mawja al-sakhiba*, 264–65.
80. Merleau-Ponty and Neruda also figured strongly; al-'Azzawi, *Al-Ruh al-hayya*, 51; Mahdi, *Al-Mawja al-sakhiba*, 22.
81. Al-'Azzawi, *Al-Ruh al-hayya*, 122–23.
82. Musawi, *Reading Iraq*, 113.
83. For critiques of iltizam that emerged in the early 1960s, see *Al-Adab*, March 1962, 109; Badawi, "Commitment," 870; Muhammad Adib al-'Amari, "al-Haya wa-l-iltizam," *Al-Adib*, April 1962, 2; Muhammad Adib al-'Amari, "al-Ilham wa-l- iltizam," *Al-Adib*, July 1962, 2; Muta' Safadi, "Multazimun am muta'assibun?," *Al-Adab*, February 1960, 61. Even as far as Bahrain, uncommitted writers were attacked for their position; Qasim Hadad, "'An al-iltizam," in *Tahawwulat mafhum al-iltizam fi-l-adab al-'Arabi al-hadith*, ed. Muhammad Barada (Beirut: Dar al-Fikr al-Mu'asir, 2003), 126–32. Suhayl Idris rushed to defend his original cause in its pure Sartrean interpretation, arguing that he preached for iltizam and not for ilzam (coercion); Suhayl Idris, "Adabuna la thawri," *Al-Adab*, January 1960, 1–2.
84. This was quite evident, for instance, in the contents of one of its cultural mouthpieces, which, in the face of a full-scale assault on the monarchy, published far-fetched articles such as "Some observation and experiments on sex alteration" and "When will we eat algae?" See *Al-Mu'allim al-Jadid*, June 1957, 50–54, and September 1957, 81–85.
85. Muta' Safadi, "Crisis of the Contemporary Arab Hero," in *Contemporary Arab Political Thought*, ed. Anouar Abdel-Malek (London: Zed Books, 1983), 107.
86. Ibid., 104.
87. Ibid., 104–5.
88. Ibid., 105.
89. Even a retired *adib* invoked the idea that that Arab literature should become world literature; 'Abbas Mahmud al-'Aqqad, "Adabuna al-'Arabi sa-yakun adaban 'alamiyyan," *Al-Hilal*, January 1959, 20–23. See personal correspondence between Badr Shakir al-Sayyab and Suhayl Idris from June 19, 1954, in al-Samarra'i, *Rasa'il al-Sayyab*, 109.

CHAPTER SIX

1. For a comprehensive overview of these ideological threads, see ʿAbd al-Ilah Balqaziz, ed., *Al-Thaqafa al-ʿArabiyya fi-l-qarn al-ʿishrin: Hasila awwaliyya* (Beirut: Markaz Dirasat al-Wahda al-ʿArabiyya, 2011), 205–48, 303–26.
2. Arthur, *Unfinished Projects*, 69.
3. Ibid., 30.
4. Ibid.
5. Noureddine Lamouchi, *Jean-Paul Sartre et le Tiers Monde: Rhétorique d'un discourse anticolonialiste* (Paris: L'Harmattan, 1996), 41–57.
6. Suhayl Idris, preface to Sartre's "Nizam al-Istiʿamar al-Faransi fi-l-Jazaʾir," *Al-Adab*, June 1956, 3.
7. Picon Gaëtan, "Zaʿim al-falsafa al-wujudiyya, Jan-Bul Sartar," *Al-Adib*, May 1954, 72–75.
8. Robert Young, "Preface," *Interventions: International Journal of Postcolonial Studies* 3, no. 1 (2001): 129.
9. Ibid., 127–28.
10. Ibid., 138.
11. Ibid.
12. Arthur, *Unfinished Projects*, 66.
13. Ibid.
14. Jan-Bul Sartar, "Nizam al-Istiʿamar," 78.
15. Sayigh, *Risalat al-mufakkir al-ʿArabi*, 119.
16. Jean-Paul Sartre, "Colonialism Is a System," *Interventions: International Journal of Postcolonial Studies* 3, no. 1 (2001): 129.
17. Young, "Preface," *Interventions*, 129.
18. Ibid., 140.
19. Jan-Bul Sartar, "Mujannadun yashhadun," *Al-Adab*, August 1957, 6–9. On the resistance of French intellectuals to the war, see Le Sueur, *Uncivil War*, 28–54; Jan-Bul Sartar, *ʿAruna fi-l-Jazaʾir*, translated by Suhayl Idris and ʿAida Idris (Nazareth: Al-Kitab al-ʿArabi, 1960), 64.
20. Suhayl Idris, "Nahnu wa Sartar," *Al-Adab*, December 1964, 1–3; see also Lamouchi, *Jean-Paul Sartre et le Tiers Monde*, 77–108.
21. Arthur, *Unfinished Projects*, xix.
22. On this affair, see Judith Surkis, "Ethics and Violence: Simone de Beauvoir, Djamila Boupacha, and the Algerian War," *French Politics, Culture and Society* 28, no. 2 (Summer 2010): 38–55.
23. See, for instance, Shukri Ghali, "Nakarazuf: Faylusuf al-azma al-Faransiyya," *Al-Adab*, May 1960, 22–25, 74–77.
24. Over this issue and the party's support of the war in Algeria, in 1956 Césaire quit the French Communist Party (the PCF); see Aimé Césaire, "Letter to Maurice Thorez," *Social Text* 28, no. 2 103 (Summer 2010): 145–52.
25. See CIA analysis of Polish debates and, in particular, the antiexistentialist position of Adam Schaff: "Communist Revisionism and Dis-

sidence," November 2, 1960, Summary Number 2486, CIA-RDP78-00915R001200120007-8, NARA, Washington, DC, USA.

26. Al-ʿAlim, "Al-Hurriyya wa-l-iltizam," 226.
27. Ibid., 236.
28. Ibid.
29. Ibid., 227.
30. Summarized from Georg Lukács's critical 1949 essay "Existentialism" in *Marxism and Human Liberation: Essays on History, Culture and Revolution*, ed. Georg Lukács (New York: Dell, 1973), 243–66; and George Novack, "Basic Differences between Existentialism and Marxism," in *Existentialism versus Marxism: Conflicting Views on Humanism*, ed. George Novack (New York: Dell, 1966), 317–40.
31. For a critical discussion of *The Critique*, see Arthur, *Unfinished Projects*, 77–117.
32. Claude Lanzmann, *The Patagonian Hare*, 338–39. Fanon's biographer mentions a different timeline for their meeting; David Macey, *Frantz Fanon: A Biography* (New York: Verso, 2012), 448–50.
33. Fuʾad Zakariyya, "Al-Jadl bayna al-wujudiyya wa-l-marksiyya," *Al-Fikr al-Muʿasir*, June 1965, 24–27.
34. Mutaʿ Safadi, "Sartar bayna al-wujudiyya wa-l-marksiyya," *Al-Adab*, December 1964, 4–6, 73.
35. On the rise of human rights, see Moyn, *The Last Utopia*.
36. Mutaʿ Safadi, "Sartar bayna," 4–6, 73.
37. Jurj Tarabishi, *Sartar wa-l-Marksiyya* (Beirut: Dar al-Taliʿa, 1964), 7–8.
38. Ibid., 8–9.
39. Ibid., 9–10.
40. Ibid., 13–14.
41. See introduction and opening quote from the Egyptian Socialist Charter (1962) by translator ʿAbd al-Munʿim al-Hifni in Jan-Bul Sartar, *Al-Marksiyya wa-l-thawra* (Cairo: al-Dar al-Misriyya, n.d.), 3–13.
42. Tarabishi, *Sartar wa-l-Marksiyya*, 11–12.
43. Al-ʿAzzawi, *Al-Ruh al-hayya*, 78.
44. Tarabishi, *Sartar wa-l-Marksiyya*, 189.
45. Al-Bayyati had a pioneering role in a serious Iraqi "effort to identify with foreign poets, including Persian, Turkish, Russian, American, English, Spanish, Latin American and French. Hence, we come across poems that take their titles from specific names, like Neruda, Lorca, and Nâzim Hikmat." Musawi, *Reading Iraq*, 131.
46. Al-Bayyati, *Tajribati al-shiʿriyya*, 15.
47. Ronald Aronson, "Albert Camus," in *Stanford Encyclopedia of Philosophy*, ed. Edward N. Zalta, last modified spring 2012, http://plato.stanford.edu/archives/spr2012/entries/camus/, accessed July 2014.
48. See Ronald Aronson, *Camus and Sartre: The Story of a Friendship and the Quarrel That Ended It* (Chicago: University of Chicago Press, 2004).

49. ʿAbd al-Wahhab al-Bayyati, "Ila Albir Kamu," in *Diwan ʿAbd al-Wahhab al-Bayyati* (Beirut: Dar al-ʿAwda, 1972), 1:640–42.

50. Nâzim Hikmet, *Maʾsat al-insan al-muʿasir fi shiʿr ʿAbd al-Wahhab al-Bayyati* (Cairo: Matbaʿat al-Dar al-Misriyya, 1966).

51. Nuhad al-Takarli, "Albir Kami wa masir al-insan," *Al-Adib*, May 1954, 3–7, 75. Such a reading was consistent with the translation of Camus's work into Arabic. For instance, in the anonymous "Al-Suqut," *Al-Adab*, September 1956, 51.

52. However, a chapter from *The Rebel* was translated by ʿAida Matarji in 1945; Albir Kami, "Al-Qissa wa-l-thawra," *Al-Adab*, May 1953, 20–23; Albir Kami, *Al-Insan al-mutamarrid* (Beirut: Manshurat ʿUwaidat Matbaʿat Karam, 1963).

53. Imil Suwayri, "Al-ʿAdilun," *Al-Adab*, January 1954, 41.

54. ʿAbd al-Munʿim al-Hifni, *Albir Kami: Hayatuhu, adabuhi, masrahiyatuhu, falsafat fannihi* (Cairo: Dar al-Mufakkir, 1963), 151–254.

55. Al-Bayyati, *Tajribati al-shiʿriyya*, 17, 23.

56. Ibid., 20.

57. Ibid., 21.

58. On al-Bayyati's life, see "Abd al-Wahhab al-Bayyati: Poet," in *Crosshatching in Global Culture: A Dictionary of Modern Arab Writers*, ed. John Donohue and Leslie Tramontini (Beirut: Orient-Institut der DMG Beirut, 2004), 1:234–38.

59. Al-Bayyati, *Diwan ʿAbd al-Wahhab al-Bayyati*, 1:176–79, 214–15, 255, 259–62, 279–80, 287–88, 289–90, 313–15, 337–79, 380–82, 385–86.

60. Al-Bayyati, *Tajribati al-shiʿriyya*, 31.

CHAPTER SEVEN

1. "Al-Raʾis wa huwa yahda wisam al-jumhuriyya," *Al-Jumhuriyya*, June 16, 1959, 1; "Baʿthat Kuba ʿinda wusuliha," *Al-Ahram*, June 16, 1959, 1, 6; "Raʾis wafd Kuba," *Al-Ahram*, June 19, 7; "Wafd Kuba fir Ghaza," *Al-Ahram*, June 19, 7. *Ruz al-Yusuf*, June 15, 1959, 5.

2. Mohamed Hasanayn Haykal, *The Cairo Documents* (New York: Doubleday, 1973), 343.

3. "Al-Raʾis wa huwa yahda," 1; "Baʿthat Kuba ʿinda wusuliha," 1, 6; *Ruz al-Yusuf*, June 15, 1959, 5.

4. Egypt's cotton-based economy and Cuba's tobacco- and sugar-based economy shared meaningful similarities; "Kuba tutabbiqu nizam li-l-islah al-ziraʿi," *Al-Jumhuriyya*, June 17, 1959; *Al-Ahram*, June 18, 19, and 20, 1959; *Al-Jumhuriyya*, June 18, 1959, 6.

5. Paco Ignacio Taibo, *Guevara, Also Known as Che* (New York: St. Martin's Press, 1997), 282.

6. Haykal, *The Cairo Documents*, 344.

7. Ibid.

8. Jon Lee Anderson, *Che Guevara: A Revolutionary Life* (New York: Grove Press, 1997), 425–34.

9. 'Abdallah 'Abd al-Da'im, *Al-Watan al-'Arabi wa-l-thawra* (Beirut: Dar al-Adab, 1963), 200.

10. Jurj Hanna, *Al-Insan al-'Arabi qadimuhu wa-jadiduhu* (Beirut: Dar al-'Ilm li-l-Malayin 1964), 131.

11. "'Abdallah 'Abd al-Da'im, 1924–2008," in *Iktashif Suriyya*, http://www.discover-syria.com/bank/235, accessed July 5, 2015; 'Azm, interview.

12. 'Abdallah 'Abd al-Da'im, *Al-Jil al-'Arabi al-jadid* (Beirut: Dar al-'Ilm li-l-Malayin, 1961), 32–61 and elsewhere.

13. Qustantin Zurayq, *Hadha al-'asr al-mutafajjir: Nazarat fi waqi'ina wa-waqi' al-insaniyya* (Beirut: Dar al-'Ilm li-l-Malayin, 1963); Ibrahim Abu Rabi', *Contemporary Arab Thought*, 296–317. For a broader historical perspective of youth and revolution, see Erlich, *Youth and Revolution*.

14. 'Abd al-Da'im, *Al-Watan al-'Arabi*, 22.

15. Ibid., 235–49.

16. Jean-Paul Sartre, *Sartre on Cuba* (New York: Ballantine Books, 1961), 14; 'Abd al-Da'im, *Al-Watan al-'Arabi*, 235–49; 'Abdallah 'Abd al-Da'im, "'Asifa 'ala al-sukkar," *Al-Adab*, April 1962, 2–4, 79.

17. Kepa Artaraz and Karen Luyckx, "The French New Left and the Cuban Revolution 1959–1971: Parallel Histories?," *Modern and Contemporary France* 17, no. 1 (February 2009): 67–82.

18. See Al-Jazeera News interview with Malik al-Turki in which Safadi speaks of his generation's relation to existentialism and self-creation; http://www.aljazeera.net/NR/exeres/08EE14B0-680D-4CD7-9FA7-1902997CBC55.htm, accessed July 9, 2015.

19. Muta' Safadi, *Al-Thawri wa-l-'Arabi al-thawri: Dirasa fikriyya qawmiyya li-namadhij al-thawriyyin al-gharbiyyin wa-l-'Arab* (Beirut: Dar al-Tali'a, 1961), 71.

20. Ibid., 20–21, 24.

21. For a discussion of the intellectual supremacy of Beirut over Cairo, see "Al-Qahira am Bayrut?," *Al-Adab*, August 1960, 69.

22. Muta' Safadi, *Hizb al-ba'th: Ma'sat al-mawlid, ma'sat al-nihaya* (Beirut: Dar al-Adab, 1964), 11, 15–18, 27–32, 153–56; Muta' Safadi, "Mitafiziqa al-thawra," *Al-Adab*, September 1964, 5–6, 75–77. For a review of Safadi's argument about intellectuals who collaborated with the terror of the Ba'th, see Salah 'Isa, "Al-Muthaqqafun bayna al-irhab wa-l-thawra," *Al-Adab*, September 1964, 68–73 and response by 'Abd al-Rahman Gunayyim, "Al-Muthaqqafun bayna al-irhab wa-l-thawra," *Al-Adab*, October 1964, 67–78.

23. On this topic, see Fleming, "Sartre on Violence," 20–40; Neil Roberts, "Fanon, Sartre, Violence, and Freedom," *Sartre Studies International* 10, no. 2 (2004): 139–60.

24. Jonathan Judaken, "Introduction," *Situating Existentialism*, 28.

25. Jan-Bul Sartar, "Mu'adhabu al-ard," *Al-Adab*, February 1962, 2–4, 49–53.

26. Muhammad Zunaybar, *Franz Fanun aw maʿrakat al-shuʿub al- mutakhallifa* (Beirut: Dar al-Kitab, 1963), 34–35.

27. Ibid., 57, 60, 77–78.

28. Frantz Fanon, *The Wretched of the Earth*, trans. Constance Farrington (New York: Grove Press, 1963), 303; for the Arabic version, see Franz Fanun, *Muʿadhabu al-ard* (Damascus: Muʾassasat al-Kutub al-Suriyya, 1968), 197.

29. Helmi Sharawy, "Memories on African Liberation (1956–1975): A Personal Experience from Egypt, Part I," *Pamvazuka News*, May 19, 2011, issue 530.

30. Zach Levey, "The Rise and Decline of a Special Relationship: Israel and Ghana, 1957–1966," *African Studies Review* 46, no. 1 (April 2003): 155–77; Levey, "Israel's Entry to Africa, 1956–1961," *Diplomacy and Statecraft* 12, no. 3 (September 2001): 87–114.

31. Levey, "Israel's Entry," 88.

32. Ben Gurion also wrote in very colonial terms of "the privilege—which is therefore also a duty—of assisting backward and primitive people," quoted in Samuel Decalo, *Israel and Africa: Forty Years, 1956–1996* (Gainesville: University Press of Florida, 1998), 6.

33. Levey, "The Rise and Decline," 155–77; Levey, "Israel's Entry," 87–114.

34. Ibid., 104.

35. Levey, "The Rise and Decline," 158.

36. Sharawy, "Memories on African Liberation."

37. Levey, "The Rise and Decline," 159.

38. For a profile of Fathia Nkrumah, see Gamal Nakruma, "Farewell to All of That: Fathia Nkrumah," in *Al-Ahram Weekly*, September 14–20, 2000, http://weekly.ahram.org.eg/2000/499/profile.htm, accessed June 15, 2015.

39. Levey, "The Rise and Decline," 163–64; Levey, "Israel's Strategy in Africa, 1961–1967," *International Journal of Middle East Studies* 36, no. 1 (February 2004): 72, 74; Michael W. Williams, "Nkrumah and the State of Israel," *Trans Africa Forum* 7, no. 1 (Spring 1990): 39–54.

40. Robert Young, *Postcolonialism: An Historical Introduction* (Oxford: Blackwell, 2001), 44–56.

41. For the Cold War history of Congo, see Westad, *The Global Cold War*, 136–43; Lise Namikas, *Battleground Africa: Cold War in the Congo, 1961–1965* (Stanford, CA: Stanford University Press, 2013).

42. Tareq Ismael, *The U.A.R. in Africa: Egypt's Policy under Nasser* (Evanston, IL: Northwestern University Press, 1971), 204.

43. Muhammad Faʾiq was Nasser's special assistant for African affairs; Muhammad Faʾiq, *ʿAbd al-Nasir wa-l-thawra al-Ifriqiyya* (Beirut: Dar al-Wahda, 1984), 139–69.

44. Westad, *The Global Cold War*, 139.

45. Helmi Sharawy, an assistant in the Egyptian African Bureau, recalled that "the picture of the assassinated Lumumba and his family as refugees in Egypt had an impact on our public opinion far in excess of any enthusiastic speeches." Sharawy, "Memories on African Liberation."

46. For the most detailed record of this affair, see Ludo de Witte, *The Assassination of Lumumba*, trans. Ann Wright and Renée Fenby (London: Verso, 2001).

47. For ʿAli Shariʿati's report, see Rahnema, *An Islamic Utopian*, 120.

48. Faʾiq, *ʿAbd al-Nasir wa-l-thawra al-Ifriqiyya*, 165.

49. Originally published in French as "Lumumba et le néo-colonialisme" (1963); Jean-Paul Sartre, "The Political Thought of Patrice Lumumba," in *Colonialism and Neo-colonialism*, trans. Azzedine Haddour (London: Routledge, 2006), 222.

50. Zach Levey, "Israel's Involvement in the Congo, 1958–1968: Civilian and Military Dimensions," *Civil Wars* 6, no. 4 (Winter 2003): 14–36; Faʾiq, *ʿAbd al-Nasir wa-l-thawra al-Ifriqiyya*, 68–70; Owen Sirrs, *A History of the Egyptian Intelligence Service: A History of the Mukhabarat, 1910–2009* (London: Routledge, 2010), 86–87.

51. Levey, "Israel's Strategy in Africa," 72.

52. Jamal ʿAbd al-Nasir, *Al-Istiʿmar: Min aqwal al-raʾis Jamal ʿAbd al-Nasir* (Cairo: Maslahat al-Istiʿlamat, 1964), 92, 94–96, 99–103; Jamal Hamdan, *Al-Istiʿmar wa-l-tahrir fi-l-ʿalam al-ʿArabi* (Cairo: Dar al-Qalam, 1964); Taha Mahmud Sidqi, *Istiʿmar al-jadid fi-l-watan al-ʿArabi* (Damascus: al-Amana li-Ittihad al-Muhamin al-ʿArab, 1968); Nawwar ʿAbdallah, *Muʾamarat al-istiʿmar al-jadid* (Cairo: Dar al-Hana li-l-Tibaʿa, 1962).

53. Lamouchi, *Jean-Paul Sartre et le Tiers Monde*, 126–31, 235–37.

54. Ben Etherington, "An Answer to the Question: What Is Decolonization? Frantz Fanon's *The Wretched of the Earth* and Jean-Paul Sartre's *Critique of Dialectical Reason*," *Modern Intellectual History* 13, no. 1 (February 2015): 1–28.

55. Patrick Seale, "The War in Yemen," *New Republic*, January 26, 1963, http://www.newrepublic.com/article/world/the-war-yemen, accessed June 20, 2015.

56. Quoted in Jesse Ferris, *Nasser's Gamble: How Intervention in Yemen Caused the Six-Day War and the Decline of Egyptian Power* (Princeton, NJ: Princeton University Press, 2013), 24.

57. Ibid., 176.

58. Paul Dresch, *A History of Modern Yemen* (Cambridge: Cambridge University Press, 2000), 102. For a discussion of casualties and costs, see Ferris, *Nasser's Gamble*, 190–99.

59. See especially Ferris, *Nasser's Gamble*, 102–72.

60. Ibid., 220.

61. Dresch, *A History of Modern Yemen*, 99.

62. Though the decision to grant independence to South Arabia was taken already in 1965, doing so by means of full withdrawal with no military treaty was new; Ferris, *Nasser's Gamble*, 252–53.

63. Dresch, *A History of Modern Yemen*, 110.

64. ʿAbd al-Nasir, *Al-Istiʿmar*, 112, 121.

65. Quoted in Ferris, *Nasser's Gamble*, 216.

66. On the relationship between the wars, see ibid., 7.

67. Haykal, *The Cairo Documents*, 347, 356; Rosemari Mealy, *Fidel and Malcolm X* (Melbourne: Ocean View Press, 1993).

68. Taibo, *Guevara*, 405.

69. On Sabri 'Abdallah, see "Social Science in the Public Interest," *Baheyya: Egypt Analysis and Whimsy* [blog], November 7, 2006, http://baheyya .blogspot.com/2006/11/social-science-in-public-interest.html, accessed June 29, 2015.

70. "Hiwar ma Arnistu Jafara," *Al-Tali'a*, April 1965, 79–88.

71. Haykal, *The Cairo Documents*, 348–49, 354.

72. Ibid., 349.

73. Ibid., 353.

74. Ibid., 356.

75. For the full account of Che's mission in Congo, see Anderson, *Che Guevara*, 630–69.

76. Yezid Sayigh, *Armed Struggle and the Search for State: The Palestinian National Movement, 1949–1993* (New York: Oxford University Press, 1997), 95–142.

77. On the center and its Zionist publications, see Jonathan Marc Gribetz, "When the Zionist Idea Came to Beirut: Judaism, Christianity, and the Palestine Liberation Organization's Translation of Zionism," *International Journal of Middle East Studies* 48, no. 2 (May 2016): 243–66.

78. Fayiz Sayigh, *Zionist Colonialism in Palestine* (Beirut: Research Center, Palestinian Liberation Organization, 1965), v.

79. Harold Karan Jacobson, "The United Nations and Colonialism: A Tentative Appraisal," *International Organization* 16, no. 1 (December 1962), 37–56; Shira Robinson, *Citizens Strangers: Palestinians and the Birth of Israel's Liberal Settler State* (Stanford, CA: Stanford University Press, 2013), 198n22. For the UN resolution, see "Declaration on the Granting of Independence to Colonial Countries and Peoples: Adopted by General Assembly resolution 1514 (XV) of 14 December 1960," http://www.un.org/en/decolonization/ declaration.shtml, accessed June 29, 2015.

80. Sayigh, *Zionist Colonialism in Palestine*, 1.

81. Ibid., 21.

82. Ibid., 22.

83. Ibid., 24.

84. Ibid., 46.

85. Ibid., 51.

86. Ibid., 52.

87. Seeing meaningful similarities between Algeria and Palestine was a relatively new argument; Suhayl Idris, "Filastin wa-l-Jaza'ir," *Al-Adab*, October 1963, 1.

88. See Keith Feldman, *A Shadow over Palestine: The Imperial Life of Race in America* (Minneapolis: University of Minnesota Press, 2015), 37–43.

89. In the 1950s *The Voice of the Arabs* employed Leopold von Mildenstein, Joseph Goebbels's propaganda agent for the Middle East during World War II, who advised the station on anti-Jewish propaganda. Another adviser to the station was former SS officer Johannes von Leer; Sirrs, *A History of the Egyptian*, 104; Meir Litvak and Esther Webman, *From Empathy to Denial: Arab Responses to the Holocaust* (New York: Columbia University Press, 2009), chapter 3.

90. For a study and a debate about the Egyptian liberal tradition's opposition to fascism and Nazism, see Gershoni, *Arab Responses to Fascism and Nazism* and Gershoni and Jankowski, *Confronting Fascism in Egypt.*

91. Lutfi al-Khuli, "Aichman bayna al-Naziyya wa-l-Sahyuniyya," *Al-Ahram*, April 12, 1961, 8.

92. Ibid.

93. Ibid.

94. Sayigh, *Zionist Colonialism in Palestine*, 26–27; see also Lutfi al-Khuli, "Nahnu wa Isra'il: Haqiqat mawqifina," *Al-Ahram*, May 18, 1961, 8.

95. For a sociological perspective on this process, see Jeffrey Alexander, "On the Social Construction of Moral Universals: The 'Holocaust' from War Crime to Trauma Drama," in *Cultural Trauma and Collective Identity*, ed. Jeffrey Alexander et al. (Berkeley: University of California Press, 2004), 196–26; Alan Rosenbaum, ed., *Is the Holocaust Unique? Perspectives on Comparative Genocide* (Boulder, CO: Westview Press, 2001).

96. See Odette Guitard, "Alger ou la désunion Afro-Asiatique," *Annuaire de l'Afrique du Nord* 4 (1966), 49–61.

97. Mark Berger, "After the Third World? History, Destiny and the Fate of Third Worldism," *Third World Quarterly* 25, no. 1 (2004): 9–39.

98. Richard Wolin, *The Wind from the East: French Intellectuals, the Cultural Revolution, and the Legacy of the 1960s* (Princeton, NJ: Princeton University Press, 2010), 325.

99. Ibid., 329.

100. Gadkar-Wilcox, "Existentialism and Intellectual Culture," 377–95.

CHAPTER EIGHT

1. Although, according to Levinas's biographer, Sartre asked, "But who is Levinas?," we know that, already in the 1930s, Sartre had been introduced to Edmund Husserl's phenomenology by way of reading Levinas. Shlomo Malka, *Imanuel Levinas: Biographia*, trans. Daniela Yoel (Tel Aviv: Resling, 2008), 293.

2. Arthur, *Unfinished Projects*, 147–53.

3. Jonathan Judaken, *Jean-Paul Sartre and the Jewish Question: Anti-Antisemitism and the Politics of the French Intellectual* (Lincoln: University of Nebraska Press, 2006), 190.

4. Ibid., 190.

5. Ibid.

6. Badawi, *Sirat hayati*, 1:200.

7. Al-Sharif, "Sartar fi-l-Qahira," 161–62.

8. Jean-Paul Sartre, "Khitab maftuh," *Al-Ahram*, February 25, 1967, 1.

9. Suhayl Idris, "Ahlan bi Sartar wa Simon," *Al-Adab*, March 1967, 1.

10. Ibid.

11. "Marhaban bi Sartar wa Bufwar fi-l-Qahira," *Al-Ahram*, February 26, 1967, 7.

12. *Ruz al-Yusuf*, February 27, 1967, 50; *Al-Akhbar*, March 5, 1967, 16.

13. The other Egyptian writer with whom they were familiar was Albert Qusayr; 'Abd al-Malik Khalil, "Al-Mumaththilun al-Misriyyun fahimu masrahiyyati," *Al-Akhbar*, February 1, 1967, 9; Beauvoir, *All Said and Done*, 365.

14. "Al-Duktur Taha Husayn yatahaddath ila al-Jumhuriyya," *Al-Jumhuriyya*, March 14, 1967, 12.

15. Khalil, "Al-Mumaththilun al-Misriyyun," 9.

16. "Sartar damir al-'asr: 'Adad mumtaz," *Al-Fikr al-Mu'asir*, March 1967; *Al-Tali'a*, February 1967.

17. The most complete Arab dossier on Sartre and Beauvoir's lifetime work was published by *Al-Tali'a*: "Milaf khas 'an Sartar," *Al-Tali'a*, February 1967.

18. El-Samman, *Egypt: From One Revolution to Another*, 64.

19. 'Abd al-Malik Khalil, "Ziyarat Sartar," *Akhir Sa'a*, March 8, 1967, 16.

20. Lanzmann, *The Patagonian Hare*, 383.

21. Khalil, "Ziyarat Sartar," 16.

22. Ibid. In 2003 Muhammad Abu al-Ghar argued that Sartre never published the book he promised; Muhammad Abu al-Ghar, *'Ala hamish al-rihla* (Cairo: al-Hay'a al-Misriyya al-'Amma li-l-Kitab, 2003), 215–17.

23. Beauvoir, *All Said and Done*, 379.

24. Lanzmann, *The Patagonian Hare*, 383; Lanzmann, interview.

25. Al-Samman, interview.

26. Al-Samman, *Awraq 'umri*, 120.

27. El-Samman, *Egypt: From One Revolution to Another*, 67; al-Samman, interview.

28. Beauvoir, *All Said and Done*, 379.

29. 'Abd al-Wahhab, "Ziyara li-misr," 60.

30. Al-Samman, *Awraq 'umri*, 124.

31. Khalil, "Al-Mumaththilun al-Misriyyun," 9.

32. Al-Sharif, "Sartar fi-l-Qahira," 165.

33. For Sartre's full text, see "Dawr al-muthaqqafin fi-l-mujtama' al-mu'asir," *Al-Tali'a*, April 1967, 118–28.

34. "Al-Qism al-thalith," *Al-Tali'a*, April 1967, 143.
35. Ibid., 142.
36. "Al-Kutab yunaqishun Sartar hawla Brecht wa tatawwur al-masrah al-Misri," *Al-Jumhuriyya*, March 8, 1967, 12.
37. Jaroslav Stetkevych, interviewed by the author in New York City, May 8, 2011.
38. Simone de Beauvoir, "Dawr al-mar'a fi-l-'asr al-hadith," *Al-Tali'a*, April 1967, 130.
39. Ibid.
40. Ibid., 133.
41. Ibid.
42. Ibid., 131, 133–34.
43. Al-Samman, *Awraq 'umri*, 121.
44. "Al-Qism al-thalith," *Al-Tali'a*, April 1967, 140.
45. Ibid.
46. Ibid., 141.
47. Ibid.
48. Ibid., 142.
49. Beauvoir, *All Said and Done*, 378.
50. Ibid.
51. Ibid., 377.
52. "Faylasufat al-jins al-thani fi-l-Qahira," *Al-Ahram*, February 26, 1967, 3.
53. Beauvoir, *All Said and Done*, 372.
54. Isma'il al-Mahdawi, "Sartar ya'taliqu 'ala hadith li Mahmud Amin al-'Alim," *Al-Jumhuriyya*, March 3, 1967, 10.
55. Isma'il al-Mahdawi, "Al-Hurriyya al-wujudiyya fi-l-sanawat al-akhira kanat nazwa," *Al-Jumhuriyya*, March 5, 1967, 5.
56. Ibid.
57. Al-Mahdawi, "Sartar ya'taliqu," 10.
58. "Ma'a al-'ummal," *Al-Tali'a*, April 1967, 145.
59. Ibid.
60. Ibid.
61. Cohen-Solal, *Sartre: A Life*, 250–51, 291.
62. Al-Mahdawi, "Sartar ya'taliqu," 10.
63. Isma'il al-Mahdawi, "Jawlat al-fikr," *Al-Jumhuriyya*, March 2, 1967, 16.
64. Ibid.
65. Lucian Sayf, "Radd 'ala kitab Sartar naqd al-mantiq al-dialeqtiqi," *Al-Hilal*, February 1967, 78–94.
66. Shirin Abu al-Naja, ed., *Min awraq Shahinda Maqlad* (Cairo: Dar Mirit, 2006), 131–34.
67. Ibid., 132.
68. Ibid., 131–34.
69. Abu al-Ghar, *'Ala hamish al-rihla*, 215.
70. Ibid., 215–16.

71. Ibid., 215–17; Khayr Mansur, "Ziyarat al-sayyid al-faylasuf," *Al-Quds al-'Arabi*, January 7, 2006, 10.
72. Abu al-Ghar, *'Ala hamish al-rihla*, 217.
73. Beauvoir, *All Said and Done*, 377.
74. Khalil, "Ziyarat Sartar," 16.
75. Lanzmann explained on Sartre's behalf that the philosopher could not come to Beirut because of his engagement with the Russell Tribunal. For a different version of this anecdote, see 'al-Sharif, "Sartar fi-l-Qahira," 165.
76. Lanzmann, *The Patagonian Hare*, 384.
77. "Sartar wa-l-ma'sa fi Ghaza," *Akhir Sa'a*, March 15, 1967, 70.
78. "Ma'a al-sha'b al-Filastini fi Ghaza," *Al-Tali'a*, April 1967, 147.
79. Beauvoir, *All Said and Done*, 380.
80. Lanzmann, *The Patagonian Hare*, 385.
81. 'Abd al-Wahhab, "Ziyara li-Misr," 59–60; 'al-Sharif, "Sartar fi-l-Qahira," 166.
82. Al-Samman, *Awraq 'umri*, 115.
83. Beauvoir, *All Said and Done*, 381.
84. Lanzmann, *The Patagonian Hare*, 385.
85. Ibid., 169; al-Samman, *Awraq 'umri*, 115.
86. "Sartar faylasufan," *Al-Tali'a*, February 1967, 123.
87. Al-Samman, *Awraq 'umri*, 115.
88. Ibid., 116–17.
89. Beauvoir, *All Said and Done*, 381.
90. Ibid.
91. Ibid.
92. Ibid.
93. Ibid., 382.
94. Lanzmann intimated to al-Adab's correspondent that the reason behind his depressive mood was his sister's death; 'al-Sharif, "Sartar fi-l-Qahira," 173–74.
95. While touring Liberation Province, an exemplary state-led project of development and social rehabilitation, an official told Lanzmann, "Tell our enemies and our friends of the work we are carrying out." Beauvoir, *All Said and Done*, 376.
96. Al-Samman, *Awraq 'umri*, 115.
97. For a list of intellectuals who were present in Gaza, see "Al-Qism al-thalith," *Al-Tali'a*, April 1967, 138.
98. Beauvoir, *All Said and Done*, 382.
99. Lanzmann, interview; Lanzmann, *The Patagonian Hare*, 384, 386.
100. Georges Philippe Friedmann, *The End of the Jewish People?* (Garden City, NY: Doubleday, 1967).
101. Lanzmann, *The Patagonian Hare*, 386.
102. Ibid., 26.
103. Ibid., 28.

104. Ibid., 29.
105. Amnon Kapeliuk, "Sartre in the Arab Press," *New Outlook* 10, no. 4 (May 1967): 31.
106. Mu'nis 'Abd al-Salam, "Qissa 'an al-sha'b al-yahudi wa-l-shabaka," *Al-Ba'th*, March 19, 1967, 8.
107. Al-Samman, *Awraq 'umri*, 113.
108. Isma'il al-Mahdawi, "Misr balad la yanam," *Al-Jumhuriyya*, March 14, 1967, 2.
109. Quoted in *Al Ha-Mishmar*, March 22, 1967, 1, 3.
110. Edvin Eitan, "Ha-shagrirut ha-tsarfatit hehrima," *Yediot Ahronot*, March 9, 1967, 10; Shlomo Nakdimon "Ein manos me hahzrat plitim," *Yediot Ahronot*, March 20, 1967, 2.
111. Amos Keinan, "Ha-Sofrim baim ha-sofrim baim," *Yediot Ahronot*, March 17, 1967, 12.
112. Eitan, "Ha-shagrirut," 10.
113. Ely Ben Gal, *Mardi chez Sartre: Un hebreu a Paris, 1967–1980* (Paris: Flammarion, 1992), 15.
114. *Yediot Ahronot*, March 15th, 1967: 5.
115. Ibid.
116. Evidence of this can be found everywhere in Lanzmann's autobiography, *The Patagonian Hare*.
117. Sartre repeated his position about Israel's right to exist during his first week in Israel; *Yediot Ahronot*, March 19, 1967, 2.
118. Lanzmann, *The Patagonian Hare*, 387.
119. Ibid., 386–87; Lanzmann, interview.
120. Ben Gal, *Mardi chez Sartre*, 24–28.
121. Ya'ari to Flapan, April 17, 1967, folder 2, 20.7-96, YY, Givat Haviva, Israel.
122. "Sarter lomed me Shalev," *Yediot Ahronot*, March 27, 1967, 5.
123. Ben Gal, *Mardi chez Sartre*, 40.
124. In a meeting with the secretary general of the Association of Women Workers, Beauvoir took a critical note of the condition of Israeli women. She was also unimpressed with the division of labor between men and women in the kibbutz; Ben Gal, *Mardi chez Sartre*, 83; Beauvoir, *All Said and Done*, 389, 384–98.
125. Ben Gal, *Mardi chez Sartre*, 82.
126. Ibid., 79–80.
127. "Sartar yarfudu ziyarat al-qita'at al-'askariyya al-Sahyuniyya," *Al-Ba'th*, March 29, 1967, 1.
128. Yishayahu Ben Porat, "Ha-lavyanim ha Yehudim," *Yediot Ahronot*, April 14, 1967, 10.
129. Ben Gal, *Mardi chez Sartre*, 80; Lanzmann, *The Patagonian Hare*, 386.
130. Tawfiq Ziyad, "Sartar, wa nahnu, wa-l-niza' al-'Arabi al-Isra'ili," *Al-Jadid*, April 1967, 4; see also Saliba Khamis, "Ziyarat Sartar wa Simun di Bufwar," *Al-Jadid*, March 1967, 2, 43.

131. Ariel Ginai, "Sarter," *Yediot Ahronot*, March 26, 1967, 19.

132. Yossef Elgazi, who accompanied the couple on their tour to Nazareth on behalf of the Israeli Communist Party, interviewed over telephone by the author, July 12, 2012.

133. "Sarter siyer," *Yediot Ahronot*, March 28, 1967, 9; Ariel Ginai, "Sarter mithamek me sihot," *Yediot Ahronot*, March 16, 1967, 3; Shlomo Nakdimon, "Sarter bitel," *Yediot Ahronot*, March 22, 1967, 2; *Al Ha-Mishmar*, March 23, 1967, 1.

134. Judaken, *Jean-Paul Sartre and the Jewish Question*, 194; see also "Jean-Paul Sartre et Simone de Beauvoir en Israël," *Cahiers Bernard Lazare*, May 10, 1967, 4–20.

135. The scholar Menachem Brinker, who was present in the meeting, interviewed by the author, June 2, 2016.

136. Ben Gal, *Mardi chez Sartre*, 33.

137. Meir Yanai, "Lama hitrapsut?," *Yediot Ahronot*, March 28, 1967, 14; "Madua bitel Sarter et bikuru be Tzahal?," *Yediot Ahronot*, March 29, 1967, 14; Avraham Mazuz, "Trufat hapele shel Sarter," *Yediot Ahronot*, April 7, 1967, Seven Days Magazine sec., 2.

138. Ziva Yariv, "Agudat ha super-menim," *Yediot Ahronot*, March 21, 1967, 11; Arye Zimuki, "Bikur Sarter ve ha-proporzia," *Yediot Ahronot*, March 24, 1967, n.p.; "Sarter nishaar yadid ha-Aravim," *Yediot Ahronot*, April 7, 1967, Seven Days Magazine sec., 18; *Haaretz*, March 24, 1967, 10.

139. Though both were on the Left, the radical Uri Avneri was a nemesis of MAPAM; *Haolam Hazeh* and *Yediot Ahronot*, March 21, 1967, 2.

140. "Simon de Buvar," in "Bikur Sarter," Ministerial Office of Zalman Aran, Ministry of Education, folder ג-10: 5597, 71.1/3-10, ISA, Jerusalem.

141. Beauvoir, *All Said and Done*, 388.

142. Ibid., 389; "Jean-Paul Sartre et Simone de Beauvoir en Israël," 7.

143. Tuvia Rivner, interviewed by the author in Israel, December 21, 2014; Hava Yas'ur, wife of the late kibbutz philosopher Avraham Yas'ur, who wrote prolifically about Sartre, interviewed by the author in Israel, December 21, 2014.

144. Zimuki, "Bikur Sarter," n.p.

145. Bornstein Heini, *Mi-Bazel 'ad lehavot ha-Bashan: Derekh hayim* (Israel: Yad Ya'ari, 2015), 154–60.

146. "Yesh lachem zhut," *Al Ha-Mishmar*, March 19, 1967, 1, 3.

147. Zimuki, "Bikur Sarter," n.p.

148. That was one of the reasons for which the tribunal eventually convened in Sweden and not in Algeria as originally planned. For the battle over Grossman's nomination, see Flapan to Ya'ari, April 23, 1967, folder 2, 20.7-95, YY, Givat Haviva, Israel.

149. Ben Gal, *Mardi chez Sartre*, 83.

150. "Jean-Paul Sartre et Simone de Beauvoir en Israël," 4–20.

151. Ibid., 6.

152. Edvin Eitan "Al ha-aravim lehakir be Israel," *Yediot Ahronot*, March 30, 1967, 3.

153. Lanzmann, *The Patagonian Hare*, 70–92 and elsewhere.

CHAPTER NINE

1. "Qararat al-mu'tamar al-kabir," *Al-Thawra*, April 1, 1967, 6.

2. Riyad Najib al-Rayyis, "Filastin: Idha lam yakunu," *Al-Nahar*, March 29, 1967, 8; "Tawsiya bi idanat Isra'il," *Al-Quds*, March 29, 1967, 7.

3. On this scandal, see Elizabeth Holt, "'Bread or Freedom': The Congress for Cultural Freedom, the CIA, and the Arabic Literary Journal *Hiwar* (1962–67)," *Journal of Arabic Literature* 44 (2013): 83–102.

4. "Qararat al-mu'tamar al-kabir," *Al-Thawra*, April 1, 1967, 6; "Mu'tamar al-kutab," *Al-Nahar*, March 23, 1967, 1, 8.

5. "Isra'il sa tantahi," *Al-Thawra*, April 1, 1967, 6.

6. Mu'nis 'Abd al-Salam, "Qissa 'an al-sha'b al-yahudi wa-l-shabaka," *Al-Ba'th*, March 19, 1967, 8.

7. Ibid.

8. Ibid.

9. Ibid.

10. "Marks wa Sartar wa-l-mas'ala al-Yahudiyya," *Al-Ba'th*, April 2, 1967, 3.

11. Ibid.

12. A. A., "Sartar wa-l-qadiyya al-Filistiniyya," *Al-Thawra*, February 28, 1967, 3.

13. Ibid.

14. "Marks wa Sartar wa-l-mas'ala al-Yahudiyya," *Al-Ba'th*, April 2, 1967, 3.

15. Amnon to Flapan, April 17, 1967, folder 5, 1 94-95, YY, Givat Haviva, Israel.

16. André Scemama, "Tout en faisant siennes certaines thèses sionistes," *Le Monde*, March 31, 1967, 3.

17. Flapan to editor of *Al Ha-Mishmar*, April 11, 1967, folder 4, 1 94-95, YY, Givat Haviva, Israel.

18. Amnon to Flapan, April 17, 1967, folder 5, 1 94-95, YY, Givat Haviva, Israel.

19. Ben Porat, "Ha lavyanim," 10.

20. "Sartar yaqulu fi Tal Abib ma la yaquluhu fi-l-Qahira," *Al-Quds*, April, March 30, 1967, 1.

21. Muhammad al-Jundi, "Sartar wa-l-Sahyuniyya," *Al-Thawra*, April 2, 1967, 1, 7. Simha Flapan was aware of Syrian and Palestinian reactions to this development. Flapan to Ya'ari, April 25, 1967, folder 2, 20.7-95, YY, Givat Haviva, Israel.

22. Jum'a Hammad, "Sartar . . . wa Filastin," *Al-Dustur*, April 2, 1967, 2.

23. "Jean-Paul Sartre est critiqué à Damas," *Le Monde*, April 4, 1967, 6.

24. Flapan to Ya'ari April 14, 1967, folder 2, 20.7-95, YY, Givat Haviva, Israel.

25. Ibid.

26. Flapan to Ya'ari, April 23, 1967, folder 4, 1 94-95, YY, Givat Haviva, Israel.

27. Flapan to Ya'ari, April 25, 1967, folder 2, 20.7-95, YY, Givat Haviva, Israel.

28. Flapan to Ya'ari April 14, 1967, and Flapan to Ya'ari April 25, 1967, folder 2, 20.7-95, YY, Givat Haviva, Israel.

29. Flapan to Ya'ari, April 23, 1967, folder 4, 1 94-95, YY, Givat Haviva, Israel.

30. Flapan to Ya'ari, April 14, 1967, folder 2, 20.7-95, YY, Givat Haviva, Israel.

31. "Jean-Paul Sartre et le sionisme," *Le Monde*, April 8, 1967, 5.

32. "Parashat Sarter," *Yediot Ahronot*, April 6, 1967, 2.

33. Yishayahu Ben Porat, "Sarter lo hebia klal haaracha latzionot," *Yediot Ahronot*, April 9, 1967, 2.

34. Ben Porat, "Ha lavyanim," 10.

35. Ibid.

36. Flapan to Ya'ari, April 14, 1967, folder 2, 20.7-95, Yad Ya'ari, Givat Haviva, Israel.

37. Flapan to editor of *Yediot Ahronot*, April 7, 1967, and Flapan to editor of *Al Ha-Mishmar*, April 11, 1967, folder 5, 1 94-95, Yad Ya'ari, Givat Haviva, Israel.

38. Flapan to Amnon, April 11, 1967, folder 5, 1 94-95, YY, Givat Haviva, Israel.

39. Ibid.

40. Amnon to Flapan, April 17, 1967, folder 5, 1 94-95, YY, Givat Haviva, Israel.

41. "Playboy Interview: Arnold Toynbee," *Playboy*, April 1967, 57–76, 166; cited also in Mordechai Kirshenbaum, "Ha-filosof ha-meofef," *Yediot Ahronot*, March 31, 1967, 8.

42. Muhammad al-Jundi, "Ma'rakat al-'alam al-thalith," *Al-Thawra*, June 7, 1967, 1.

43. "Risala kutibat bi-l-damm," *Al-Thawra*, May 30, 1967, 6.

44. Joan Wolf, *Harnessing the Holocaust: The Politics of Memory in France* (Stanford, CA: Stanford University Press, 2004), 31.

45. On the Treblinka Affair, see *Samuel Moyn, A Holocaust Controversy: The Treblinka Affair in Postwar France* (Waltham, MA.: Brandeis University Press, 2005); for Beauvoir's preface to Steiner's *Treblinka*, see Margaret A. Simons and Marybeth Timmermann, eds., *Simone de Beauvoir: Political Writing* (Urbana-Champaign: University of Illinois Press, 2012), 305–10.

46. Wolf, *Harnessing the Holocaust*, 1.

47. "Cinq intellectuels de gauche dénoncent violemment la politique des pays Arabes," *Le Monde*, June 2, 1967, 4.

48. Wolf, *Harnessing the Holocaust*, 26, 37.

49. Beauvoir, *All Said and Done*, 400.

50. Ben Gal, *Mardi chez Sartre*, 93.

51. Jean-Paul Sartre and Claude Lanzmann, eds., *Le conflit israélo-arabe* (Paris: Les Temps Modernes, 1967), 8.

52. Ibid., 1.
53. Ibid., 9.
54. Ben Gal, *Mardi chez Sartre*, 93.
55. For a full account of those days, see Samir Kassir and Farouk Mardam-Bey, *Itinéraires de Paris à Jérusalem: la France et le conflit israélo-arabe* (Washington, DC: Institut des études palestiniennes, 1992), 127–41.
56. For instance, the appeal by the Mouvement contre le racisme et pour l'amitié entre les peoples; "Un appel du M.R.A.P. Pour la paix," *Le Monde*, May 28–29, 1967, 3.
57. "Un appel d'intellectuels Français en faveur la paix," *Le Monde*, May 30, 1967, 4, 7; "Une conférence d'information des intellectuels Français," *Le Monde*, June 1, 1967, 3; "Cinq intellectuels," 4. *New Outlook* also published the statement on the front page of its June 1967 issue.
58. Pierre Vidal-Naquet (1930–2006) was a Jewish resistance fighter, historian, and public intellectual. He was among the first intellectuals to point out French crimes in Algeria and mobilize public opinion on behalf of Algeria's liberation. He signed the Manifesto of the 121 and had very complex relationship with Israel. For his position during the conflict, see Pierre Vidal-Naquet, "Apers," *Le Monde*, June 13, 1967, 1, 7; see also Irad Malkin, "Israël et Pierre Vidal-Naquet," in *Pierre Vidal-Naquet, un historien dans la cité*, ed. François Hartog et al. (Paris: La Découverte, 2007), 199–218. Vladimir Jankélévitch (1903–1985) was the chair of moral philosophy at the Sorbonne. Claude Roy (1915–1997) was a famous poet, journalist, writer, and a signatory of the Manifesto of the 121.
59. Kassir and Mardam-Bey, *Itinéraires de Paris à Jérusalem*, 203–10.
60. In the late 1940s, Sartre testified on behalf of Robert Misrahi who was charged with trafficking weapons to the militant Zionist organization LEHI; Kassir and Mardam-Bey, *Itinéraires de Paris à Jérusalem*, 129; Cohen-Solal, *Sartre: A Life*, 205, 284–85.
61. Nonetheless, Mayer took a strong public position against the destruction of Israel; Daniel Mayer, "Shalom," *Le Monde*, May 31, 1967, 3.
62. The Manifesto of the 121 was published in September 1960 and called on the French public to acknowledge the legitimacy of the Algerian struggle and support conscientious objectors. It was a watershed moment in the French understanding of the struggle.
63. "Cinq intellectuels de gauche," 4.
64. Ibid.; Lanzmann later wrote to *Le Monde* and protested their characterization of his position, especially with regard to the prospect of dialogue with the Arab Left. "Une Lettre de M. Lanzmann," *Le Monde*, June 13, 1967, 6.
65. "Communistes et Socialistes font des analyses contradictoires," *Le Monde*, May 26, 4; Beauvoir, *All Said and Done*, 401. For the pro-Arab Left, see Kassir and Mardam-Bey, *Itinéraires de Paris à Jérusalem*, 161–65.
66. Georges Friedmann, "La Dette," *Le Monde*, June 7, 1967, 7.

67. Lanzmann, interview.
68. Lutfi al-Khuli, *Hiwar maʿa Bartrand Rasil wa Jan-Bul Sartar* (Cairo: Dar al-Maʿarif, 1968), 76.
69. Avneri, *Optimi*, 538.
70. Suhayl Idris, "Nantaziru min Sartar mawqifan wahidan," *Al-Adab*, April–May 1980, 7, originally published in *Al-Adab*, August 1967.
71. Muʿin Basisu, "Jan-Bul Staynbak," *Al-Thawra*, June 3, 1967.
72. Idris, "Nantaziru min Sartar," 7; N. A. "Al-ʿIraq tamnaʿ Sartar wa Bufwar," *Al-Thawra*, June 2, 1967, 1.
73. Hamid ʿAbd al-Qadir, "li-Madha huriqat kutub Jab-Bul Sartar bi al-Jazaʾir?," *Jazaʾiris*, March 20, 2010, http://www.djazairess.com/elmoustakbel/1004581, accessed August 27, 2015.
74. Intelligence Memorandum, June 2, 1967, "Arab-Israeli Situation Report," Central Intelligence Agency, CIA-RDP79T00826A002000010078-8, NARA, Washington, DC, USA.
75. For their positions, see Jacques Berque, "Pour une solution du problème Palestinien," *Le Monde*, June 2, 1967, 4; Maxime Rodinson, "Vivre avec les Arabes," *Le Monde*, June 4–5, 1967, 1, 5.
76. Al-Khuli, *Hiwar maʿa Bartrand Rasil wa Jan-Bul Sartar*, 78.
77. After 1967 Rodinson and Berque established a special research committee on Palestine; Gérard D. Khoury, "Maxime Rodinson et la constitution du Grapp (Groupe de recherche et d'action pour la Palestine)," *Matériaux pour l'histoire de notre temps* 4, no. 96 (2009): 28–37.
78. Al-Khuli, *Hiwar maʿa Bartrand Rasil wa Jan-Bul Sartar*, 75–77.
79. Josie Fanon, "À-propos de Frantz Fanon, Sartre, le racisme et les Arabes," *El Moudjahid*, June 10, 1967, 6.
80. Ibid.
81. Ibid.; see 1968 and 1970 editions without Sartre's introduction; Frantz Fanon, *Les damnés de la terre* (Paris: François Maspero, 1968, 1970); originally quoted in Michel Contat, *The Writings of Jean-Paul Sartre* (Evanston, IL: Northwestern University Press, 1974), 1:396; see also Lamouchi, *Jean-Paul Sartre et le Tiers-Monde*, 157–58; Judaken, *Jean-Paul Sartre and the Jewish Question*, 196.
82. Sartre and Lanzmann, *Le conflit israélo-arabe*, 11.
83. For example, Simha Flapan, "Le dialogue entre socialistes arabes et israéliens est une nécessité historique," in Sartre and Lanzmann, *Le conflit israélo-arabe*, 559–602.
84. Ali el-Samman, "Pourquoi le «non» au dialogue?," in Sartre and Lanzmann, *Le conflit israélo-arabe*, 359–70.
85. *Min al-fikr al-Sahyuni al-muʿasir* (Beirut: Markaz al-Abhath, Munazzamat al-Tahrir al-Filastiniyya, 1968).
86. Maxime Rodinson, "Israel: a Colonial Fact," *Al-Maʿrifa*, September 1967, 20–43.
87. Lanzmann, interview.

88. That was the headline in the daily *Al-Ahram*, June 7, 1967, 1; Beauvoir, *All Said and Done*, 402.
89. See headline in *Le Monde*, June 7, 1967, 1. According to Israeli reports, many Arab students in Paris also disbelieved that the Arabs had been defeated; Yehusu' Kreitzman, "Skira 'al hilchei ruah," June 13, 1967, Ministry of Foreign Affairs, folder 1708/8—צה, 93.2/6-136, ISA, Jerusalem.
90. Al-Khuli, *Hiwar ma'a Bartrand Rasil wa Jan-Bul Sartar*, 78.
91. Beauvoir, *All Said and Done*, 402.
92. "Les Étudiants Arabes s'adressent au Général de Gaulle," *Le Monde*, June 7, 1967, 4.
93. Al-Khuli, *Hiwar ma'a Bartrand Rasil wa Jan-Bul Sartar*, 78.
94. Ibid., 78. However, I was unable to locate this source.
95. Ibid., 79.
96. Beauvoir, *All Said and Done*, 402.
97. Ibid., 402.
98. Ibid., 405.
99. Denis Charbit, "Les Raisons d'une fidélité: Simone de Beauvoir, Israël et les Juifs," *Simone de Beauvoir Studies* 17 (2000–2001): 48–63.
100. Al-Khuli, *Hiwar ma'a Bartrand Rasil wa Jan-Bul Sartar*, 81.
101. Ibid., 83.
102. Ibid., 84.
103. Ibid., 85.
104. Ibid., 87–88.
105. Ibid., 88–90.
106. Ibid., 90–92.
107. Ibid., 92.
108. Ibid.
109. Ibid., 93.
110. Ibid.
111. Ibid., 102.
112. Ibid., 109.
113. Ibid., 113.
114. Al-Sharif, "Sartar fi-l-Qahira," 179.
115. *Al-Adab* also published the text; see Idris, "Nantaziru min Sartar," 8.
116. Ibid.
117. Ibid.
118. The Paris office of the Arab League asked the Russell Tribunal to acknowledge the similarities between the Middle East and Vietnam; "La Ligue Arabe Demande Au Tribunal Russell 'Une Enquête au jugement' contre Israël," *Le Monde*, June 14, 1967, 4.
119. Idris, "Nantaziru min Sartar," 9.
120. The most complete history of the al-Khuli family can be found in the blog of family member Hamdi 'Abd al-Qadr al-Khuli, http://halkholy.com/family_alkholy.htm, accessed November 13, 2012; see also "Lutfi El-Kholi,

1927–1999," *Al-Ahram Weekly*, February 11–17, 1999, http://weekly.ahram .org.eg/1999/416/kholi.htm, accessed November 13, 2012.

121. Ibrahim 'Amr, "Ma ba'd Sartar," *Al-Hilal*, January 1968, 19, 22.

122. Judaken, *Jean-Paul Sartre and the Jewish Question*, 150.

123. Thomas Anderson, *Sartre's Two Ethics: From Authenticity to Integral Human-ity* (Chicago: Open Court, 1993) and Arthur, *Unfinished Projects*.

124. Quoted in Bourg, *From Revolution to Ethics*, 316; and Anderson, *Sartre's Two Ethics*, 112.

EPILOGUE

1. *Al-Hayat*, February 27, 2002; see also *Al-Sharq al-Awsat*, July 26, 2002.

2. Badawi, *Sirat hayati*, 1:182.

3. Ibid., 200.

4. As Sa'id Lawindi put it, "Badawi: the existentialist philosopher who escaped to Islam." Sa'id Lawindi, *'Abd al-Rahman Badawi: Faylasuf al-wujudiyya al-harib ila al-Islam* (Cairo: Markaz al-Hadara, 2001).

5. Ann Fulton, *Existentialism in America, 1945–1963* (Evanston, IL: North-western University Press, 1999).

6. See Henri Lauzière, *The Making of Salafism: Islamic Reform in the Twentieth Century* (New York: Columbia University Press, 2015).

7. Samir Kassir, *Being Arab* (London: Verso, 2013).

8. Arthur Marwick, *The Sixties: Cultural Revolution in Britain, France, Italy, and the United States, 1958–1974* (New York: Oxford University Press, 1998), 3–4.

9. Ibid.

10. See a report on a June 14, 1967, *Al-Jumhuriyya* editorial that called to liquidate Western culture. N.A., "Le Journal 'Al Goumhouriya' Préconise la Liquidation de la Culture Occidentale en Égypte," *Le Monde*, June 15, 1967, 2.

11. For a discussion of the war, see Kassab, *Contemporary Arab Thought*, chapter 1.

12. There is, however, some evidence to the contrary, as in networks of politi-cal support that existed between Tunisia and Paris. Burleigh Hendrickson, "March 1968: Practicing Transnational Activism from Tunis to Paris," *International Journal of Middle East Studies* 44, no. 4 (November 2012): 755–74.

13. Khilnani, *Arguing Revolution*, 3.

14. Bourg, *From Revolution to Ethics*; Kristin Ross, *May '68 and Its Afterlives*; Camille Robcis, "May '68 and the Ethical Turn in French Thought," *Mod-ern Intellectual History* 11, no. 1 (2014): 267–77.

15. Ian Birchall, "Third World and After," *New Left Review* 80 (March–April 2013): 151.

16. Pascal Bruckner, *The Tears of the White Man: Compassion as Contempt*, trans. William R. Beer (New York: Free Press, 1986).
17. Birchall, "Third World and After," 154.
18. Ghassan Kanafani, *Adab al-muqawama fi Filastin al-muhtala* (Beirut: Dar al-Adab, 1966); Shukri Ghali, *Adab al-muqawama* (Beirut: Dar al-afaq al-jadida, 1969).
19. For UNESCO's resolution, see "Implementation of the resolutions of the General Conference and decisions of the Executive Board concerning the protection of cultural property in Jerusalem," Records of the General Conference Eighteenth Session, Paris, October 17 to November 23, 1974, pp. 59–60, http://www.unesco.at/bildung/basisdokumente/empfehlung1974_intverst.pdf, accessed November 13, 2015. Beauvoir reacted to UNESCO's decision by accepting the Jerusalem Prize. Simons and Timmermann, *Simone de Beauvoir*, 295–304.
20. Mu'in Basisu, "Jan-Bul Sartar yutliqu al-sawarikh . . . ," *Al-'Usbu' al-'Arabi*, December 16, 1974, 73. I thank Esmat Elhalaby for this reference.
21. Judaken, *Jean-Paul Sartre and the Jewish Question*, 184, 200–201.
22. Ora Armoni, "Ha Yehudi Ha Noded," *Atar Ha Kibutzim* (official publication of the *Kibutz Movement*), October 12, 2005, http://www.kibbutz.org.il/itonut/2005/haver/051012_ben-gal.htm, accessed November 13, 2015.
23. Pierre Bourdieu, "Un sociologue dans le monde Rencontre avec Pierre Bourdieu," *Revue d'études palestiniennes* 22 (Winter 2000): 11.
24. Joseph Massad, "Sartre, European Intellectuals and Zionism," *Electronic Intifada*, January 31, 2003, https://electronicintifada.net/content/sartre-european-intellectuals-and-zionism/4384, accessed September 3, 2015.
25. Farouk Mardam-Bey, "French Intellectuals and the Palestine Question," *Journal of Palestine Studies* 43, no. 3 (Spring 2014): 26–39; Kassir and Mardam-Bey, *Itinéraires de Paris à Jérusalem*.
26. Said, "Diary," *London Review of Books* 22, no. 11 (June 1, 2000): 42–43, http://www.lrb.co.uk/v22/n11/edward-said/diary, accessed September 28, 2015.
27. See Jan-Bul Sartar, *Ta'ammulat fi-l-mas'ala al-Yahudiyya*, trans. Hatim al-Jawahiri (Cairo: Rawafid li-l-Nashr wa-l-Tawzi', 2016). I thank Samy Ayoub for the grocery-store reference.
28. Ilyas Khuri recognizes his debt to Arab existentialism, and Adonis still invokes Sartre as a model for emulation; Ilya Khuri, "Al-Adab wa al 'amal al-fida'i," *Al-Jazeera* interview with Sami Kulayb, January 2007, http://www.aljazeera.net/programs/pages/5c9adb75-8430-4e19-afcb-4c119d8ac428, accessed November 12, 2015; and Adonis, "La Sartar fi-l-'alam al-Islami, bal fuqaha'," opinion piece published in *Al-Mudun*, February 5, 2015, http://www.almodon.com/culture/5534278f-63cf-4f18-9751-d87416b01ad4. In contrast, in some political quarters, Sartre's Arab legacy became so distorted that contemporary Islamists genuinely believe

that Sartre was "a Jew who promoted the goals of world Jewry"; Sulay-man al-Kharashi, "Sartar wa arauhu al-falsafiyya fi-l-wujudiyya," *Muntada al-Tawhid*, September 2004, http://www.eltwhed.com/vb/showthread.php ?t=1863, accessed November 12, 2015.

29. "Ghiyab Sartar," *Al-Adab*, April–May 1980, 2.

30. Some of this material had already been republished in 1977 as part of The Best of Al-Adab series. Suhayl Idris, ed., *Mawaqif wa qadaya adabiyya* (Beirut: Dar al-Adab, 1977).

Selected Translations

This is a partial list of translations of the works of Jean-Paul Sartre and Simone de Beauvoir from 1946 to 1970. It does not include dozens of Arabic commentaries on Sartre, Beauvoir, and existentialism.

Arabic title and date of translation	Original French title	Translator
Al-Dawwama (1946). In the 1950s and 1960s it was retranslated under multiple titles such as *Al-Abwab al-muqfala, Jalsa sirriyya*, and *La mafar.*	Jean-Paul Sartre, *Huis clos* (1944)	First translation by Hashim al-Husayni (Beirut: Dar Maktabat al-Haya). Later translations by Fawziyya Mahran, Mujahid ʿAbd al-Munʿim Mujahid, and others.
Al-Wujudiyya falsafa insaniya (1954) and *Al-Wujudiyya Madhhab Insani* (1964)	Jean-Paul Sartre, *L'Existentialisme est un humanisme* (1946)	First translation by Hana Dimyan (Dar Beirut). Second translation by ʿAbd al-Munʿim al-Hifni (Cairo: Matbaʿat al-Dar al-Misriyya).
"Nizam al-Istiʿamar al-Faransi fi-l-Jazaʾir," *Al-Adab*, June 1956	Jean-Paul Sartre, "Le colonialisme est un système" (1956)	Suhayl Idris and ʿAida Matraji (Beirut: Dar al-Adab).
Ma al-adab? (1961) and *Ma al-adab?* (1962)	Jean-Paul Sartre, *Qu'est-ce que la littérature?* (1948)	Muhammad Ghunaymi Hilal
Ma huwa al-adab? (1964)	Jean-Paul Sartre, *Qu'est-ce que la littérature?* (1948)	Second translation by Jurj Tarabishi (Beirut: Al-Maktab al-Tijari).
Al-adab al-multazim (1965)	Jean-Paul Sartre, *Qu'est-ce que la littérature?* (1948)	Third translation by Jurj Tarabishi (Beirut: Dar al-Adab).
ʿAruna fi-l-Jazaʾir (1960)	Jean-Paul Sartre, selection of articles on Algeria from *Situations IV, V*	Suhayl Idris and ʿAida Matraji (Beirut: Dar al-Adab)
ʿAsifa ʿala sukkar (1960)	Jean-Paul Sartre, *Ouragan sur le sucre* (1960)	Mujahid ʿAbd al-Munʿim Mujahid (Beirut: Dar al-Adab).

Arabic title and date of translation	Original French title	Translator
Nazriyya fi infialat (1960)	Jean-Paul Sartre, Esquisse d'une théorie des émotions (1939)	Sami Mahmud ʿAli and ʿAbd al-Salam al-Qaffash (Cairo: Dar al-Maʿarif).
Ana wa Sartar wa-l-hayat (1961)	Simone de Beauvoir, La force de l'âge (1960)	ʿAida Matraji (Beirut: Dar al-Adab).
Al-muthaqqafun (1961)	Simone de Beauvoir, Les Mandarins (1954)	Jurj Tarabishi (Beirut: Dar al-Adab).
Durub al-hurriyya (1962)	Jean-Paul Sartre, Chemins de la liberté (1945)	Suhayl Idris and ʿAida Matraji (Beirut: Dar al-Adab).
Al-Shaytan wa-l-ilah al-tayyib (1962)	Jean-Paul Sartre, Le Diable et le bon Dieu (1951)	Beirut: Dar al-Ittihad.
Al-baghi al-fadila wa mawta bi-la qubur: Masrahiyatan (1962)	Jean-Paul Sartre, La putain respectueuse (1946), Morts sans sepulture (1946)	Suhayl Idris and Jalal Matraji (Beirut: Dar al-Adab).
Al-Marksiyya wa-l-thawra (1962), Al-Madhab al-madi wa-l-thawra (1960s), and Al-maddiya wa-l-thawra: Dirasat falsafiyya (1966)	Jean-Paul Sartre, Matérialisme et revolution (1947)	First translation by ʿAbd al-Munʿim al-Hifni (Cairo: Dar al-Misriyya). Second translation by Sami Drubi and Jamal Atasi (Damascus: Dar al-Yaqza al-ʿArabiyya). Third translation by ʿAbd al-Fattah Didi (Beirut: Dar al-Adab).
Al-Jidar (1963)	Jean-Paul Sartre, Le mur (1939)	ʿAbd al-Munʿim al-Hifni (Beirut: Dar Maktabat al-Haya).
Muhawarat fi-l-Siyasa (1963)	Jean-Paul Sartre, Entretien sur la politique (with David Rousset et Gérard Rosenthal, 1948)	Jurj Tarabishi (Beirut: Dar al-Adab).
Waqiʿ al-fikr al-Yamini (1963)	Simone de Beauvoir, "La pensée de droite, aujourd'hui" (1956)	Jurj Tarabishi (Beirut: Dar al-Taliʿa).
Al-Istiʿmar al-jadid (1964)	Jean-Paul Sartre, selections from Situations V	Suhayl Idris and ʿAida Matraji (Beirut: Dar al-Adab).
Quwwat al-ashyaʾ (1964)	Simone de Beauvoir, La force des choses (1963)	ʿAida Matraji (Beirut: Dar al-Adab).
Tarikh hayt taghiya (1964)	Jean-Paul Sartre, L'Engrenage (1948)	ʿAbd al-Munʿim al-Hifni (Beirut: Dar al-Mufakkir).
Nikrasuf (1964)	Jean-Paul Sartre, Nekrassov (1955)	ʿAbd al-Munʿim al-Hifni (Beirut: Dar al-Mufakkir).
Shabah Stalin (1965)	Jean-Paul Sartre, "Le fantôme de Staline" (1957)	Suhayl Idris and ʿAida Matraji (Beirut: Dar al-Adab).
"Jumhuriyyat al-samt: Abhath fi-l-hayat wa-l-fann" (1965)	Jean-Paul Sartre, "La république du silence" (1944)	Jurj Tarabishi (Beirut: Dar al-Adab).
Al-Wujud wa-l-ʿadam (1966)	Jean-Paul Sartre, L'Être et le néant (1943)	ʿAbd al-Rahman Badawi (Beirut: Dar al-Adab).

Arabic title and date of translation	Original French title	Translator
Al-Suwar al-Jamila: Riwaya (1967)	Simone de Beauvoir, *Les belles images* (1966)	'Aida Matraji (Beirut: Dar al-Adab).
Al-dhubab (1960s)	Jean-Paul Sartre, *Les mouches* (1943)	Muhammad al-Qassas (Beirut: Dar Maktabat al-Haya).
Kiyan (1960s)	Jean-Paul Sartre, *Kean* (1954)	'Abd al-Mun'im al-Hifni
Sujana' Ataluna (1960s)	Jean-Paul Sartre, *Les séquestrés d'Altona* (1959)	'Abd al-Mun'im al-Hifni
Nisa' Tarruda (1960s)	Jean-Paul Sartre, *Les troyennes* (1965)	Wahid al-Naqqash (Beirut: Dar al-Adab).
Al-Ghithyan (1950s)	Jean-Paul Sartre, *La nausée* (1938)	Suhayl Idris (Beirut: Dar al-Adab).
Difa' 'an al-Muthaqqafin (1973)	*Plaidoyer pour les intellectuels* (1972)	Jurj Tarabishi (Beirut: Dar al-Adab).

Between 1970 and 2011, dozens of translations and retranslations of Beauvoir's and Sartre's work appeared. In March 2016, seventy years after its original date of publication, Sartre's *Réflexions sur la question juive* was finally translated into Arabic.

| *Ta'ammulat fi-l-mas'ala al-Yahudiyya* (2016) | Jean-Paul Sartre, *Réflexions sur la question juive* (1946) | Hatim al-Jawahiri (Cairo: Rawafid li-l-Nashr wa-l-Tawzi'). |

Bibliography

MANUSCRIPT COLLECTIONS

Fayez A. Sayegh Collection (FSC), J. Willard Marriott Library's Aziz A. Atiya Library, University of Utah, Salt Lake City, Utah, USA.
Israel State Archive (ISA), Ministry of Foreign Affairs and Ministry of Education, Jerusalem, Israel.
National Archives and Records Administration (NARA), Washington, DC, USA.
Yad Ya'ari, Hashomer Hatzair Research and Documentation Center & Hakibbutz Hartzi Movement Archive (YY), Givat Haviva, Israel.

NEWSPAPERS, MAGAZINES, AND JOURNALS

Adab wa Naqd
Akhir Sa'a
Al-Adab
Al-Adib
Al-Ahram
Al-Ahram al-'Arabı
Al-Akhbar
Al-Ba'th
Al-Dustur
Al-Fikr al-Mu'asir
Al Ha-Mishmar
Al-Hayat
Al-Hilal
Al-Jadid
Al-Jumhuriyya
Al-Katib

Al-Katib al-Misri
Al-Ma'rifa
Al-Mu'allim al-Jadid
Al-Nahar
Al-Quds
Al-Quds al-'Arabi
Al-Safir
Al-Sharq al-Awsat
Al-Tali'a
Al-Tariq
Al-Thaqafa al-Wataniyya
Al-Thawra
Al-'Usbu' al-'Arabi
Al-Wasat
El Moudjahid
Haaretz

Haolam Hazeh	Playboy
Hiwar	Shi'r
Le Monde	Yediot Ahronot

ARABIC AND HEBREW SOURCES

'Abd al-Da'im, 'Abdallah. *Al-Jil al-'Arabi al-jadid*. Beirut: Dar al-'Ilm li-l-Malayin, 1961.

———. *Al-Watan al-'Arabi wa-l-thawra*. Beirut: Dar al-Adab, 1963.

'Abdallah, Muhammad 'Abd al-Halim. *Qadaya wa ma'arik adabiyya*. Cairo: Dar al-Sha'b, 1974.

'Abdallah, Nawwar. *Mu'amarat al-isti'mar al-jadid*. Cairo: Dar al-Hana li-l-Tiba'a, 1962.

'Abd al-Mun'im Mujahid, Mujahid. *'Asifa 'ala al-'asr*. Beirut: Dar al-Adab, 1965.

'Abd al-Nasir, Jamal. *Al-Isti'mar: Min aqwal al-ra'is Jamal 'Abd al-Nasir*. Cairo: Maslahat al-Isti'lamat, 1964.

Abu al-Ghar, Muhammad. *'Ala hamish al-rihla*. Cairo: al-Hay'a al-Misriyya al-'Amma li-l-Kitab, 2003.

Abu al-Naja, Shirin, ed. *Min awraq Shahinda Maqlad*. Cairo: Dar Mirit, 2006.

'Aflaq, Michel. *Fi Sabil al-Ba'th*. 4th ed. Beirut: Dar al-Tiba'a wa-l-Nashr, 1970.

———. *Ma'rakat al-masir al-wahid*. Beirut: Dar al-Adab, 1963.

'Alim, Mahmud Amin al-. "Al-Hurriyya wa-l-iltizam 'inda Sartar." In *Ma'arik fikriyya*, edited by Mahmud Amin al-'Alim, 226–37. Cairo: Dar al-Hilal, 1970.

———. "Husayn Muruwwa fi rihlatihi al-thalath." In *Husayn Muruwwa: Fi masiratihi al-nidaliyya fikran wa mumarsa*, 31–40. Beirut: Dar al-Farabi, 1997.

'Alim, Mahmud Amin al-, and 'Abd al-'Azim Anis. *Fi-l-Thaqafa al-Misriyya*. Cairo: Dar al-Thaqafa al-Jadida, 1989.

Amin, Samir. *Mudhakarati*. Beirut: Dar Saqi, 2006.

'Aqqad, 'Abbas Mahmud al-. *'Aqa'id al-mufakkirin fi-l-qarn al-'ishrin*. Cairo: Maktabat Gharib, 1968.

———. *Bayna al-kutub wa-l-nas*. Beirut: Dar al-Kutub al-'Arabi, 1966.

'Atiya, Salah, ed. *Taha Husayn wa ma'raktuhu al-adabiyya*. 2 vols. Cairo: Dar al-Jumhuriyya li-l-Sahafa, 2008.

'Atiyya, Ahmad Muhammad. *Anwar al-Ma'dawi: Asrihihu al-adabi wa asrar ma'satihi*. Riyad: Dar al-Mirrikh, 1988.

Avneri, Uri. *Optimi*. Tel Aviv: Yediot Ahronot, 2014.

'Azza, Badr. *Al-Muthaqqaf wa-l-sulta*. Cairo: Dar al-Jumhuriyya li-l-Sahafa, 2014.

'Azzawi, Fadil al-. *Al-Ruh al-hayya: Jil al-sittinat fi-l-'Iraq*. Damascus: Dar al-Thaqafa li-l-Nashr, 1997.

Ba'albaki, Layla. *Ana ahya*. Beirut: Dar Majallat Shi'r, 1963.

Badawi, 'Abd al-Rahman. *Dirasat fi-l-falsafa al-wujudiyya*. Cairo: Maktabat al-Nahda al-Misriyya, 1966.

———. *Humum al-shabab*. Cairo: Maktabat al-Nahda al-Misriyya, 1946.

———. *Al-Insan al-kamil fi-l-Islam*. Cairo: Maktabat al-Nahda al-Misriyya, 1950.

———. *Al-Insaniyya wa-l-wujudiyya fi-l-fikr al-'Arabi*. Cairo: Maktabat al-Nahda al-Misriyya, 1947.

———. *Sirat hayati*. 2 vols. Beirut: al-Mu'assasa al-'Arabiyya li-l-Dirasat wa-l-Nashr, 2000.

———. *Al-Zaman al-wujudi*. Cairo: Maktabat al-Nahda al-Misriyya, 1955.

Balkhayri, Ahmad. *Al-Muthaqqaf wa-l-sulta: Mawaqif wa rihanat*. Rabat: Dar al-Tawhidi li-l-Nashr wa-l-Tawzi', 2013.

Balqaziz, 'Abd al-Ilah, ed. *Al-Thaqafa al-'Arabiyya fi-l-qarn al-'ishrin: Hasila awwaliyya*. Beirut: Markaz Dirasat al-Wahda al-'Arabiyya, 2011.

Barada, Muhammad. "Tahawwulat mafhum al-iltizam fi-l-adab al-'Arabi al-hadith." In *Tahawwulat mafhum al-iltizam fi-l-adab al-'Arabi al-hadith*, edited by Muhammad Barada, 7–47. Beirut: Dar al-Fikr al-Mu'asir, 2003.

Bayyati, 'Abd al-Wahhab al-. *Diwan 'Abd al-Wahhab al-Bayyati*. 3 vols. Beirut: Dar al-'Awda, 1972.

———. *Tajribati al-shi'riyya*. Beirut: Manshurat Nizar Qabbani, 1968.

Bennabi, Malek. *Fikra al-Ifriqiyya al-Asyawiyya fi daw' mu'tamar Bandunj*. Translated by 'Abd al-Sabur Shahin. Cairo: Maktabat Dar al-'Uruba, 1957.

Bornstein, Heini. *Mi-Bazel 'ad lehavot ha-Bashan: Derekh hayim*. Israel: Yad Ya'ari, 2015.

Bufwar, Simun di. *Al-Jins al-akhar*. Translated by 'Ali Sharaf al-Din. Beirut: al-Maktaba al-Hditha li-l-Tiba'a wa-l-Nashr, 1979.

Dakrub, Muhamd. "Kalimat 'an Husayn Muruwwa wa 'an al-farh bi jadid al-akhirin." In *Husayn Muruwwa shahadat fi fikrihi wa nidalihi*, 153–70. Beirut: Dar al-Farabi, 1981.

Fa'iq, Muhammad. *'Abd al-Nasir wa-l-thawra al-Ifriqiyya*. Beirut: Dar al-Wahda, 1984.

Fanun, Franz. *Mu'adhabu al-ard*. Damascus: Mu'assasat al-Kutub al-Suriyya, 1968.

Fathi, Ibrahim. "Al-Sira al-dhatiyya al-siyasiyya li-'Abd al-'Azim Anis." *Alif: Journal of Comparative Poetics*, no. 22 (2002): 90–91.

Hadad, Qasim. "'An al-iltizam." In *Tahawwulat mafhum al-iltizam fi-l-adab al-'Arabi al-hadith*, edited by Muhammad Barada, 126–32. Beirut: Dar al-Fikr al-Mu'asir, 2003.

Hakim, Tawfiq al-. *Al-Ta'duliyya: Madhhabi fi-l-haya wa-l-fann*. Cairo: Maktabat al-Adab, 1955.

Hamdan, Jamal. *Al-Isti'mar wa-l-tahrir fi-l-'alam al-'Arabi*. Cairo: Dar al-Qalam, 1964.

Hanna, 'Abbud. *Al-Madrasa al-waqi'iyya fi-l-naqd al-'Arabi al-hadith*. Damascus: Wizarat al-Thaqafa wa-l-Irshad al-Qawmi, 1978.

Hanna, Jurj. *Al-Insan al-'Arabi qadimuhu wa-jadiduhu*. Beirut: Dar al-'Ilm li-l-Malayin 1964.

————. *Maʿna al-thawra*. Beirut: Dar Bayrut, 1957.

Hifni, ʿAbd al-Munʿim al-. *Albir Kami: Hayatuhu, adabuhi, masrahiyatuhu, falsafat fannihi*. Cairo: Dar al-Mufakkir, 1963.

Hikmet, Nâzim. *Maʾsat al-insan al-muʿasir fi shiʿr ʿAbd al-Wahhab al-Bayyati*. Cairo: Matbaʿat al-Dar al-Misriyya, 1966.

Husayn, Taha. *Khisam wa naqd*. Beirut: Dar al-ʿIlm li-l-Malayin, 1977.

————. *Mustaqbal al-thaqafa fi Misr*. Cairo: Matbaʿat al-Maʿarif, 1938, 2 vols.

Husayni, Ishaq. *Azmat al-fikr al-ʿArabi*. Beirut: Dar Bayrut, 1954.

Idris, Samah. *Raʾif Khuri wa turath al-ʿArab*. Beirut: Dar al-Adab, 1986.

Idris, Suhayl. *Dhikrayat al-adab wa-l-hubb*. Beirut: Dar al-Adab, 2002.

————, ed. *Mawaqif wa qadaya adabiyya*. Beirut: Dar al-Adab, 1977.

Kami, Albir. *Al-Insan al-mutamarrid*. Beirut: Manshurat ʿUwaidat Matbaʿat Karam, 1963.

Kanafani, Ghassan. *Adab al-muqawama fi Filastin al-muhtala*. Beirut: Dar al-Adab, 1966.

Khatibi, ʿAbd al-Kabir al-. "Dumuʿ Sartar." In *Sartar wa-l-fikr al-ʿArabi al-muʿasir*, edited by Ahmad ʿAbd al-Halim ʿAtiya, 79–104. Beirut: Dar al-Farabi, 2011.

Khuli, Lutfi al-. *Hiwar maʿa Bartrand Rasil wa Jan-Bul Sartar*. Cairo: Dar al-Maʿarif, 1968.

Lamuchi, Nur al-Din. "Sartar wa-l-siraʿ al-ʿArabi al-Israʾili." In *Sartar wa-l-fikr al-ʿArabi al-muʿasir*, edited by Ahmad ʿAbd al-Halim ʿAtiya, 105–26. Beirut: Dar al-Farabi, 2011.

Lawindi, Saʿid. *ʿAbd al-Rahman Badawi: Faylasuf al-wujudiyya al-harib ila al-Islam*. Cairo: Markaz al Hadara, 2001.

Maʿalla Muhammad, Nadim. *Al-Adab al-masrahi fi Suriyya: Nashʾatuhu, tatawwuruh*. Damascus: s.n., 1982.

Madkur, Ibrahim. "Mustafa ʿAbd al-Raziq: raʾis madrasa." In *Al-Shaykh al-akbar Mustafa ʾAbd al-Raziq: mufakkiran wa adiban wa muslihan*, 5–11. Cairo: Al-Hayʾa al-Misriyya al-ʿAmma li-l-Kitab, 1982.

Mahdi, Sami. *Al-Mawja al-sakhiba: Shiʿr al-sittiniyat fi-l-ʿIraq*. Baghdad: Dar al-Shuʾun al-Thaqafiyya al-ʿAmma, Wizarat al-Thaqafa wa-l-Iʿlam, 1994.

Malka, Shlomo. *Imanuel Levinas: Biographia*. Translated by Daniela Yoel. Tel Aviv: Resling, 2008.

Mardan, Husayn. *Al-Aʿmal al-nashriyya*. 2 vols. Baghdad: Dar al-Shuʾun al-Thaqafiyya al-ʿAmma, 2009.

Min al-fikr al-Sahyuni al-muʿasir. Beirut: Markaz al-Abhath, Munazzamat al-Tahrir al-Filastiniyya, 1968.

Moreh, Shmuel. *Ha ilan ve ha ʿanaf: Ha sifrut ha ʿaravit ha hadasha ve yetziratam ha sifrutit shel yotzei Iraq*. Jerusalem: Magnes, 1997.

Mubarak, Muhammad. *Al-Jabiri: Bayna Turuhat Lalande wa Jan-Biyajih*. Beirut: al-Muʾassasa al-ʿArabiyya li-l-Dirasat wa-l-Nashr, 2000.

Murad, Yusuf. Review of *Al-Zaman al-wujudi*, by ʿAbd al-Rahman Badawi. *Majallat ʿilm al-nafs* 1, no. 1 (June 1945): 80.

Muruwwa, Husayn. *Dirasat naqdiyya fi daw' al-manhaj al-waqi'i*. Beirut: Maktabat al-Ma'arif, 1965.

———. *Qadaya adabiyya*. Cairo: Dar al-Fikr, 1956.

Musa, Salama. *Al-Adab li-l-sha'b*. Cairo: Mu'assasat al-Khanji, 1961.

———. *Ha'ula' 'allamuni*. Cairo: Dar al-Jil li-l-Tiba'a, 1966.

———. *Ma hiya al-nahda?* Cairo: al-Hay'a al-Misriyya al-'Amma li-l-Kitab, 1993.

Rahib, Hani al-. *Al-Mahzumun*. Beirut: Dar al-Adab, 1961.

Sabr 'Arab, Muhammad, and Ahmad Zakariyya al-Shalaq, eds. *Awraq Taha Husayn wa murasalatahu*. 2 vols. Cairo: Dar al-Kutub wa-l-Watha'iq al-Qawmiyya, 2007.

Safadi, Muta'. *Hizb al-ba'th: Ma'sat al-mawlid, ma'sat al-nihaya*. Beirut: Dar al-Adab, 1964.

———. *Al-Thawri wa-l-'Arabi al-thawri: Dirasa fikriyya qawmiyya li-namadhij al-thawriyyin al-gharbiyyin wa-l-'Arab*. Beirut: Dar al-Tali'a, 1961.

Samarra'i, Majid al-, ed. *Rasa'il al-Sayyab*. Beirut: al-Mu'assasa al-'Arabiyya li-l-Dirasat, 1994.

Samman, 'Ali al-. *Awraq 'umri: Min al-malik ila 'Abd al-Nasir wa-l-Sadat*. Cairo: Al-Maktab al-Misri al-Hadith, 2005.

Sartar, Jan-Bul. *'Aruna fi-l-Jaza'ir*. Translated by Suhayl Idris and 'Aida Idris. Nazareth: Al-Kitab al-'Arabi, 1960.

———. *Al-Marksiyya wa-l-thawra*. Translated by 'Abd al-Mun'im al-Hifni. Cairo: al-Dar al-Misriyya, 1962.

———. *Ta'ammulat fi-l-mas'ala al-Yahudiyya*. Translated by Hatim al-Jawahiri. Cairo: Rawafid li-l-Nashr wa-l-Tawzi', 2016.

Sayigh, Anis. *Anis Sayigh 'an Anis Sayigh*. Beirut: Riyad al-Rayyis li-l-Kutub wa-l-Nashr, 2006.

Sayigh, Fayiz 'Abdullah. *Ila ayna? Bahth tahlili naqdi fi mawqif al-hizb al-Suri al-qawmi al-ijtima'i min al-fikr wa-l-din wa-hurriyyatuhu*. Beirut: Dar al-Kitab, 1947.

———. *Risalat al-mufakkir al-'Arabi*. Beirut: Majallat al-Ahad, 1955.

Sayyab, Badr Shakir al-. *Kuntu shuyu'iyyan*. Cologne: Manshurat al-Jamal, 2007.

Shahada, Khuri. *Al-Adab fi-l-maydan*. Damascus: Matba'at Dimashq, 1950.

Sharif, 'Aida al-. "Sartar fi-l-Qahira." In *Sartar wa-l-fikr al-'Arabi al-mu'asir*, edited by Ahmad 'Abd al-Halim 'Atiya, 151–82. Beirut: Dar al-Farabi, 2011.

Shukri, Ghali. *Adab al-muqawama*. Beirut: Dar al-Afaq al-Jadida, 1969.

Sidqi, Taha Mahmud. *Isti'mar al-jadid fi-l-watan al-'Arabi*. Damascus: al-Amana li-Ittihad al Muhamin al-'Arab, 1968.

Sulayman, Nabil. *Al-Idiyulujiya wa-l-adab fi Suriyya, 1967–1973*. Beirut: Dar Khaldun, 1974.

Ta'i, 'Abd al-Husayn Salih al-. *Jadaliyat al-'alaqa bayna al-muthaqqaf wa-l-sulta*. London: Dar al-Hikmah, 2013.

Talhami, Dawud. "'Ala daw' liqa' ma'a al-faylasuf al-Faransi: Sartar wa-l-mas'ala al-Filastıniyya." *Shu'un Filastıniyya* 12 (1972): 66–72.

Tarabishi, Jurj. *Sartar wa-l-Marksiyya*. Beirut: Dar al-Tali'a, 1964.

Zakariyya al-Shilaq, Ahmad. *Al-Shaykh Mustafa 'Abd al-Raziq wa mudhakaratihi: 'Aql mustanir tahta al-'amama*. Cairo: al-Hay'a al-Misriyya al-'Amma li-l-Kitab, 2006.

Zuhayr, Muhammad, and Jamil al-Kutbi. *Al-Muthaqqaf al-'Arabi wa-l-sulta*. Cairo: Matabi' al-Ahram, 1995.

Zunaybar, Muhammad. *Franz Fanun, aw, ma'rakat al-shu'ub al- mutakhallifa*. Beirut: Dar al-Kitab, 1963.

Zurayq, Qustantin. *Hadha al-'asr al-mutafajjir: Nazarat fi waqi'ina wa-waqi' al-insaniyya*. Beirut: Dar al-'Ilm li-l-Malayin, 1963.

ENGLISH AND FRENCH SOURCES

"Abd al-Wahhab al-Bayyati: Poet." In *Crosshatching in Global Culture: A Dictionary of Modern Arab Writers*, edited by John Donohue and Leslie Tramontini, 1:234–38. Beirut: Orient-Institut der DMG, 2004.

Abdel-Malek, Anouar. *Egypt: Military Society; The Army Regime, the Left, and Social Change under Nasser*. New York: Random House, 1968.

Abdul-Salaam Yacoob, Yousif. "Vanguardist Cultural Practices: The Formation of an Alternative Cultural Hegemony in Iraq and Chile, 1930s–1970s." PhD diss., University of Iowa, 1988. Retrieved from http://ezproxy.lib .utexas.edu/login?url=http://search.proquest.com.ezproxy.lib.utexas.edu/docview/303695333?accountid=7118.

Aghacy, Samira. "Lebanese Women's Fiction: Urban Identity and the Tyranny of the Past." *International Journal of Middle East Studies* 33, no. 4 (2001): 503–23.

Ajami, Fuad. *The Arab Predicament: Arab Political Thought and Practice since 1967*. Cambridge: Cambridge University Press, 1981.

Alexander, Jeffrey. "On the Social Construction of Moral Universals: The 'Holocaust' from War Crime to Trauma Drama." In *Cultural Trauma and Collective Identity*, edited by Jeffrey Alexander, Ron Eyerman, Bernard Giesen, Neil J. Smelser, and Piotr Sztompka, 196–263. Berkeley: University of California Press, 2004.

Allan, Michael. *In the Shadow of World Literature: Sites of Reading in Colonial Egypt*. Princeton, NJ: Princeton University Press, 2016.

Allen, Roger, and Issa J. Boullata, eds. *The Arabic Novel since 1950: Critical Essays, Interviews, and Bibliography*. Cambridge, MA: Dar Mahjar, 1992.

Allman, Jean. "Phantoms of the Archive: Kwame Nkrumah, a Nazi Pilot Named Hanna, and the Contingencies of Postcolonial History-Writing," *American Historical Review* 118, no. 1 (2013): 104–29.

Anderson, Jon Lee. *Che Guevara: A Revolutionary Life*. New York: Grove Press, 1997.

Anderson, Thomas. *Sartre's Two Ethics: From Authenticity to Integral Humanity*. Chicago: Open Court, 1993.

Ang Mei Sze, Jennifer. *Sartre and the Moral Limits of War and Terrorism.* New York: Routledge, 2010.

Appadurai, Arjun. *Modernity at Large: Cultural Dimensions of Globalization.* Minneapolis: University of Minnesota Press, 1996.

Armitage, David. "The International Turn in Intellectual History." In *Rethinking Modern European Intellectual History,* edited by Darrin McMahon and Samuel Moyn, 232–33. New York: Oxford University Press, 2014.

Arnaldez, R. "Al-Insān al-Kāmil." In *Encyclopaedia of Islam,* 2nd ed., edited by P. Bearman, T. Bianquis, C. E. Bosworth, E. van Donzel, and W. P. Heinrichs. Leiden: Brill, 2011. Consulted online on April 5, 2017. http://dx.doi.org.ezproxy.lib.utexas.edu/10.1163/1573-3912_islam_COM _0375.

Aronson, Ronald. *Camus and Sartre: The Story of a Friendship and the Quarrel That Ended It.* Chicago: University of Chicago Press, 2004.

Artaraz, Kepa, and Karen Luyckx. "The French New Left and the Cuban Revolution 1959–1971: Parallel Histories?" *Modern and Contemporary France* 17, no. 1 (February 2009): 67–82.

Arthur, Paige. *Unfinished Projects: Decolonization and the Philosophy of Jean-Paul Sartre.* New York: Verso, 2010.

Badawi, Abdurahman. *Le problème de la mort dans la philosophie existentielle.* Cairo: Institut Français d'archéologie Orientale, 1964.

Badawi, M. Mustafa. "Commitment in Contemporary Arabic Literature." *Cahiers d'histoire mondiale* 14, no. 4 (1972): 859–79.

———. *A Short History of Modern Arabic Literature.* Oxford: Clarendon, 1993.

Badr, Ali. *Papa Sartre.* Translated by Aida Bamia. Cairo: American University Press, 2009.

Bahoora, Haytham. "Baudelaire in Baghdad: Modernism, the Body, and Husayn Mardan's Poetics of The Self." *International Journal of Middle East Studies* 45, special issue 2 (May 2013): 313–29.

Bailkin, Jordanna. "Where Did the Empire Go? Archives and Decolonization in Britain." *American Historical Review* 120, no. 3 (June 2015): 884–89.

Bair, Deirdre. *Simone de Beauvoir: A Biography.* New York: Touchstone, 1990.

Bashkin, Orit. "Nationalism as a Cause: Arab Nationalism in the Writings of Ghassan Kanafani." In *Nationalism and Liberal Thought in the Arab East Ideology and Practice,* edited by Christoph Schumann, 92–112. London: Routledge, 2010.

———. *The New Babylonians: A History of Jews in Modern Iraq.* Stanford, CA: Stanford University Press, 2012.

———. *The Other Iraq: Pluralism and Culture in Hashemite Iraq.* Stanford, CA: Stanford University Press, 2008.

———. "Representations of Women in the Writings of the Intelligentsia in Hashemite Iraq, 1921–1958." *Journal of Middle East Women's Studies* 4, no. 1 (2007): 53–82.

Bassey, Magnus. "What Is Africana Critical Theory or Black Existential Philosophy?" *Journal of Black Studies* 37, no. 6 (July 2007): 914–35.

Batatu, Hanna. *The Old Social Classes and the Revolutionary Movements of Iraq: A Study of Iraq's Old Landed and Commercial Classes and of Its Communists, Ba'thists, and Free Officers*. London: Saqi Books, 2004.

Bayly, Christopher. *Recovering Liberties: Indian Thought in the Age of Liberalism and Empire*. Cambridge: Cambridge University Press, 2011.

Beauvoir, Simone de. *All Said and Done*. New York: Putnam, 1974.

Beinin, Joel. *The Dispersion of Egyptian Jewry: Culture, Politics and the Formation of a Modern Diaspora*. Berkeley: University of California Press, 1998.

Ben Gal, Ely. *Mardi chez Sartre: Un hebreu a Paris, 1967–1980*. Paris: Flammarion, 1992.

Berger, Mark. "After the Third World? History, Destiny and the Fate of Third Worldism." *Third World Quarterly* 25, no. 1 (2004): 9–39.

Bertholet, Denis. *Sartre*. Paris: Plon, 2000.

Beshara, Adel. *Lebanon: The Politics of Frustration—the Failed Coup of 1961*. New York: Routledge, 2005.

———. *Syrian Nationalism: An Inquiry into the Political Philosophy of Antun Sa'adeh*. Beirut: Bissan, 1995.

Birchall, Ian. "Third World and After." *New Left Review* 80 (March–April 2013): 151–60.

Boullata, Issa. "Badr Shakir al-Sayyab and the Free Verse Movement." *International Journal of Middle East Studies* 1, no. 3 (July 1970): 248–58.

Bourg, Julian. *From Revolution to Ethics: May 1968 and Contemporary French Thought*. Montreal: McGill-Queen's University Press, 2007.

Bouwer, Karen. *Gender and Decolonization in the Congo: The Legacy of Patrice Lumumba*. New York: Palgrave, 2010.

Brennan, James. "Radio Cairo and the Decolonization of East Africa, 1953–1964," in *Making a World after Empire: The Bandung Moment and its Political Afterlives*, edited by Christopher Lee, 173–195. Athens: Ohio University Press, 2010.

Bruckner, Pascal. *The Tears of the White Man: Compassion as Contempt*. Translated by William R. Beer. New York: Free Press, 1986.

Byrne, Jeffrey. *Mecca of Revolution: Algeria, Decolonization, and the Third World Order*. New York: Oxford University Press, 2016.

Cachia, Pierre. "The Critics." In *Cambridge History of Arabic Literature*, edited by M. M. Badawi, 417–42. Cambridge: Cambridge University Press, 1992.

———. "Husayn Taha (1889–1973)." In *Routledge Encyclopedia of Arabic Literature*, edited by Julie Scott Meisami and Paul Starkey, 297. New York: Routledge, 2010.

———. *An Overview of Modern Arabic Literature*. Edinburgh: Edinburgh University Press, 1990.

Césaire, Aimé. "Letter to Maurice Thorez." *Social Text* 28, no. 2 103 (Summer 2010): 145–52.

Charbit, Denis. "Les raisons d'une fidélité: Simone de Beauvoir, Israël et les Juifs." *Simone de Beauvoir Studies* 17 (2000–2001): 48–63.

Christofferson, Michael Scott. *French Intellectuals against the Left: The Antitotalitarian Moment of the 1970s.* New York: Berghahn Books, 2004.

Cohen, Bernard. "Alexandre Koyré (1892–1964)." *Isis* 57, no. 2 (Summer 1966): 157–66.

Cohen, G. A., "The Structure of Proletarian Unfreedom," *Philosophy and Public Affairs* 12, no. 1 (Winter 1983): 3–33.

Cohen-Solal, Annie. *Sartre: A Life.* Translated by Anna Cancogni. New York: Pantheon Books, 1987.

Colla, Elliott. "Badr Shākir al-Sayyāb, Cold War Poet." *Middle Eastern Literatures* 18, no. 3 (2015): 247–63.

Connelly, Matthew. *A Diplomatic Revolution: Algeria's Fight for Independence and the Origins of the Post–Cold War Era.* Oxford: Oxford University Press, 2002.

Contat, Michel. *The Writings of Jean-Paul Sartre.* Evanston, IL: Northwestern University Press, 1974.

Cooper, David. *Existentialism: A Reconstruction.* Oxford: Blackwell, 1990.

Cooper, Frederick. *Citizenship between Empire and Nation: Remaking France and French Africa, 1945–1960.* Princeton, NJ: Princeton University Press, 2014.

———. *Colonialism in Question: Theory, Knowledge, History.* Berkeley: University of California Press, 2005.

———. *Decolonization and African Society: The Labor Question in French and British Africa.* Cambridge: Cambridge University Press, 1996.

Craps, Stef, and Gert Buelens. "Introduction: Postcolonial Trauma Novels." *Studies in the Novel* 40, nos. 1–2 (Spring–Summer 2008): 1–12.

Creswell, Robyn. "Tradition and Translation: Poetic Modernism in Beirut." PhD diss., New York University, 2012. Retrieved from http://ezproxy.lib .utexas.edu/login?url=http://search.proquest.com.ezproxy.lib.utexas.edu/ docview/992988836?accountid=7118.

Dabashi, Hamid. *Theology of Discontent: The Ideological Foundation of the Islamic Revolution in Iran.* New York: New York University Press, 1993.

Davies, Howard. *Sartre and "Les Temps Modernes."* Cambridge: Cambridge University Press, 1987.

Davis, Eric. *Memories of State: Politics, History and Collective Identity in Modern Iraq.* Berkeley: University of California Press, 2005.

Dawisha, Adeed. *Arab Nationalism in the Twentieth Century: From Triumph to Despair.* Princeton, NJ: Princeton University Press, 2003.

Decalo, Samuel. *Israel and Africa: Forty Years, 1956–1996.* Gainesville: University Press of Florida, 1998.

Descombes, Vincent. *Modern French Philosophy.* Translated by L. Scott-Fox and J. M. Harding. Cambridge: Cambridge University Press, 1998.

Desmond, Stewart. "Contacts with Arab Writers." *Middle East Forum* 37, no. 1 (January 1981): 19–21.

DeYoung, Terri. *Placing the Poet: Badr Shakir al-Sayyab and Postcolonial Iraq.* Albany: State University of New York Press, 1998.

Di-Capua, Yoav. "Arab Existentialism: A Lost Chapter in the Intellectual History of Decolonization." *American Historical Review* 17, no. 4 (October 2012): 1061–91.

———. *Gatekeepers of the Arab Past: Historians and History Writing in Twentieth-Century Egypt.* Berkeley: University of California Press, 2009.

———. "Homeward Bound: Husayn Muruwwah's Integrative Quest for Authenticity." *Journal of Arabic Literature* 44, no. 1 (2013): 21–52.

Dresch, Paul. *A History of Modern Yemen.* Cambridge: Cambridge University Press, 2000.

Efrati, Noga. *Women in Iraq: Past Meets Present.* New York: Columbia University Press, 2012.

El-Samman, Aly. *Egypt: From One Revolution to Another; Memoir of a Committed Citizen under Nasser, Sadat, and Mubarak.* London: Gilgamesh, 2012.

Elshakry, Marwa. *Reading Darwin in Arabic, 1860–1950.* Chicago: University of Chicago Press, 2013.

El Shakry, Omnia. "The Arabic Freud: The Unconscious and the Modern Subject." *Modern Intellectual History* 11, no. 1 (April 2014): 89–118.

———. "History without Documents: The Vexed Archives of Decolonization in the Middle East." *American Historical Review* 120, no. 3 (June 2015): 920–34.

———. "Youth as Peril and Promise: The Emergence of Adolescent Psychology in Postwar Egypt." *International Journal of Middle East Studies* 43, no. 4 (November 2011): 591–610.

Eppel, Michael. *Iraq from Monarchy to Tyranny: From the Hashemites to the Rise of Saddam.* Gainesville: University Press of Florida, 2004.

Erlich, Haggai. *Youth and Revolution in the Changing Middle East, 1908–2014.* Boulder, CO: Lynne Rienner, 2015.

Etherington, Ben. "An Answer to the Question: What Is Decolonization? Frantz Fanon's *The Wretched of the Earth* and Jean-Paul Sartre's *Critique of Dialectical Reason*." *Modern Intellectual History* 13, no. 1 (February 2015): 1–28.

Fanon, Frantz. *Les damnés de la terre.* Paris: François Maspero, 1968 and 1970.

———. *The Wretched of the Earth.* Translated by Constance Farrington. New York: Grove Press, 1963.

Farouk-Sluglett, Marion, and Peter Sluglett. "The Transformation of Land Tenure and Rural Social Structure in Central and Southern Iraq, c. 1870–1958." *International Journal of Middle East Studies* 15, no. 4 (November 1983): 491–505.

Feldman, Keith. *A Shadow over Palestine: The Imperial Life of Race in America.* Minneapolis: University of Minnesota Press, 2015.

Ferris, Jesse. *Nasser's Gamble: How Intervention in Yemen Caused the Six-Day War and the Decline of Egyptian Power.* Princeton, NJ: Princeton University Press, 2013.

Firat, Alexa. "Cultural Battles on the Literary Field: From the Syrian Writers Collective to the Last Days of Socialist Realism in Syria." *Middle Eastern Literatures* 18, no. 2 (2015): 153–76.

Flapan, Simha. "Le dialogue entre socialistes arabes et israéliens est une nécessité historique." In *Le conflit israélo-arabe*, edited by Jean-Paul Sartre and Claude Lanzmann, 559–602. Paris: Les Temps Modernes, 1967.

Fleming, Michael. "Sartre on Violence: Not So Ambivalent?" *Sartre Studies International* 17, no. 1 (2011): 20–40.

Flynn, Robert. *Sartre: A Philosophical Biography*. Cambridge: Cambridge University Press, 2014.

Friedmann, Georges Philippe. *The End of the Jewish People?* Garden City, NY: Doubleday, 1967.

Fulton, Ann. *Existentialism in America, 1945–1963*. Evanston, IL: Northwestern University Press, 1999.

Gadkar-Wilcox, Wynn. "Existentialism and Intellectual Culture in South Vietnam." *Journal of Asian Studies* 73, no. 2 (May 2014): 377–95.

Gershoni, Israel, ed. *Arab Responses to Fascism and Nazism: Attraction and Repulsion*. Austin: University of Texas Press, 2014.

Gershoni, Israel, and James Jankowski. *Confronting Fascism in Egypt: Dictatorship versus Democracy in the 1930s*. Stanford, CA: Stanford University Press, 2010.

Gershoni, Israel, and Amy Singer. "Introduction: Intellectual History in Middle Eastern Studies." *Comparative Studies of South Asia, Africa and the Middle East* 28, no. 3 (2008): 383–84.

Gheissari, Ali. *Iranian Intellectuals in the Twentieth Century*. Austin: University of Texas Press, 1998.

Ginat, Rami. *Egypt's Incomplete Revolution: Lutfi al-Khuli and Nasser's Socialism in the 1960s*. London: Frank Cass, 1997.

Ginat, Rami, and Meir Noema. "Al-Fajr al-Jadid: A Breeding Ground for the Emergence of Revolutionary Ideas in the Immediate Post–Second World War." *Middle Eastern Studies* 44, no. 6 (November 2008): 867–93.

Giordani, Angela. "*Shi'r* and the Other Revolution of the Arab Fifties." Unpublished seminar paper, University of Texas at Austin, 2010.

Gleijeses, Piero. *Conflicting Missions: Havana, Washington, and Africa, 1959–1976*. Chapel Hill: University of North Carolina Press, 2002.

Gordon, Hayim. *Naguib Mahfouz's Egypt: Existential Themes in His Writings*. New York: Greenwood Press, 1990.

Gordon, Lewis. *Existentia Africana: Understanding Africana Existential Thought*. London: Routledge, 2000.

———. "The Problem of Biography in the Study of the Thought of Black Intellectuals." *Small Axe: A Caribbean Journal of Criticism* 2, no. 2 (September 1998): 47–63.

———. *What Fanon Said: A Philosophical Introduction to His Life and Thought*. New York: Fordham University Press, 2015.

Greif, Mark. *The Age of the Crisis of Man: Thought and Fiction in America, 1933–1973*. Princeton, NJ: Princeton University Press, 2015.

Gribetz, Jonathan. "When the Zionist Idea Came to Beirut: Judaism, Christianity, and the Palestine Liberation Organization's Translation of Zionism." *International Journal Middle East Studies* 48, no. 2 (May 2016): 243–66.

Guha, Ranajit. *Dominance without Hegemony: History and Power in Colonial India*. Cambridge, MA: Harvard University Press, 1997.

Guitard, Odette. "Alger ou la désunion Afro-Asiatique." *Annuaire de l'Afrique du Nord* 4 (1966): 49–61.

Hafez, Sabry. *The Quest for Identities: The Development of the Modern Arabic Short Story*. London: Saqi, 2007.

Haidar, Otared. *The Prose Poem and the Journal Shi'r: A Comparative Study of Literature, Literary Theory and Journalism*. Reading, UK: Ithaca Press, 2008.

Haj, Samira. *The Making of Iraq, 1900–1963: Capital, Power, and Ideology*. Albany: State University of New York Press, 1997.

Hamil, Mustafa. "Mohamed Zafzaf's al-Mar'a wa-l-Warda or the Voyage North in the Postcolonial Era." *International Journal of Middle East Studies* 38, no. 3 (August 2006): 417–30.

Hanafi, Hasan. "Phenomenology and Islamic Philosophy." In *Phenomenology World-Wide: Foundations, Expanding Dynamisms, Life-Engagements; A Guide for Research and Study*, edited by Anna-Teresa Tymieniecka, 318–21. Dordrecht: Kluwer Academic, 2002.

Handal, Nathalie, ed. *The Poetry of Arab Women: A Contemporary Anthology*. Translated by Husain Haddawy. New York: Interlink Books, 2001.

"Hani al-Rahib." In *Crosshatching in Global Culture: A Dictionary of Modern Arab Writers*, edited by John Donohue and Leslie Tramontini, 2:928–30. Beirut: Orient-Institut der DMG, 2004.

Hanoosh, Yasmeen. "Contempt: State Literati vs. Street Literati in Modern Iraq." *Journal of Arabic Literature* 43, nos. 2–3 (2012): 372–408.

Harlow, Barbara. "Reading of National Identity in the Palestinian Novel." In *The Arabic Novel since 1950: Critical Essays, Interviews, and Bibliography*, edited by Issa J. Boullata and Roger Allen, 89–106. Cambridge, MA: Dar Mahjar, 1992.

———. "Return to Haifa: 'Opening the Borders' in Palestinian Literature." *Social Text*, nos. 13/14 (Winter–Spring 1986): 3–23.

Haykal, Mohamed Hasanayn. *The Cairo Documents*. New York: Doubleday, 1973.

Hendrickson, Burleigh. "March 1968: Practicing Transnational Activism from Tunis to Paris." *International Journal of Middle East Studies* 44, no. 4 (November 2012): 755–74.

Hering, Jean. "In Memoriam: Alexander Koyré." *Philosophy and Phenomenological Research* 25, no. 3 (March 1965): 453–54.

Herivel, John. "Alexandre Koyré (1892–1964)." *British Journal for the History of Science* 2, no. 3 (June 1965): 257–59.

Heter, Storm. *Sartre's Ethics of Engagement: Authenticity and Civic Virtue*. London: Continuum, 2006.

Holt, Elizabeth. "'Bread or Freedom': The Congress for Cultural Freedom, the CIA, and the Arabic Literary Journal Ḥiwār (1962–67)." *Journal of Arabic Literature* 44 (2013): 83–102.

Hourani, Albert. *Arabic Thought in the Liberal Age 1798–1939*. Cambridge: Cambridge University Press, 1989.

Husry, Khaldun al-. "The Iraqi Revolution of July 14th 1958." *Middle East Forum* 41, no. 1 (1965): 25–28.

Immerman, Richard, and Petra Goedde, eds. *The Oxford Handbook of the Cold War*. Oxford: Oxford University Press, 2013.

Ismael, Tareq. *The Rise and Fall of the Communist Party in Iraq*. New York: Cambridge University Press, 2008.

———. *The U.A.R. in Africa: Egypt's Policy under Nasser*. Evanston, IL: Northwestern University Press, 1971.

Isstaif, Abdul-Nabi. "Going beyond Socialist Realism, Getting Nowhere: Luwis 'Awad's Cross-Cultural Encounter with the Other." In *Tradition, Modernity, and Postmodernity in Arabic Literature: Essays in Honor of Professor Issa J. Boullata*, edited by Kamal Abdel-Malek and Wael Hallaq, 113–40. Leiden: Brill, 2000.

Jabra, Jabra Ibrahim. "The Palestinian Exile as Writer." *Journal of Palestine Studies* 8, no. 2 (Winter 1979).

———. *Princess Street: Baghdad Memories*. Translated by Issa Boullata. Fayetteville: The University of Arkansas Press, 2005.

Jacobson, Harold Karan. "The United Nations and Colonialism: A Tentative Appraisal." *International Organization* 16, no. 1 (December 1962): 37–56.

Jacquemond, Richard. *Conscience of the Nation: Writers, State, and Society in Modern Egypt*. Translated by David Tresilian. Cairo: AUC Press, 2008.

Jad, Ali. *Form and Technique in the Egyptian Novel, 1912–1971*. London: Ithaca Press, 1983.

"Jean-Paul Sartre et Simone de Beauvoir en Israël." *Cahiers Bernard Lazare*, May 10, 1967, 4–20.

Johnson, Amy. *Reconstructing Rural Egypt: Ahmed Hussein and the History of Egyptian Development*. Syracuse, NY: Syracuse University Press, 2004.

Judaken, Jonathan. *Jean-Paul Sartre and the Jewish Question: Anti-Antisemitism and the Politics of the French Intellectual*. Lincoln: University of Nebraska Press, 2006.

———. "Sisyphus's Progeny: Existentialism in France." In *Situating Existentialism: Key Texts in Context*, edited by Jonathan Judaken and Robert Bernasconi, 89–122. New York: Columbia University Press, 2012.

Judaken, Jonathan, and Robert Bernasconi, eds. *Situating Existentialism: Key Texts in Context*. New York: Columbia University Press, 2012.

Judt, Tony. *Past Imperfect: French Intellectuals, 1944–1956*. Berkeley: University of California Press, 1992.

————. *Postwar: A History of Europe since 1945*. New York: Penguin, 2005.

Kanafani, Ghassan. *Men in the Sun*. Translated by Hilary Kilpatrick. Cairo: American University Press, 1991.

Kapeliuk, Amnon. "Sartre in the Arab Press," *New Outlook* 10, no. 4 (May 1967): 29–33.

Kapila, Shruti, and Faisal Devji, eds. "An Intellectual History for India." Special issue, *Modern Intellectual History* 4, no. 1 (2007).

Kassab, Suzanne Elizabeth. *Contemporary Arab Thought: Cultural Critique in Contemporary Perspective*. New York: Columbia University Press, 2009.

Kassir, Samir. *Being Arab*. London: Verso, 2013.

Kassir, Samir, and Farouk Mardam-Bey. *Itinéraires de Paris à Jérusalem: La France et le conflit israélo-arabe*. Washington, DC: Institut des études palestiniennes, 1992.

Kennedy, Dane. "Imperial History and Post-colonial Theory." In *The Decolonization Reader*, edited by James D. Le Sueur, 1–22. New York: Routledge, 2003.

Khilnani, Sunil. *Arguing Revolution: The Intellectual Left in Postwar France*. New Haven, CT: Yale University Press, 1993.

Khoury, Gérard D. "Maxime Rodinson et la constitution du Grapp (Groupe de recherche et d'action pour la Palestine)." *Matériaux pour l'histoire de notre temps* 4, no. 96 (2009): 28–37.

Khuri-Makdisi, Ilham. *The Eastern Mediterranean and the Making of Global Radicalism, 1860–1914*. Berkeley: University of California Press, 2010.

Kleinberg, Ethan. *Generation Existential: Heidegger's Philosophy in France, 1927–1961*. Ithaca, NY: Cornell University Press, 2005.

Klemm, Verena. "Different Notions of Commitment (*Iltizam*) and Committed Literature (*al-adab al-multazim*) in the Literary Circles of the Mashriq." *Middle Eastern Literatures* 3, no. 1 (January 2000): 51–62.

————. *Literarisches Engagement im arabischen Nahen Osten: Konzepte und Debatten*. Würzburg: Ergon, 1998.

Kockelmans, Joseph J. "Phenomenology." In *Cambridge Dictionary of Philosophy*, edited by Robert Audi, 664–66. Cambridge: Cambridge University Press, 1999.

Kumar, Aishwary. *Radical Equality: Ambedkar, Gandhi, and the Risk of Democracy*. Stanford, CA: Stanford University Press, 2015.

Labib, Zuwiyya Yamak. *The Syrian Social Nationalist Party: An Ideological Analysis*. Cambridge, MA: Center for Middle Eastern Studies of Harvard University, 1966.

Lamouchi, Noureddine. *Jean-Paul Sartre et le Tiers-Monde: Rhétorique d'un discourse anticolonialiste*. Paris: L'Harmattan, 1996.

Lanzmann, Claude. *The Patagonian Hare*. New York: Farrar Straus and Giroux, 2012.

Lazarus, Neil. *The Postcolonial Unconscious*. Cambridge: Cambridge University Press, 2011.

Lazreg, Marnia. *Torture and the Twilight of Empire: From Algiers to Baghdad.* Princeton, NJ: Princeton University Press, 2007.

Le Sueur, James. *Uncivil War: Intellectuals and Identity Politics during the Decolonization.* Philadelphia: University of Pennsylvania Press, 2001.

Levey, Zach. "Israel's Entry to Africa, 1956–1961." *Diplomacy and Statecraft* 12, no. 3 (September 2001): 87–114.

———. "Israel's Involvement in the Congo, 1958–1968: Civilian and Military Dimensions." *Civil Wars* 6, no. 4 (Winter 2003): 14–36.

———. "Israel's Strategy in Africa, 1961–1967." *International Journal of Middle East Studies* 36, no. 1 (February 2004): 71–87.

———. "The Rise and Decline of a Special Relationship: Israel and Ghana, 1957–1966." *African Studies Review* 46, no. 1 (April 2003): 155–77.

Levine, Andrew. "Foundations of Unfreedom." *Ethics* 88, no. 2 (January 1978): 162–72.

Lévy, Bernard-Henri. *Sartre: The Philosopher of the Twentieth Century.* Cambridge: Polity Press, 2003.

Litvak, Meir, and Esther Webman. *From Empathy to Denial: Arab Responses to the Holocaust.* New York: Columbia University Press, 2009.

Litvin, Margaret. *Hamlet's Arab Journey: Shakespeare's Prince and Nasser's Ghost.* Princeton, NJ: Princeton University Press, 2011.

Lloyd, David. "Colonial Trauma/Postcolonial Recovery?" *Interventions: International Journal of Postcolonial Studies* 2, no. 2 (2000): 212–28.

Lonsdale, John. "Anti-colonial Nationalism and Patriotism in Sub-Saharan Africa." In *Oxford Handbook of the History of Nationalism,* edited by John Breuilly, 318–37. Oxford: Oxford University Press, 2013.

Loya, Arieh. "Poetry as a Social Document: The Social Position of the Arab Woman as Reflected in the Poetry of Nizar Qabbani." *International Journal of Middle East Studies* 6, no. 4 (October 1975): 481–94.

Lukács, Georg. *Marxism and Human Liberation: Essays on History, Culture and Revolution.* New York: Dell, 1973.

Macey, David. *Frantz Fanon: A Biography.* New York: Verso, 2012.

Machut-Mendecka, Ewa. *Studies in Arabic Theatre and Literature.* Warsaw: Dialog, 2000.

Malik, Habib. "The Reception of Kierkegaard in the Arab World." In *Kierkegaard's International Reception,* edited by Jon Stewart, 41–49. Farnham, UK: Ashgate, 2009.

Malkin, Irad. "Israël et Pierre Vidal-Naquet." In *Pierre Vidal-Naquet, un Historien dans la Cité,* edited by François Hartog, Pauline Schmitt Pantel, and Alain Schnapp, 199–218. Paris: La Découverte, 2007.

Manjapra, Kris. *Age of Entanglement: German and Indian Intellectuals across Empire.* Cambridge, MA: Harvard University Press, 2014.

Mansour, Wisam. "Arab Women in Nizar Kabbani's Poetry." *Comparative Studies of South Asia, Africa and the Middle East* 25, no. 2 (2005): 480–86.

Mardam-Bey, Farouk. "French Intellectuals and the Palestine Question." *Journal of Palestine Studies* 43, no. 3 (Spring 2014): 26–39.

Marr, Phebe. *The Modern History of Iraq.* Boulder, CO: Westview, 2004.

Marwick, Arthur. *The Sixties: Cultural Revolution in Britain, France, Italy, and the United States, 1958–1974.* New York: Oxford University Press, 1998.

Matera, Marc. *Black London: The Imperial Metropolis and Decolonization in the Twentieth Century.* Berkeley: University of California Press, 2015.

Mealy, Rosemari. *Fidel and Malcolm X.* Melbourne: Ocean View Press, 1993.

Mehrez, Samia. *Egyptian Writers between History and Fiction.* Cairo: American University Press, 1994.

Meijer, Roel. *Secular Liberal and Left-Wing Political Thought in Egypt 1945–1958.* London: Routledge, 2002.

Meretoja, Hanna. *The Narrative Turn in Fiction and Theory: The Crisis and Return of Storytelling from Robbe-Grillet to Tournier.* London: Palgrave, 2014.

Meyer, Stefan. *The Experimental Arabic Novel.* Albany: State University of New York Press, 2001.

Micklethwait, Dwight Christopher. "*Faits Divers*: National Culture and Modernism in Third World Literary Magazines." PhD diss., University of Texas at Austin, 2011. Retrieved from http://catalog.lib.utexas.edu/search/t ?SEARCH=Faits+Divers%3A+National+Culture+and+Modernism+.

Mishra, Pankaj. *From the Ruins of Empire: The Intellectuals Who Remade Asia.* New York: Farrar, Straus and Giroux, 2012.

Mitoma, Glen. "Charles H. Malik and Human Rights: Notes on a Biography," *Biography: An Interdisciplinary Quarterly* 33, no. 1 (Winter 2010): 222–41.

Mohsen, Fatima. "Debating Iraqi Culture: Intellectuals between the Inside and the Outside." In *Conflicting Narratives: War, Trauma and Memory in Iraqi Culture*, edited by Stephan Milich, Friederike Pannewick, and Leslie Tramontini, 5–24. Wiesbaden, Germany: Reichert, 2012.

Montasser, Adel. *La Répression anti-démocratique en République Arabe Unie.* Paris: Temps modernes, 1961.

Moreh, Shmuel. "Free Verse." In *Encyclopedia of Arabic Literature*, edited by Julie Scott Meisami and Paul Stakey. Oxford: Routledge, 2010.

Moyn, Samuel. *A Holocaust Controversy: The Treblinka Affair in Postwar France.* Waltham, MA: Brandeis University Press, 2005.

———. *The Last Utopia.* Cambridge, MA: Harvard University Press, 2012.

Moyn, Samuel, and Andrew Sartori. "Approaches to Global Intellectual History." In *Global Intellectual History*, edited by Samuel Moyn and Andrew Sartori, 3–32. New York, Columbia University Press, 2015.

Mudimbe, V. Y. *The Invention of Africa: Gnosis, Philosophy, and the Order of Knowledge.* Bloomington: Indiana University Press, 1988.

Mufti, Malik. *Sovereign Creations: Pan-Arabism and Political Order in Syria and Iraq.* Ithaca, NY: Cornell University Press, 1996.

Murdoch, Alexandre John. "Koyré 1892–1964." *Proceedings and Addresses of the American Philosophical Association* 38 (1964–1965): 98–99.

Musawi, Muhsin. *Reading Iraq: Culture and Power in Conflict.* London: I. B. Tauris, 2006.

——. "The Socio-Political Context of the Iraqi Short Story, 1908–1968." In *Statecraft and Popular Culture in the Middle East,* edited by Eric Davis and Nicholas Gaverieldes, 202–27. Gainesville: University Press of Florida, 1991.

Namikas, Lise. *Battleground Africa: Cold War in the Congo, 1961–1965.* Stanford, CA: Stanford University Press, 2013.

Nietzsche, Friedrich. *The Use and Abuse of History.* New York: Bobbs-Merrill Company, 1957.

"Nizar Qabbani." In *Crosshatching in Global Culture: A Dictionary of Modern Arab Writers,* edited by John Donohue and Leslie Tramontini, 2:883. Beirut: Orient-Institut der DMG, 2004.

Novack, George, ed. *Existentialism versus Marxism: Conflicting Views on Humanism.* New York: Dell, 1966.

Omri, Mohamed-Salah. *Nationalism, Islam and World Literature: Sites of Confluence in the Writings of Maḥmūd al-Masʿadī.* Abingdon, UK: Routledge, 2006.

Ostle, Robin. "Maḥmūd al-Masʿadī and Tunisia's 'Lost Generation.'" *Journal of Arabic Literature* 8 (1977): 153–66.

Pursley, Sarah. "A Race against Time: Governing Femininity and Reproducing the Future in Revolutionary Iraq, 1945–63." PhD diss., City University of New York, 2012. Retrieved from http://ezproxy.lib.utexas.edu/login?url= http://search.proquest.com.ezproxy.lib.utexas.edu/docview/1018426654 ?accountid=7118.

Rahnema, Ali. *An Islamic Utopian: A Political Biography of Ali Shariʿati.* London: I. B. Tauris, 1998.

Reid, Donald. *Cairo University and the Making of Modern Egypt.* Cambridge: Cambridge University Press, 1990.

Rhiannon, Goldthorpe. "Understanding the Committed Writer." In *Cambridge Companion to Sartre,* edited by Christina Howells, 140–77. Cambridge: Cambridge University Press, 1992.

Robcis, Camille. "May '68 and the Ethical Turn in French Thought." *Modern Intellectual History* 11, no. 1 (2014): 267–77.

Roberts, Neil. "Fanon, Sartre, Violence, and Freedom." *Sartre Studies International* 10, no. 2 (2004): 139–60.

Robinson, Shira. *Citizens Strangers: Palestinians and the Birth of Israel's Liberal Settler State.* Stanford, CA: Stanford University Press, 2013.

Rockmore, Tom. *Heidegger and French Philosophy: Humanism, Antihumanism and Being.* London: Routledge, 1995.

Rosenbaum, Alan, ed. *Is the Holocaust Unique? Perspective on Comparative Genocide.* Boulder, CO: Westview Press, 2001.

Ross, Kristin. *May '68 and Its Afterlives.* Chicago: University of Chicago Press, 2002.

Roth, Michael. *Knowing and History: Appropriations of Hegel in Twentieth-Century France.* Ithaca, NY: Cornell University Press, 1988.

Ruder, Cynthia. "Socialist Realism." In *Encyclopedia of Russian History*, edited by James Millar, 4:1415–19. New York: Macmillan, 2004.

Ruocco, Monica. *L'intellettuale arabo tra impegno e dissenso: analisi della rivista libanese al-Ādāb*. Rome: Jouvence, 1999.

Russell, Bertrand. *Yours Faithfully, Bertrand Russell: A Lifelong Fight for Peace, Justice, and Truth in Letters to the Editor*. Chicago: Open Court, 2002.

Safadi, Muta. "Crisis of the Contemporary Arab Hero." In *Contemporary Arab Political Thought*, edited by Anouar Abdel-Malek, 103–7. London: Zed Books, 1983.

Samman, Ali el-. "Pourquoi le «non» au dialogue?" In *Le conflit israélo-arabe*, edited by Jean-Paul Sartre and Claude Lanzmann, 359–70. Paris: Les Temps Modernes, 1967.

Sandford, Stella. "Going Back: Heidegger, East Asia and 'The West.'" *Radical Philosophy* 120 (July–August 2003): 11–22.

Santorini, Ronald. *Sartre on Violence: Curiously Ambivalent*. University Park: Pennsylvania State University Press, 2003.

SARTEC, ed. *Iraq Contemporary Art*. Lausanne: SARTEC, 1977.

Sartre, Jean-Paul. "Colonialism Is a System." *Interventions: International Journal of Postcolonial Studies* 3, no. 1 (2001): 127–40.

———. "The Political Thought of Patrice Lumumba." In *Colonialism and Neo-colonialism*. Translated by Azzedine Haddour, 87–114. London: Routledge, 2006.

———. *Sartre on Cuba*. New York: Ballantine, 1961.

Sartre, Jean-Paul, and Claude Lanzmann, eds. *Le conflit israélo-arabe*. Paris: Les Temps Modernes, 1967.

Sayigh, Fayiz. "Existential Philosophy: A Formal Examination." PhD diss., Georgetown University, 1950. Retrieved from http://ezproxy.lib.utexas.edu/login?url=http://search.proquest.com.ezproxy.lib.utexas.edu/docview/301812305?accountid=7118.

———. "Personal Existence: An Essay." Master's thesis, American University of Beirut, 1945.

———. "Self-Examination and Arab Youth." Address to the Fourth Annual Convention of the Organization of Arab Students in the United States, University of Wisconsin, Madison, September 6, 1955.

———. *Understanding the Arab Mind*. New York: Organization of Arab Students in the United States, 1953.

———. *Zionist Colonialism in Palestine*. Beirut: Research Center, Palestinian Liberation Organization, September 1965.

Sayigh, Yezid. *Armed Struggle and the Search for State: The Palestinian National Movement, 1949–1993*. New York: Oxford University Press, 1997.

Schmidt, Elizabeth. "Top Down or Bottom Up? Nationalist Mobilization Reconsidered, with Special Reference to Guinea (French West Africa)." *American Historical Review* 110, no. 4 (2005): 975–1014.

Schumann, Christoph. "The Generation of Broad Expectations: Nationalism,

Education, and Autobiography in Syria and Lebanon, 1930–1958." *Die Welt des Islams* 41, no. 2 (July 2001): 174–205.

Scott, David. *Conscripts of Modernity: The Tragedy of Colonial Enlightenment.* Durham, NC: Duke University Press, 2004.

Shabout, Nada. *Modern Arab Art: Formation of Arab Aesthetics.* Gainesville: University Press of Florida, 2007.

Sharabi, Hisham. *Embers and Ashes: Memoir of an Arab Intellectual.* Northampton, MA: Olive Branch Press, 2008.

———. *Nationalism and Revolution in the Arab World: The Middle East and North Africa.* Princeton, NJ: Van Nostrand, 1966.

Sharawy, Helmi. "Memories on African Liberation (1956–1975): A Personal Experience from Egypt, Part I." *Pamvazuka News*, no. 530, May 19, 2011.

Shaw, Shereen Hamed. "A Study of Tawfiq al-Hakim's Equilibrium Doctrine and Philosophical Narratives." PhD diss., University of Liverpool, 2015. Retrieved from http://ezproxy.lib.utexas.edu/login?url=http://search .proquest.com.ezproxy.lib.utexas.edu/docview/1780172044?accountid= 7118.

Shepard, Todd. *The Invention of Decolonization: The Algerian War and the Remaking of France.* Ithaca, NY: Cornell University Press, 2006.

———. "Of Sovereignty: Disputed Archives, 'Wholly Modern' Archives, and the Post-decolonization French and Algerian Republics, 1962–2012." *American Historical Review* 120, no. 3 (2015): 869–83.

Simah, David. *Four Egyptian Literary Critics.* Leiden: Brill, 1974.

Simons, Margaret, and Marybeth Timmermann, eds. *Simone de Beauvoir: Political Writing.* Urbana-Champaign: University of Illinois Press, 2012.

Sirrs, Owen. *A History of the Egyptian Intelligence Service: A History of the Mukhabarat, 1910–2009.* London: Routledge, 2010.

Smith, Charles. *Islam and the Search for Social Order in Modern Egypt: A Biography of Muhammad Husayn Haykal.* Albany: State University of New York Press, 1983.

Subrahmanyam, Sanjay. "Global Intellectual History beyond Hegel and Marx." *History and Theory* 54, no. 1 (February 2015): 126–37.

Surkis, Judith. "Ethics and Violence: Simone de Beauvoir, Djamila Boupacha, and the Algerian War." *French Politics, Culture and Society* 28, no. 2 (Summer 2010): 38–55.

Taibo, Paco Ignacio. *Guevara, Also Known as Che.* New York: St. Martin's Press, 1997.

Taylor, Charles. *The Ethics of Authenticity: Malaise of Modernity.* Cambridge, MA: Harvard University Press, 1991.

Tresilian, David. "Isma'il Sabri 'Abdullah: Mapping the Arab Future." *Al-Ahram Weekly*, July 4, 1991.

Wahba, Mourad. "Contemporary Moslem Philosophies in North Africa." In *African Philosophy: An Anthology*, edited by Emmanuel Chukwudi Eze, 50–55. Oxford: Blackwell, 2000.

Westad, Odd Arne. *The Global Cold War: Third World Intervention and the Making of Our Times*. Cambridge: Cambridge University Press, 2007.

Wilder, Gary. *Freedom Time: Negritude, Decolonization, and the Future of the World*. Durham, NC: Duke University Press, 2015.

———. *The French Imperial Nation-State: Negritude and Colonial Humanism between the Two World Wars*. Chicago: University of Chicago Press, 2005.

Williams, Michael W. "Nkrumah and the State of Israel," *TransAfrica Forum* 7, no. 1 (Spring 1990): 39–54.

Witte, Ludo de. *The Assassination of Lumumba*. Translated by Ann Wright and Renée Fenby. London: Verso, 2001.

Wolf, Joan. *Harnessing the Holocaust: The Politics of Memory in France*. Stanford, CA: Stanford University Press, 2004.

Wolin, Richard. *The Wind from the East: French Intellectuals, the Cultural Revolution, and the Legacy of the 1960s*. Princeton, NJ: Princeton University Press, 2010.

Young, Robert. *Postcolonialism: An Historical Introduction*. Oxford: Blackwell, 2001.

———. Preface to *Interventions: International Journal of Postcolonial Studies* 3, no. 1 (2001): 127–28.

———. "Sartre: The African Philosopher." In *Colonialism and Neocolonialism*, by Jean-Paul Sartre, ix–xxvii. London: Routledge, 2006.

———. *White Mythologies: Writing History and the West*. London: Routledge, 1990.

"Yusuf al-Khal, Poet, Critic." In *Crosshatching in Global Culture: A Dictionary of Modern Arab Writers*, edited by John Donohue and Leslie Tramontini, 2:606–9. Beirut: Orient-Institut der DMG, 2004.

Zevin, Alexander. "Critique of Neo-colonial Reason," *New Left Review* 70 (July–August 2011): 141–42.

Zhang, Chi. *Sartre en Chine, 1939–1976: Histoire de sa réception et de son influence*. Paris: Éditions Le Manuscrit, 2008.

Index

'Abd al-'Azim Anis. *See* Anis, 'Abd al-'Azim

'Abd al-Da'im, 'Abdallah. *See* Da'im, 'Abdallah 'Abd al-

'Abdallah, 'Isma'il Sabri, 65, 129, 189

'Abd al-Raziq, Mustafa, 52–53

Abu al-Ghar, Muhammad, 211

Adonis ('Ali Ahmad Said), 120–21, 315n28

'Aflaq, Michel, 112, 148, 165

Africa: battle for postcolonial, the Arab-Israeli conflict and, 179–82; the Congo crisis, 181–85; Yemen, conflict in, 38, 176, 186–88, 190, 230

Africana thought, 262n16

Ahmad, Muhammad Sa'id, 129

Al-Adab: communism, hostility to, 87–90; creation of, 67–68; editorial welcoming Sartre to Egypt, 199; free verse poetry in, 138–39; the generational clash between literary critics and, 83; literary criticism, call for revolution in, 86–91; al-Mala'ika as the only woman on the board of, 139; Pan-Arab state, championing of, 113–14; postcolonial intelligentsia and, 86; production of by Suhayl and 'Aida Matraji Idris, 5, 64; regional competition for the best Arabic novel of the year, 122; special commemorative is-sue on the occasion of Sartre's death, 259–60

Al-Ahram: Badawi's dissertation de-fense as news, 47; al-Samman's interview with Sartre, 37–39; Sartre's trip to Egypt and, 34, 199

Algeria: as an Arab cause, 114; Manifesto of the 121, 311n62; questioning of Sartre's position on, 234; Sartre and, 18, 158, 208; universality of problems in, 171

Al-Hayy al-Latini (Idris), 66

'Alim, Mahmud Amin al-: on Arab existentialism, 13; Badawi, as student of, 54–55; biographi-cal sketch of, 6; competition to influence public life, role in, 106; Egyptian repression of, 112, 129; existentialism, discrediting of and incompat-ibility with Marxism, 159–60, 162, 208; Husayn, intellectual battles against, 80–86, 103–4; Muruwwa, meeting with, 280n22; on political commit-ment, 131; political responsi-bility, debate with existential-ists regarding, 38; socialist literary criticism, claim for the prominence of, 103; support for, 103

Al-Katib al-Misri, 58–60, 63, 91

Allen, Woody, 143